C. S. LEWIS

C. S. LEWIS

A BIOGRAPHY

A. N. WILSON

COLLINS
8 Grafton Street, London w1
1990

William Collins Sons & Co. Ltd
London · Glasgow · Sydney · Auckland
Toronto · Johannesburg

BRITISH LIBRARY CATALOGUING IN PUBLICATION DATA

Wilson, A. N. *1950–*
C. S. Lewis: a biography.
1. Fiction in English. Lewis, C. S. (Clive Staples),
1898–1963
I. Title
823'.912

ISBN 0 00 215137 5

First published in Great Britain 1990
Copyright © A. N. Wilson 1990

Photoset in Linotron Janson by
Rowland Phototypesetting Ltd
Bury St Edmunds, Suffolk
Printed and bound in Great Britain by
William Collins Sons & Co. Ltd, Glasgow

For Ruth

CONTENTS

ILLUSTRATIONS

between pages 126 and 127
Jack Lewis as a child (Bodleian Library, Oxford)[1]
Flora Lewis (© Marion E. Wade Center)[2]
Watercolour drawing of the Little Master (Collins/Harcourt Brace Jovanovich)[3]
Albert Lewis, *c*.1881 (© Marion E. Wade Center)
Jack and Albert Lewis, 1918 (© Marion E. Wade Center)
Jack Lewis in the Little End Room, 1919 (© Marion E. Wade Center)
Mr and Mrs Kirkpatrick, 1920 (© Marion E. Wade Center)
Jack Lewis with Paddy Moore, 1917 (© Marion E. Wade Center)
Jack Lewis with Maureen and Mrs Moore, 1927 (© Marion E. Wade Center)

between pages 254 and 255
New Buildings, Magdalen College, Oxford (Thomas Photos, Oxford)
Charles Williams (Elliott & Fry)
J. R. R. Tolkien (Lafayette)
Jack and Warnie Lewis in Ireland, 1949 (© Marion E. Wade Center)
Manuscript leaf from *Surprised by Joy* (Bodleian Library, Oxford)[4]
Joy Lewis, *c*.1957 (Curtis Brown, London)
C. S. Lewis at Magdalen, 1947 (© Arthur Strong)

[1] MS Eng. lett c.220/2 f.14
[2] Marion E. Wade Center, Wheaton College, Illinois
[3] This illustration appeared in *Boxen: The Imaginary World of the Young C. S. Lewis*
[4] Dep. d.241 f.22

THE QUEST
FOR A WARDROBE

A child pushed open the door of the wardrobe so as to hide in it. It was, however, no ordinary wardrobe. It was hung with fur coats. The child pressed on further through the dark recesses of the cupboard, pushing aside the soft folds of fur and discovering beyond them a new world. What crunched beneath the feet was not mothballs but snow. Lucy had discovered Narnia.

Millions of readers throughout the world have been thrilled by this moment in C. S. Lewis's story *The Lion, the Witch and the Wardrobe* and have gone on to read the six other stories which he wrote about that other world behind the wardrobe, the world of Narnia. The powerfulness of the stories derives in part from the immediacy of Lewis's rough-hewn style, but more, surely, from the fact that this image touches something so very deep in so many people.

'If everything on earth were rational,' someone remarks in Dostoyevsky's novel *The Brothers Karamazov*, 'nothing would happen.' Nothing much would appear to have happened in the life of C. S. Lewis, who for his entire adult life was a scholar and teacher at Oxford and Cambridge in England. He did not mix in the world, with famous or fashionable people. His days were filled with writing and reading and domestic chores. And yet books about him continue to pour from the presses on both sides of the Atlantic.

This phenomenon can only be explained by the fact that his writings, while being self-consciously and deliberately at variance with the twentieth century, are paradoxically in tune with the needs and concerns of our times. Everything on earth is not rational, and attempts to live by reason have all failed. The world has changed more radically in the last hundred years than in any previous era of history. Old values and certainties have been destroyed; religions have collapsed. In such a world, a voice which appears to come from the old world and to speak with the old sureness will have an obvious appeal. Lewis's attempts to justify an old-fashioned Christian orthodoxy have made him an internationally celebrated and reassuring figure to those believers who have felt betrayed by the compromises of the mainline Christian churches. Lewis, to the amazement of those who knew him in his lifetime, has become in the quarter-century since he died something very like a saint in the minds of conservative-minded believers.

It is not the rational Lewis who makes this enormous appeal, the Lewis who lectured on medieval and Renaissance literature with such superb fluency and wide-ranging erudition to generations of English students. It is the Lewis who plumbed the irrational depths of childhood and religion who speaks to the present generation.

Though all Freud's theories about the origins of consciousness may be disavowed, this remains the century of Freud. We have learnt that our lives are profoundly affected by what happened to us when we were very young children, and that wherever we travel in mind or body we are compelled to repeat or work out the drama of early years. If this were a work of psychoanalysis or literary theory, I should feel compelled to test *The Lion, the Witch and the Wardrobe* by the theories of the human mind which have been adopted and discarded by psychoanalysts and philosophers in the last hundred years. But these are not areas which admit of rational enquiry, even if I were qualified to explore them, and Lewis himself would have been equally anxious to remind us of the whole European philosophical tradition since Plato which has attempted in the language of metaphysics to account for our sense that we do not belong in this world, that we are pilgrims and strangers here, homesick for another place where one day we shall be truly ourselves.

Two journeys, made in the course of my researches for this biography, have brought home to me more vividly than any others the strange nature of my task.

The first was to Belfast in Northern Ireland. For those who are not Irish, their first glimpse of modern Belfast is a shock. Much of its ancient prosperity, derived from its magnificent shipyards, has gone. There is widespread unemployment and poverty. Walking the streets of the working-class districts of the city one is confronted by distressing images of human irrationality. Even the kerbstones shriek of their religious and political allegiance. Protestant, Unionist streets are painted red, white and blue in praise of the Queen and the Reformation. Catholic, Nationalist streets are daubed white, green and orange for Ireland and the Pope. In no place on earth does it seem truer that Christ came to bring not peace, but a sword. The post offices and police stations are barricaded like fortresses. There is no prospect here of the rational prevailing. Every week that passes, a bomb explodes or a gun is fired because of ancient, atavistic religious prejudice.

It would not be the best place in the world to take a non-believer in the hope of persuading him or her that Christianity was a very ennobling belief, but it is a very good place for a Christian to recognize what a small part reason plays in most human lives; and it might very well prompt the visitor, and even more the resident, to hope that some form of Christianity could be expounded which was the agreed and good thing which all Christians hold in common, the set of unchanging and saving beliefs which Lewis named *Mere Christianity*.

Driving out of the beleaguered city into the suburbs is immediately to encounter a different, happier world, a prosperous middle-class place which knows no violence; big, comfortable houses built to sustain and celebrate the simple happiness of family life. Down one such leafy road, you will find the house built by a Belfast police solicitor named Albert Lewis in 1905. It was in this lumpy Edwardian villa that C. S. Lewis and his brother Warren spent the most crucial period of their lives. Climbing up the small back staircase, I reached a landing on the second floor of the house, and there at the end of the corridor I found the 'Little End Room' where the boys had escaped from the grown-ups and indulged their childhood games.

For Lewis himself, it was not a house with happy memories, for it was here that the catastrophe of his life took place: the death of his mother on 23 August 1908, when Lewis was nine years old. The loss was something which he bottled up within himself, unable to appease it through the emotionally stultifying years of boarding-school education in England. In terms of his emotional life, the quest for his lost mother dominated his relations with women. His companion for over thirty years was a woman old enough to be his mother; and when she died it was not long before, like a Pavlovian dog trained to lacerate his heart with the same emotional experiences, he married a woman whose circumstances were exactly parallel to those of his own mother in 1908 – a woman dying of cancer who had two small sons.

Standing in the Little End Room, I realized that I was beginning to come to terms with the Lewis phenomenon, and why it had such a hugely popular appeal. I had thought to go there merely in order to soak up 'atmosphere'. I realized that what Lewis was seeking with such painful earnestness all his life was not to be found in this house; nor had it ever been, for any of the time he had lived there after his mother's death. Without the capacity to develop an 'ordinary' emotional life, based on a stable relationship with parents, Lewis was driven back and back into the Little End Room, 'further up and further in'.

It would have been good to see the wardrobe in Belfast, but it was not there. To see that, I journeyed over three and a half thousand miles to a small liberal arts college in the suburbs of Chicago: Wheaton College, Illinois. Between the two journeys I had spent months reading Lewis, and hours talking to those who knew him. An image of what he was actually like, as a man, was by now vividly clear to me. The reasons why many of his Oxford colleagues had disliked him were obvious. He was argumentative and bullying. His jolly, red, honest face was that of an intellectual bruiser. He was loud, and he could be coarse. He liked what he called 'man's talk', and he was frequently contemptuous in his remarks about the opposite sex. He was a heavy smoker – sixty cigarettes a day between pipes – and he liked to drink deep, roaring out his unfashionable views in Oxford bars. This – the 'beer and Beowulf' Lewis – was understandably uncongenial to those of a different temperament. But I had also learnt that he was a kind and patient teacher, a loyal friend, a magnificently astute and intelligent conversationalist who had read much and who had the capacity to fire his hearers with a longing to read his favourite authors for themselves. Few of his friends had ever heard Lewis allude to his inner life, and even his religion was more to be taken for granted than to be aired in conversation. The gatherings of cronies in pubs or college rooms had no feeling of an evangelical prayer group. Two members of that celebrated group, known as the Inklings, have told me that there was always an air of English embarrassment when the subject of religion cropped up, and that Lewis's activities as a religious broadcaster and writer were not something with which his fellow-Christians in the Inklings felt at ease. These men knew almost nothing of the Lewis who had emerged in my reading of private letters and diaries. They knew nothing from him of his childhood trauma, little of his two great emotional attachments to women, and next to nothing of his spiritual journey, even though one of these men, Hugo Dyson, had been responsible in part for persuading Lewis to abandon atheism and become a Christian.

C. S. Lewis the popular Christian apologist, who was reaching so many readers in Europe and the United States, was a phenomenon who had a life of his own in the minds of the reading public. His friends did know that this activity had generated an enormous band of admirers and enquirers, who wrote to Lewis from every corner of the globe and could be sure of getting a written reply.

Lewis did not ask to become a cult figure, but by writing so faithfully to his correspondents, he allowed the cult to build up. For many, including the penfriend he eventually married, the author of *The Screwtape Letters* and *Mere Christianity* was a guru or spiritual master who might be expected to provide *Answers to Life's Problems*. That is not the title of one of Lewis's books. It is the title of a book by Dr Billy Graham, the most famous alumnus of Wheaton College, Illinois. As you approach the college, you see on your left an enormous Greek Revival building known as the Billy Graham Center, built in honour of the famous evangelist. It is hard to imagine Billy Graham enjoying C. S. Lewis's company at any length, though I believe the two met during one of Dr Graham's crusades in England. Lewis was impatient with puritanism and disliked non-smokers or teetotallers. He liked to talk of books, books, books, and he would not have shared any of Dr Graham's political enthusiasms. But the wardrobe from Little Lea has come to repose at Wheaton College, Illinois.

The Marion E. Wade Center on the upper floor of the college library is devoted to the memorabilia of various Christian writers: George MacDonald, T. S. Eliot, Dorothy L. Sayers, Charles Williams, J. R. R. Tolkien, C. S. Lewis and his brother Warren. The library has also recently acquired the papers of that veteran journalist and cynic Malcolm Muggeridge, and here the faithful may see Muggeridge's portable typewriter kept, like the body of Lenin, in a glass case.

A portrait of C. S. Lewis, painted by T. M. Williams, smiles down on the reading room. It has the same glowing unreality as pious paintings of Thérèse of Lisieux or the Sacred Heart, adorning convent walls in days now gone. Hard by, in a glass display cabinet, are Lewis's beer tankards and pipes, which in this abstemious atmosphere seem out of place. I worked at the table which, a brass plate informed me, had been in Lewis's college rooms at Magdalen and subsequently in the dining-room at his house in Oxford, The Kilns. Dorothy L. Sayers and T. S. Eliot and many other famous people, it was claimed, had used this table. I had been reading Lewis, and talking to those who had known him, for the better part of twenty years, and doing serious research into his life for two years. I have come across no possible occasion when T. S. Eliot, with whom Lewis did not enjoy very cordial relations, would have used this table. What does it matter? The same sort of rationalist objections could be made about supposed relics of the True Cross. A piece of furniture stood in the corner of the room, carved by Lewis's grandfather. It was the wardrobe. At Wheaton, one has stepped through the wardrobe into the world of make-believe.

Not long before my visit to Wheaton, a book by Kathryn Lindskoog had been drawn to my attention entitled *The C. S. Lewis Hoax*. It was published in Oregon in 1988 and it makes disturbing reading. Since its central thesis has been disproved, I imagine that it will not be published in Great Britain, though it was bought by a British publisher at the Frankfurt Book Fair in 1988. Lindskoog claims that one of Lewis's feebler posthumous works, a semi-obscene piece of science fiction called *The Dark Tower*, a continuation of his space trilogy, was not in fact the work of Lewis at all, but a forgery by someone else. A manuscript of this depressing fragment is deposited in the Bodleian Library in Oxford and experts have made it clear beyond doubt that it is written in Lewis's hand. Nevertheless, Lindskoog's book is concerned with a much wider issue than the authorship of *The Dark Tower*. It amounts to one of the most vitriolic personal attacks on a fellow-scholar, Walter Hooper, that I have ever read in print.

As Lyle W. Dorsett, the curator of the Marion E. Wade Center, concedes, Lindskoog has gone too far in her assaults on Hooper's good name. Her notions of a forged *Dark Tower* are mistaken, and some of her other assertions – for example, that the title given by

Hooper to Lewis's letters to Arthur Greeves, *They Stand Together*, is a piece of pederastic argot – are wide of the mark. For those of us who have known Hooper for a very long time, however, there are moments in Lindskoog's diatribe where we recognize bits of truth. Hooper does, as Lindskoog asserts, like people to believe that he knew Lewis much better and much longer than was really the case.

The details of Lindskoog's book are unimportant to the general reader. What strikes an outsider is how violently the C. S. Lewis devotees seem to dislike one another. From very early days, there has been a Great Schism in their camp. It is notoriously difficult for those outside the borders of a religious dispute to describe with accuracy the sticking points involved, and if I attempted a detailed analysis of the Lewis feuds I should probably fall into as many errors as if I were to attempt a discourse on the difference between Shiite and Sunni Moslems.

Some of the quarrels had to do with the holdings of Lewis manuscripts. Walter Hooper, an American resident in Oxford, was anxious that a complete Lewis collection, either in original manuscript form or on microfiche, should be available to scholars in the Bodleian Library. The late Clyde S. Kilby, who was largely responsible for building up the Lewis collection at Wheaton, agreed to a proposal that there should be a free exchange between Wheaton and the Bodleian until a dispute arose about some letters. 'Then all smiles stopped together.'

Walter Hooper, who has had the task of editing most of Lewis's posthumous works and working directly with Lewis's estate and publishers, has come in for the brunt of criticism from his fellow-countrymen back across the water, but over the years it has become clear that the quarrels are not merely about Hooper's own role in Lewis's life or about the ownership of various bits of paper. Two totally different Lewises are being revered by the faithful, and it is this which makes the disputes so painfully acrimonious. Hooper was for many years an extreme Anglo-Catholic priest, but has subsequently become a Roman Catholic. He presides over weekly meetings of the C. S. Lewis Society in Oxford where papers are read and discussions held by interested parties, mainly students. It is not an exclusively High Church group, but there is a distinctly Catholic bias in Hooper's interpretation of Lewis which not everyone who knew the man would find completely believable. Most noticeably peculiar in Hooper's picture of his hero is his belief in the Perpetual Virginity of C. S. Lewis. There is very direct evidence, both from Lewis's brother-in-law Dr Davidman and from Lewis's own pen, that Lewis was not a virgin and that his marriage was consummated. It would also be amazing, though no evidence is forthcoming either way, if Lewis's thirty-year relationship with Mrs Moore was entirely asexual. Ordinary biographical criteria, however, are not allowed by Hooper to apply, since for him Lewis has become a sort of Catholic saint, and one can hardly believe in a Catholic saint both of whose sexual relationships were with women who had husbands still living. Therefore, when Lewis wrote in *A Grief Observed* that he and his wife were lovers, that they had 'fallen in love', that 'a noble hunger, long unsatisfied, met at last its proper food', that she was his 'mistress', that 'we were one flesh', that 'no cranny of heart or body remained unsatisfied', he was in fact writing a work of fiction. Hooper has a natural bent for hero-worship, and because he believes celibacy to be a high virtue he cannot believe that Lewis and his wife were, as the man himself wrote, 'a sinful woman married to a sinful man'.

In the United States, among Lewis's Protestant devotees, there is an analogous awkwardness about his passion for alcohol and tobacco. Some of Lewis's American publishers actually ask for references to drinking and smoking to be removed from his work, and one has the strong feeling that this is not so much because they themselves disapprove of the activities as because they need a Lewis who was, against all evidence, a non-smoker and a lemonade-drinker.

It is the need which awakens the image, and once the image has been set up and revered, and emotion has been poured into it, there is something profoundly painful about the idea of anyone worshipping a different icon, or threatening to demolish all the icons. Lewis idolatry, like Christianity itself, has resorted to some ugly tactics as it breaks itself into factions. Hard words are used on both sides, and there is not much evidence of Christian charity when the war is at its hottest. In their libraries and periodicals, the differing Lewis factions have conceived for one another an enmity which would do Screwtape proud, and it provides a strange parallel to the sort of unhinged sectarian disputes which have dogged Lewis's native Belfast for the last sixty years.

When we step beyond the wardrobe door, we expect battles. Witches and monsters will threaten our subconscious until we reach the longed-for consummation when change itself stands still and Aslan is King for ever.

A writer who can evoke such reactions is worthy of scrutiny, and scrutiny of a particular kind. When I had seen Belfast and Wheaton, I saw the extent of the problem facing Lewis's biographer. Some time before, staying in the south of France with Christopher Tolkien, the son of J. R. R. Tolkien, I took down from the shelf a copy of Lewis's book *Letters to Malcolm, Chiefly on Prayer*. Here was evidence, if any was needed, of how one of Lewis's closest friends reacted to his last work of piety. The book is not 'about prayer', Tolkien writes in the margin, 'but about Lewis praying'. 'But', he adds on the fly-leaf, 'the whole book is *always interesting*. Why? Because it is about Jack, by Jack, and that is a topic that no one who knew him well could fail to find interesting even when exasperating.'

I myself never knew Lewis, though I have known many people who did, and I have never failed to find their memories of the man interesting. Like Tolkien, I am puzzled. Why? In the same marginal note, Tolkien continues, 'The book is in fact entirely *egocentric*, by which I do not mean that C.S.L. worshipped himself or was a proud or vain man, overesteeming his own worth or wisdom. But I do mean that as must be the case with anyone who essays autobiography, under any form, he found C.S.L. an absorbing topic.'

Lewis was in fact an obsessive autobiographer. Most of his later books are, as Tolkien says, all about himself, and he also wrote copiously on the subject to his many correspondents. Yet few writers have ever been less introspective: this is the paradox. He was not vain, but he had a capacity to project images of himself into prose; sometimes, one feels, without quite realizing what he was doing. It is these images which have such posthumous staying power. For me, the most attractive Lewis is the author of *English Literature in the Sixteenth Century*, a fluent, highly intelligent man talking about books in a manner which is always engaging. This itself is a self-projection. Reading the book, you feel you know what it was like to hear him talk. This is ten times truer of his religious books, and since many readers will associate Lewis's tone of voice with some of their deepest and most profoundly felt religious moments, there is no wonder that they guard their images of him jealously.

Lewis himself, in his own words that 'sinful man', wrote in his most devastatingly personal book *A Grief Observed* that 'All reality is iconoclastic. The earthly beloved, even in this life, incessantly triumphs over your mere idea of her. And you want her to; you want her with all her resistances, all her faults, all her unexpectedness. That is, in her foursquare and independent reality. And this, not any image or memory, is what we are to love still, after she is dead.'

This book is not intended to be iconoclastic, but I will try to be realistic, not only because reality is more interesting than fantasy, but also because we do Lewis no honour to make him into a plaster saint. And he deserves our honour.

ONE

ANTECEDENTS

Clive Staples Lewis was born on 29 November 1898 in the city of Belfast. More than most men, he was the product of his upbringing and ancestry. Throughout his adult life he remained constantly preoccupied with his own childhood. Moreover the companion of his infancy, Warren Hamilton Lewis, his elder brother by three years, lived with him for the greater part of his life. Their comradeship outlasted the vicissitudes of love and friendship.

But C. S. Lewis did more than carry the *memories* of his childhood in Northern Ireland into grown-up life. Many of his most robustly distinctive qualities were manifestly ones of inheritance.

It is always tiresome for a child to be told by older relations that his personal characteristics are the results of genetics. It implies that the child is no more than a collection of bits – one grandfather contributing the nose, another the golfing handicap, an aunt on the mother's side contributing the ear for languages or the eye for painting. Surely the child must feel he is more than the sum of his ancestors' parts. And indeed C. S. Lewis was very much more than a mixture of Hamilton and Lewis chromosomes. When we turn back to the close of the nineteenth century, however, and meet Lewis's grandparents and parents, the family likenesses are too overwhelming to miss.

Lewis's mother was Florence Hamilton, always known as Flora. Her father, Thomas Hamilton (1826–1905), was a bluff Church of Ireland clergyman whose father had been the Rector of Enniskillen and whose grandfather, the Right Reverend Hugh Hamilton, had been the Bishop of Ossory. C. S. Lewis and his brother were rather proud of this episcopal ancestor. They had more ambivalent feelings about their grandfather when they read his surviving writings and papers. He had been a naval chaplain in the Baltic during the Crimean War and he was well travelled in Europe. But his copious travel journals were repulsive to Warren, partly because of their 'constant and irritating employment of outworn literary cliche', but more because of 'his intense religious bigotry, which was not . . . palliated as being in the spirit of his age'.

Among the beliefs which the Reverend Thomas Hamilton shared with a high proportion of Protestants in Northern Ireland was the idea that the Roman church was 'composed of the Devil's children'. Indeed he doubted whether it was possible for a Roman Catholic to be saved. What was so typical of Thomas Hamilton, however, was that he managed to sustain this belief for four years as Anglican chaplain in Rome. While he was there he wrote a long essay entitled 'What saith the Scripture – an Inquiry of what it is that the Bible teaches concerning the future state of the Lost'. Hamilton advanced the interesting view that, in effect, only the saved survive. When the Bible says that the damned suffer eternal punishment it must mean punishment eternal in its effects. They do not go on suffering continuously. They are snuffed out, they cease to be. Precisely similar preoccupations were to haunt the mind of Thomas's grandson, Clive Staples Lewis, when he came to write his theological reflections.

While Thomas Hamilton was living in Rome, incidentally, something occurred which entered into family legend and eventually formed a seed for C. S. Lewis's most famous story. Hamilton's daughter Flora – C. S. Lewis's mother – was then a little girl. One afternoon she and some grown-ups escaped the scorching heat of the pavement by walking into a church. Under one of the altars there was the body of a saint lying in a glass case. While no grown-up was looking, Flora distinctly saw this figure open her eyelids. Just as when Lucy comes back from the other side of the wardrobe and discovers that everyone thinks Narnia is a product of her imagination, so the Hamiltons failed to believe in Flora's 'miracle'. The difference between Flora and Lucy was that Flora did not herself believe that she had witnessed anything miraculous. 'I thought it was done by cords pulled by a priest behind the alter [sic].' Nevertheless, the pattern of the story – a little girl who has seen a wonder in which the rest of her family refuse to believe – is structurally the same as that of *The Lion, the Witch and the Wardrobe*.

After their spell in Rome, the Hamiltons returned to Ireland and Thomas Hamilton became the Rector of St Mark's, Dundela, on the outskirts of Belfast, a position which he occupied until his retirement in 1900 (he died in 1905). St Mark's is an impressively large church designed by the Tractarian architect William Butterfield. By the subdued standards of the Church of Ireland, it is rather 'High'.

Those who knew Thomas Hamilton, while being a little overwhelmed by his theological pugnacity, were fond of his company. He was flawlessly eloquent, and he was no ascetic. He had a love of hearty eating and drinking, and was addicted to jaunts, his favourite occupation being walking tours with male friends. He could be thunderingly tactless, but he had a heart of gold. His daughter Flora was an intelligent young woman who had gained an honours degree in mathematics at the Queen's University, Belfast – an unusual achievement for a woman in those days.

In 1894, Thomas Hamilton at length consented to give his daughter's hand in marriage to a solicitor in the Belfast police courts called Albert Lewis. 'Rarely has a Jacob served more arduously for his Rachel than did Albert,' Warren Lewis was to write about his parents' courtship. 'And many years afterwards he frequently recited with indignant amusement the various embarrassments which he suffered on those trips.'

Perhaps one reason why the Reverend Thomas Hamilton had doubts about Albert Lewis was that he was only *just* a gentleman. 'His grandfather', C. S. Lewis remembered, 'had been a Welsh farmer, his father, a self-made man, had begun life as a workman, emigrated to Ireland and ended as a partner in the firm of Macilwaite & Lewis, 'Boiler makers, Engineers and Iron Ship Builders'.[1] What we do not learn from *Surprised by Joy*, C. S. Lewis's spiritual autobiography, is that grandfather Lewis, like grandfather Hamilton, was a fluent writer. Richard Lewis was not just an engineer or a businessman. When he was working for the Cork Steamship Company he spent his evenings reading papers to the men on such subjects as 'A Special Providence' and 'On Jonah's Mission to Nineveh' and 'Whether man will or no'. Richard Lewis wrote, 'God's purposes, whether of justice or mercy shall be carried out ... True, God has threatened the sinner, but from the character the Bible gives of Him, His threatenings are all to be applied conditionally. His will is that all shall be saved ...'

Richard Lewis did not only write theological essays. He also made up primitive science-fiction stories to amuse his children – stories, for example, in which a Mr Timothy Tumbledown advertises for 'a good telescope that will show the inhabitants of the moon life size. Also a selenographical machine to enable the undersigned to construct an aeronautic cable from Tycho to Vesuvius as he is anxious to find out the different geological strata of the moon.'

Once again, here are characteristics for which C. S. Lewis was conspicuous latently present in one of his grandfathers. He, like Richard Lewis, was a man whose idea of a good evening's entertainment was reading a paper on Free Will and Divine Providence and whose private delight was in children's literature and scientific fantasy.

Albert Lewis, the son of Richard and the father of our subject, is one of the most important characters in the story. He was a 'character', and that in two senses. First, he was a strongly marked and in many ways eccentric individual, highly imaginative, bombastic, literate and eloquent. But secondly, and much more confusingly, Albert Lewis also became a 'character' in literature. Anyone who has read *Surprised by Joy* will recognize the portrait of C. S. Lewis's father as a comic masterpiece. When we turn back from *Surprised by Joy* to the Lewis family papers we find not that C. S. Lewis has exactly speaking lied about his father but that he has left so much out of the picture and painted it from a position of such uncontrollable prejudice that it is something of a shock to encounter Albert Lewis on his own terms and read his speeches, poems, letters and notebooks.

A clever, highly imaginative boy, Albert had been educated at Lurgan College, County Armagh, where his headmaster, a brilliant young logician called W. T. Kirkpatrick, formed and retained throughout life a high view of his capabilities. Perhaps Kirkpatrick, who himself enjoyed fiercely conducted intellectual contests, was responsible for fostering the direction of Albert's career. After Lurgan, Albert went down to Dublin to study law at the firm of Maclean, Boyle & Maclean. Initially he intended to read for the Bar but, presumably because his father did not have the means to support him, he returned to Belfast after qualifying in 1885 and started his own law firm as a solicitor. The law for Albert Lewis was to have been the platform or starting point for a career in politics.

We are speaking of a period when the whole land of Ireland, from

County Kerry to County Antrim, was part of Great Britain in the way that Scotland and Wales are today. Albert Lewis, like the majority of Irish Protestants, was ardently keen that this state of things should be maintained. The talk of Home Rule for Ireland was by his standards dangerous nonsense. In 1882 he said in a speech in Dublin, when he was only nineteen, 'I believe the cause of Irish Agitation to be on the one hand the Roman Catholic religion and on the other the weakness and vacillation and the party selfishness of English ministers [i.e. of the Crown].' The English politician he loathed the most was Gladstone, whom he once called 'that disingenuous and garrulous old man' and who in his support for Irish Home Rule was, Albert Lewis thought, being simply mischievous. 'Mr Gladstone, like another celebrated character, "cries havoc and lets loose the dogs of war"' – i.e. the terrorists and revolutionaries of Sinn Fein.

But Albert Lewis, in spite of his high promise, was never to sit in the House of Commons in Westminster. He spent most of his career as a prosecuting solicitor in the police courts in Belfast, pouring into the frequently trivial cases which came before him all his gifts of oratory, his considerable powers of argument and debate, and his rich vein of humour. Indeed it was his sense of humour, C. S. Lewis believed, which somehow or other made Albert Lewis's political career unmanageable.

He was a master of the anecdote, a fund of improbable stories, many of which for him epitomized the tragicomedy of what it meant to be Irish. One of the more bizarre 'wheezes' (as he habitually termed these stories and observations) concerned an occasion when he was travelling in an old-fashioned train of the kind which had no corridor, so that the passengers were imprisoned in their compartments for as long as the train was moving. He was not alone in the compartment. He found himself opposite one other character, a respectable-looking farmer in a tweed suit whose agitated manner was to be explained by the demands of nature. When the train had rattled on for a further few miles, and showed no signs of stopping at a station where a lavatory might have been available, the gentleman pulled down his trousers, squatted on the floor of the railway carriage and defecated. When this operation was complete, and the gentleman, fully clothed, was once more seated opposite Albert Lewis, the smell in the compartment was so powerful as to be almost nauseating. To vary, if not to drown the odour, Albert Lewis got a pipe from his pocket and began to light it. But at that point the stranger opposite, who had not spoken one word during the entire journey, leaned forward and censoriously tapped a sign on the window which read NO SMOKING. For C. S. Lewis, this 'wheeze' of his father's always enshrined in some insane way a truth about Northern Ireland and what it was like to live there.

Perhaps it was his ability to recite such stories which meant that Albert Lewis would never be a politician. He was a strange combination of rhetorical comedy and inner piety and emotionalism. If Albert Lewis was the mustachioed comedian whose favourite drink was whiskey and water and who could keep any company in stitches with his skills as a raconteur – imitating all the different voices as he spun out his tall stories – he was also the soulful poet who loved to be alone and to confront the mystery of things. As he wrote in 1882:

> I hate the petty strifes of men
> Their ceaseless toil for wealth and power:
> The peace of God in lonely glen
> By whispering stream at twilight hour
> Is more to me than prelates' lawn
> Than stainless ermine, gartered knee,
> I wait Christ's coronation morn
> And rest, my God, through faith in Thee.

Albert Lewis's piety was deep and unchanging. For all his political distaste for the power of the Roman church, he had none of Thomas Hamilton's feeling that Catholics were not really Christians. This is made clear by another of his wheezes, written down after he had attended a funeral in Belfast. He came back from the cemetery in a carriage with one Protestant and two Catholics. It had been a Catholic funeral, conducted in Latin, but the Protestant was a man of sufficient learning to have understood the words *Pater Noster*. Leaning forward to his Catholic friends, this Protestant said – 'I heard the priest say that old prayer "Our Father". I should like to ask you a question. Did we steal that prayer from your church or did you steal it from us?' Albert Lewis was astonished. He said quietly, 'We both "stole" it from our Saviour . . .' Living in Ulster compelled the serious believer to cling to 'mere Christianity', that is, to those parts of the faith which both sides held in common, not those parts of it which were divisive.

This was Albert Lewis, the man who married Flora Hamilton on 29 August 1894. 'I wonder whether I do love you? I am not quite sure,' she had written to him the previous year. Although she came to feel that 'I am very fond of you and . . . I should never think of loving anyone else', it would seem as though Albert was 'the more loving one'. Perhaps because of his gifts as a comedian, or his small stature, or his thick moustaches, Albert Lewis, though a fundamentally serious man, was doomed to be regarded as a figure of fun by those whom he loved best.

TWO

EARLY DAYS
1898–1905

'I fancy happy childhoods are usually forgotten,' C. S. Lewis was to write in later life. 'It is not settled comfort and heartsease but momentary joy that transfigures the past and lets the eternal quality show through.' But his own childhood, or the first nine years of it, was happy and not so much forgotten as mythologized.

Albert and Flora Lewis made their first marital home in a substantial semi-detached house called Dundela Villas. They were still within reach, if not in the parish, of St Mark's, Dundela, the church where they were married and where Thomas Hamilton, Flora's father, was the parson. Albert's father, too, was nearby. Their marriage was not, like some unions, a breaking-away from parents and background. Rather it was a strengthening of their roots. Ulster, conservative, Protestant, middle-class Ulster, was the world into which their children were born and to which they completely belonged.

There were two children of the marriage – both boys. Warren Hamilton Lewis was born on 16 June 1895 and his younger brother Clive Staples on 29 November 1898. The Lewises liked nicknames and pet-names. Flora – itself a variant on her baptismal name of Florence – was sometimes called Doli by her husband. She called Albert Ali or Lal. Warren Hamilton Lewis quickly became Warnie, Badger, Badgie or Badge. Clive Staples was from an early age known as Jacks, Jacko, Jack, Kricks or Klicks, as well as being affectionately referred to by Warnie as 'It'.

When he began to emerge from babyhood Jacks discovered that he had two great friends – Warnie and their nurse Lizzie Endicott. 'There was no nonsense about "Lady nurses" in those days. Through Lizzie we struck our roots into the peasantry of County Down.'[1]

These peasant roots were as vigorously Protestant as those of the more genteel Hamiltons and the Lewises.

'Now mind out there, Master Jacks,' he remembered his nurse saying as she took his hand on a walk, 'and keep your feet out of the puddles. Look at it there, all full of dirty wee popes.' He remembered Lizzie taking his hand and peering with him into the filthy puddle, flecked with bits of mud. A 'wee pope' in Lizzie's vocabulary meant anything dirty or distasteful. In later life, when he befriended English Roman Catholics, C. S. Lewis would sometimes try to explain to them what it was like to have been brought up in Protestant Ulster. It was hearing the word 'pope' and being supplied by the irrational involuntary part of the brain with an image not of a bishop in a triple crown but of a filthy puddle.[2] Although C. S. Lewis denied that the 'Puritania' of his fantasy *The Pilgrim's Regress* was to be identified with the North of Ireland, it plainly was so, even if his parents were not in the narrow sense 'puritanical'. Heaven and hell, if only in a fantastical way, seemed closer here than they would have done in an English suburb of comparable date and gentility. In the suburb of Strandtown where they were living there was a mad clergyman called Russell. Once when Albert Lewis was smoking a cigarette in the road, he met Russell, who stopped, pointed down and thundered, 'Plenty of smoke down there,' then, pointing upwards, 'None up there!' and walked rapidly away.[3]

Yet in *The Pilgrim's Regress* this dread of hell is tempered with pure humbug, as when John, the Pilgrim, is asked by the Steward (i.e. the Clergy) whether he has broken any of the rules imposed on the human race by the Landlord (i.e. God).

John's heart began to thump and his eyes bulged more and more, and he was at his wit's end when the Steward took the mask off and looked at John with his real face and said, 'Better tell a lie, old chap, better tell a lie. Easier for all concerned,' and popped the mask on his face all in a flash. John gulped and said quickly, 'Oh no, sir.' 'That is just as well,' said the Steward through the mask. 'Because you know, if you did break any of them and the Landlord got to know of it, do you know what he'd do to you? . . . He'd take you and shut you up for ever and ever in a black hole full of snakes and scorpions as large as lobsters – for ever and ever. And besides that, he is such a kind, good man, so very, very kind, that I am sure you would never want to displease him.[4]

The caricature of Lewis's boyhood Protestantism is here unmistakable and, as the mask of the Steward makes clear in his allegory of the matter, the very fact that the doctrine of hell was believed in by decent, amiable people, who enjoyed their beer and their whiskey, made it harder, not easier, for his imagination to absorb. This was the air he breathed as a child, the religion he imbibed with his mother's milk. Moreover, because, by the turn of the century, the Irish crisis was reaching a head, Protestantism found itself very much on the defensive. It was clear to any intelligent observer that the Catholic Irish wanted Home Rule and that eventually they would get it. But where would this leave the Protestants, and in particular those Protestants who formed the overwhelming majority of the population in the six counties of the North of Ireland? Like the theology, this situation was something Lewis grew up with long before he was able to articulate or understand it. Before he knew what the speeches were *about*, he was aware of his father, a glass of whiskey and water in his hand, thunderously denouncing the English government; he was aware of his religiously obsessed old grandfather Lewis and servant Lizzie's dread of the Catholics, who by all accounts were advancing and making gains month by month.

But there was also a growing awareness of Belfast as a place. 'This was in the far off days when Britain was the world's carrier and the Lough was full of shipping. The sound of a steamer's horn at night still conjures up my whole boyhood.'[5] An early treat was being taken for walks across to Harland & Wollfs the shipbuilders when the White Star Liner *Cedric* was being built in 1902.[6]

And as well as the water, Lewis could see hills from the nursery window – 'What we called "the Green Hills"; that is, the low line of the Castlereagh Hills. They were not very far off but they were to children, quite unattainable. They taught me longing – *Sehnsucht*; made me for good or ill, and before I was six years old, a votary of the Blue Flower.'[7]

Before leaving the nursery at Dundela Villas, mention should be made of two experiences, unremarkable in themselves but striking for the manner in which Lewis's imagination has photographed them.

The first is one of horror – a book which contained a picture of a midget child, a sort of Tom Thumb, threatened by a stag beetle very much larger than himself. It was a primitive sort of 'pop-up' book. The horns of the beetle were strips of cardboard separate from the plate so that you could make them open and shut like pincers. From this early terror, Lewis derived his violent distaste for insects. It was his first experience of real fear and psychological pain, and interestingly enough he associates it in his own writings with his mother: *How a woman ordinarily so wise as my mother could have allowed this abomination into the nursery is difficult to understand.*

Lewis's mother is a shadowy figure in his autobiography. Beyond telling us that she was well educated and rather better born than his father, he has almost nothing to say about her as a person. In the *Lewis Papers*, the compilation of family letters and diaries made by Warren Hamilton Lewis during the 1930s, Mamy as they called her is canonized as we should expect. The strange little association between his own terror of the beetle and the wisdom or otherwise of his mother may be without significance in the story of C. S. Lewis, but there are to be other occasions in his story where love and pain, women and fear are found in conjunction.

His second nursery memory is equally pregnant with association. The sense of longing or *Sehnsucht*, the dawning of that Romantic yearning which he was to call Joy, began in his memory when the nursery door opened and his brother Warnie brought in 'the lid of a biscuit tin which he had covered with moss and garnished with twigs and flowers so as to make it a toy garden or a toy forest – that was the first beauty I ever knew . . . As long as I live my imagination of Paradise will retain something of my brother's toy garden.'[8]

The comradeship between Warnie and Jacks was deep from the earliest days, and appears to have been largely unaffected by the three-year difference in their ages. Probably the manifest difference in their levels of intelligence helps to account for this since Jacks, by far the cleverer of the two, was from a very early age able to keep up with Warnie's level of reading, as well as to share his toys and fantasies. Both of them looked back on their nursery days together at Dundela Villas as an idyll. And it was out of that nursery that the passion for reading and writing developed which was to be their most striking characteristic in grown-up days. For C. S. Lewis the man, the happiest times were spent either reading or writing or talking about reading and writing with his brother or brother-substitutes.

An early book-memory for C. S. Lewis was the publication of Beatrix Potter's *Squirrel Nutkin* when he was five and Warnie was seven. 'It troubled me with what I can only describe as the Idea of Autumn. It sounds fantastic to say that one can be enamoured of a season but that is something like what happened.' To Beatrix Potter, doubtless, C. S. Lewis owed the inspiration for his earlier essays in fiction, some of which were made when he was five or six. While Warnie, the future soldier and historian, was drawing ships and trains and writing histories of India, Jacks was inventing a place called Animal-land, peopled with 'dressed Animals'. But these creatures were wholly unlike the subdued, ironical creations of Beatrix Potter. They were full-square portraits of the grown-ups surrounding Jacks and Warnie.

Well before Jacks was seven years old, the two brothers had developed the habit of mythologizing the grown-ups, whose highly coloured antics both amused them and threatened the security of their alliance. They had inherited from their father the power to distort and fictionalize other people so that we, looking back at the Lewis family of that era, have the greatest difficulty in distinguishing between what any of them were actually like and the fantastical shape they assumed in the two brothers' collective memory. The fact that the grown-ups were always a threat, as well as a comic turn, emphasized the sharp outlines of memory's caricature.

And the threat which they were hatching all through the nursery years was the threat of school. The choice which lay before Albert and Flora Lewis was whether to educate Jacks and Warnie as Irishmen or whether to turn them into English gentlemen. Several factors must be borne in mind here. One is that the 'Irish situation' from the Protestant point of view was getting worse and worse: that is to say that the formation of some form of Irish Catholic Republic independent of the English Crown looked more and more likely, and there was no certainty whatsoever at the time that the Province of Ulster (the Protestant six counties of the North) would be any more capable of retaining its links with Great Britain than the counties of the south. To anyone in favour of retaining the Union, but pessimistic about its future, the lure of an English education for their children would have seemed particularly strong.

Then again, there was an element of snobbery in the decision. If the Hamiltons could boast a long line of respectable parsons and even a bishop in the blood, Flora's mother's family was even grander. They were related to Sir William and Lady Ewart of Glenmachan House, one of the gracious 'ascendancy' mansions with which Ireland had been adorned since the eighteenth century. The Lewises were frequent and welcome guests on this particular 'rich man's flowering lawns': a far cry from the world of Grandfather Lewis's childhood. The urge to gentrify itself which is endemic in the British middle class made it all the more difficult to contemplate giving the boys anything but 'the best'. And 'the best' in this context meant an English private school.

Neither Flora nor Albert Lewis knew anything about English schools, which was why they consulted Albert's old headmaster from Lurgan College, W. T. Kirkpatrick or 'Kirk'. Albert had been one of Kirk's favourite pupils, as is made clear by the extremely sentimental letters which survive from the older to the younger man: 'When you recall the days we spent in Lurgan, shall I confess it? Tears dim my usually tranquil vision.'[9]

As far back as 1900, Kirkpatrick had enlisted Albert's services as a lawyer in a matter of characteristic pettiness. Kirkpatrick, who was a wealthy man with private means, had retired early (aged fifty-one) and gone to live in England so that his only son could read electrical engineering at Manchester University while still living with his parents at home. Before leaving Ireland he had taken a clock to be cleaned by a man named Brown of Rosemary Street, Belfast. The clockmaker had spoilt the clock and Kirkpatrick had subsequently spent £3. 6s. having it repaired in Manchester. He was now trying to reclaim the money from the Irish clockmaker and was prepared if necessary to go to law.

It was in the course of this strange affair that he made contact once more with Albert Lewis and the flood of his affection, together with an avaricious desire to screw the last penny from the clockmaker, gushed from his pen. 'It was a privilege to have you for a pupil . . . I never forget you and never can. I felt instinctively that you had some sparks of the divine fire.'

When Warnie approached the age when he might be sent to school, it was natural that Flora and Albert Lewis should consult the oracle.

What about Campbell College, the best school in Belfast? Flora was evidently in favour, having been educated, and well educated, without having to go away. But Kirkpatrick's advice was firm. 'Pray convey my regards to your wife. I don't think she would be satisfied with her boy going to Campbell as a day pupil, and in any case it will be good for the boy himself to be away, and look to his home as a holiday-heaven [sic].'[10] This letter was written in October 1904. Kirkpatrick's view of the matter was itself wildly irrational, for he was obviously capable of retaining in his head a snobbish, headmasterly veneration for English boarding schools and at the same time a healthy Irish vision of how appalling they are. This is revealed in a rather nasty letter he wrote to Albert Lewis somewhat later:

> When the black day comes that the mother's darling must leave home, that he has so long bullied, some school is sought to break the fall. What shall it be? O, there are plenty. Demand soon creates supply. There are schools where everything is done for the little dears, where graduates are kept to help them trundle hoops and wipe their noses, where every luxury is guaranteed. True the charge is a bit stiff, but what of that? What are money considerations when weighed against the tears and sobs of separation? And then there is the appeal to snobbery, which never fails. The boys are all of a nice social grade. So they whisper: but as a matter of fact they are more likely to be the sons of PARVENU shopkeepers and the rich business class.[11]

Kirkpatrick here, with typical *saeva indignatio*, fires to left and right. By any rule of logic this should have dissuaded the Lewises from the very idea of an English boarding school, particularly since, when he was asked for the name of a specific prep school (i.e. a school for the seven-to-thirteen age group), Kirkpatrick was unable to supply a single one; nevertheless, in the mysterious way that these things happen, the correspondence of the Headmaster with his beloved old pupil had sealed the fate of the two little boys. But before that was to happen, there was another monumental change in their lives. They moved house.

THREE

LITTLE LEA
1905–1908

Albert Lewis was coming up in the world. Little Lea was a substantial house which he had built himself, with the intention of retiring from his solicitor's practice at the age of about fifty and going in 'mildly for Literature or Public Life – such as Town Council or Harbour Board'.[1]

C. S. Lewis recalled that

> My father, who had more capacity for being cheated than any man I have ever known, was badly cheated by his builders; the drains were wrong, the chimneys were wrong, and there was a draught in every room. None of this, however, mattered to a child. To me, the important thing about the move was that the background of my life became larger.[2]

This house, with its long book-lined corridors, its ugliness ('we never saw a beautiful building nor imagined a building could be beautiful'), and above all its roominess, was the background for all the Lewis brothers' subsequent imaginative experiences. In memory, they returned to it again and again – above all to the 'Little End Room', an attic sitting-room which was created for them as a refuge from the grown-ups. Warnie, however, had less than a month of the new house before being sent away to boarding school. They moved in on 21 April 1905, and on 10 May he was sent off to Wynyard House near Watford. 'Warren left home for school tonight for the first time,' Albert wrote in his diary. 'Fearful wrench for me. Badge behaved very pluckily. Flora took him over. May God bless the venture.'[3]

In the last resort, the Lewises, like many middle-class parents, had chosen a school for their son 'blind', relying not on their own sense or experience but on the advice of an educational 'agency' in London called Gabbitas & Thring. This curious institution has the dual purpose of finding both staff to teach in private schools and parents trusting enough to put their children in these teachers' charge. Since a high proportion of English writers have at one stage or another been obliged to earn their living as schoolmasters, it is not surprising that the agency has been so often mentioned in the pages of mid-twentieth-century literature. W. H. Auden dubbed it Rabbitarse & String, while Evelyn Waugh used it as the catalyst by which his first fictional hero, Paul Pennyfeather, was transformed into an usher at Llanabba Castle. In *Decline and Fall*, the agency is called Church & Gargoyle.

> 'We class schools, you see, into four grades: Leading School, First-rate School, Good School, and School. Frankly,' said Mr Levy, 'School is pretty bad.'[4]

Wynyard was to turn out to be no better than 'School', but this was a fact that Jack Lewis was not to discover for himself until nearly three years had elapsed. Up to that point he had the run of Little Lea; and he was educated entirely at home. His governess was called Miss Harper, and his mother herself took charge of teaching him French and Latin. He seems to have disliked his governess – who was a Presbyterian. A theological lecture interspersed between the sums was one of his first intimations that there was Another World in which Christians were supposed to believe. He preferred the other world of his own invention, and by the time he was nine he had already assembled a considerable *œuvre*, chiefly relating to Animal-land and the dressed animals, but also including a number of plays. Those looking in this early juvenilia for signs of the later Lewis will be disappointed. There is none of the sense in it which you get in the Narnia stories of 'another world', of the numinous or the strange. Worse, his childish fantasies are really rather dull. What sets them apart is their fluency, and the fact that they reveal him as a precise, attentive reader. 'My invented world was full (for me) of interest, bustle, humour and character. But there was no poetry, even no romance in it. It was almost astonishingly prosaic.'[5] He thought this meant he was training himself to be a novelist but it would be truer

to see in the juvenilia Lewis training himself to be a critic. The stories
and plays are at their liveliest when he is echoing another writer. In
the stage directions to *Littera Scripta*, for instance, a play he wrote
much later (at the age of thirteen), there is all the unactable novelistic
quality of Shaw: 'Mr Bar in evening dress is standing in the open
drawing-room doorway, with his back to the stage. He is a stout,
cheerful little fellow, who carries an atmosphere of impudence and
unpaid bills.'[6]

To the end of his days Lewis was a brilliant parodist – always the
sign of a good critic. The stories reveal not that he was trying to
escape the grotesque (as he saw it) world of servants and relations,
but that he would best come to terms with them when he had
re-invented them in the pages of his notebooks. In addition to his
parents and Miss Harper, there were Maude the maid, Martha the
cook and his old grandfather Lewis, who came to live in the house in
April 1907, a prematurely senile presence, muttering psalms to himself
in an upstairs bedroom. For much of the time from 1905 until 1907,
Jacks was left alone, wallowing in books. When he wasn't reading he
was either missing Warnie, away at school, and writing him letters,
or thinking about the games they would play when he got home.

'Hoora!' he wrote in 1907. 'Warnie comes home this morning. I
am lying in bed waiting for him and thinking of him, before I know
where I am I hear his boots pounding on the stairs, he comes into my
room, we shake hands and begin to talk.' He wrote that when he was
nine, but he could easily have written it when he was twenty-nine or
fifty-nine.

Little Jacks himself we can glimpse in his fragment of autobiography
– 'My life during the Xmas holidsas of 1907 by Jacks or Clive Lewis
author of "Building of the Promanad", "Toyland" "Living races of
Mouse-Land" etc. Dedicated to Miss Maude Scott.'

I begin my life after my 9th birthday, on which I got a book from
Papy and a post-card album from Mamy. I have a lot of enymays,
however there are only 2 in this house they are called Maude and
Mat. Maude is far worse than Mat but she thinks she is a saint. I
rather like Mat, but I HATE Maude, she is very nasty and bad
tempered, also very ugly, as you can see in the picture . . .

Having disposed of the servants, our young author turns his attention to his parents. 'Mamy is like most middle-aged ladys, stout, brown hair, spectacles, kniting her chief industry etc. etc. I am like most boys of 9 and I am like Papy, bad temper, thick lips, thin and generaly wearing a jersy.' The thick lips were to strike others later in life. 'Oh, he was a brute,' one of his colleagues in the English Faculty at Oxford once recalled. 'You could always tell when he was going to start an argument, he would push forward his thick lower lip.'

His knowledge of his close resemblance to his own father was to leave Lewis. Albert would become a more and more fantastical creature in his son's imagination – perhaps in fact. But in those tranquil Little Lea years before the great calamity befell them all, and before Jacks entered puberty, there were times of great happiness. The leisurely Irish quality of Albert's life is captured by one of his wheezes about a neighbouring peer who annually allowed a cricket match in his park. The luncheon provided on these occasions was so generous that in the afternoon 'there were few steady men on the field'. The wicketkeeper was one of the few who had remained sober, and when the drunken batsman lurched out several yards from the pitch to meet his ball and missed it, the wicketkeeper clearly stumped him. 'How's that, umpire?' he said to the umpire, who was steadying himself on a bat. To which the umpire replied, 'What the hell is it your business? Go on with the bloody match.'

These were not only the days when such amusing things happened; they were also the days when the family still laughed about Albert's 'wheezes'. The house moreover became more and more prosperous and comfortable. In May 1907, a telephone was installed.[7] The first person Jacks tried to ring was a neighbour of about his age called Arthur Greeves who, like Warnie, was to be a constant in his life. The Greeves family were flax-spinners – the chief industry of Belfast apart from shipbuilding. Jacks's friendship with Arthur was not to blossom until they were in their teens. In early boyhood, Warnie was really his only friend, the one with whom he shared his fantasies. And it was noticeable that from an early age the younger brother dominated over the elder. There is real forceful bossiness in the letter he wrote to Warnie in May 1907 after the telephone was installed. 'I have got an adia [sic] you know the play I was writing. I think we will try and act it with new stage don't say annything about it not being dark, we will have it upstairs and draw the thick curtains and the night one, the scenery is rather hard but still I think we shall do it.'

Warnie was by now twelve years old and his parents were starting to wonder about where he should be educated after Wynyard. Luckily, advice was to hand from old Mr Kirkpatrick, whose litigious nature had not been satisfied with suing a clockmaker for spoiling his clock. A few years later a parent who had entrusted Kirkpatrick with the tuition of a son had been slow in paying an agreed fee and Kirkpatrick had once more enlisted Albert Lewis's help as a solicitor to extract the money from the defaulter. Albert Lewis himself had not required a cash payment for this service. A greater reward, as he told his old teacher, would be to hear Kirkpatrick's views on the relation between morality and religion. Kirkpatrick wrote back that

> it is a subject too wide, too vast, too dependent on time, place, heredity and social conditions to be treated adequately in a letter. It would take a SYMPOSIUM, or, as Cicero preferred to call it, a Convivium, to touch even on some aspects of what must always be the most profoundly interesting of all questions that deal with man's spiritual nature and future destiny in the world.[8]

Albert had to be content, instead, with receiving Kirkpatrick's advice about a suitable school for Warnie. Winchester was 'out of the question', Cheltenham and Rugby were both possibilities. Indeed, Albert even got to the point of writing to a housemaster at Rugby and seeing if his boy could have a place there. Shrewsbury looked tempting. 'You will do worse,' Kirkpatrick advised, 'especially if your boy is literary.' It looked, however, as if Rugby would be the school for Warnie. But before that time, the sky darkened over Little Lea, and the paradise which young Jacks was inhabiting there with his parents and brother and servants and books was shattered for ever. For Albert Lewis 1908 was a year of unbelievable sorrows. Flora Lewis became seriously ill, and cancer was diagnosed. Since nurses were required night and day, Albert Lewis was compelled to ask his father, who had been living with the family for a year, to move out of Little Lea. Richard Lewis made the move in March. On 24 March he suffered a serious stroke and on 2 April he died. This was the first death of the year.

Flora lasted another four months. Jack remembered the night when he was ill:

> crying both with headache and toothache and distressed because my mother did not come to me. That was because she was ill too: and what was odd was that there were several doctors in her room and voices and comings and goings all over the house and doors shutting and opening. It seemed to last for hours. And then my father, in tears, came into my room and began to try to convey to my terrified mind things it had never conceived before.

It is hard to know whether it was worse to be Jacks, in the midst of all this suffering, or Warnie, away at school in England and terrified that his mother might at any minute die before he had the chance to see her for the last time.

'My dear son,' Albert warned him in a letter written shortly after Warnie's thirteenth birthday, 'it may be that God in his mercy has decided that you will have no person in the future to turn to but me.' Warnie's response was brave. 'Write as often as you can and tell me all you can about Mammy. It is beastly for me here not being able to tell what is going on from day to day.'[9]

In the event, she was to die in the summer holidays. By 11 August it was obvious that she did not have long to live. From her bedroom she could hear in the distance the Orange Lodge practising for the Apprentices' march, blowing pipes and banging drums with what seemed like cruel force. 'It's a pity that it takes so long to learn that tune,' she murmured. By the night of 20 August she had been wandering for a while in her talk, but she suddenly grasped Albert's hand and said to the nurse, 'Nurse, when you get married see that you get a good man who loves you and loves God.'

The next night she was more composed, and again Albert sat up with her. 'I spoke to her (nor was it the first time by any means that a conversation on heavenly things had taken place between us),' he wrote, 'sometimes begun by her, sometimes by me, of the goodness of God. Like a flash she said, "What have we done for him?" May I never forget that. She died at 6.30 on the morning of the 23rd August, my birthday. As good a woman, wife and mother, as God has ever given to man.'[10]

On Flora's mantelpiece there was a calendar with a Shakespearean quotation for each day of the year. The quotation for the day on which she died was from the fifth act of *King Lear*:

> Men must endure
> Their going hence, even as their coming hither:
> Ripeness is all.

Albert, who had lost his father and his wife in the space of four months, was to suffer a third blow only a fortnight later when his elder brother Joe also died.

Albert's grief over the summer had made him a poor companion to his sons, and he was now in no position, emotionally, to look after them on his own. Perhaps if he had been forced to do so by financial circumstances, things would have been different. 'His nerves had never been of the steadiest,' C. S. Lewis mercilessly recalled, 'and his emotions had always been uncontrolled. Under the pressure of anxiety his temper became incalculable; he spoke wildly and acted unjustly.' This disturbing passage in *Surprised by Joy* implies that in the weeks leading up to Flora's death, the survivors all hurt one another in an irremediable way. Albert's outbursts of rage against Jacks were not forgiven. 'During these months the unfortunate man, had he but known it, was really losing his sons as well as his wife.' It had already been decided that Jacks should accompany Warnie back to Wynyard School.

FOUR

SCHOOLS
1908–1914

Presumably there is no paediatrician or child psychologist in the world who would recommend that a nine-year-old boy, within a fortnight of his mother's death, should be sent away from home; and not merely sent away from home, but sent to another country, to a school run on harshly unfeeling lines. But this is what happened to C. S. Lewis. The experience was made all the more painful by his father's sobbing on the quayside in Ireland as he bade the boys farewell, and by the boys' not having the ability to express whatever it was they felt. Forty years later, Jacks said he had felt merely 'embarrassed and self-conscious', and hated the discomfort of his school uniform – an Eton collar, a black coat, knickerbockers which buttoned at the knee.

After an overnight crossing of the Irish Sea, during which Warnie was seasick, they arrived at Liverpool, and C. S. Lewis 'reacted with immediate hatred' to the sight of England. With a deep part of himself, he was always to remain a stranger there. As the train made its progress from the North of England down to London, he felt he was entering a world of Stygian dullness. The English accents all around him 'seemed like the voices of demons'.[1]

At Euston, they changed trains, and made the short journey – some twenty minutes – to Jack's first school, Wynyard House, Watford, in the county of Hertford.

It was an unprepossessing place, being merely a couple of semi-detached, yellow-brick, suburban houses. There were fewer than twenty pupils, eight or nine of whom, like the Lewis brothers, were boarders. In his first letter home to his father, Jack was prepared to look on the bright side. 'I cannot of course tell you yet but I think I shall like this place,' he wrote. 'Misis [sic] Capron and the Miss Caprons are very nice and I think I will be able to get on with Mr.

Capron though to tell the truth he is rather eccentric.'² This remark
was an understatement. The headmaster of Wynyard House, the
Reverend Robert Capron, was a bad-tempered and capricious man
who was especially unkind to those boys whom he suspected of having
low social origins. The boys called him Oldie. He was rather a
handsome figure in a vaguely Teutonic mould, with a short grey
beard, moustaches and thick grey hair. 'I have seen him', Warnie
remembered later, 'lift a boy of twelve or so from the floor by the
back of his collar, and holding him at arm's length as one might a
dog, proceed to refresh the unfortunate youth's memory by applying
his cane to his calves.'³ It is hard to tell whether Warnie had told his
parents of the horrors of Wynyard House and they had ignored him,
or whether it took the more trenchant Jacks, who was infinitely more
articulate, and used to all home comforts, to protest at Capron's ways.
Only a fortnight after relaying his sunny hope that he would like
Wynyard, Jack was writing to Albert, 'My dear Papy, Mr. Capron
said something I am not likely to forget – "Curse the boy" (behind
Warnie's back) because Warnie did not bring his jam to tea, no one
ever heard such a rule before. Please may we not leave on Saturday?
We simply CANNOT wait in this hole until the end of term . . .
Your loving son Jack.'⁴

But for one reason or another, they stayed. The brothers loathed
Capron and his mincing, affected manner of speech. *Oh* was *Eoh*, *beer*
was *be-ah*. For his part Capron persistently picked on Warnie. He
asserted that Warnie was lazy, a cheat, and – the final outrage which
nearly *did* cause Albert Lewis to withdraw his sons when he heard of
it – that he had a cousin in the Canadian Mounted Police. It is not
possible, at this distance, to discover either how Capron dreamed up
this fanciful notion, or why it was deemed so offensive.

C. S. Lewis remained obsessed by Wynyard for the rest of his life.
Although he spent only eighteen months as a pupil there, he devoted
nearly a tenth of his autobiography to describing it, in the most lurid
terms, as a 'concentration camp'. He went further, and called it Belsen.
Wynyard was important as the place where he first became conscious
of two things which must have already formed part of the texture of
his Irish childhood. Here he met them in unfamiliar English guises:
corporal punishment and Christianity. 'Everyone talks of sadism
nowadays,' Lewis wrote in his autobiography (Do they? the reader

23

naturally replies), '. . . but I question whether Capron's cruelty had any erotic element in it.' The question he does not ask is to what extent Capron's floggings contributed to his own, Lewis's, erotic development. Capron flogged the boys indiscriminately – for getting sums wrong (and there were a lot of sums on the curriculum at Wynyard), for breaking the innumerable rules of the place – and sometimes for no reason at all. During one term, Capron's wife died, and it had the effect of making him even more indiscriminately violent: so much so that his son, known as Wee-wee to the boys, felt obliged to apologize on his father's behalf – an apology which in itself was an excruciating torture to Jack, who had 'learnt to fear and hate emotion'.

Almost the most interesting thing about Lewis's memories of Wynyard, however, is his assertion that Capron was the first person to teach him undiluted Christianity, 'as distinct from general "up-lift"'. The impression given in *Surprised by Joy* is that he grew up in a religiously wishy-washy household. No emphasis is given to his father's profound piety, nor to the theological preoccupations of grandfather Lewis, who wandered about the corridors of Little Lea muttering psalms. It was at Wynyard that he began seriously to pray, to read the Bible and to attempt seriously to obey his conscience.

His initial reaction to the school religion, however, was less than favourable. Capron took the boys to worship at the church of St John's, Watford, an Anglo-Catholic shrine very little different, when judged from the Ulster viewpoint, from the abominations of Rome herself. 'In this abominable place of Romish hypocrites and English liars,' Jack wrote at the time, 'the people cross themselves, bow to the Lord's table (which they have the vanity to call an altar) and pray to the Virgin.' But when he looked back on it from the perspective of middle age, and when he had more or less adopted this 'Romish' style of religion for himself, he decided that 'the effect . . . was entirely good'.[5]

The psychosexual effects of living under a reign of terror, where everything was punishable by the cane; the effects, moreover, of having been introduced to this system at the very moment when he had lost his mother and begun to 'fear and hate emotion' – all these were to make themselves felt in Lewis's later development. For the time being, he reacted as he was always to react to grown-ups with whom he was unable to make friends. He made Capron into a monster. It may very well be the case that the man *was* a monster, but since we may only view him through the creative lens of the Lewis brothers' memory, there is no knowing what he was like in other people's minds. To judge from the fact that Warnie, of good average intelligence, had sunk back badly in his school work by the time he went on to public school, we may believe them when they bemoan the academic standard at Wynyard House. In memory the place was like Doctor Grimstone's school in *Vice Versa*. The tyranny which Capron exercised, not only over the boys but also over his own grown-up children, seems like something in Victorian fiction, though in many ways he sounds more like a character in Ivy Compton-Burnett than one in F. Anstey.

Both boys were so unhappy at Wynyard that they wrote to their father with the suggestion that they should go to Campbell College, a day school in Belfast. 'Jack and I have been thinking it over,' Warnie wrote, 'and we both think we would like to go to Campbell College. Of course, as you say the boys may not be gentlemen, but no big school is entirely composed of gentlemen, and I think English boys are not so honest or gentlemanly as most Irish ones.'[6]

Poor Albert was too wrapped up in the after-effects of bereavement to give intelligent attention to the education of his sons. He continued to struggle on with his work in the police courts, and this brought solace. But in solitude he was seized with irrational fears, and hypochondria began to take a grip on him. He was convinced, for example, that he was diabetic, and no number of visits to the doctor, followed by tests and negative results, would put his mind at rest. He was just not in a position to make a decision. He wrote to Capron suggesting that he should withdraw his sons from Wynyard, but not being on the spot, and being constitutionally unable to stray from home to investigate the school for himself, he accepted Capron's word that all was well. In the event it was to Capron, rather than to his older mentor Kirkpatrick, that Albert Lewis entrusted the choice of Warnie's public school. Capron made the perfectly sensible suggestion that Warnie should be sent to Malvern College, and in the autumn term of 1909 to Malvern he went.

This would have been the moment for Jack to leave Wynyard, but Capron was by now in desperate straits and he played on the gullible Mr Lewis to persuade him to leave Jack in his care. In fact, his beatings and canings had grown so extreme that a parent had brought a High Court action against Capron, and the scandal caused by this meant that his pupils dwindled to nine in number, of whom one was Jack. The case was dropped, but it left Capron a ruined man, and in the end, since he was a priest in orders, he looked about for a cure of souls. He became the rector of Radstock in Hertfordshire, and died in 1911 aged sixty. His epitaph was composed of two words – JESU MERCY.

In 1910, then, C. S. Lewis was separated from one of the great monsters in his life, but memory lovingly cultivated Capron until, larger than life, he was ready to step on to the pages of *Surprised by Joy*. The very year that Wynyard collapsed, 1910, was also memorable for one of the key theatrical experiences of the Lewis brothers' lives. In the Christmas vacation, their second cousin, Hope Ewart, took them to see Barrie's *Peter Pan*. It is one of the Grand Conspicuous Omissions in Lewis's autobiography that he says nothing about this experience which, to judge from the *Lewis Papers*, was momentous. For there was no children's story more apposite to his life than that of the little boy who *could* not grow up, and who had to win his immortality by an assertion of metaphysical improbabilities – in this case a belief in fairies.

After the collapse of Wynyard, Jack achieved his wish of being sent to Campbell College for the autumn term of 1910. It was here that the English master, J. A. McNeill, introduced him to Matthew Arnold's *Sohrab and Rustum* – 'much the most important thing' to have happened to him while he was at the school, so far as Lewis himself was concerned. In *Surprised by Joy* he makes a point about his discovery of that poem which holds good for the development in personal literary taste of many another reader:

> Parrot critics say that *Sohrab* is a poem for classicists, to be enjoyed only by those who recognise the Homeric echoes . . . For me, the relation between Arnold and Homer worked the other way. I knew nothing of Homer; when I came, years later, to read the Iliad, I liked it partly because it was for me reminiscent of *Sohrab*.[7]

Doubtless all this was true, but like so much else in the autobiography it throws dust in the reader's eyes, and withholds from us the great, obvious fact about *Sohrab* – the fact about it which must have made its immediate and colossal appeal to Jack Lewis when he read it on the verge of his adolescence. It is the story of a father and son who have been separated. The father, without realizing Sohrab's identity, accepts the challenge of the Tartar chieftain, who is in fact his son. On the misty banks of Oxus, fog-bound as Belfast in November, father and son fight their archetypal combat, and the son is slain. There was quite as much in this story as there was in *Peter Pan* for young Jack to feast upon. After only a few weeks of Campbell, however, he fell ill. Poor health had always dogged his childhood. It could be said that he had come to regard periodic bouts of illness as the norm. Even in the days of his mother's lifetime, there had been delicious periods of fever and bad throats during which he was laid up, able to do nothing – what did he ever like doing better? – but read. At Wynyard, his health had become even worse, and in 1909 there had been an operation on his adenoids. In November 1910, Albert Lewis withdrew Jack from Campbell and decided that he should go to school in the same town as Warnie. He was not old enough yet to go to public school.

Gabbitas & Thring were once again consulted, and this time they came up with Cherbourg, a small preparatory school directly overlooking the College where Jack was destined one day to be a scholar. In January 1911, the two brothers set off for Malvern.

These Malvern days had, for them both, a quality of bitter-sweet when they looked back on them from the perspectives of manhood. Great Malvern is a Victorian spa town, nestling on the sunless side of a magnificent row of hills which stretch from the south-western tip of Worcestershire into Herefordshire. Those who built the town were either European mountain-dwellers (Swiss, Austrian, German) or English people who wished to recapture their own pleasure in the Alps or the Tyrol. Fanciful gables and evergreen gardens adorn the suburban roads. Opposite the Gothic railway station which (until a regrettable fire in 1985) was redolent of a mountain halt in the Vaud Canton, towers the Gothic splendour of the Ladies' College, formerly the Imperial Hotel where Victorian gentlefolk came for the water-cure. The list of those who submitted to this obviously bogus therapy (it involves being wrapped in a wet sheet and exposed to the open air) is impressive, and includes Tennyson and Thackeray. It was the popularity of Malvern as a health spa which made parents of the middle classes believe that it would be a suitable place for their children to be educated. Hence the presence there of the Boys' College (where Warren Lewis was), a sham medieval structure founded in 1862 in imitation of the older public schools, as well as a number of similar establishments for girls, and a host of little preparatory schools. To this day, these spawn all over the hillside as a puzzling testimony to the fact that English parents do not enjoy the company of those whom they have taken the trouble of bringing into the world.

Cherbourg, the school where Jack Lewis spent the period from January 1911 to June 1913, was a large white stucco building overlooking the College. Its architecture was reminiscent of villas on the Italian lakes. There were seventeen boys, three assistant masters, and a matron called Miss Cowrie, to whose lax religious views (she dabbled with theosophy and what Lewis later called 'the whole Anglo-American Occultist tradition') readers of *Surprised by Joy* are invited to attribute the loss of the author's boyhood Christian faith. This is the chapter of Lewis's autobiography which rings least true. Three things, he tells us, contributed to the collapse of the Christianity which he had imbibed from Oldie Capron at Wynyard. One was the wishy-washy spiritual nonsense of 'dear Miss C.'; another was the alleged sophistication of a young master called 'Pogo', who was 'dressy' and told the boys all about the famous actresses in London. The third factor was his advance in studying the classics.

> Here, especially in Virgil, one was presented with a mass of religious ideas; and all teachers and editors took it for granted from the outset that these religious ideas were sheer illusion . . . The impression I got was that religion in general, though utterly false, was a natural growth, a kind of endemic nonsense into which humanity tended to blunder. In the midst of a thousand religions, stood our own, the thousand and first, labelled True. But on what grounds could I believe this exception?[8]

While this third objection to Christianity rings true as a thought which troubled him at the age of twelve, the other two do not. We feel too strongly the presence of the middle-aged Lewis looking back on the Peter Pan, pubescent boy-Lewis and being horrified by his 'loss of faith, of virtue, of simplicity'. The passages, for example, where he describes his longing to abandon Christianity because of an over-scrupulous terror that he was not sufficiently concentrating on his prayers, while they may be true in general, are far too specifically recalled to be plausible. The details are too sharp. His saying that he hates himself for becoming at this period a 'prig' and a 'snob' is really another way of saying that he hates himself for having grown up at all.

For the truth is that he was an intelligent and gifted boy, whose range of reading and whose capacity to appreciate literature (and, to a lesser extent, music) were uncommonly advanced. For him, the great personal 'renaissance' or imaginative discovery of this period of his life was what he came to call Northernness. What he means by this is expounded in one of the most eloquent passages in *Surprised by Joy*:

A vision of huge, clear spaces hanging above the Atlantic in the endless Twilight of a Northern summer, remoteness, severity . . . and almost at the same moment I knew that I had met this before, long, long ago, (it hardly seems longer now) in *Tegner's Drapa*, that Siegfried (whatever it might be) belonged to the same world as Balder and the sunward-sailing cranes.

This aesthetic experience which came upon Lewis 'almost like heart-break' was prompted merely by glimpsing in some literary periodical the words *Siegfried and the Twilight of the Gods* and an Arthur Rackham illustration to that volume. In the decade before the First World War, when a Victorian passion for all things Teutonic and Northern still gripped the British middle class, it is hardly surprising that all this should have come Lewis's way. This was the era of the haunting music-hall song 'Speak to Me, Thora', the sentiments of which exactly coincide with Lewis's boyhood epiphany:

I stand in a land of roses,
But I dream of a land of snow.
When you and I were happy
In the days of long ago . . .

29

He had only to read the words *Twilight of the Gods* and he was able to recover 'the knowledge that I had once had what I now lacked for years, that I was returning at last from exile and desert lands to my own country'.

None of this would perhaps have taken root so forcefully in the imagination had Albert Lewis not been a man of some musical taste, who took the boys to the opera and the ballet whenever they were performed at the Belfast Hippodrome, and who also gave them a gramophone. It was through gramophone-record catalogues that C. S. Lewis first discovered Wagner, and his essay on 'the great Bayreuth Master', written when he was barely thirteen, is by far the most remarkable production of his early years – a thousand times more impressive than his plays or his Animal-land fantasies.

One sees what the middle-aged Lewis meant about the twelve-year-old being a prig and a snob. All the same, the expressions of that priggishness and snobbery are well turned, as when he says of Wagner that 'He has not been, nor ever will be, appreciated by the mass: there are some brains incapable of appreciation of the beautiful except when it is embodied in a sort of lyric prettiness.' What impresses about the essay is the thoroughness with which Lewis, merely by listening to gramophone records and following the stories, had learnt to appreciate the great Wagnerian *Ring* cycle and *Parsifal*, 'his last and greatest work'. He disdained *Tannhäuser*, in which Wagner was 'led away into the tinselled realms of tunefulness', but considered *Tristan* unsurpassed as drama by anything the world had ever seen. 'Once having grown to love Wagner's peculiar richness of tone and the deep meaning of his music and the philosophy of his dramatic poems, all other composers seem but caricatures and ghosts.'[9]

The masters at Cherbourg cannot have failed to recognize that they had in their midst a child prodigy. It would seem too as if this was the period of his childhood when he was most able to mix with other boys on their own terms. He tells us that he made friends with the children at Cherbourg, as he had not at Wynyard. And the school magazine records that he even played for the school cricket eleven (though, given that there were only seventeen boys in the school, it may have been impossible to avoid this). He played twelve innings and his highest score was ten. The author of the sports page described Lewis as a 'stonewaller . . . only very moderate in the field'.

When the time came for him to sit the scholarship examination to Malvern College, Lewis once again fell ill. He had to take the exams in bed, in the school sanatorium. In spite of, or perhaps because of, this, he was awarded a scholarship to Malvern College. The boys of Cherbourg were given a holiday – which took the form of an outing to the British Camp (the Ancient British enclosure to the west of the town where Caractacus made his last stand against the Romans), followed by an excellent tea. At home, his father bought Jack an *édition de luxe* of Kipling's works signed by Kipling himself. 'I am not making too much of the scholarship,' Albert wrote to his son. 'It is not the scholarship I am so proud of but the circumstances in which it was won.' He signed this letter, as he so often and truthfully did, 'Your ever loving Paps'. But the love was no longer reciprocated. Albert, who was intensely lonely without his boys during the school terms, would wait eagerly for Warnie and Jack to return from Malvern. They would be three chums, all boys together. But this was not what his sons wanted. Albert's 'wheezes', stored up in memory and written down in his notebooks, were not what they wanted to hear.

He was bursting to tell his tales. Like the occasion in the police courts when he found himself prosecuting a girl called Maria Volento for allegedly assaulting a man in her father's ice-cream parlour. Assuming her to be an Italian with no grasp of English, Albert was almost certain that she would need the assistance of an interpreter; but he began to question her in English, very slowly, 'in the best nursery style'.

'Just try to explain in your own words what happened to you last night.'

Her reply, in the broadest Ulster brogue, was: 'Thon fella [pointing at the prisoner] clodded a tumbler at me and it wud have hut me only I deuked ut.'[10]

But to his sons, his self-confessed tendency to get hold of the wrong end of the stick was merely exasperating. In addition to conversational crossed wires and misapprehensions, he was capable of pure *non sequiturs*. 'Did Shakespeare spell his name with an E at the end?' asked Warnie. 'I believe – ' said Jack, but Albert interrupted: 'I very much doubt if he used the Italian calligraphy *at all*.'[11]

The portrait of Albert Lewis which emerges from *Surprised by Joy* is devastatingly cruel.

'Liberty Hall, boys, Liberty Hall,' as he delighted to quote. 'What time would you like lunch?' But we knew only too well that the meal which would otherwise have been at one had already been shifted in obedience to his lifelong preference to two or even two thirty; and that the cold meats which we had liked had been withdrawn in favour of the only food our father ever voluntarily ate – hot butcher's meat, boiled, stewed or roast . . . and this to be eaten in mid afternoon in a dining room that faced south

– on a day when the summer sun 'was blistering the paint' on the hot garden seats.

In time, everything about Albert came to annoy Jack and Warnie. When Albert was dead, Jack looked back with nostalgia to 'home and the way we hated it and the way we enjoyed hating it'. Warnie, likewise, remembered 'Saturday evening tram-rides and visits to the Hippodrome with late supper afterwards'. But even these were a torment to Jack. He did not really enjoy the popular music-hall songs or musical comedies which gave such innocent pleasure to his father and brother. And when Albert got them tickets for some 'popular' opera such as *Carmen*, Jack could now loftily consider it completely inferior to Wagner. 'One of the most noticeable results of the advent of Wagner's works in England is the rather paradoxical fact that he has made much more popular than they formerly were the lyrical operas to which he was so much opposed,' the young essayist of Cherbourg had written.[12] 'They're doing Carmen and Maritana,' Albert told Jack enthusiastically, 'and others that you and Warnie would rather like to hear.'[13] Looking back on it all, Jack was to confess, 'I thought Monday morning, when he went back to his work, the brightest jewel in the week.'[14]

So much for 'our father', as Albert is repeatedly called in the autobiography. In the autumn term of 1913, Jack began his career at Malvern College. The Lewis family's relations with the school were already strained. Warnie's career there had on the whole been happy and successful. He had submitted himself to the public-school system, played games and recovered some of the ability (which had been quite lost at Wynyard) of concentrating on academic tasks. He had even had some interesting contemporaries in the school, though perhaps the most interesting, the future novelist Michael Arlen (author of such amusing comedies as *The Green Hat*), made almost no impression on him whatsoever. In those days Arlen 'was still an Armenian boy called Koyoumgjain' and, as Warnie recalled, 'He made no mark of any kind at school, being merely one of a trinity of "dagoes" of whom the other two were also in my house.'[15]

So successful was Warnie's career at school that there had even been talk of his becoming the head boy, when, in the summer of 1913, disaster had struck. He was caught smoking (a habit to which both Lewis brothers had been devoted for a number of years now) and asked to leave. After a certain amount of special pleading by Albert Lewis, it was agreed that Warnie would not actually be sacked, on condition that he voluntarily withdrew himself from the school by the next term. It was a great blow to his pride, and potentially a great setback to his professional life. For he had decided (or it had been decided for him) that he should go into the Army, and for this it was necessary to prepare for the entrance examination to the Officer Training College at Sandhurst. Since he could no longer do this at school, where could he go? In his distress, Albert naturally turned to his old mentor Mr Kirkpatrick, who had by then moved to a house near Great Bookham in Surrey. For the first time in years, the brothers were separated. While Warnie went off to stay with Kirkpatrick, Jack began the adventure of public-school life on his own.

There is perhaps nowhere that the English appear more odious than within the confines of public schools. Lewis, who still nursed all his anti-English prejudice (though the beauty of the Malvern Hills did something to mitigate it), found little to love among his coevals. Above all, he hated the 'fagging' system – the notion, abolished now in the majority of boarding schools in England, but still widespread until ten or twenty years ago – that the junior boys of thirteen and fourteen should act as the servants of the older boys of seventeen or eighteen. Warren, who had thoroughly absorbed the public-school ethos, once remarked that 'if junior boys weren't fagged, they would become insufferable.' Jack answered the charge that it was mere pride and self-conceit in the fags which made the fagging system objectionable by transferring it to an adult context.

If some neighbouring V.I.P. had irresistible authority to call on you for any service he pleased at any hour when you were not in the office – if, when you came home on a summer evening, tired from work and with more work to prepare against the morrow, he could drag you on to the links and make you his caddy till the light failed – if at last he dismissed you unthanked with a suitcase full of his clothes to brush and clean and return to him before breakfast, and a hamper full of his foul linen for your wife to wash and mend – and if, under his regime, you were not always perfectly happy and contented, where could the cause lie except in your own vanity?[16]

It is interesting, incidentally, that someone who could see so clearly what was wrong with the fagging system in the course of this devastating analogy could not see that to all intents and purposes this was what the privileged classes were doing to the lower classes in the first half of the twentieth century.

Coming at a moment of particularly rapid physical growth in Lewis, the whole school system exhausted him. Like his frog-hero, Lord John Big, 'weary and depressed by over-work, despirited [sic] by his failures on the field and unpopular among his fellows who could not bear the comparison with so deligent [sic] a classmate, he led an unpleasant life. He returned home for his first holyday [sic] full of knowledge, bearing more than one prize and sadly broken in spirit.'[17]

Lewis's cleverness, his academic ability, probably made it harder for him to settle into the rough and tumble of life at Malvern. He had grown used to small schools and (at Cherbourg) to being the much-prized prodigy. At the Coll (as the boys called Malvern College) numbers were much greater, and different standards applied. To be popular there, you needed to be good at games and preferably, if you were young, pretty. Lewis appears to have had no trace of homosexuality in his make-up, and he had no wish to become a Tart, as the more desirable younger boys were called. He was physically clumsy. He once remarked that his whole life would have been different if he had not had thumb joints which did not bend in the middle. This physical peculiarity, inherited from his father, made him a poor craftsman, and did not improve his skill at catching balls when they were thrown at him.

Yet however much he loathed the boorishness of his fellow-collegians (and he was nearly always to dislike colleagues), Lewis did find things to love about Malvern. First, there was the Latin master,

Harry Wakelyn Smith, known to the boys as Smugy. (The first syllable was pronounced to rhyme with *fugue*.) Not only did he improve Jack's Latin and start him on the road to Greek with the *Bacchae* of Euripides (a play Jack was to love for the rest of his days); more important than that, his lessons were little outposts of civilization in an otherwise barbarous world. Smugy was a greasy-haired, bespectacled figure, vaguely frog-like in appearance, who was a friend of the composer Sir Edward Elgar, many of whose finest pieces of music had been composed when walking or riding on the Malvern Hills. Once, on a walk, Jack came upon the cottage where Elgar had lived. Smugy 'told us that Elgar used to say he was able to read a musical score in his hand and hear in his mind not only the main theme of the music, but also the different instruments and all the side currents of sound. What a wonderful state of mind!'[18]

Smugy's grateful pupil was to remember the honey-toned manner in which he read aloud the poets: not just Virgil, Horace and Euripides, but the great English poets too. 'He first taught me the right sensuality of poetry, how it should be savoured and mouthed in solitude. Of Milton's "Thrones, Dominations, Princedoms, Virtues, Powers," he said, "That line made me happy for a week." '[19]

Malvern had its good points. 'If I had never seen the spectacle which these coarse, brainless English schoolboys present, there might be a danger of my sometimes becoming like that myself.' Apart from Smugy's classroom, the other welcome refuge was the well-stocked College library, known as the Gurney. There in the summer term, with bees buzzing at the open windows, Lewis discovered the *Corpus Poeticum Boreale*. He followed up Smugy's suggestion and began to read Milton on his own. He read Yeats, and wrote home eagerly to Papy, or the P'daytabird as the boys had started to call Albert,* for a Yeats of his own.[20] Through Yeats he discovered Celtic mythology, while on his own he continued to be possessed by Northernness, and moved on from Wagner to read Mallet's *Northern Antiquities*, *Myths of the Norsemen* and *Myths and Legends of the Teutonic Race*. He was even composing a Northern tragedy of his own, in the form of a Euripidean drama. It was to be called *Loki Bound*. Lewis's Loki rebels against the All-father Odin, not out of pride and malice, as in the

---

* As a result of his Irish pronunciation of the word 'potato'.

Prose Edda, but because he loathes the cruelty of the world which Odin has made. He is the first of the great anti-father figures in Lewis's poetry. In the drama he stands against Thor, a brutally orthodox oaf who, in his loyalty to Odin, reflects the unthinking conservatism of the powerful older boys at the Coll – 'bloods' as they were called.

But even as his fluent pen moved across the page in the Gurney and the bees buzzed outside the window, Lewis knew that the order of his release had been approved. He could be happy in the knowledge that his father did not insist upon his returning to Malvern in the autumn. His first summer term there was also to be his last. The P'daytabird had come up with a scheme which was almost unbelievably good news as far as Jack was concerned. At fifteen years old, he was to be withdrawn from school, and allowed to continue his education under his father's great master, William Kirkpatrick.

It was the summer of 1914. More than Lewis's schooldays were over. A whole era, not only in his life, but also in the world, had come to an end. He would always feel that he belonged to that old world. In the barbarous world which was struggling to be born, he would be an alien.

FIVE

THE GREAT KNOCK
1914–1917

Shortly before the beginning of his last term as a schoolboy, Lewis had been told that his Belfast neighbour Arthur Greeves was convalescing from some illness and would welcome a visit. In 1907, it may be remembered that the telephone had no sooner been installed in the house than young Jacks wanted to speak to Arthur down the line. But their friendship had remained a thing of pure neighbourliness, without blossoming into any sort of spiritual or intellectual intimacy.

It was in April or May 1914, with his head full of the epic of *Loki Bound* and H. M. A. Guerber's *Myths of the Norsemen*, that Jack knocked on the Greeveses' front door and was shown upstairs to Arthur's bedroom. He found the boy sitting up in bed. On the table beside him lay a copy of . . . *Myths of the Norsemen*.

'Do *you* like that?' he asked.

'Do *you* like that?' Arthur replied.

It was not long before the two boys were exchanging their thoughts about the whole world of Norse mythology, so excited to discover this mutual interest that they were almost shouting. 'Both knew the stab of Joy, and . . . for both, the arrow was shot from the North.'[1]

Lewis had already learnt, in his brother's company, the joy of what he later termed the first great love, that of Affection. During his conversation with Arthur Greeves, he discovered the second love, that of Friendship. 'Many thousands of people have had the experience of finding the first friend, and it is none the less a wonder; as great a wonder (*pace* the novelists) as first love, or even greater.'[2]

The friendship of his own sex was one of the great sources of Joy in Lewis's life; and it was always axiomatic with him that friendship *began*, and perhaps continued, with two men 'seeing the same truth'. By many people of a less cerebral disposition, it is not considered necessary to *agree* with their friends on points of literary judgement, or even of theology. Lewis thought that it was; or perhaps it would be truer to say that he thought that he thought that it was. In point of fact, his friendship with Arthur Greeves was to outlast many changes of view on both sides.

The friendship with Greeves occupied a position of unique importance in Lewis's life, for geographical and practical reasons. Like Lewis, Greeves was the son of a Belfast middle-class household which had nothing to do with the world of Oxford or London, where Lewis was to achieve his fame. Greeves, though highly intelligent and bookish, was not destined to go to university. His friendship with Lewis was kept going by letter. Both were prodigiously fluent and regular correspondents, and their letters to one another continued from 1914 until a few weeks before Lewis's death in 1963. Sadly, Arthur Greeves' side of the correspondence has been destroyed, but the Lewis letters to Greeves (published as *They Stand Together*, 1979) provide an invaluable insight into Lewis's imaginative growth. The greater part of his intellectual journeyings, as well as many of his emotional experiences, were confided to Greeves. Moreover since Lewis, already a self-confessed follower of the Romantic movement in literature, was highly self-conscious, the letters to Greeves helped him not merely to disclose but also to discover himself. It was in writing to Greeves that he decided, very often, the sort of person he wanted to be. We could very definitely say that if it had not been for Arthur Greeves, many of Lewis's most distinctive and imaginatively successful books would not have been written. The letters were the dress rehearsal for that intimate and fluent manner which was to make Lewis such a successful author. The early stuff which he wrote for himself, such as *Loki Bound*, is almost entirely unreadable. In the letters to Greeves, he learnt to write for an audience.

By September 1914, the Archduke had been shot in Sarajevo, and the great European powers had drifted inexorably into war. Warren Lewis, who had been a prize cadet at Sandhurst (21st out of 201 candidates) found himself being rushed through his officers' training course. By November he was in France with the Fourth Company of the Seventh Divisional Train of the British Expeditionary Force. It was a war which was to change everything; not only the disputed territories of the Prussian empire, but also much bigger things – like the position of the social classes in Europe and the position of women in society. Ireland, too, was to be changed irrevocably by the turmoil in which Britain found itself.

Jack Lewis, as he entered his teenage years, was put into an idyllic position of isolation, far from Belfast and the Western Front. On 19 September 1914, he stepped off the train at Great Bookham, Surrey, and encountered the legendary Mr Kirkpatrick. The old schoolmaster was sixty-six years old. He and his wife had enjoyed having Warnie to live with them while he prepared for the Sandhurst exams: 'A nicer boy I never had in the house.'[3] But from the beginning, the relationship with Jack was more special.

Kirkpatrick wrote to his beloved pupil Albert Lewis, 'When I first saw him on the station I had no hesitation in addressing him. It was as though I was looking at yourself once more in the old days at Lurgan.'[4] Kirkpatrick's letters to Albert over the years had been fulsome and emotional: 'A letter from you carries the mind across the vistas of the years and wakens all the cells where memory slept . . .'[5] His relationship with Albert's sons was to be more distant and old-fashioned. It was not surprising, therefore, that the boys seized on this to provide yet another example of the P'daytabird getting things hopelessly wrong. Albert recalled being squeezed as a boy by the Great Knock and having his youthful cheeks rubbed by his 'dear old whiskers'. But when Jack got off the train, his cheeks tingling with anticipation, something very different happened. 'Anything more grotesquely unlike the "dear old Knock" of my father's reminiscences could not be conceived.'[6]

The old man himself confessed to being deeply moved by the appearance of Clive Lewis (as far as history discovers the matter, Kirkpatrick was the only person who ever called Lewis by his baptismal name). But the Knock's devotion to the boy took the form not of tears and kisses, but of a well-developed act which he obviously enjoyed adopting. Lewis accused his father of transforming the real Kirkpatrick into a figure hopelessly unlike the reality. From all the evidence which survives, we can see that the Great Knock of *Surprised by Joy* is quite as much an imaginative projection as the Victorian sentimentalist beloved of Lewis's father.

Kirkpatrick's letters to Albert were real enough. When they are not dripping with syrupy endearments about his former pupils, they thunder with all the irrational force of an angry man reading the newspapers about the Hun, the Catholics, the Conservative Party and anyone else he disapproves of. But for Jack Lewis, the Great Knock was to be the embodiment of pure logic, the man who sacrificed everything – social niceties, good manners, even the pleasure of conversation – to a passionate desire to get things right. Even as they were strolling from the station, Jack was discovering, or creating, this magnificent character. He remarked that he was surprised by the scenery of Surrey, which was much wilder than he had expected.

'Stop!' shouted the Knock. 'What do you mean by wildness and what grounds had you for not expecting it?' By a series of Socratic thrusts, Kirkpatrick managed to show Lewis that his remarks were wholly meaningless and that he had no grounds whatsoever for expressing an opinion about a subject (the scenery of Surrey) of which he had hitherto known nothing. As Lewis remarks, 'Born a little later, he would have been a Logical Positivist.'[7]

Kirkpatrick's teaching techniques, when it came to studying litera-ture, were no less remarkable. Lewis arrived on a Saturday. On Monday morning at nine o'clock, Kirkpatrick opened the *Iliad* and read aloud the first twenty lines, chanting it in his pure Ulster brogue. Then he translated the lines into English, handed Lewis a lexicon and told him to go through as much of it as he had time for. With any less able child, this would have been a disastrously slapdash method of instruction. But it was not long before Lewis began trying to race Kirkpatrick, seeing if he could not learn a few more lines of Homer than his master. Before long, he was reading fluently and actually thinking in Greek. The same method was applied to the Latin poets. Eventually, while he was living at Gastons (as the Knock's house was called), Lewis was to read his way through the whole of Homer, Virgil, Euripides, Sophocles and Aeschylus, as well as the great French dramas, before branching out into German and Italian. In all these areas, Kirkpatrick's methods were the same. After the most rudimen-tary instruction in the grammar of the languages, Jack was reading *Faust* and the *Inferno*.

They were very happy times for Kirkpatrick himself. His letters to Albert about the boy are glowing and full of appreciation for Jack's qualities of mind; they are exact in their analysis of what was so remarkable about him, throughout his life, as a literary critic. 'It is the maturity and originality of his literary judgements which is so unusual and surprising. By an unerring instinct he detects first rate quality in literary workmanship and the second rate does not interest him in any way.'[8]

In religion, Kirkpatrick was an old-fashioned nineteenth-century rationalist, whose favourite reading consisted of Frazer's *Golden Bough* and Schopenhauer. Nevertheless, he remained very distinctly an Ulster Presbyterian atheist. Jack noticed with amusement that Kirkpatrick always did the garden in a slightly smarter suit on Sundays.

Albert hoped that neither of his boys had been infected by the 'Gastons heresies'. Warren's religion appeared to have survived Kirkpatrick's atheistical society. Indeed, when he was at Sandhurst at the beginning of 1914, he had written home to bewail the atmosphere in the chapel there – 'that easy, bored, contemptuous indifference which is so hard to describe, but which you would understand perfectly if you had any experience of the products of the big public schools'.[9]

By the close of the year, Warnie was in France and so he missed Jack's confirmation service, which was held, at Albert's suggestion, at St Mark's, Dundela. Jack and his father were now so estranged that Jack did not feel able to tell his father that he did not believe in God and did not wish to go through with the ceremony. Even after he had turned back to Christianity himself, Lewis did less than justice to Albert's position.

> It would have been quite impossible to drive into his head my real position. The thread would have been lost almost at once and the answer implicit in all the quotations, anecdotes, and reminiscences which would have poured over me would have been one I then valued not a straw – the beauty of the Authorised version, the beauty of the Christian tradition and character.[10]

This is to suggest that Albert mainly valued Christianity as an aesthetic or national tradition. His letter to Warnie at the Western Front describing Jack's confirmation shows him, by contrast, to have been a profoundly committed Christian. After an account of the 'very impressive' service Albert continues:

41

Don't take this further word amiss, dear Badge. I am not going to preach a sermon. I know that you are living a hard life and that a battle field is not the best place for the Christian witness to flourish. But don't altogether forget God, and turn in thought at times to remember that you too have been confirmed in Christ.[11]

Jack Lewis went through the ceremony knowing that he was enacting a lie, and he hated himself for so doing. His actual belief, strengthened by contact with the 'Gastons heresies' and Frazer's *Golden Bough*, was that religion, 'that is all mythologies',[12] sprang into being in order to explain phenomena by which primitive man was terrified – thunder, pestilence or snakes. In a similar fashion, great men such as Heracles, Odin or Yeshua ('whose name we have corrupted into Jesus') came to be regarded as gods after their deaths. 'Superstition of course in every age has held the common people but in every age the educated and thinking ones have stood outside it, though usually outwardly conceding to it for convenience.' Arthur Greeves, who was a devout Christian, did not agree, and the letters between the two friends on the subject were so intense that they eventually agreed not to discuss the matter. In the letters of young C. S. Lewis the atheist we find all the bombast and dialectic which was one day to be turned on its head in defence of the faith. 'Strange as it may appear, I am quite content to live without believing in a bogey who is prepared to torture me for ever and ever if I should fail in coming up to an almost impossible ideal.'[13]

It was, he believed, from Kirkpatrick that he learnt dialectic, just as it was from Smugy that he had learnt grammar and rhetoric. Kirkpatrick was in fact dismayed by how little grammar (Greek and Latin) Lewis had learnt. He was astonished, for example, that the boy did not know the Greek accents. But it may have been true that some of his forceful dialectic techniques got passed on to his pupil. For example, not many months after the outbreak of the First World War, Kirkpatrick observed of the Liberal Government:

If after eight years of experience, they did not grasp the German menace, they are convicted of stupidity: if they did know it, and never informed the nation or made military preparations to meet it, they are guilty of moral cowardice and neglect of the highest national interests. They may choose which horn of the dilemma they prefer but escape from one or the other is impossible.[14]

This was precisely the kind of argument Lewis was to employ later in life to persuade people to accept the divinity of Christ.

But if he learnt dialectic from Kirkpatrick, he probably did not learn much about the relations between the sexes or the emotional life. The Kirkpatricks were unsuitably matched. Tea parties, bridge and gossip were Mrs Kirkpatrick's favourite occupations. Lewis manages to make them sound pointless, even slightly esoteric activities, but the majority of middle-class women lived in this way, and one might wonder what was wrong with their doing so. Mrs Kirkpatrick did her best to keep Jack amused. She read French novels with him in the evenings. She took him up to London to see the Russian ballet.[15] She even introduced him to Virginia Woolf's *The Voyage Out*, making him resolve to 'look out for anything else she writes'. (He added, in Virginia Woolfish mode, 'A moth has flown into my mantle and broken it.')[16] But none of this could stop him regarding Mrs Kirkpatrick as a 'vulgar little woman'. He hated her when she returned from shopping expeditions and told 'triumphantly how she snubbed some poor devil of a shopwalker. Ugh!'

Little Lea, since 1908, had been an all-male household. In the following six years Jack was at all-male boarding schools. His first opportunity to share in the life of a domestic household with a man and a woman had led him to Mrs Kirkpatrick. His scorn of her was doubtless learnt from her misogynistic husband, who, it was said, had only married her to fill the housekeeper's room at Lurgan. It was an unhappy model to grow up with: the clever man matched with a woman who, though evidently no fool, had to be written down as a fool to satisfy her husband's ego and explain his dislike of her.

Nor, though he wrote it up as an idyll afterwards, was life at Gastons all fun. For much of the time he was terribly bored, as he confided both to Arthur Greeves and to his pocket diary. 'Got very bored in the morning', 'Am bored', 'A dull day'[17] are all typical entries. However deeply studious he was, it was a strange way for a boy of sixteen or seventeen to be living. This worried Kirkpatrick, and for short spells he tried the experiment of having another pupil to live in the house with Lewis. This never worked, partly because the boy concerned was always far beneath Lewis's intellectual level, and so could not possibly have shared lessons with him; partly because Lewis had simply grown accustomed to being on his own. 'A damned fellow pupil of my own age and sex – isn't it the limit!'[18]

Mrs Kirkpatrick tried the experiment of introducing him to girls. For example, there was a family of Belgian refugees evacuated to Great Bookham, and for a period Lewis affected to be smitten by one of the girls of the family. By now, his correspondence with Greeves contained a good deal of covert confidences about sex. 'How could young adolescents really be friends without it?'[19] as he reflected in middle age. Arthur Greeves was homosexual. Lewis, knowing that he wasn't, assumed himself to be a simple heterosexual and even supplied Arthur with details of assignations with the Belgian girl which he afterwards admitted he had fabricated.[20] Most of the 'real' sexual experiences which they shared related, unsurprisingly, to masturbation.

The 'ordinary' experience of going to cafés or dances and falling in love with the girl over the garden fence or at the next desk in school was not to be Lewis's. In one of the most revealingly characteristic of all the letters he wrote in his teenage years, he said to Greeves:

> You ask whether I have ever been in love: fool as I am, I am not quite such a fool as that. But if one is only to talk from first hand experience on any subject, conversation would be a very poor business. But though I have no personal experience of the thing they call love, I have what is better – the experience of Sappho, of Euripides, of Catullus, of Shakespeare, of Spenser, of Austen, of Brontë, of, of, – anyone else I have read.[21]

'Jack Lewis loved books!' his Oxford friend Hugo Dyson used to say, in his huge booming voice, causing all heads in a bar to turn in his direction.[22] In some ways, this obvious truth was the most important thing about Lewis. 'Though I have no personal experience . . . I have what is better . . .' Most of Lewis's important experiences were, in fact, literary ones. They happened when he was holding a book or a pen in his hand.

Since Lewis died, the professional world of English Literature studies in universities and learned periodicals has been dominated by various formalist critics (most of whom he would have abominated) exploring the curious relationship between text and reader. Reading is not a simple exercise. Very often, the simplest 'understanding' of a text would turn out in another person's eyes to be a 'misreading' of it. Reading is a creative exercise, an exercise in the imagination. It constitutes an experience in itself. Perhaps there are many imaginative, religious or emotional areas where it actually makes very little sense to distinguish between 'real' or 'personal' experiences, and things we have 'only' read about in books. These are matters to which Lewis, in later life, was to devote thought. How much is the bookish man distinguishable from his imagined self, the self he projects into the books he reads?

When he looked back on his life at Great Bookham, there was one great reading experience which outshone all others, and which certainly constitutes a personal experience every bit as important as his encounters with the Belgian girl or Mrs Kirkpatrick. In some ways it was more important than his acquaintanceship with Kirkpatrick himself.

This occurred at the beginning of March 1916, when quite by chance on the station bookstall at Great Bookham, he happened to pick up a copy of *Phantastes* by George MacDonald. After only a few pages he knew at once that he was in for 'a great literary experience'.[23]

George MacDonald was to be so important a figure in Lewis's life, and *Phantastes* such a great milestone in his inner journey, that some word of exposition is required here. Can we explain *why* the book meant so much to him, became almost a holy text in his imagination, and – most characteristic – a touchstone by which to judge whether other people were, or were not, 'of the brethren'?

'All was changed . . . I had not the faintest notion what I had let myself in for by buying *Phantastes*.'[24]

Many of Lewis's admirers must have rushed eagerly to the pages of MacDonald and felt a grave disappointment at what they found there. For MacDonald supremely lacks Lewis's greatest quality – that of readability, the simple ability to write prose in such a manner that one wants to keep on turning the pages. It is this which accounts for the obscurity into which MacDonald's reputation fell after his death in 1905, at the age of seventy-nine. But Lewis was surely right to discern in him one of the most original imaginations in the whole of English literature. *Phantastes* is not, strictly speaking, a story. It is an imagined dream or vision in which the hero, Anodos (which means in Greek 'No Way'), wakes up and finds that his bedroom is not as he remembered it. From the wash-basin a stream is flowing on to the carpet. The carpet is now bright-green grass, and a tiny stranger offers to lead him through a small section of his writing desk into the world of Faery (MacDonald was a friend of Lewis Carroll). In the company of this fairy, who turns out to be his lost grandmother, he enters a world of potent symbols and archetypical images, and sets out on various quests for a perfect woman, part lover, part mother-figure. One of these is the beauteous marble lady – very possibly MacDonald's lost mother, who by a dreadful 'weaning' abandoned her child by dying when he was only eight.

MacDonald is the missing link between Spenser's *Faerie Queene* and the writings of Freud and Jung. He seems to have the supreme gift, in his fairy stories, of writing unselfconsciously about the subconscious: not only describing what it is like to be in a subconscious dream-state, but also, without any spelling-out of the obvious, high-lighting the meaning of these mentally subterranean journeyings. One of MacDonald's favourite sayings came from Novalis: 'Our life is no dream, but it ought to become one and perhaps will.' He is the great chronicler of the inner life, the mapper-out of what takes place when the subconscious is allowed free range and – in dream or fantasy – tells us stories about ourselves which with our conscious minds we would not necessarily understand or might not be strong enough to bear. MacDonald's entire *œuvre* has been described as 'a life-time effort of mourning' the traumatic losses of his boyhood, above all the death of his mother. Lewis, when he first read *Phantastes*, could have had no idea that MacDonald's early history was so like his own.[25] MacDonald's genius is to draw archetypes to which we all respond. But this story made a particular appeal to Lewis: the young man with No Way in the world, pursuing images of selfhood, images of womanhood, images of loss, images of death.

Later, he was to see that reading *Phantastes* had been something much more than a literary experience. Indeed, Lewis never blinded himself to the fact that in technical, literary terms MacDonald is not necessarily 'a good writer'. And in one sense, the wanderings of Anodos were no different from many of the other worlds and enchanted places which he had met with in favourite authors from Spenser to William Morris and Yeats. 'But in another sense all was changed. I did not yet know (and I was long in learning) the name of the new quality, the bright shadow that rested on the travels of Anodos. I do now. It was Holiness. For the first time the songs of the sirens sounded like the voice of my mother or my nurse.'[26]

For the previous eight years, Lewis had been bottling up the emotion which he had most needed to let out: grief for his mother. The experience of boarding school immediately after Flora died and the stiff-upper-lip schoolboy atmosphere in which the emotions were suspected and tears were thought cissy had led to a profound stiffening and hardening throughout his being. MacDonald was the first person who touched Lewis sufficiently to let him see what he needed. It is no surprise that, upon reading *Phantastes*, Lewis heard a sound like the voice of his mother. Meanwhile, his mentor and teacher Kirkpatrick was giving his mind to what the future might hold for this most gifted youth. Two things struck him as obvious and, given the way things turned out, we should commend Kirkpatrick's foresight.

Early on, he had noted that 'Clive is an altogether exceptional boy.'[27] Later, he had told Albert Lewis that Clive 'was born with the literary temperament and we have to face the fact with all it implies. This is not a case of early precocity showing itself in rapid assimilation of knowledge and followed by subsequent indifference or even torpor. As I said before it is the maturity of his literary judgements which is so unusual and surprising.'[28]

Albert asked what career this pointed to, and Kirkpatrick replied that they should consider the Bar (i.e. being an advocate or attorney in court) as 'the career marked out for Clive by nature and destiny . . . He has every gift, a goodly presence, a clear resonant voice, an unfailing resource of clear and adequate expression.'

So, he was to turn out as a literary man and an advocate. This was true. But in neither case was he to fulfil Kirkpatrick's prophecy as he or Albert expected. His skills as an advocate were eventually to be used in the area of Christian apologetics; his literary skills in the areas of criticism, essays, science fiction and children's stories.

In his late teens, Jack himself was convinced that he was going to become a poet, and this was a conviction which he carried with him until the late 1920s. Between Easter 1915 and Easter 1917, he wrote fifty-two poems, all about on a par with 'The Hills of Down':

> I will abide
>   And make my Dwelling here
> Whatso betide
>   Since there is more to fear
> Out yonder. Though
>   This world is drear and wan
> I dare not go
>   To dreaming Avalon,
> Nor look what lands
>   May lie beyond the last
> Strange sunset strands
>   That gleam when day is fast
> I' the yearning west
>   Nor seek some faery town
> Nor cloud land lest
>   I lose the hills of Down
> The long low hills of Down.

It is extraordinary that someone who, as Kirkpatrick observed, had such an unfailing eye for the excellent in other poets could have gone on writing poetry of such appalling quality. True, large numbers of people write bad poetry in their teens. But Lewis went on and on doing so, apparently convinced that he was going to turn into a poet in the same class as W. B. Yeats.

Not that he imagined he would be able to make a living out of poetry. He realized that he was expected to do something with his life, and the next stage in the life of a clever person inevitably looked like university. By the close of 1916, when he was just eighteen years old, he was ready to sit the scholarship examination for Oxford, and on 4 December he arrived in the town where, with periods of exile, he was to spend the rest of his life. This was the Oxford which existed before the building of the Cowley motor works and the expansion of the place into a mixture of modern industrial town and 'shopping centre' into which the old University buildings now appear to have been slotted by chance. The Oxford which Lewis saw was an unspoilt

Gothic paradise. True, there were dull suburbs growing up around what Gerard Manley Hopkins, the Oxford Jesuit poet, had called its 'base and brickish skirt'. But encircling it all there were open fields and meadows. No motor-car disturbed its tranquil streets. From college entrances hobbled old men in gowns who had known Dr Pusey and Dr Pattison. 'This place has surpassed my wildest dreams,' Lewis wrote. 'I never saw anything so beautiful, especially on these frosty moonlight nights; though the Hall at Oriel [College] where we do the papers is fearfully cold at about four o'clock in the afternoons. We have most of us tried with varying success to write in our gloves.'[29]

Oxford is a collegiate university. To gain entrance there you have to be accepted by a college. The exact method of entrance to the colleges has varied over the years. When Lewis was sitting for the scholarship, there was a central pool from which the more brilliant candidates could be drawn. New College – in those days a place still very largely inhabited by boys who had been to Winchester – turned him down, but he was accepted at University College. After Christmas in Belfast, Lewis passed through Oxford for an interview with the Master of 'Univ' (as the college is invariably called), who explained that though he had been accepted as a scholar of the college, he had not yet matriculated as a member of the University. To do this, he would have to pass an examination called Responsions, which involved some elementary mathematics. If he passed this exam in March, then he could come up to Univ in the Trinity Term (i.e. April to June) of 1917.

It was a tedious chore, but he went back to the Kirkpatricks to brush up his (never very strong) mathematics. It was during this period that he started Italian and German. It was also during this period that he began to disclose to Arthur some of his more bizarre sexual preferences and fantasies.

In January 1917, his hand wobbles and he apologizes for his poor handwriting, poor because 'it is being done across my knee'. The very phrase is enough to set off in his mind a train of sado-masochistic reflections: '"Across my knee" of course makes one think of positions for whipping: or rather not for whipping (you couldn't get any swing) but for that torture with brushes. This position, with its childish nursery associations would have something beautifully intimate and also very humiliating for the victim.'[30] He began to sign his name

Philomastix ('Lover of the whip'). He enjoyed fantasies about Arthur Greeves's sister who should be 'punished . . . to the general enjoyment of the operator and to the great good of her soul', and about some other girl in Belfast whose large bottom was 'shaped with an intolerable grace . . . Ah me! if she had suffered indeed half the stripes that have fallen upon her in imagination she would be well disciplined.'[31] He also enjoyed, and recommended, the *Confessions* of Jean-Jacques Rousseau. 'Altogether "a really rather lovely" book. His taste is altogether for suffering rather than inflicting: which I can feel too, but it is a feeling more proper to the other sex.'

These distractions did nothing to impair Lewis's academic achievements, and he began his first term as an undergraduate at Oxford. It might readily be supposed that there was a tremendous contrast between the total solitude of Great Bookham and the merry life of Oxford; but by its own standards Oxford was strangely deserted. At Univ there were only twelve men in college[32] and the hall was no longer used for dinner. The students ate in a small lecture room. Lewis was given an enormous sitting room all for himself. It was thickly carpeted with a profusion of rugs and furnished in stupendous style, with richly carved oak tables and a grand piano. A fire was burning in the grate, and his scout (college servant) had put the kettle on to boil on a gas ring. This was his first glimpse of college life. The room he had been given, including its furniture, belonged to 'a tremendous blood who is at the front'.[33]

For the reason Oxford was so empty was that it was 1917, and nearly all the young men were in Flanders and France, fighting in the trenches. The war was going badly for the Allies, and conscription had by now been introduced. Since he was an Irishman, Lewis was not obliged to enlist, but he volunteered to do so. This meant that, although he was technically a student, he was in effect a trainee officer in the British Army. The Dean of the college refused to map out any plan of reading for Lewis 'on the grounds that the Corps will take me all my time'.

Still, in that first Oxford term at Univ, there was a chance to wander about and drink in the atmosphere of the place. One alumnus of the college had been Percy Bysshe Shelley – another atheist poet. He had actually been sent down from Oxford for his atheism, but after his death the college had accepted a remarkable statue of him which is housed beneath a blue dome. Lewis believed that Greeves would have loved it. 'I pass it every morning on the way to my bath. On a slab of black marble, carved underneath with weeping muses, lies in white stone the nude figure of Shelley, as he was cast up by the sea – all tossed into curious attitudes with lovely ripples of muscle and strained limbs. He is lovely.' Then – since the thought of naked loveliness will obviously raise the question of whether Lewis has masturbated recently, he adds, 'No – not since I came back. Somehow I haven't thought of it.'

As well as naked figures in marble, there were naked figures in the flesh at 'Parson's Pleasure', a stretch of the River Cherwell where men could bathe 'without the tiresome convention of bathing things'. It was to be one of his favourite spots for many years to come. And, as well as the newly discovered delights of architecture, there were libraries and bookshops such as he had never known before.

It was a beautifully, unreally happy first term, made the more poignant by the knowledge that sooner or later training would start in earnest and he would be sent off to the Western Front. On 3 June, he passed Robert Bridges, the Poet Laureate, in the street and would dearly have loved to speak to him.[34] But by 10 June term was over and he was moved to Keble College, which had been requisitioned as a military barracks. 'It is a great change to leave my own snug room at Univ for a carpetless room, with beds without sheets or pillows, kept miserably tidy and shared with another cadet, at Keble,' he wrote. The other cadet was a schoolboy who had only just left Clifton College in Bristol. Like Lewis, he was an Irishman, but that was not the reason he had been put to share with him. It was simply that their names came together on the alphabetical list. The other cadet, 'though he was a little too childish', was 'quite a good fellow'. His name was Edward Francis Courtenay Moore, known to his friends as Paddy. Lewis could not possibly have guessed that this purely casual arrangement was to be one of the most important things which ever happened to him, something which was to shape and influence the rest of his life.

SIX

THE ANGEL OF PAIN
1917–1918

Lewis and the other boys were about to take part in trench warfare. The training they received was heartlessly casual. After only a few weeks' drill at Keble, he was given some leave and returned to Univ, the only man in the college. 'I spent a long time wandering over it, into all sorts of parts where I had never been before, where the mullioned windows are dark with ivy that no one has bothered to cut since the war emptied the rooms they belong to. Some of these rooms were dust-sheeted, others were much as their owners had left them . . .' The important thing was that he did not go home to Ireland during this spell of leave. There were reasons for that. The journey, properly speaking, took two days. The Irish channel was patrolled by U-boats and there was the danger of the packet being hit by a torpedo. But the most important reason was that he did not love his father, and he did not want to go home. Albert Lewis, for his part, though worried sick, and angry that Jack's brilliant career should be interrupted by the demands of soldiering, could not stir himself to visit his son in Oxford, even though Jack more than once invited him. Albert had a dread which was almost pathological of leaving the office routines. He hated travel. Also, unknown at this point to either of his sons, he had started to drink very heavily. He contented himself with writing letters to his Member of Parliament, Colonel Craig, trying to get Jack transferred to the Royal Artillery.

It was natural, at this anxious period when the comforts of a true home were precisely what a boy needed, that Jack should have happily joined in with Paddy Moore's people who visited him regularly from Bristol: his twelve-year-old sister Maureen and his mother Janie, a pretty blonde Irishwoman of forty-five. In August, Warnie got a short spell of leave from the Western Front, and Jack was persuaded to go back to Strandtown to spend the week with him. He had reached the point where he could not bear to see his father *à deux*, but with his still-loved brother it was a different matter. On 21 August, Warnie went back to France and Jack returned to Oxford for his only piece of practical training for trench warfare – a three-day bivouac in Wytham Woods. It was wet weather – 'Our model trenches up there will provide a very unnecessarily good imitation of Flanders mud,' he quipped to his father. To read on the boat, the P'daytabird had lent him a novel called *The Angel of Pain* by E. F. Benson which he now wanted back. 'I will send you the Angel of Pain in a few days: just at present my friend Mrs. Moore has borrowed it.'[1]

Albert could not possibly have guessed that from now onwards Mrs Moore's presence at Jack's side was to be almost constant. At the end of September he got a month's leave, and chose to spend nearly all of it with Paddy Moore and his family at 56 Ravenswood Road, Redlands, Bristol. 'On Monday, a cold (complete with sore throat) which I had developed at Oxford went on so merrily that Mrs. Moore took my temperature and put me to bed,' he wrote home. When the cold was better, he only had a week in which to dash home and see his father.

The experience of being mothered, for the first time in his life since he was nine years old, was having a profound effect on Jack. The feelings of affection were not one-sided. Jack's personality, which had so charmed Kirkpatrick, was also having a strong effect on Mrs Moore.

That October, Paddy Moore and Lewis were parted. Lewis was gazetted to the Somerset Light Infantry and Paddy was assigned to a different regiment. But it was obvious that the links between Mrs Moore and Lewis were not to be severed. She wrote to Albert, 'Your boy, of course, being Paddy's room mate, we know much better than the others, and he was quite the most popular boy of the party; he is very charming and most likeable, and won golden opinions from everyone . . .' But from no one more than from Janie Moore herself. Where was Mr Moore, whom she referred to as 'The Beast'? Somewhere in Ireland, it was thought. Jack was given to understand that he had treated her badly and failed to give her enough money. The Lewis family knew nothing of this and assumed that Mrs Moore was a widow.

They had no idea that there was any crisis brewing in Jack's life either of an emotional or of a practical character. In fact, he was about to be sent off to war. The call came in November. He was given forty-eight hours' leave, after which he would be sent to France. Naturally, he went to Bristol to stay with Mrs Moore, and telegraphed to his father: 'HAVE ARRIVED IN BRISTOL ON 48 HOURS LEAVE. REPORT SOUTHAMPTON SATURDAY, CAN YOU COME BRISTOL? IF SO MEET AT STATION. REPLY MRS MOORE'S ADDRESS 56 RAVENSWOOD ROAD REDLANDS BRISTOL.' To many parents, the significance of 'REPORT SOUTHAMPTON SATURDAY' would have been obvious: Southampton was where the troopships sailed from. But to Irish Albert, who had never sailed from Southampton, only from Liverpool or Belfast, the words meant nothing. He could not allow himself to believe that the words meant what they said. So he wired back 'DONT UNDERSTAND TELEGRAM, PLEASE WRITE. P.' By letter Jack spelt it all out. 'Forty-eight hours is no earthly use to a person who lives in Ireland and would have to spend two days and nights travelling. Please don't worry. I shall probably be a long time at the base as I have had so little training in England.'

By the time this letter reached Strandtown, Jack was in France. Albert found the news overwhelming. 'It has shaken me to pieces.' He did not realize how it had shaken Jack, nor how his failure to come and say goodbye at that crucial emotional moment had helped to sever a few more threads of affection binding the son to his father and to his home. He could not have seen how much the shape of things to come was foreshadowed in the hasty scribble which he held in his hand as he trudged, half-drunk, from one empty room to the other at Little Lea. *'Can't write more now,'* Jack had said, *'must go and do some shopping.'* There can have been few other young officers in the British Isles at that period who, with only hours to spare before leaving for an almost certain death in the trenches, were required to perform menial domestic tasks. But it was to be part of Lewis's relationship with Mrs Moore from the beginning that he 'must go and do some shopping'.

By the time of his nineteenth birthday, he was in the front-line trenches, near the village of Arras. Christmas was spent there. Back at Little Lea, Albert spent the day alone. He went to the early service at St Mark's. 'At times I was unable to repeat the responses. It is something more than sentiment and early associations that comforts a sorrowful man in this Holy Eucharist and leads him to look forward with firmer faith to the safety and salvation of those he loves . . .'[2] He nevertheless felt furious with Jack for not responding to Colonel Craig's attempts to get the boy transferred to an artillery regiment. Jack, however, had his reasons. 'I must confess that I have become very attached to this regiment. I have several friends whom I should be sorry to leave and I am just beginning to know my men and understand the work.'

School had been a nightmare which everyone expected him to enjoy. No one pretended that you should enjoy the Army, and this mysteriously made it more bearable.[3] He found the camaraderie of the men, and of the senior officers, who were not in the least like the bloods of Malvern, much more to his taste. Even the trenches were not as bad as he had feared. 'They are very deep, you go down them by a shaft of about 20 steps; they have wire bunks where a man can sleep quite snugly and braziers for warmth and cooking.'[4] The trenches were also a place where 'a man', at least this man, could read. That January found him deeply absorbed in '*Adam Bede* and *The Mill on the Floss*, which I like even better'.

In February, he went down with trench fever, or pyrexia – with a high temperature, and many of the symptoms of influenza. He was transferred to the Red Cross Hospital at Treport and wrote home for 'some cheap edition of Burton's *Anatomy of Melancholy*'.[5] The hospital was a converted hotel, and the discovery of clean sheets, pretty nurses and above all *books* was very welcome to the patient. The only drawback to the place was that his room-mate was conducting a love affair with one of the nurses, and kept him awake. 'I had too high a temperature to be embarrassed but the human whisper is a very tedious and unmusical noise.'[6] When the amorous room-mate departed, Lewis was left on his own and read a volume of G. K. Chesterton's essays. Here, too, was to be a great influence, almost comparable in scale and importance with George MacDonald; but for the time being he merely enjoyed Chesterton as a wit and stylist, without being quite aware of what it was that he was swallowing with the thrusts and paradoxes. 'A young man who wishes to remain a sound atheist cannot be too careful of his reading.'[7]

Once he was better, he had to put his books down and return to the Front. On one occasion, he took sixty German prisoners – 'that is, discovered to my great relief that the crowd of field-grey figures who suddenly appeared from nowhere all had their hands up'.[8] He now began to taste the horror of the war. The corpses everywhere recalled the deadness of his dead mother. Days were passed squelching in thigh-length gumboots through the mud while facing enemy fire. Almost as much as the bullets, the soldiers dreaded the barbed wire. Merely to tear your boot on the wire was to fill it with muddy water. As the spring days advanced, the Germans increased their offensive, determined to make one last grand Wagnerian gesture of defiance against their almost inevitable defeat. During the battle of Arras on 15 April 1917, Lewis was on Mount Bernenchon. He was standing near his dear friend Sergeant Ayres when a shell exploded. It killed Ayres outright and the splinters from it hit Lewis in the leg, the hand, the face and just under the arm. This last splinter touched his lung and momentarily winded him. When he found that he was not breathing, he concluded that this was death. The intelligence dawned on him dully – inspiring neither fear nor courage. In fact, it was not death but that fate which all English soldiers coveted – a wound not of great gravity, but sufficiently serious to remove the victim from the scene of conflict: in other words, 'a Blighty'.

After a short spell in the Liverpool Merchants' Mobile Hospital, Étaples, he was taken home, and by 25 May he was able to wire to his father: AM IN ENDSLEIGH PALACE HOSPITAL ENDSLEIGH GARDENS LONDON. JACK. He followed up the telegram with a letter asking his father to come over and visit him for a few days. Albert was himself laid up with severe bronchitis at the time. Even so, given the fact (repeatedly revealed in his surviving diaries) that he was desperately worried about his boy, it is remarkable that he was unable to stir himself for a hospital visit when the bronchitis was clear.

Mrs Moore was not so diffident, and came to London at once to be near Jack. She was extremely worried about the fate of her own son, Paddy, who had been reported 'missing'. Before they had been separated and sent off to different regiments, Paddy and Jack had made a pact: in the event of one or the other's death, the survivor would 'look after' the bereft parent of the one who had been killed. Mrs Moore's daughter Maureen distinctly remembered this solemn undertaking being made by the two eighteen-year-old boys.[9]

To what extent Paddy Moore would have been a welcome guest at

Little Lea in the event of Jack's death, let alone able to 'look after' Albert Lewis, was never put to the test, for it was Moore who was lost, and Lewis who survived. After a few weeks in the End-sleigh Palace Hospital, Jack was well enough to get up, and he took the opportunity for a Sunday outing from London to Great Bookham.

> Even to go to Waterloo was an adventure full of memories, and every station I passed on the way down seemed to clear away another layer of time that had passed, and bring me back to the old life. Bookham was at its best; a mass of green, very pleasing to one 'that has been long in city pent' . . . I opened the gate of Kirk's garden almost with stealth, and went on past the house to the vegetable garden and the little wild orchard with the pond where I had sat so often on hot Sunday afternoons, and there among the cabbages in his shirt and Sunday trousers, sure enough, was the old man, still digging and smoking his horrible pipe . . .[10]

The Kirkpatricks welcomed home the wounded soldier; Mrs Moore had welcomed him; but Albert still did nothing. One explanation may be found in a little incident which occurred several months later when Arthur Greeves happened to call at Little Lea and put his head round the study door. He found Albert slumped in a chair, very red in the face. 'I'm in great trouble, you'd better go away,' he said. Jack's harsh gloss on this sentence was, 'No evidence as to what this "great trouble" was has ever been forthcoming so I think we may with probability if not quite certainty breathe the magic word ALCOHOL.'[11] He was still a boy. Alcohol was still a subject of mirth. Its nightmares – very forceful in his family – lay in the future.

It would not appear that Greeves said anything about Albert's peculiar behaviour in his letters to Jack. The two friends were back to 'normal' as correspondents, swapping opinions about books, while from Greeves's side there were confidences about his emotional and sexual preferences. Before going to the wars, Lewis had expanded upon his own taste, in imagination at least, for sado-masochism, and a fellow-Irishman called Butler, an old boy of Campbell College, had put him on to the Marquis de Sade. Arthur's tastes were still develop-ing along homosexual lines. From Endsleigh Palace Hospital, Lewis had written to him, 'I admit the associations of the word paederasty are unfortunate but you should rise above that.'[12]

How far Lewis was able to indulge any of his sexual tastes must remain something of a mystery. We are at a point in his life where in his own account of the matter a great but almost exhibitionistic silence is observed. 'One huge and complex episode', he wrote in *Surprised by Joy*, 'will be omitted. I have no choice about this reticence. All I can or need say is that my earlier hostility to the emotions was very fully and variously avenged.'[13] That he fell in love with Mrs Moore, and she with him – probably during the period when she was visiting him in hospital, and frantic with worry about Paddy – cannot be in doubt. Neither of them was a Christian believer, nor were they bound by any code of morality which would have forbidden them to become lovers in the fullest sense of the word. True, she was still married to the Beast, and would go on being married to him for the duration of her long association with C. S. Lewis. While nothing will ever be proved on either side, the burden of proof is on those who believe that Lewis and Mrs Moore were *not* lovers – probably from the summer of 1918 onwards. 'When I came first to the University,' Lewis tells us with typical hyperbole, 'I was as nearly without a moral conscience as a boy could be . . . of chastity, truthfulness and self-sacrifice, I thought as a baboon thinks of classical music.'[14]

As the months went on, feelings between the father and son, who had not seen one another since Jack's return from France, grew less and less amiable. Albert complained to Warnie about the silences of 'that young scoundrel IT'. For his part, Jack complained to his father, 'It is four months now since I returned from France and my friends suggest laughingly that "my father in Ireland" of whom they hear, is a mythical creation like Mrs. 'Arris.' Albert took the Mrs 'Arris joke in very poor part, and not unnaturally felt that his son and Mrs Moore had been jeering at him behind his back. Jack, with the pomposity of youth, felt constrained to justify himself: 'I do not choose my friends among people who jeer, nor has a tendency to promiscuous confidence ever been one of my characteristic faults.' His father was aware that he had been negligent. 'No doubt Jacks thinks me unkind and that I have neglected him,' he wrote to Warnie. 'Of course that fear makes me miserable . . . I have never felt so limp and depressed in my life.'[15] Warnie assured him that everyone understood that the solicitor's office could not be neglected. But Jack never did quite understand this, and the estrangement of that summer of 1918 was to leave wounds as lasting as those sustained at Arras. In September 1918 it was confirmed that Paddy Moore had indeed been killed, and Albert Lewis wrote a letter of condolence to the bereaved mother. Janie Moore wrote back:

I just lived my life for my son and it is very hard to go on now . . . Of the five boys who came out to us so often at Oxford, Jack is the only one left . . . Jack has been so good to me. My poor son asked him to look after me if he did not come back. He possesses for a boy of his age such a wonderful power of understanding and sympathy. He is not at all fit yet and we can only hope will remain so for a long time [sic].

Presumably the last, somewhat 'Irish', sentence means that she hopes Jack will continue to be regarded as a convalescent and not be sent back to the slaughter of the Front.

His wound was still troubling him in October when he was sent to the Officers' Command Depot in Eastbourne, Sussex. Mrs Moore took her daughter to lodgings in Eastbourne so as to be near him. Lewis and Mrs Moore were mutually dependent. Whatever other ingredients there might have been in their relationship, one which made sense to talk about was that of the mother and the son. Janie Moore had gained a son. She always spoke of him as her adopted son and this, in effect, was what he was. By a route of tortuous coincidences, the wounds which had been inflicted on him in August 1908 with the death of Flora were now to be given a chance to heal. Anodos had kissed the marble statue and she had come to life.

As for the other wound, his hospitalization and enforced convalescence had provided Lewis with precisely the right degree of leisure for some literary activity. He had set off to France with a pocket-book full of his own poems, and in the course of the year he had added to them. Since being taken back to Blighty, he had rearranged these verses – all lyrics – into a cycle which he wanted to call *Spirits in Prison*, taken from the First Epistle of St Peter, where Christ went 'and preached unto the spirits in prison'. The lyric cycle is not markedly religious in tone, but it is striking that, even in his 'atheistical' phase, the young poet should have looked to the New Testament for his title.

He sent it off to publishers, and by September he heard 'the best of news',[16] that it had been accepted for publication. His editor, C. S. Evans, arranged for him to have an interview in October with William Heinemann himself. Lewis found Heinemann 'a fat little old man with a bald head, apparently well read and a trifle fussy – inclined to get his papers mixed up and repeat himself'.

Heinemann said, 'Of course, Mr Lewis, we never accept poetry unless it is really good.'[17]

Whether this was an attempt to convince himself, or whether Heinemann really meant it, we shall never know. The publishers not only accepted *Spirits in Prison* for publication; they also assured Lewis that John Galsworthy, the novelist and author of *The Forsyte Saga*, would give it some publicity in his magazine *Reveille*, in which a selection of work by contemporary poets was promised. 'You'll be in very good company,' Evans assured Lewis, 'for we have poems by Robert Bridges, Siegfried Sassoon and Robert Graves in the same number.'[18] Actually, much to Lewis's chagrin, Galsworthy decided not to include any of Lewis's poems in the next number of *Reveille*, so clearly not everyone shared Heinemann's glowing opinion of the young poet.

Albert Lewis was proud, but he did not allow paternal pride to blind him to the poor quality of the work. He said that 'for a first book – and of poetry – written by a boy not yet twenty it is an achievement. Of course we must not expect too much from it.' That would seem to be the sanest judgement of the book that there is. Albert, the catholic and voracious reader, also pointed out to his son that there was already a novel by Robert Hichens called *Spirits in Prison* and that he would do well to choose a different title. It was duly changed to *Spirits in Bondage*. Lewis did not publish it under his own name, but under that of Clive Hamilton – his own first name and his mother's surname. Nevertheless, by some absurd oversight, he appeared in the Heinemann catalogue as George S. Lewis. Galsworthy did eventually relent, and in the February 1919 issue of *Reveille* he published Lewis's poem 'Death in Battle'. The book had the quietest, tamest of receptions, much to the poet's disappointment, but this did nothing to diminish his sense that a poet, first and foremost, was what he was.

In November 1918, the dread that he might be transported from Eastbourne back to the Western Front was lifted. The Armistice was signed. 'It is almost incredible that the war is over, isn't it?' he wrote to Greeves. 'Not to have that "going back" hanging over my head all the time.' Holidays with no school term to cloud them, the condition of being perpetually at home, these were to become images in his mind of the heavenly places. Life was returning to normal. He spent Christmas in Ulster, but in an important sense Belfast was not any longer home. When he resumed his undergraduate career at Oxford in the new year, he did not go alone.

SEVEN

UNDERGRADUATE

1919–1922

Lewis returned to University College, Oxford, in January 1919. Because of his experiences in the war, he was excused the matriculation requirements, Responsions and Divinity. Had he chosen to do so, he could also have dispensed with the first of his public examinations, Honour Moderations, 'Mods' (that is to say, Latin and Greek Literature), and proceeded straight to the second part of the Classics course, Ancient History and Philosophy (Literae Humaniores, or Greats). He had decided, however, upon an academic career, and was advised that for this he would do better to take the whole course.

Many of the books, perhaps most of them, that he was studying for Mods were already familiar to him. Being a naturally fluent reader with a brilliant teacher in W. T. Kirkpatrick, he would probably have been equipped to get a good mark in Mods in his last month at Great Bookham. The first four terms of his Oxford life were therefore a delightful opportunity to taste again, and at greater leisure, at familiar wells. For example, at Gastons, he had read through the *Bacchae* of Euripides in Greek and compared it with the poetic English rendering, which he much admired, of Gilbert Murray. At Oxford, he had the chance to attend lectures on the *Bacchae* by Murray himself – the brilliant young Australian who had become a Professor of Greek at Glasgow in his early twenties and had now returned to his old university to occupy the Regius Chair of Greek. 'He is a real inspiration,' Lewis wrote, 'quite as good as his best books, if only he did not dress so horribly, worse even than most dons.'[1]

Other intellectual stimulation came from his membership of an undergraduate society called the Martlets, a group that met once a week in term-time to discuss a subject of common interest and hear one of their members read a paper. An essay which particularly took

62

Lewis's fancy was one on the poetry of Henry Newbolt, read by a man called Basil Wyllie. 'I hadn't thought the subject *very* promising but he quoted a great many good things I hadn't known – especially a queer little song about grasshoppers.'[2] When we follow Lewis's reading over his first couple of terms, it is sometimes hard to remember that he is at this point studying Latin and Greek rather than English Literature. Gibbon, Shakespeare's *King John* and *Troilus and Cressida* ('a very good play'), Layamon's *Brut* and Wace in the Everyman translation and an unnamed book of philosophy which took him eight weeks to read were all devoured in his first term, on top of his Latin and Greek authors. 'Of course there is very little time for ordinary reading, which has to be confined to the week-end as it was at Kirk's.'[3]

They were happy days, spent basking in the pleasures of peace-time, the beauty of the college buildings and, as spring turned into summer, the beauty of Oxford itself.

'It is perfectly lovely now both in town and country – there are such masses of fruit trees all white,' he wrote in June 1919.

One big cherry tree stands in the Master's garden just below my windows and a brisk wind this morning has shaken down masses of leaves that lay like snowflakes on the bright smooth grass. Then beyond the lawn you see the gable end of the chapel. I usually go and bathe before breakfast now at a very nice place up the Cherwell called 'Parsons Pleasure'. I always swim (on chest) down to a bend, straight towards the sun, see some hills in the distance across the water, then turn and come again to land going on my back and looking up at the willow trees above me.[4]

As if the pleasures of mind and sense were not enough, he was also expanding his circle of friendship. Eric Dodds, his fellow-Irishman, destined one day to succeed Gilbert Murray as Regius Professor of Greek, was Lewis's exact contemporary at Univ. They differed radically over the Irish question – Dodds being a fanatical Home Ruler who refused to stand up for the National Anthem; but they liked each other and were stimulated by each other's company. A. K. Hamilton Jenkin, later to be known as an authority on Cornwall, was another friend made at this juncture. 'I learned from him that we should attempt a total surrender to whatever atmosphere was offering itself at the moment, in a squalid town to seek out those very places where its squalor rose to grimness and almost grandeur, on a dismal day to find the most wet and dripping wood, on a windy day to seek the windiest ridge.' Another friend met in his first year of residence at Univ was Owen Barfield, an undergraduate at Wadham College. The First Friend, Lewis believed, is like Arthur Greeves, the man who becomes an *alter ego* and who shares your tastes. 'But the Second Friend is the man who disagrees with you about everything.'[5] Lewis was to say that Barfield changed him a good deal more than he did Barfield, and this was probably true. The thing they disagreed about most forcefully was religion, Barfield being set on the course which was to lead him to embrace theosophy, and Lewis at this stage still being an ardent atheist.

Lewis appeared to be enjoying an archetypal undergraduate career in ancient and beautiful surroundings. But in fact his routines were completely different from those of his fellow-collegians. True, he rose at six-thirty, bathed, attended chapel (which was still compulsory for undergraduates) and had his breakfast in hall. Then he went to lectures and libraries and tutorials, and had lunch (bread, cheese and beer) brought over to his room by a college servant. But at 1 p.m. without fail, he got on his bicycle and pedalled over Magdalen Bridge, up Headington Hill and into the dingy little suburban thoroughfare near the mental hospital. There at Number 28 Warneford Road, in the house of a lady of High Church persuasion by the name of Featherstone, Mrs Moore and her daughter Maureen had taken up their abode. 'They are installed in our "own hired house" (like St. Paul only not daily preaching and teaching). The owner of the house has not yet cleared out and we pay a little less than the whole for her still having a room.'[6]

It is the 'we' in this paragraph from a letter to Arthur Greeves which must give the reader pause. Lewis is now twenty years old, and dependent (in those days before university grants) on an allowance from his father. This allowance was meant to cover the expenses of one young man living in college. Instead, it was made to stretch (in those months when cheques were not forthcoming from the Beast) to pay the rent for Mrs Moore and her daughter. Here was a commitment indeed.

Nor was it merely a financial one. From the very beginning of his relationship with Janie Moore, Lewis involved himself in all her domestic arrangements – the cleaning, the cooking, the shopping, as well as the schoolwork of the little girl. 'He's as good as an extra maid,'[7] Mrs Moore once said of him. Moreover, because the arrangement was so makeshift, there was no permanence in any of the domestic arrangements which they made. They lived from hand to mouth. Between 1918 and 1923 they had nine different addresses, traipsing disconsolately from one set of rented rooms to the next, and always finding something wrong when they got there. Some places objected to Maureen's noisy music practice. Some were by their nature temporary. In others doubts were cast on the relationship between Mrs Moore and her 'adopted son' and they moved on to avoid scandal.

For all this domestic life of Lewis's in his undergraduate days had to remain a closely guarded secret. Nowadays, nearly all the colleges in Oxford are open to both sexes, and no disgrace attaches to the two sexes consorting together. Things were very different until at least 1960. In 1919, the older dons could just about remember the days when college fellows had to be celibate. Even though marriage was now permitted them, an atmosphere of celibacy prevailed. Scholars of colleges were under an obligation of celibacy. Nor was this entirely a formality. Failure to attend breakfast in your college could result in being 'gated', that is confined to the college for a period of anything from a week to a term. To have slept out of college was a very serious offence. To be shown to have associated with a member of the opposite sex was yet more serious. Six years after Lewis began his career at Univ, another poet whose first volume had been published before he arrived at Oxford was rusticated – sent away for a term – because of his association with a married woman in Maidenhead. '"I hope, Mr. Quennell, you do not know as much about Mrs. X as *we* do," remarked the Vice Chancellor with a gently dismissive sigh . . . The Oxford I knew was still a semi-monastic institution; some of the dons clearly detested women; and the only kind of moral offence they condoned were discreetly managed homosexual passions.'[8]

If Lewis's domestic arrangements had been known to the college authorities or to the Vice-Chancellor of the University, there is no doubt at all that they would have been considered most irregular. True, there had been oddities before in the history of the University.

John Ruskin's mother had taken up residence in the High Street when he was an undergraduate at Christ Church. Robert Hawker, the future vicar of Morwenstowe and author of 'And Shall Trelawney Die', had arrived to be an undergraduate as a married man (as it happened to a woman twenty years his senior who was also his godmother). But Mrs Moore was neither Lewis's wife nor his mother, and though she may have been something just as innocent, it would have put his entire career in jeopardy had the authorities known about her. He would certainly never have had any hope of a college fellowship; even in the 1950s, Oxford dons who were deemed to have led irregular lives with the opposite sex found themselves 'resigning' their fellowships.

They were jealous of their time together. In early days, there was a significant little quarrel between Maureen Moore, her mother and Lewis. An unshakable part of the Sunday routine was that Maureen should be sent out to church in the morning, leaving her mother and Lewis for a precious hour together on their own. She did not much enjoy going and had from the first resented her mother's being prepared to allow life to revolve around Jack. Maureen's life had never been stable, but since Lewis had come on the scene, what stability it once possessed had been lost for ever. Since 1919, she had been moved from school to school, and from lodging house to lodging house: Bristol, Eastbourne, London, Oxford. Her mother was prepared to take her anywhere, so long as she could be near Jack.

One week, she decided to rebel against the church routine. Why should she always go to church alone? Her mother and Jack never went to church. She refused to go. Their reaction was vehement. She must go out and leave them alone. Unwillingly, furiously, she went. In later years, when Lewis himself had become a regular churchgoer, Maureen wistfully looked back on this apparent over-reaction and wondered if it was the beginning of his return to the practice of Christianity. As a child, it did not occur to her to ask why a young man might wish sometimes to be left alone with her mother.[9]

In addition to what Maureen, or Oxford, might make of the relationship between Lewis and Mrs Moore, there was the question of what Belfast would make of it. Although Lewis did his best to conceal from his father the full extent of his involvement with Mrs Moore, Albert was no fool; and as a police-court solicitor he naturally viewed the thing in a lurid light.

'If Jacks were not an impetuous, kind-hearted creature who could be cajoled by any woman who has been through the mill I should not be so uneasy,' he wrote to Warnie. 'Then there is the husband whom I have always been told is a scoundrel – but the absent are always to blame – somewhere in the background, who some of these days might try a little aimiable [sic] blackmailing.'[10] Warnie, when he got this letter, was 'greatly relieved to hear that Mrs. Moore HAS a husband'. He made two sound points in reply to his father's fears. '(1) Mrs. Moore can't marry Jacks (2) Mr. Moore can't blackmail him because "IT" hasn't enough money to make it a paying risk.'[11]

Jack, for his part, felt an intense awkwardness about the fact that he had, in effect, cut loose from home and thrown in his lot with Mrs Moore and Maureen. Guilt made him hostile, and the more conscious he became that his father disapproved of the Mrs Moore set-up, the more venomous his hostility became. 'Haven't heard from my esteemed parent for some time; has he committed suicide yet?' he asked Greeves in one letter of June 1919, and in July he wrote, 'I hope you are avoiding my father as much as possible.'[12]

As the summer term at University College came to an end, the question had naturally arisen of where, and with whom, Jack would spend the Long Vacation (from June until October). He wanted to be with Mrs Moore, but could not admit the extent of his involvement with her. Why could he not come to Ireland as usual? was the cunning request of both Albert and Warnie, neither of whom liked the sound of Mrs Moore *at all*. Jack parried, 'Where could you pass your holiday better than in Oxford? The three of us could certainly spend our afternoons in a punt under the willows at least as comfortably as we did at Dunbar and the Mitre, honoured with so many famous ghosts, would be an improvement on the Railway Hotel.'[13]

He felt torn. He both did, and did not, want to admit to himself that the childhood days at Little Lea had come to an end. In the event the vacation was a compromise, with Jack moving to and fro between his two homes, trying in each to pretend that the other did not exist. At the end of July, he and Warnie made a visit to Gastons to see the Kirkpatricks, and on their way back stayed in London to see a show – *The Maid of the Mountains*, with Bertram Wallis and José Collins. They then went back to Ireland together. In spite of various happy outings with their mother's relations, the Ewarts and the Hamiltons (and a jaunt to Island Magee), the atmosphere at home was tense. A major quarrel developed between Jack and his father, and by the end of August Jack had returned to Oxford to reside in 'lodgings' – Uplands, Windmill Road, Headington – with Mrs Moore and Maureen. The quarrel rumbled on by letter throughout the late summer and early autumn. 'I must ask you', Jack implored, 'to believe that it would have been easier for me to have left those things unsaid. They were as painful to me as they were to you.'[14]

It would be fascinating to know from Jack's tutors at University College how much any of these tensions were reflected either in his work or in his general demeanour during tutorials and at college meals. But no such record survives. All we know is that by the spring of 1920 he was ready to sit Honour Moderations, and to be placed very surely in the First Class. 'I was very sorry to hear that I had allowed you first to learn the news about Mods from a stranger,' he wrote home to his father. 'I had put off writing until I was clear of Oxford.'[15]

This letter, like nearly all the letters he wrote to his father at this period, reflects an agony of guilt about their quarrel and separation. The guilt was something which he was never, quite, able to expunge. He always regarded this spell of angry estrangement from Albert as 'the blackest chapter of my life'.[16]

'Clear of Oxford' in that last letter meant that he was enjoying a walking holiday in Somerset 'with a friend'. The friend, of course, was Mrs Moore. By the end of his next term, when he had started to study ancient history and philosophy for Greats, Lewis was completely wrapped up in a happy combination of academic work and domestic absorption in Mrs Moore's doings and affairs. Ireland, which was in the grip of a civil war which threatened to destroy the entire Protestant population, seemed remote during the happy Oxford summer of 1920. 'I cannot understand the Irish news at all,' he wrote airily.[17] This was the period when he came closest to an estrangement not only from the P'daytabird, but also from his beloved brother Warnie. Snatching a bit of leave from the Army, Warnie arrived in Oxford and was surprised to read, 'I am afraid this is rather an unfortunate day for you to come up as I am taking a child' (Maureen, of course) 'to a matinée and shall not therefore be able to see you until rather late.' This from his closest companion and friend. No feeling of apology accompanied this note, left at Warnie's hotel, because by now Jack took it for granted that Mrs Moore and her family took precedence over everything. He added insult to injury by saying 'another time if possible you should warn me for duty earlier.' Seeing his brother had become a 'duty'.[18]

Warnie was nevertheless insistent about keeping open lines of communication with Jack, and in September 1920 he made Jack come on holiday with him to Ulster. Dreadful rows took place during this time between Jack and his father. When the boy had gone back to Oxford his father licked his wounds in the pages of his diary.

I still think I was very badly – not to say insultingly and contemptuously treated by Jacks. It is questionable whether I did a wise thing in submitting as I did, but it would have made me miserable for the rest of my life to have had an open rupture and forbidden him the house. But such weakness with some natures is traded upon and made to justify further insult and disrespect.[19]

There can be little doubt, once he lost control and tempers flared, that Jack Lewis could take a delight in tormenting his victim. One of his more sinister dreams, recorded at about this period, was of Mrs Moore and himself in a street off the Cowley Road, one of the poorer, slummier streets in East Oxford.

We each had a man wrapped in sacking and helmeted with a biscuit tin, and we are throwing them up in the air to kill them with the fall. When that failed it became one man whom we succeeded in murdering (I am not sure how. I think by drumming his head on the pavement) and the rest of the dream consists of fearful anxiety lest we should be discovered.[20]

Thanks to Warnie, some semblance of a relationship between Albert and Jack was maintained. Jack went home, for example, for Christmas 1920, and accompanied his brother to church; and a flow of dutiful letters were sent back to Little Lea from Oxford.

Against this troubled emotional background, Lewis continued to read the ancient historians and the philosophers, and to see friends such as Barfield. The subject which now interested him most was philosophy; it appealed to that side of his nature which was born of the police-court solicitor and nourished at the feet of the Great Knock: the side which liked to argue, to dispute, to analyse, to indulge in intellectual cut and thrust. He began to nurse ambitions that he would become a professional philosopher and a fellow of one of the colleges. Meanwhile the side of his nature which read George MacDonald and W. B. Yeats, which saw visions and dreamed dreams, poured itself out in poetry, and he began to execute a large mythical work entitled *Dymer*.

His academic prowess showed no signs of waning. In the spring of 1921, he wrote an essay on Optimism, which was awarded the Chancellor's English Essay Prize and declaimed before the assembled University grandees, Doctors, Professors and Heads of House, at the annual Encaenia in June. While he was writing the essay, he also had two memorable encounters with one of his heroes, W. B. Yeats, who had taken up residence at 4 Broad Street, Oxford.

The meetings with Yeats made a deep impression and he wrote them up for the benefit of both Arthur Greeves and his own father. He was struck by the rare, bogus-mystical ambience which the poet, then aged about sixty, had constructed around himself. Visitors were shown up a narrow staircase, lined with pictures by Blake – mainly illustrations to the *Book of Job* and *Paradise Lost*. There they found a room whose flame-coloured curtains were drawn shut, and whose only form of light derived from large, flickering six-foot candles of the kind normally seen on a church altar. Mrs Yeats reclined on a sofa, while the visitors sat around on hard upright chairs and listened to the oracular figure of Yeats himself, huge, fat, and with an affected voice which sounded almost as much French as it did Irish.[21] 'I understood the Dr. Johnson atmosphere for the first time – it was just like that, you know, we all sitting round, putting in judicious questions while the great man played with some old seals on his watch chain and talked.'[22]

On Lewis's first visit the talk, highly uncongenial to the young atheist visitor, was all of magic and apparitions. The Jesuit Master of Campion Hall, Father Martindale, SJ, provided a skeletal presence in the flickering candlelight while Yeats prosed about the Hermetic books, lunar meditations, and the practice of magic which he said he had learnt from Bergson's sister. It amazed Lewis the rationalist that intelligent people could be sitting about in a circle in Oxford and talking of the supernatural as if it were soberly true, and the incident was to have a deep effect on his imagination. Twenty years later, Lewis himself was to be the centre of just such a circle, discussing spirits and spiritualities with Charles Williams. Now Yeats was immediately transformed into the magician in Lewis's own poem *Dymer*, and many years later Lewis drew on Yeats when he was describing the bulky mysterious figure of Merlin, the morally ambivalent wizard-ruffian of *That Hideous Strength*. 'It is a pity', Jack wrote to his father, 'that the real romance of meeting a man who has written great poetry and who has known William Morris and Tagore and Symonds should be so overlaid with the sham romance of flame-coloured curtains and mumbo-jumbo.'[23]

Silliness, sham and mumbo-jumbo have never been absent from the Oxford scene. Only a few yards down the street from Yeats's house, the Reverend Montague Summers was writing his great book about vampires (of which he claimed to have first-hand knowledge). Lewis would not have been able to echo W. H. Auden's view of Yeats: 'you were silly like us'. Lewis's generation, the men who came straight back from the trenches to pursue their studies at the University, were too relieved to be alive, and too emotionally shocked, to be able to indulge in the wild, liberating silliness either of their elders, like Yeats, or of the younger generation who were about to appear in Oxford – the heroically silly generation of Harold Acton, Evelyn Waugh and the Hypocrites Club. Lewis's undergraduate life, even without the presence of Mrs Moore, was prosaic, almost suburban. Those who do not have the sound of exploding shells still echoing in their dreams, and the memory of decaying young corpses forever present in their memories, might well be inclined to impatience with Lewis's cult of the ordinary. It was at this period, in some dingy room in Headington, that he laid down his book and wrote a poem which, though indefensible from an aesthetic point of view, was unquestionably written from the heart:

> Thank God that there are solid folk
> Who water flowers and roll the lawn
> And sit and sew and talk and smoke
> And snore through all the summer dawn . . .

Oh happy people, I have seen
No verse yet written in your praise,
And truth to tell, the time has been
I would have scorned your easy ways.

But now through weariness and strife
I learn your worthiness indeed,
The world is better for such life
As stout, suburban people lead.

The tragedy of Albert Lewis's life was that his son had to learn this
lesson not in his own suburban house at Strandtown, but in rented
accommodation with his 'adopted mother'. It has become customary
for those who write about Lewis to speak of his fondness for Mrs
Moore and the domestic routines in which she involved him as a
tyranny which he endured with a martyr's patience. Almost any
domestic routine which involves more than one person can be viewed
in this light; and it is unquestionable that Mrs Moore was a demanding
companion whose desire for Lewis to be involved in the smallest
detail of her life did not diminish with the years. But though she may
have given him more than he bargained for, it would be unfair to her
memory to deny that she was providing something which he very
much needed and wanted.

Mrs Moore was demanding, but she was also generous. Much of
the shopping and fetching was only necessary because she wanted to
entertain and to give people meals. She was naturally gregarious.
Children and animals loved her. She was spontaneously affectionate
– witness the occasion when she was asked to do jury service at the
Oxford Crown Court and was upbraided by the court officials for
being found sitting outside in the corridor with her arm around the
defendant, comforting him in his nervous sorrow. She asked much,
but she also gave much. She was entirely lacking in English 'reserve'.
If one wants to know what she meant to the young Lewis one should
not read only the accounts of her written by Warnie when he was
a jealous, crusty bachelor and she had grown into a querulous
old woman. One should read the vision in *The Great Divorce* of
a Great Lady surrounded by a procession of angels, children and
animals.

'Who are all these young men and women on each side?'

'They are her sons and daughters.'

'She must have had a very large family, sir.'

'Every young man or boy that met her became her son – even if it was only the boy that brought the meat to her back door. Every girl that met her was her daughter.'

'Isn't that a bit hard on their own parents?'

'No. There *are* those that steal other people's children. But her motherhood was of a different kind ... Few men looked on her without becoming in a certain fashion her lovers. But it was the kind of love that made them not less true but truer to their own wives.'

'And how ... but hullo! What are all those animals? A cat, two cats – dozens of cats. And all those dogs ... why, I can't count them. And the birds. And the horses.'

'They are her beasts.'

'Did she keep a sort of zoo? I mean, this is a bit too much.'

'Every beast and bird that came near her had its place in her love. In her they became themselves.'[24]

At about the time when Lewis was sitting in the candlelight at the feet of Yeats, William Kirkpatrick died, aged seventy-one. Lewis was stricken by the news and imagined the Great Knock confronting the Almighty with the Voltairean alexandrine, 'Je soupçonne entre nous que vous n'existez pas,' or telling Aristotle (this was a real Kirkian remark which he once made) that his logic had 'the distinction of never having been the slightest use to any human being'.[25] None of Lewis's Oxford tutors was to make an impression upon him which was comparable with the impression made by Kirkpatrick. With Kirk he had felt the Romance of Ideas and the excitement of dialectic. And – an important feature of his religious development – while Kirkpatrick was alive, there could probably have been no question of his pupil – who had absorbed wholesale the 'Gastons heresies' – departing from the high old Victorian atheistic line. It was no doubt with a sad sense of how proud the Knock would have been that Jack Lewis collected his Chancellor's English Essay Prize and, the following summer of 1922 (having spent the May before his exams nursing Maureen Moore's influenza), a First Class degree in Greats.

EIGHT

HEAVY LEWIS

1922–1925

With a First in Mods, a First in Greats and the Chancellor's English Essay Prize, Lewis began to look eminently employable. In fact, like all but the most conceited young men, he despaired of getting started in the world, and regarded the possibility of finding permanent academic preferment as remote. Towards the end of his final term of Greats, his tutors put several offers of temporary employment in his way. Farquharson, at Univ, got him a job as private tutor to a family on Boar's Hill, on the outskirts of Oxford, but he did not follow it up. Carritt, his philosophy tutor, pointed out a vacancy in the Classics Department at Reading University – £300 per annum for a lectureship, 'apply E. R. Dodds, Head of their Classical Department'. 'I wondered if this might not be Eric Dodds, the drunken Sinn Feiner and friend of Theobold Butler's who had been at Univ. Going into town I met Carritt in the library and found that this was so.' This job was actually offered to Lewis, but he withdrew when he discovered that it would necessitate living in Reading, half an hour from Oxford by train. Had he been a free agent, he probably would have taken the Reading job. But it was not desirable to move Maureen Moore, who was by now happily settled at Headington School for Girls, so conveniently near their present suburban Oxford lodgings. It would have been a 'thousand pities' to change Maureen's school for a year. As well as continuing well with her music, Maureen had recently been elected house captain of cricket for day girls: 'an event', Lewis noted, 'which has hardly turned her head'.[1] The schoolgirl's needs dictated the student's prospects, and because he was in love with Oxford, he was happy that this should be so. He looked over some of the examination papers required for getting into the civil service and decided 'Greats' was child's play compared with them.[2] He would not, in any event, have wanted to become a civil servant in London.

These circumstances narrowed the field. Indeed, but for the very distinctive nature of Lewis's position at this date, the story which follows might have been very different. Rich as his imagination was, it had not yet seen its truest modes of expression; brilliantly workable as his mind was, he had not yet discovered, though it was obvious to Kirkpatrick within a week's acquaintance, the precise nature of what he was good *at*; remarkably mature as in some ways he was, in all the most crucial ways he remained unformed. What happened in the next two or three years was to be of lasting consequence. It therefore matters intensely that Lewis's relationships with his father and with Mrs Moore made him see his circumstances in a manner which would have struck any outside observer as distorted.

Once it had become clear that Lewis was clever enough to hope for an Oxford fellowship, his father said that he would continue to provide him with adequate financial support until the right post materialized. Lewis tried to persuade himself that this was not the case, but it was re-emphasized for him not only by his father's written assurances, but also by Lily Ewart, a relation who came to live near Oxford at about this time and who was delegated by Albert Lewis to make the position clear. Jack, who was by now in the grip of an uncontrollable love-hatred of his father, with a very marked bias, whenever they actually met, towards hatred, longed to be rid of parental support. So long as he depended on Albert's money, the tension was acute. Moreover that income was not sufficient to meet the needs of three people.

Poverty only increased Mrs Moore's obsession with domestic chores. She was not a lazy woman. She was persistent in trying to do unnecessary tasks, thereby forcing Jack, out of guilt, to do them himself. This domestic obsession continued even when paid help was available. For example, when they had engaged a woman to help with cleaning and polishing, Jack came home to find that Mrs Moore and the woman were both polishing an upstairs wardrobe. When he came downstairs and tried to concentrate on his work, he heard 'an awful crash' and rushed up to see what had happened. Mrs Moore had somehow or other managed to pull down the wardrobe on top of her. When it had been set to rights she still insisted that she must go on polishing it:

After tea she went on again and said I could not help: finally she came down quite breathless and exhausted. This put me into such a rage against poverty and fear and all the infernal net I seemed to be in that I went out and mowed the lawn and cursed all the gods for half an hour. After that (and it was about as far down as I have got yet) I had to help with rolling linoleums and by the time we got to supper a little before ten, I was tired and sane again.[3]

It was to escape this 'net' that Lewis looked for a fellowship and financial independence from his father. In his final term of Greats he had an interview with the Master of Univ who recommended him to stay on for an extra year and take a degree in English Literature. This would mean that, while he pursued his career as a philosopher, he could offer teaching in the expanding English School. Accordingly, in the academic year 1922–23, he laid aside his classical and philosophical texts and concentrated on those books which had always been the consuming passion of his leisure hours – Layamon's *Brut*, Chaucer, Malory, Spenser, Shakespeare, Milton, Wordsworth.

He also had his first taste of the men and women who were to be his colleagues for half a lifetime in the English Faculty: Professor H. C. Wyld, who had been taught to pronounce 'Oxford English' by a sister of Dr Pusey and whose lectures on the history of the language took a wildly aggressive tone with his audience – '*You're* the sort of people who would say *waist-coat*';* and Percy Simpson, whose overpowering halitosis distracted his students' attention from the finer points of textual criticism.[4]

'English' as an academic discipline was still in its infancy. In Oxford, it was regarded with some suspicion, at least until the middle years of this century. It is symptomatic of the way in which the subject was regarded that not until 1953 was a Professor of English appointed at Oxford who had read English Literature as a first undergraduate degree. Until that point, nearly all the English dons had themselves read History, Classics or some such obviously meaty subject. The feeling abroad was that English was not really a man's subject – more suitable for girls. It was too nebulous in its intellectual range. Criticism as a pseudo-science had scarcely begun and when it did so, in other

* i.e. rather than use the old-fashioned gentlemanly pronunciation 'westcut'.

universities, it was not welcomed at Oxford. English Literature was studied there, in Lewis's time as an undergraduate, from a relentlessly philological and historical point of view.

He revelled in this. He loved learning Old English with Miss Wardale of St Hugh's College, author of an Old English grammar. He enjoyed taking all his favourite authors in chronological order and seeing how they fitted in with their historical background and times. And his own career is not a bad justification for the study of English as a university discipline. Without it, Lewis would not have been the man he became. It gave him a little push in the direction of becoming himself, the true self who would one day write the books which made him so popular. Classical Mods had confirmed his knowledge of and love for the great texts of Rome and Greece which were always to form so large a part of the furniture of Lewis's mind. Greats had sharpened his wits to the point where he thought not only that he was a philosopher, but that life and its problems could be adequately explained by purely cerebral means. English was to restore to him with inescapable force the message which he had been hearing haphazardly but forcibly ever since he became addicted to reading as a small child in Northern Ireland. This was the knowledge that human life is best understood by the exercise not only of the wit, but also of the imagination; that poets and moral essayists and novelists, with their rounded sense of human experience, have perhaps more to teach us than logicians; that while no academic, and indeed no individual pursuing the truth, can dare to discard the rigour of logic, this is no more than an instrument. Lewis had felt the truth of this when he read *Squirrel Nutkin* and had the feeling of autumn-ness tugging at his heart; when the grand romance of Northernness had captured him through Wagner; when *Phantastes* had awakened in him thoughts too deep for tears; and when the great English poets had provided him with food which was more than just simple 'entertainment'. Reading English, in other words, compelled Lewis to come to grips with something much more fundamental than mere examination answers on the history of literature. It confronted him with questions which would not go away about the nature of Man, questions which infuriatingly formed themselves into religious shapes.

I was deeply moved by the *Dream of the Rood*; more deeply still by Langland; intoxicated (for a time) by Donne; deeply and lastingly satisfied by Thomas Browne. But the most alarming of all was George Herbert. Here was a man who seemed to me to excel all the authors I had read in conveying the very quality of life as we actually live it from moment to moment; but the wretched fellow, instead of doing it all directly, insisted on meditating it through what I would still have called 'the Christian mythology'. On the other hand, most of the authors who might be claimed as precursors of modern enlightenment seemed to me very small beer and bored me cruelly. I thought Bacon (to speak frankly) a solemn pretentious ass, yawned my way through the Restoration Comedy, and having manfully struggled on to the last line of *Don Juan* wrote on the end leaf 'Never again.' The only non-Christians who seemed to me really to know anything were the Romantics and a good many of them were tinged with something like religion, even at times with Christianity. The upshot of it all could nearly be expressed in a perversion of Roland's great line in the *Chanson* –
Christians are wrong but all the rest are bores.[5]

It is odd to find Byron boring, but *chacun à son goût*. Even if one finds him uncongenial, it is hard to feel that 'bore' is quite the right word to describe the poet of *Don Juan*, or, come to that, other non-Christian writers such as Gibbon, Hume or Hazlitt. The vigour of the sentiment, as so often in Lewis, disguises the unfairness of the argument. Until the mid-eighteenth century, most writers in the English language were Christians. It is no more surprising that the author of *The Dream of the Rood*, or Edmund Spenser, or George Herbert were Christians than it is surprising that the best Arab poets have happened to be Moslems. Had Lewis chosen to bring literary history up to date, into an era with an intellectual climate in which serious-minded people might not be Christians, he might have seen how flimsy his argument was. He himself, for example, had enjoyed the works of Virginia Woolf. Is she a 'bore' compared with a Christian writer like, say, Sheila Kaye-Smith? Is James Joyce an inherently more boring writer than his believing contemporaries? Once we have framed that question, we prepare ourselves for a strange lack of development in Lewis's reading tastes. His fascination with what he deemed to be Christian literature provided him with a good excuse for taking no apparent cognizance of the fact that a profound change had taken place, during his generation, in the human consciousness, and in Western art and literature. The development which is loosely termed 'modernism', reflected in the poetry of Pound and Eliot, the novels of Joyce, was something which, however uncongenial Lewis might have found it, surely deserved his attention as a literary historian. In most of his writing about literature, however, and in all his teaching, he appears to have chosen to turn a blind eye to these authors, justifying his ignorance of the 'moderns' in ideological, rather than aesthetic, terms.

No doubt this rooted conservatism had something to do with his uncontrollable nostalgia for childhood and his longing, at some unconscious level, to be back in the Little End Room. In latter days, he made rather a 'thing' of preferring children's books to grown-up literature. At the time, the stirrings caused in his heart by the old Christian authors were matched by the curious fact that not only in his reading, but also among his friends, he found it true that 'the rest' were bores, and the Christians were those who most engaged his imagination.

The friendships he had made with fellow-undergraduates at Univ while he was reading Greats were none of them particularly deep or long-lasting. It was surely symptomatic of the distance he kept that he did not learn his nickname in College until he had been there nearly four years. 'Coming back to College I heard with interest what is I suppose my nickname. Several Univ. people whom I don't know passed me. One of them, noticing my blazer, must have asked another who I was, for I heard him answer, "Heavy Lewis".'[6] The anecdote reveals not only that he was a stranger to them, but that *their* identity was not of the smallest interest to *him*. With the friends he made when he began to study English literature it was quite otherwise.

It is by no means the case that he fell in with a crowd who were specifically religious or 'holy'. He was, however, among a group of men, mainly of his own age, who had been through the war and who were led, by their study of literature, into a consideration of wider matters of concern than paper-logic. Professor George Gordon presided over a group which met regularly at Exeter College, and to which Lewis attached himself. It included F. W. Bateson, Nevill Coghill and others. A good example of the tenor of the discussions was an evening on 1 June 1923, when a student called Strick, whom Lewis had never esteemed very highly, read a paper of amazing excellence on tragedy. 'It was more on life than on letters,' Lewis recorded. Considerations of the *theory* of tragedy, as expressed in the writings of critics like Bosanquet and Bradley, gradually passed, in the course of the evening, to talk of Masefield, and 'then to war reminiscences between Gordon, Strick, Coghill and me'.[7]

Nevill Coghill, like Lewis, was an Irishman. He was strikingly handsome, and rather well born, coming from an ascendancy family in County Cork. The first time he met Lewis, he asked him if he were Catholic, 'which made me suspect that he might be one himself'.[8] The question had more edge to it than Lewis at first supposed, since Coghill, as a 'Protestant' in the South which, even as they spoke, was turning itself into a republic, had suffered violent experiences of the 'troubles' at first hand. His house in County Cork had been invaded by a Republican mob who dragged him outside and threatened him with lynching. They had let him go, only to call him back again, and put him in front of a firing squad of revolvers. Then he was released. It was, he said, more terrifying than anything which had happened to him during the war.[9]

Coghill, though not a Catholic in the Irish sense of the term – that is, a member of the Roman Church – was nevertheless a believer in the Catholic creeds enshrined in the prayer book of the Church of Ireland. It was a shock to Lewis to find a man who was so urbane and so charming, yet who shared with Arthur Greeves and Owen Barfield the mental quirk of believing in another world. On one occasion, he said to Lewis that he thought that William Blake was 'really inspired'. When he went on to say, 'in the same sense as Joan of Arc', Lewis found himself saying, 'I agree, in exactly the same sense.' Then, realizing that they had entered dangerous waters, the logician in Lewis added, 'But we may mean different things.' Coghill immediately replied, 'If you are a materialist.' Lewis apologized for quibbling but wanted to say that it depended what was meant by 'materialistic'. It did indeed. It depended much more than Lewis at that juncture could imagine.

Coghill was not a logician, but he was in many ways more grown-up than Lewis. He remembered the boyish enthusiasm with which Lewis took up the study of Old English and how once, when the two of them were out on a walk in the country, Lewis's passion for *The Battle of Maldon* had led him to declaim the climactic speech of the poem, that of Byrhtnoth, leader of the doomed Saxon warriors who held the causeway against the onslaught of Vikings:

Hige sceal þe heardra, heorte þe cenre
Mod sceal þe mare, þe ure maegen lytlaþ!

(Will shall be tougher, heart braver, courage the more as our strength grows less.)

On another occasion, Coghill said that Mozart had remained like a boy of six all his life. Lewis's disarmingly revealing response was that he thought nothing could be more delightful. 'He replied (and quite right) that he could imagine many things more delightful.'[10]

Gordon's discussion group, Coghill's friendship and the stimulation of the English course were the positive features of that year. Equally forceful in the formation of Lewis's future character were the darker sides of life. Strick, the man who had read the brilliant essay on Tragedy, entered into a tragedy of his own; unable to shake off the memories of the trenches, he had a nervous breakdown. Much nearer home, Mrs Moore's brother, Dr Askins, was descending into insanity. Askins had brought his family to live at Iffley, a village just outside Oxford. While the Lewises were worrying about Jack throwing himself away on an unknown married woman who might – for all they knew – be a blackmailer, it is possible that the Askinses were worried that the impulsive, passionate, warm-hearted Janie was unsuitably involved with a young man. As it turned out, Dr Askins – 'the Doc' as Lewis always called him – was a highly congenial man, and Lewis often liked to walk down to Iffley to see him. By now, some of Lewis's friends – Barfield, Greeves – had been introduced to the Moores and the Askinses and formed part of the same circle.

What none of them – least of all Mrs Moore – knew about the Doc was that he had contracted syphilis during his own student days; and by 1923 the disease had got to his brain. Afterwards, when his diary came to be transcribed by Warnie into the *Lewis Papers*, Jack maintained that the idea of Doc's syphilis had been a mere delusion.[11]

It was felt to be real at the time. One day in February 1923, the Doc lunched with Lewis and Mrs Moore in Headington. Lewis then accompanied the Doc back to Iffley on foot. As they walked along, they discussed the afterlife, and it became apparent that this was no 'ordinary' discussion of the kind which Lewis might have had with Barfield or Coghill. The Doc was convinced that he was going to hell. Demons were saying things inside his head, horrible blasphemies and obscenities which were causing him torment. 'He was walking very stiffly.'[12] Three days later Mrs Moore summoned her doctor, who examined Askins and pronounced him doomed, incurably, to 'lunacy and death'. That night, the Doc had a bad fit – 'Rolling on the floor and shrieking that he was damned for ever and ever. Screams and grimaces unforgettable.' Dr Hichens returned, and Lewis had to hold Askins on the floor, dripping with sweat, while chloroform was administered. 'He'd got as strong as a horse. He was ages going over: and kept on imploring us not to shorten his last moments and send him to Hell sooner than need be.' It was in these circumstances that Lewis was trying to prepare essays on *The Owl and the Nightingale* for Miss Wardale and on Elizabethan literature for his other English tutor, F. P. Wilson. 'For painfulness I think this beats anything I've seen in my life.' With the Doc and his wife [?] Mary in the house, Lewis was now obliged to rest on the sofa. His own bed was being slept in by 'Rob', the Doc's son. To use the word 'sleep' for those weeks would be to distort language. He hardly slept at all, for all the noise and worry, and almost the only moments of true repose which he enjoyed were when he was able to slip into Mrs Moore's bed after she had 'just vacated it' for the afternoon. For reasons which now seem obscure, they were not able to find an appropriate asylum for the Doc for over two weeks, and there were intense worries about his pension coming through. Eventually, a mental hospital was found in Henley, and Lewis and Rob drove the Doc over there on 12 March 1923. When he got home, Jack found Mrs Moore completely exhausted. Mary – dubbed the She-Wolf by Lewis – said that she wanted to buy Lewis a present in recognition for all his kindness. 'I had thought it was not in her power to annoy me more, but this was the last straw.' He stomped out of the house and bought himself a large whisky and soda.[13]

Lewis felt himself changed by the Doc experience. The Doc had been, in the loose sense of the term, a Romantic, a man who had appealed to the side of Lewis's nature which loved Wagner, as well as to the side which liked to hear Barfield or Yeats speak of the occult. The Doc, in his time, had been interested in spiritualism, theosophy, yoga. Now, 'I thought I had seen a warning. It was to this, this raving on the floor, that all romantic longings and unearthly speculations led a man in the end . . . Safety first, thought I: the beaten track, the approved road, the centre of the road, the lights on . . . For some months after that nightmare fortnight, the words "ordinary" and "humdrum" summed up everything that appeared to me most desirable.'[14]

If the humdrum and the ordinary were what he craved, Mrs Moore was more than capable of supplying his wants. The diary which he kept during his final undergraduate year is a catalogue of tedious chores, performed in the intervals of working on his English literature essays, or on his own poetry. 'After lunch I sat down to work on *Dymer*,' is a typical entry. 'I had just started in high hopes when I was called upstairs to help in fixing up the curtains in D's rooms which, having been fixed with rawlplugs, come down in an avalanche about once a week.'

Mrs Moore is always referred to as 'D' in the diary and no one living appears to know why. Jack's mother was sometimes called Doli by his father; it is possible that the son called his adopted mother by the same endearment. Friday, 27 April 1923 saw Jack working on Old English until the moment when he was required to carry an old cast-iron wringer, a miniature mangle, into the centre of Oxford by bus, with the instruction to see if it could be exchanged in a certain shop for a lawnmower. Since the shop did not want it, he had to carry the mangle back up Headington Hill. He was then, in the same afternoon, told that Mrs Moore had lost her purse, and sent back into Oxford to enquire after it at the bus station. Each of these journeys would have taken in the region of twenty minutes into town and twenty minutes out again. It would be easy to suppose that the diary is a catalogue of complaints about this ceaseless succession of chores, but no breath of complaint about 'D' ever occurs in their pages. Readers who suppose that he is complaining about Mrs Moore are imagining what they would feel like if they had to rush out of a lecture, buy some margerine (sic) for Mrs Moore and cycle up Headington

Hill with it before they went to their next academic assignment. But as readers of *The Allegory of Love* were to be reminded thirteen years later, 'to leap up on errands, to go through heat or cold, at the bidding of one's lady, or even of any lady, would seem but honourable and natural to a gentleman of the thirteenth or even of the seventeenth century; and most of us have gone shopping in the twentieth with ladies who showed no sign of regarding the tradition as a dead letter.'[15]

The routine evidently did nothing to diminish his competence as an examinee. Almost his last bit of reading before he sat for English Schools was *King Lear*, and he made the highly characteristic observation: 'No critic has noticed what a beastly old man Lear is until he is quite broke.' At about the same time, Lewis had a dream that Miss Wardale, his Old English tutor, was helping him to escape his own father. There could be no doubt, in either his conscious or subconscious mind, about the likeliness of his success in the English Schools. The papers in the event were surprisingly tough, and Lewis boiled with anger after the exams at what he regarded as a number of unfair questions. 'Neither for Mods nor Greats did I ever meet cads for lecturers and malicious papers as I have done in this. I hope more than ever for a first if only to defeat the old men.'[16] Chief of the old men in the English Faculty that Lewis hated was Percy Simpson, the editor of Ben Jonson. Needless to say, Lewis got his First, in the summer of 1923; but a few years were to pass before he was able to get his revenge on the 'old men'. Lewis's philosophy tutor, E. F. Carritt, recounted to him a conversation which had taken place at the high table of Univ. A philosopher who had examined in the Schools remarked to Carritt, 'One of your young men seems to think Plato is always wrong.' 'Oh,' said Carritt, 'is it Simpson?' 'No.' 'Blunt? Hastings?' 'No. Man called Lewis, seems an able fellow anyway . . .'[17]

It was one of those apparently trivial exchanges which, once repeated, took on significance. As soon as Carritt had told his pupil about it, Lewis became convinced that he would one day succeed as a professional philosopher. In the eighteen months which followed his triumph in the English Schools, Lewis considered his options. Harwood wrote urging him to consider taking the All Souls exam. Had he done so, he would have won a research fellowship for seven years at a college which had no undergraduates and been able to concentrate on reading and research pure and simple. This was never to be his destiny. For him, reading and writing – the two things which made life worth living – always had to be squeezed in between domestic life and the requirements of teaching. There was the possibility of teaching Philosophy at Trinity College, but that was a job he missed. In the autumn of 1923, in dire need of funds, he undertook to prepare an unpromising ex-schoolboy for the scholarship exam:

LEWIS: Well, S., what Greek authors have you been reading?

BOY (cheerfully): I can never remember. Try a few names and I'll see if I get any.

LEWIS (a little damped): Have you read any Euripides?

BOY: No.

LEWIS: Any Sophocles?

BOY: Oh yes.

LEWIS: What plays of his have you read?

BOY (after a pause): Well – the *Alcestis*.

LEWIS (apologetically): But isn't that by Euripides?

BOY (with genial surprise of a man who finds £1 where he thought there was only a ten-shilling note): Really. Is it now? Then by Jove I *have* read some Euripides.

In the lives of most teachers there is some such dispiriting exchange. Luckily for Lewis, his old college came to the rescue. Carritt was given a year's professorship at Ann Arbor University, Michigan, and the new Master of Univ, Sir Michael Sadler, asked Lewis if he would step into the breach and do the teaching. This meant that he had his first job – as a temporary lecturer in philosophy at his old college. Philosophy more than most disciplines thrives on the tutorial system, that is to say, on conversation; and it was during this year when he taught nothing but philosophy that Lewis was able to question whether he still thought that Plato was 'always wrong'. Among all the popular twentieth-century writers in English, Lewis is conspicuous for the number of times he appears to believe that Plato is right; we must assume that the beginnings of this momentous conversion took place during his discussions with his Univ pupils.

By the following year, 1924, he was considering applying for the Philosophy fellowship at St John's College, and was going to offer them, in proof of his worth, a dissertation on Bertrand Russell's *Worship of a Free Man*. Lewis had been arrested by this book because in its pages 'I found a very clear and noble statement of what I myself believed a few years ago. But he does not face the real difficulty – that our ideals are after all a natural product, facts with a relation to all other facts, and cannot survive the condemnation of the fact as a whole.'[18] Reading Russell, in short, compelled him to reconsider the great questions which had been posed by Socrates and Plato in Athens four centuries BC. What is the Good? If the universe is what the nineteenth-century materialists believed it to be, and if human beings are no more than physical phenomena within it, to be scattered as soon as their brain cells are interfered with or their bodies decay, then how can they attach a hierarchy of significance to the thoughts which pass through their heads? Why are Russell's ideals any more or less lofty than those of a common criminal? Why are his brilliant discoveries about mathematics of more or less consequence than the mental ramblings of a manual labourer? Once a hierarchy of values is implied, either moral or intellectual, then you are taken outside a purely material realm into that of metaphysics.

The followers and friends of Russell, particularly Ludwig Wittgenstein, and subsequently such popularizers of Wittgenstein's early thought as A. J. Ayer, saw their way out of this string of difficulties by placing a clear no-entry sign at the turning of the road. 'The world is that which is the case.' This did not imply (for Wittgenstein, though it did for Ayer) that metaphysics was all wrong; it merely placed a drastic limitation on what philosophers could meaningfully discuss. The so-called verification principle (familiar in different forms from the time of the Cartesian philosophers in the late seventeenth century) was erected as a great totem before which thinking man was expected to bow down. A statement could not be meaningful unless it was capable of verification by some means external to itself. The only truths which passed this test were statements of a priori acceptability, such as mathematical formulae; and statements relating to our sense data, to the physical universe. The words 'science' and 'scientific', which had been given an inflated importance in the Victorian period, were now swollen yet further to embrace all truth. Questions of aesthetics, morality, and above all questions of religion were relegated to the scrap heap where language was meaningless. The areas which had concerned the noblest and most agile minds of the previous twenty-three centuries were put on one side as being not merely unimportant but actually nonsensical.

This was the philosophical world into which Lewis was about to step. Mid-twentieth-century logical positivism, with Ayer as its *enfant terrible*, was yet to flower fully. Russell was a figure who interested Lewis because he appeared to embody a phenomenon which to a lesser degree had been shown forth in old Kirkpatrick: a passionate belief in virtue, without any philosophical justification for his position.

In the year that Lewis was wrestling with these problems in his mind, his friend Barfield was following a very different course. Far from wrestling with Plato, Barfield had gone back to him with alacrity, only via the writings of Rudolph Steiner. Reading Steiner was for Barfield a profound religious awakening; it made 'the burden roll' from his back.[19] Steiner made Barfield see that there was no need to accept the Darwinian, purely materialistic interpretation of the world. The crude Darwinian view of human consciousness, for example, was that it had somehow or other 'evolved' from a succession of increasingly intelligent apes, beginning with a creature who little thought beyond where his next banana was coming from, and culminating in the President of the Royal Society. But this was only a theory and not, on the face of it, a particularly probable one. Steiner recovered from Plato the idea of consciousness and imagination as reflections of the soul or mind outside the human. For Barfield, the words of Coleridge took on new significance when the poet wrote of the imagination as the 'repetition in the finite mind of the eternal act of creation in the Infinite I AM'. The extreme disagreement between Lewis and Barfield on this matter led to the exchange of letters which they came to call *The Great War*.

Lewis was sufficiently committed to the life of the mind to see that if what Barfield was saying was true, it would profoundly affect everything. There cannot be a greater difference than that between someone who supposes that the human race (and with it all art, philosophy, science and virtue) is a mere atomic accident in a blankly meaningless universe and those who believe that there is a plan, and behind it all a design. Lewis could, as it were, feel the breath of that idea on the back of his neck, and he did not like it. This was an unhappy period of his life, dogged by uncertainty about everything.

Barfield's talk about the burden rolling from his back did not stop Lewis from wanting to hug his own burden.

> I woke up late this morning in such a state of misery and depression as I never remember to have had. There was no apparent reason. Really rather ridiculous – I found myself in tears for the first time for many a long day, while dressing . . . Read Hume's 'Of Morals'. This contains nearly all my own fallacies in Ethics – which look more fallacious in another person's language.[20]

Were it not for the distressing fact that nearly all his favourite English authors also seemed to arouse the same metaphysical speculations, he would perhaps have been happier teaching English literature. F. P. Wilson, his old tutor, thought very highly of his powers, and had urged him to pursue his studies in a B.Litt or a doctoral thesis. Lewis suggested the idea that he might like to work on 'a study of the Romantic epic from its beginnings down to Spenser, with a side glance at Ovid'.[21] This was far too broad a sweep for the essentially minimal confines of a 'research degree', and Wilson urged him to find something narrower. In fact, this idea contained the seeds of his first important book, *The Allegory of Love*. From the beginning, 'Heavy' Lewis was to be a heavyweight in the field of scholarship. Not for him, as for so many scholars, the painstakingly minute study of some small area, the discovery of more and more about less and less. Instead, the broad, general sweep, the bold, big outline, was to be his mode. It was this which would make him such a very satisfying critic for the general reader, as well as an inspired lecturer for generations of undergraduates.

Janie Moore, who worried as much as Lewis did about money and all the 'humiliations, the hardships and the waste of time that come from poverty', nevertheless had the insight to be slightly afraid of Lewis's decision to embark upon the academic life. She saw that teaching could be a grind, and she felt keenly, as Lewis did himself, that 'the creative years are slipping past me without a chance to get to my real work.' By this they both meant, Irish as they were, the great work of poetry. They were both preparing for Lewis the great Romantic poet to burst upon the world. The academic jobs were merely a way of paying the rent, unless it transpired that Lewis could find a post which gave him time for his philosophical speculations.

The academic year of 1924 passed by, and no prospect of a job in philosophy materialized. Then a fellowship in English was announced at Magdalen College. Lewis applied, and soon found himself on a shortlist of two. His rival was John Bryson, who later became the English tutor at Balliol College and an expert on portraiture, among other things. Curiously enough, Bryson was also an Ulsterman from Portadown, County Armagh, but it would have been hard to find two men more different. Bryson was an aesthete, a miniaturist, a man who worked by intuition; Lewis was large, bombastic, a dialectician as well as a Romantic. Since Magdalen was looking for a man who would also help with the teaching of philosophy, there could not have been any doubt about which of the two candidates was the more worthy. But dons, particularly dons in committee, are capable of making bizarre choices. Nothing was certain. After the academic interviews had been completed, the two candidates were invited to dine on High Table, so that their manners and conversation could be assessed. Both men were charming company, though in very different styles.

Though both were gentlemen, the dinner was not unfrightening. Lewis consulted Farquharson (the Farq) at Univ and asked him what to wear. He was told 'white tie and tails'. When he arrived, he found that everyone else around the dinner table was wearing a black tie with dinner jacket. The President of Magdalen, Sir Herbert Warren, had been tutor to the Prince of Wales, and was a byword for grand social ideas. He took to Lewis, and it may well have been this which swayed events in Lewis's favour.

Magdalen elected him, and the appointment was published in *The Times* on 20 May 1925. The next day in the local papers at home, the headline was 'HONOUR FOR BELFAST MAN'. 'The new Fellow,' readers were told, 'whose future career will be followed with great interest by his many friends, is a son of Mr. A. J. Lewis, the well-known Belfast solicitor.'[22]

The healing of relations with his father was from now onwards one of the most profound requirements of Lewis's emotional life. So long as he had been dependent on the P'daytabird, he had been unable to love him. His first act on being elected to the Magdalen fellowship was to sit down and write to Albert. Lewis had had an undergraduate career of dazzling success. He had been employed, perfectly honourably, teaching at his old college for a year, and he had now stepped into a prestigious position at one of the largest and most beautiful colleges in Oxford. When he had been anxious to go off on his own and get a job as a lecturer or a schoolmaster the family had held him back and urged him to continue to accept Albert's support, which was given quite freely and without strings attached. But to Jack, who had spent so much of his time in Janie Moore's squalid lodgings, the years since the war felt like the strugglings of a friendless pauper.

> First, let me thank you from the bottom of my heart for the generous support, extended over six years, which alone has enabled me to hang on like this. In the long course I have seen men at least my equals in ability and qualifications, fall out for the lack of it. 'How often can I afford to wait?' was everybody's question; and few of them had at their back those who were both able and willing to keep them in the field for so long. You have waited, not only without complaint but full of encouragement, while chance after chance slipped away and when the goal receded farthest from sight. Thank you again and again . . .

In the tone of all this, there is something unnatural. He writes here the words he feels that he ought to write. He does so not for the sake of pure politeness but as an emotional necessity. Something was beginning to happen to him, to his whole relationship with himself and to the way he perceived his own personality, which was to be of momentous consequence.

NINE

REDEMPTION BY PARRICIDE
1925–1929

In 1793, the Fellows of Magdalen College, Oxford, erected a large building of simple classical design on the edge of their deer park. To distinguish it from the medieval part of the college which hugs the splendid fifteenth-century cloisters, they called it New Buildings. By 1925, New Buildings had begun to look old and stately. Built from soft Headington stone, and blackened by the soot from college chimneys, it had something of the crumbly, grand appearance of a country house in Ireland. In front of the building was a neatly made formal garden. Behind and all around it was a richly planted park, in which deer grazed. Beyond it, to the east, was a meadow, thick with fritillaries in spring and surrounded by a wooded path, known (after the essayist and moralist who was a fellow of the College in the early eighteenth century) as Addison's Walk. There can be few more beautiful places in Europe. C. S. Lewis was given rooms in New Buildings and moved in shortly after the end of the summer term, 1925. He had expected to be given the rooms furnished by the College. He had no money in his bank account, and when he gazed about at the huge drawing-room, smaller inner drawing-room and large bedroom, he had no idea how he was to find the money to buy the barest essentials – a few chairs, a table, a bed. All that met his eye was the linoleum on the floor which the College bursar, in a spirit of generosity, said that he could keep.

The bed was necessary, because Lewis intended to sleep in the College, at least during the week in term-time. Why not? He was a bachelor, and this was certainly expected of him by his colleagues. The modern habit of Oxford dons' merely coming into their colleges to teach, and perhaps lunch, before cycling or driving home to their wives and children had not caught on. Most fellows would have dined in college on most nights, whether they were married or not; and the huge majority were still bachelors for whom the celibate life was the norm.

Lewis was now twenty-seven years old. Mrs Moore was fifty-three. Maureen Moore was nineteen, and when she had finished her qualifications she would become a music teacher. There was no question of Lewis abandoning the Moores, but the body does not always believe the evidence of its senses; and from this time onwards Minto (as Lewis had begun to call Janie, after a variety of sweet to which she was devoted) began to develop a series of psychosomatic conditions which strengthened the ties binding him to her side. A holiday on Exmoor in the course of that summer was dogged by her rheumatism. If it kept her awake all night, then it was only right that she should wake up Jack for fresh hot-water bottles to be applied to the afflicted areas. They consulted a doctor who told them that there was very little that could be done for a rheumatic attack.[1]

Yet those are mistaken who imagine (as, for example, Warnie did) that Mrs Moore was nothing but a distraction from the serious business of work. For one thing, although she *was* a distraction, she did try not to be. She honestly believed that she was making life easier for Jack, by providing him with a background of home, where not only were meals provided and clothes mended, but his time was also jealously guarded. She made a point of ensuring that others did not disturb him when he was at his books, even though it was not always a rule that she was able to keep herself.

> I don't think I ever saw J[ack] work more than half an hour without the cry of 'Barboys!' – 'Coming, dear!', down would go the pen, and he would be away perhaps five minutes, perhaps half an hour; possibly to do nothing more important than stand by the kitchen range as scullery maid. Then another spell of work, then the same all over again. And these were the conditions under which *Screwtape* and indeed all his books were produced.[2]

How, it may be asked, could any serious work be done in those circumstances? The answer is that in the years when Minto was in her full vigour, Lewis's flow of words was limited. A glance at the shelf containing his long list of books shows us immediately that the bulk of his work was completed when Minto was in her dotage or after she died. He was a fluent and rapid prose writer. But his first major prose work – *The Allegory of Love* – took about eight years to complete. This was the price he paid for having thrown in his lot with a person who with all her virtues – generosity, warmth of character, genuine and passionate admiration, as well as love, for Lewis himself – did not have the concept of a working day. She belonged to that great majority of intelligent human beings who think of a book as something with which to beguile the hours of solitude of an evening. After years of living with Lewis she still knew but did not know that 'a man' could regard reading as the main business of the day and everything else as an interruption.

On the other hand, if Lewis had been allowed to live in this way, though we might have had a few more mighty works of literary history from his pen, it is doubtful whether he would have written the works for which he is more popular. He is the great chronicler of the minor domestic irritation, of the annoying little trait bulking to (literally) hellish proportions. Domestic life with his father had been the training-school for this distinctively Lewisian vision. Minto not only provided him with plenty of *Screwtape*-style domestic situations. She also had a rich enjoyment of the comedy of human character, which was one of the things she shared with Lewis. For example, at the next table at the Exmoor Forest Hotel, he had overheard two people talking to each other, a 'very well bred looking old man with a dry peevish voice whom I took to be mentally deranged and a woman who was either his daughter or his nurse'. Lewis took the trouble to transcribe what he remembered of their conversation:

HE: Look at this ham. It's all cut in chunks.

SHE: Oh, do be quiet.

HE: Anyone would think they were cutting it for coal-heavers (pause) or stonebreakers. It's . . . it's . . . wasteful you know, so wasteful.

SHE: Well, you needn't worry about that, need you.

HE (savagely): Look at that. It's abominable.

SHE: Oh do be quiet. Get on with your lunch. I want to go out.

HE: What's it like out?

SHE: It's lovely.

HE: Oh yes, I know it's lovely. What I want to know is, is it cold or hot?

SHE: It was cold when I first went out, but —

HE (Interrupting): There you are, cold. I knew it was cold.

SHE: I was going to say, if you'd let me, that it was very hot before I got back.

HE (after a pause): Look at that. It's really disgraceful to cut ham like that. It was a nice ham too. Well smoked, well cured and good fibre. And they go and spoil it all by cutting it in chunks. Chunks. Just look at that (stabbing a piece and holding it up in mid-air).

SHE: Oh, do get on.

HE: (Something inaudible)

SHE: Well they've as much right here as we have. Why can't you get on and eat your lunch?

HE: I'm not going to be hustled over my lunch. Hustled. I won't let you hustle me in this way. (A pause.) Why don't you ask Mrs Ellworthy to let you make some of that nice porridge of yours.

SHE: How could I in a hotel? (They had a long argument over this.)

Then HE (almost pathetically): Why don't you eat some of this salad? It's beautifully flavoured (here his voice broke and he added almost in a whisper) – with CUCUMBER. If it wasn't for the ham . . .

And so they went on.[3]

The impulse which made Lewis transcribe the dialogue at such length was something which could have been directed into comic fiction. It was the side of Lewis which reflected his father's love of 'wheezes'. Albert's love of recording the essential transitoriness of irritation, mere human annoyingness, gives an almost stream-of-consciousness effect in the *Lewis Papers*. 'Sunday, August 10, 1913: I wish this awful man would not come into our house' is a fairly typical entry, transcribed from Albert's pocket diary. Obviously in the presence of some prize bore, Albert had scribbled this down and shoved the book across the table to Warnie or Jack. Everyone in the world has had such thoughts. The distinctive Lewisian thing was to have written them down. In Albert's 'wheezes', human beings are often behaving foolishly, but they are usually observed with some warmth. In Jack's transcriptions of such experiences, the vision of humanity is bleaker. Already, before he has found a theological universe in which to create them, they have the feeling of lost souls, fodder for hell. I suspect that Mrs Moore's sense of humour contributed much to the genuine streak of misanthropy in Lewis's nature.

In spite of this, his animus against his father was already diminishing. At the end of the vacation – in the last two weeks of September – he returned to Ulster, and Albert gratefully recorded, 'Jacks returned. A fortnight and a few days with me. Very pleasant. Not a cloud. Went to the Boat with him. The first time I did not pay his passage money. I offered, but he did not want it.'[4]

Jack Lewis was about to embark on his professional career as a college tutor at Magdalen; and since not everyone is familiar with the way Oxford functions, it might be worth explaining exactly what his work was going to entail. He did not need Albert to pay his fare on the Irish packet for, at last, he was an independent man, earning his own living. As a Fellow of Magdalen he earned £500 a year, considerably more than his father's allowance of £210. Lewis was about to embark on a three-stranded career. He would be a university lecturer, responsible for lecturing perhaps once a week; a Fellow of Magdalen, involved in the administration of the College; and, perhaps most importantly, a college tutor. He was responsible for all those men at Magdalen who were reading English. He had to prepare them for the study of Old English (Anglo-Saxon), Middle English (that is, the language and literature of England from about 1200 until 1450, including Chaucer) and all the remaining periods of English literature up to the Victorian period. He was also responsible for instructing his pupils in the History of the English Language and in philology (the growth, history and structure of words). Some of this teaching could be done in classes – the routine language work, for example. But the bulk of it was done by way of the tutorial, a weekly session in which the pupil read aloud an essay of some three thousand words to his tutor and they then discussed it. This is the distinctive method of instruction at Oxford, and it is extremely prodigal of time. If, say,

Lewis had seven pupils in one week all of whom had written an essay on Wordsworth, he would, instead of having one hour in which they all discussed Wordsworth together, have seven hours in which they all discussed Wordsworth separately.

This method of teaching, though daunting at first for the pupil, is a formative experience, the aspect of the course to which most Oxford graduates look back with most gratitude. It is not an hour in which a pupil sits learning what the tutor has to teach. It is, or should be, an hour in which the pupil gradually comes to learn to defend himself or herself in argument, to have confidence in his or her own prose style, to grow up intellectually. But it has a strange effect on the tutor. For the pupils (to keep to the same example), it is one gloriously stimulating hour in which they have the chance to pour out all that they have felt and discovered about *The Prelude*. Very few people, at nineteen or twenty, have the humility or cynicism to realize that their thoughts on any particular book will coincide with eerie exactitude to everyone else's. For the tutor it is the seventh conversation about *The Prelude* he or she has had that week. After only a very few years of teaching it becomes the twenty-first or the forty-ninth. It is small wonder that many dons (as teachers at Oxford are called; a shortening of Latin *dominus*) develop a kind of crust, a persona, a 'character' to help them through these increasingly one-sided experiences. 'O brave new world that has such people in it,' says Miranda; to which donnish Prospero replies, ''Tis new to thee.' The good Oxford tutor never forgets that ''tis new to thee.' But in order not to forget it, an element of artifice, of manner, is essential from the start.

The younger the tutor, the more this manner will be felt necessary as a defence. This is not to say that a don must affect mannerisms or artificial eccentricities as a way of keeping his distance from the pupil – though many have done this. It is more an inevitable consequence of two people (particularly people of a similar age) finding themselves sitting together week after week in a setting which, socially speaking, is hard to define. In Lewis's day, some formality was added to the proceedings by the undergraduate's wearing a gown. Nevertheless, as they both sat in upholstered armchairs or a sofa in front of a fire, there was something domestic about it. 'I'm not your schoolmaster,' Lewis once crossly remarked to a pupil. Nor quite, though, is the pupil considered the tutor's equal. Again, in Lewis's day the relationship would have begun with the pupil calling his tutor 'Sir' and the tutor calling his pupil by his surname. Later, when they came to know each other better, the pupil might graduate to calling him 'Lewis', but this would be in the case of intimates. There *is* something curiously intimate about the tutorial – about meeting regularly *à deux* to have conversations of a depth and intellectual intensity which will probably never be repeated in the pupil's life. Yet where the two do not like one another or the chemistry is wrong, the relationship will remain distant for the entire three years.

From the beginning, Lewis was a conscientious tutor who tried to keep the balance right between amiability or conviviality (not always possible between incompatible types) and his duty to the pupils to give them sufficient preparation for their examinations. Since he was also responsible for teaching a weekly class of seven young women at Lady Margaret Hall (a women's college in North Oxford) and for teaching philosophy to the undergraduates of Magdalen, his first few years at the College were strenuous.

English, as a subject, had evolved cautiously, and at Oxford, for many years, it was on the defensive. First, it was on the defensive against the Germans. It was they, shamingly, who had led the great discovery of old Germanic literature, which included the Old English texts *Beowulf*, *The Wanderer*, *The Seafarer* and the great rhythmical prose-sermons of Aelfric and Wulfstan. English scholars, all classicists or ex-classicists, hurried to catch up and prove themselves the equals of the Germans in philological and textual skill.

Then again, English at Oxford was on the defensive against the other faculties. Was English a 'proper subject' such as Law or Greek? Since any well-educated person had read *The Rape of the Lock* or *Paradise Lost*, how could English justify itself as an academic discipline? The answer was that it would make the study of literature highly historical and linguistic. In order to do well at English at Oxford, you would have to show more than a purely aesthetic aptitude. You would need to have a sound grasp of English history before you began; and you would need, at every point, to relate your study of the literature of any given period to the state and development of the language. In the earliest stages, this required a full working knowledge of the processes of Germanic philology and the history of sound-change, a branch of study which is extremely difficult to master. It calls on the speculative ability of a scientist (for the so-called laws of sound-change such as Grimm's Law and Verner's Law are, like scientific laws, working hypotheses about the development of sound); it also requires a workable memory and a simple ability to reason, to see logical consequences, an ability not always found among students of literature.

Lewis worked extremely hard at preparing this part of the course for his pupils. Needless to say, it was the part which most of them hated; they were longing to get it finished so that they could write their essays on *Hamlet* or Keats. Without a knowledge of what was happening to Germanic diphthongs and vowels in the Dark Ages, however, even a clever pupil at Oxford in those days would have done badly.

Lewis organized 'Beer and Beowulf' evenings for his pupils, during which he taught them to chant mnemonics to master the processes of sound-change:

Thus Æ to Ĕ they soon were fetchin'
Cf. such forms as ÞÆC and ÞECCEAN.

There is a kind of innocence about this which makes the modern reader, coming upon it all sixty years after the event, squirm with embarrassment. The bluffness of Lewis, which before he became a don was only part of his nature ('Heavy Lewis'), was fast hardening into a persona. The more arty and airy-fairy his pupils, the bluffer and beerier and louder he became. Magdalen, which had been Oscar Wilde's college, always attracted a fair number of rarefied and aesthetic young men, and it was on to the path of this tradition that one of Lewis's first pupils, John Betjeman, happily placed his bedroom-slippered toe.

Betjeman appeared in a pair of eccentric bedroom slippers and said he hoped I didn't mind them as he had a blister. He seemed so pleased with himself that I couldn't help saying that I should mind them very much myself but that I had no objection to *his* wearing them – a view which I believed surprised him.[5]

Betjeman liked teasing Lewis. He opted to be taught medieval Welsh as a special subject. He was perfectly entitled to do this by the statutes of the English Faculty; but there being, at that date, no one in Oxford who could teach it, Lewis had to organize a tutor from Aberystwyth to be brought to Oxford once a week by train. Sometimes Betjeman surprised Lewis by producing 'a very creditable essay'. But for the most part he was, in Lewis's eyes, an 'idle prig' who wasted his time cultivating well-born families and pretty boys and visiting exotic churches. On one occasion when he had failed to produce an essay for the third week running, Betjeman wandered sheepishly into Lewis's room and threw himself on his knees by the hearth.

'What is the matter, Betjeman?' asked Lewis.

'I'm hopeless. I've failed to produce an essay yet again. I shall be a failure, I shall have to take Holy Orders, but you see, I'm in such an agony of doubt, I can't decide.'

'What can't you decide, Betjeman?'

'Whether to be a very High Church clergyman with a short lacy surplice, or a very Low Church clergyman with long grey moustaches.'[6]

Lewis treasured this conversation in after years, but at the time he found it disconcerting and annoying. He bullied Betjeman. 'You've got no style, Betjeman,' he used to taunt the younger man. 'Why can't you go away and get some style?'[7] Betjeman asked Lewis to a number of his parties, and Lewis found their High Church pansyism fairly difficult to stomach. He saw Betjeman's qualities. It may even have been – for he was quick to spot poetic talent – that he could see where Betjeman's true genius lay. If so, it would only have increased his feeling of vulnerability and awkwardness for, until he had come to recognize that he was not going to be the greatest poet of the age after Yeats, Lewis was always hostile to poets. Betjeman introduced Louis MacNeice to him with the words 'He doesn't say much, but he's a great poet.' It prompted in Lewis the immediate feeling that MacNeice was 'absolutely silent and astonishingly ugly'.[8] He had a rooted antipathy to T. S. Eliot which, even after they had both become famous as defenders of the faith and brothers in Christ, was still hard to shake off.

When Betjeman failed his Divinity exams at the end of his first year, it would have been open to his tutor to plead for him with the College so that he could resit these comparatively unimportant exams and stay on at the University. Lewis let Betjeman sink.

Betjeman recalled the moment in his autobiographical poem, *Summoned by Bells*:

> I sought my tutor in his arid rooms,
> Who told me, 'You'd have only got a third.'

Betjeman always loathed Lewis thereafter, though as they got older they both tried to make a bit of a joke about it.

In the spring of 1926, Lewis's own secret career as a poet took a great stride forward as he completed his long narrative poem *Dymer*. He had been working on it ever since the end of the war, and showing it in whole or in part to his friends. Harwood, when he had read Canto II, had 'danced for joy', and Barfield had a very high opinion of the work. Reading *Dymer* today, it is hard to see why. It reads like Masefield on a very bad day; and one uses the word 'reads' with caution, since few people in recent times, except Lewis enthusiasts anxious to have read their way through the entire canon, can ever have bothered to press on with *Dymer*.

He had been meditating on the parricidal theme which runs through *Dymer* since he was a pupil of Kirkpatrick's. Versions of it in prose and rhyme had been written up while he was still at Gastons. After meeting Mrs Moore, the theme of a powerful female entered the story –

> Always the same . . . that frightful woman shape
> Besets the dream-way and the soul's escape.

The tale concerns a young man – Dymer – who escapes from a city – the Perfect City – which is a cross between Plato's Republic and an English public school, and becomes entangled with a hag-like older woman. She seems gay at first but she is quickly transformed, after a short lovemaking, into a Spenserian crone. From the ecstatic moment when

> He opened wide
> His arms – the breathy body of a girl
> Slid into them

he is penitent. He thinks that if he is only slavish enough in his service of the old hag, the beautiful girl to whom he once made love will come back to him:

> I would be content
> To drudge in earth, easing my heart's disgrace
> . . . If at the year's end I saw her face somewhere.

But he never finds her again, and is imprisoned in his strange mixture of tormented lust and repentance. The fruit of this mysterious union, into which Dymer has drifted, is a monster. In the latter part of the story, the monster and Dymer are involved in an Oedipal struggle, and the father is killed. By then the 'monster' has gone through many transformations, unable to decide who he is or which of his many disguises represents the true 'him'; but he can only find liberty by killing the father who sired him. 'Of course,' Lewis insisted, 'I'm not Dymer.'

Of course not. What troubles the admirer of Lewis the critic – the man who had such an eye for excellence in the poets of past ages – is that he could be capable of stanza after stanza in which the verse is deadened by flat language, repeated clumsy enjambements and sheer technical incompetence. Much of it just fails to scan correctly – very odd for someone who was lecturing and giving tutorials on English poetry. In February 1926, Lewis plucked up courage and showed the poem to his colleague in the English Faculty, Nevill Coghill. He begged Coghill to keep the matter to himself. 'I don't want it known here [i.e. at Magdalen] that I am writing "pomes" [sic].'[9]

Coghill felt that he had discovered a 'considerable poem' by 'a powerful new poet' (though 'in the Masefield tradition'), and he wrote back to Lewis in adulatory terms. Lewis felt 'as if you had given me a bottle of champagne . . . Your remarks on the Masefieldian lines go to the root of the matter – I should say the *bad* Masefieldian lines for in some points one would not in the least be ashamed to have learned from him . . .' Lewis was especially grateful that Coghill was so appreciative of Dymer's 'spiritual experiences'; and in particular that he approved of the theme of 'redemption by parricide' which Lewis feared 'would seem simply preposterous and shocking'. Coghill did more than heap praises on *Dymer*. He found a publisher for it. When

Guy Pocock of Dent read the poem, he felt 'there can be no possible question of its greatness . . . I have not read any new poetry to touch it since the publication of *The Everlasting Mercy* [by John Masefield].'[10] When the book did appear, in beautiful, almost square duodecimo format, it was adorned with a naked figure, the hero, embossed on the end board. He stretches up beyond the sun. He is there again in the frontispiece, like a figure in the Tarot cards, breaking his chains and dancing towards the spheres. Behind him, a winged, helmeted figure leans on a cruciform, phallic-looking sword.

It takes a little while for an author to realize that his book has been a complete failure. He waits and waits. Lewis anxiously opened *The Times Literary Supplement* every Friday for a year, hoping for a good notice for the poem. A favourable review did appear, but not until a year later. By then, the poem had sunk from public consciousness. It did not sell, and it made almost no impact whatsoever.

It is striking that Lewis did not want it known in College that he wrote 'pomes', but only natural that he should have looked outside Magdalen for soulmates within his own Faculty. It is the least satisfactory feature of collegiate universities that for all social and administrative purposes – meals and meetings and life in Common Room – the academics mix not with those who share their intellectual preoccupations but with people of completely different disciplines. In an ideal world this would mean that a lot of clever people, all anxious to communicate enthusiasm for their subject, would talk helpfully about it to their colleagues. In a rosy paragraph of *Surprised by Joy*, Lewis paid tribute to

> Five great Magdalen men who enlarged my very idea of what a learned life should be – P. V. M. Benecke, C. C. J. Webb, J. A. Smith, F. E. Brightman and C. T. Onions . . . In my earliest years at Magdalen I inhabited a world where hardly anything I wanted to know needed to be found out by my own unaided efforts. One or other of these could always give you a clue. ('You'll find something about it in Alanus.' 'Macrobius would be the man to try . . .' etc.)[11]

This is certainly how dons talk in the novels of Dorothy L. Sayers. Whether they did so at Magdalen in the years 1925–1929 there are few alive old enough to remember. The key phrase in Lewis's paragraph here is 'my earliest years'. He writes from the perspective of later years when the dons of Magdalen were anything but congenial society to him. Even in those early years, when honest old men were tossing out such useful snippets of information as 'Macrobius would be the man', the college did not provide soulmates of the kind Lewis always craved.

Coghill, who had been a friend since they read English together as undergraduates in 1923, was now the English tutor at Exeter College. He probably remained Lewis's best friend in the English Faculty during the early years at Magdalen. The Faculty in those days was comparatively small, and still dominated by old men who were primarily literary historians. Criticism of the kind which became popular with the pupils of I. A. Richards at Cambridge later in the century was absolutely unknown at Oxford. Reading English was really a literary way of reading History. The sort of scholarship which predominated was textual scholarship, as exemplified by Percy Simpson's monumental edition of Ben Jonson.

But there was a new broom coming into the English Faculty at this period and, although younger than Simpson, Wilson, Garrod and the rest, he appeared to be more radically reactionary. This was the Rawlinson and Bosworth Professor of Anglo-Saxon, who had been appointed to his chair at the age of thirty-two, in the same year that Lewis got his fellowship at Magdalen. His name was J. R. R. Tolkien. It was another medievalist, under Tolkien's influence, who gave utterance to the view that 'Literature stops in 1100; after that there's only books,' but they were sentiments which in a crude way echoed Tolkien's own position. A graduate of Exeter College, Oxford, Tolkien had read Classical Mods and then done a version of the English course which was rigidly philological, and did not concern itself with post-medieval literature. Much more important than this was Tolkien's vast imaginative life, one day to make him famous as author of *The Lord of the Rings*, but at this date completely hidden from all but his family and close friends. True, Tolkien's favourite books were the old books – in English, the Anglo-Saxon poets; in Icelandic, those of the Elder Edda; in Celtic, the old Welsh Triads and the Irish legends. But although he had a phenomenal gift as a philologist, and was by far the most distinguished scholar in his field of Old and Middle English, his interest in it all was very far from being 'purely academic'. It was as though an extraordinary story – a great mythology, with half-forgotten legends, languages and lore – had been unfolding in his head from the time he began to think; and his appreciation of the Old Literature was at the deepest level imaginative and creative.

An example of this can be seen in his youthful discovery of the biblical poems of the Anglo-Saxon poet Cynewulf. In the poem *Crist*, Tolkien came upon the lines:

> Eala Earendel engla berhtast
> ofer middangeard monnum sended.
>
> (Hail Earendel, brightest of the angels,
> sent to men upon Middle Earth.)

The dry-as-dust scholar, the Percy Simpson sort of scholar, would merely note here that Earendel meant 'shining ray'. Tolkien himself thought that this bright ray was the Old English word for Venus, here applied to John the Baptist, herald of the Christ. But it was not the mere surface meaning of the words which arrested him. 'I felt a curious thrill, as if something had stirred within me, half awakening from sleep. There was something very remote and strange and beautiful behind those words, if I could grasp it, far beyond ancient English.'[12]

Tolkien brought a response on this level of emotional intensity to those texts which, for the majority of the English Faculty, were the 'boring part of the course'. Indeed, when Tolkien arrived, he found that the Old English being dished up to the likes of Betjeman was in a grossly truncated form, and the poetry was mainly seen as a quarry for 'gobbets' – that is, short passages of a very few lines, used for the purposes of testing the candidates' knowledge of sound-changes. Tolkien's suggestion was that the Faculty should reform its syllabus, giving space for a proper study of the Old English poets. Since this would necessarily involve cutting out some other part of the course, he suggested stopping the syllabus at 1830, and removing the study of Victorian literature.

Lewis was strongly opposed to this move. But on his first proper encounter with Tolkien – at a meeting with English Faculty colleagues at Merton College in May 1926 – he could not help being charmed by this 'smooth, pale, fluent little chap'. At that date, as Lewis himself tells us, he had two very marked prejudices. 'At my first coming into the world I had been (implicitly) warned never to trust a Papist, and at my first coming into the English Faculty (explicitly) never to trust a philologist. Tolkien was both.'[13]

One of the first things Tolkien did after his return to Oxford in 1925 was to set up an Icelandic reading group such as he had enjoyed during his last job, as Professor of English at Leeds. The idea was that the few men in the University who could read the original language of the Edda and the Sagas should group together with those who wished to learn, and read their way through the principal texts. They called the group the Kolbitar (coal-biters), an Icelandic kenning which means those who sit around a fire. The group was quite large. It included Nevill Coghill from the beginning, and also John Bryson and George Gordon, who had supported Lewis as a candidate for the fellowship at Magdalen and became President of the college in 1928. C. T. Onions, the philologist, another fellow of Magdalen, was a founder member of the Kolbitar, and not long after it was founded two other fellows of Magdalen were asked to join: Jack Lewis and Bruce McFarlane, the historian.

It was very much Kirkpatrick's method of learning a language. Never having read a word of Norse (Old Icelandic) before, Lewis plunged in and attempted a few lines of Laxdaela Saga. For someone with a good reading knowledge of German and Anglo-Saxon, the cognate tongue of Norse offered few difficulties. Lewis, who had known the sagas in translation since Gastons days, was very happy with this further enrichment of the pleasures of reading. But he was soon to find that Tolkien had more to offer him than the chance to learn Old Norse.

Lewis himself represents the summer of 1929 as the turning point of his whole life. The fluency with which he himself wrote about this period was born out of a particular requirement. A publisher had asked him to explain, some quarter of a century after the event, how he passed from scepticism to religious belief. Minds more subtle than

Lewis's would probably have shrunk from the attempt. And those who have made similar attempts at spiritual self-chronicling have hedged their story about with provisos. 'It was not logic that carried me on,' wrote J. H. (later Cardinal) Newman in his *Apologia*. 'As well might one say that the quicksilver in the barometer changes the weather. It is the concrete being that reasons; pass a number of years and I find my mind in a new place: how? the whole man moves; paper logic is but the record of it.'[14]

There can be no doubt that the 'whole man' Lewis moved from a position of atheism in his undergraduate years to an acceptance in the early 1930s of 'mere Christianity'. In his autobiography, he tries to see how this happened to 'the whole man' – to the man who had been haunted since youth by a sense of 'Joy', to the man whose love of Autumn, of Northernness, even of his own mother, was always, as he came to feel, a longing for one without whom our hearts will find no rest. But for a handful of obvious reasons, Lewis does not draw a picture of 'the whole man' in *Surprised by Joy*. It is partly that a natural reticence made him draw a veil over the two greatest facts of his emotional history: his relationships with his father and Mrs Moore. Probably, by the time he came to write *Surprised by Joy*, his way of looking at himself had become so idiosyncratic that he was not *able* to see the significance of these two relationships in his religious, as well as in his whole emotional, development. His old friend Barfield ruefully suggested that 'at a certain stage in his life he deliberately ceased to take any interest in himself except as a kind of spiritual animus taking stock of his moral faults . . . Self knowledge for him had come to mean recognition of his own weaknesses and short-comings and nothing more.'[15] This, no doubt, was what enabled Lewis, in telling the story of his life, to separate the departments of his life, telling us only the 'spiritual' story and leaving that part of himself which Newman would have called 'the concrete man' hidden in shadows. So of his falling in love with Mrs Moore we are merely informed that 'even if I were free to tell the story, I doubt if it has much to do with the subject of this book,' and of his father's death in the late summer of 1929 that this 'does not really come into the story I am telling'.

If either of these sentences were true, the story would not have been worth telling, since the conversion would have been a purely fanciful affair which bore no relevance to Lewis at the deepest levels of his being. His reluctance to tell the full story is all of a piece with his extreme slowness, after his religious conversion, to accept Christianity, a religion which tries the heart, which searches us out and knows us. His embarrassment about self-disclosure gives the impression, belied by his other books, that he knew nothing of the mystery that grace works by means of human weakness, not by side-stepping it.

Since Lewis buried the secrets, first from himself and then from others, there is not much hope that those coming after will be able to follow the story of his conversion. He gives us a few outlines of 'paper logic' followed by a paragraph or two describing some of the religious experiences themselves.

The logical crisis went back to the time when he first started to read philosophy as an undergraduate and related to his reading of the English Idealist philosophers, as well as to his return (for the purposes of passing his exams, and later as a tutor) to the English empiricists of the eighteenth century. He had slowly, and unwillingly, come to feel the necessity of believing in an Absolute. He was driven into something 'like Berkleyanism'; and he took to feeling that there was no harm in positing the existence of some form of Absolute Spirit, so long as this was firmly distinguished from the God 'of popular religion'.

Something which focused his intellectual uncertainties at this time was reading Alexander's *Space, Time and Deity*, which introduces 'enjoyment' and 'contemplation' as technical terms. 'We do not "think a thought" in the same sense in which we "think Herodotus is unreliable". When we think a thought, "thought" is a cognate accusative (like "blow" in "strike a blow"). We enjoy the thought that Herodotus is unreliable and in so doing, contemplate the unreliability of Herodotus. I accepted this distinction at once and have ever since regarded it as an indispensable tool of thought.'[16]

It was a linchpin of Lewis's theism that thought itself was a metaphysical act; his exploration of this theme in his book *Miracles* and the subsequent heated debate between himself and a fellow-Christian philosopher, Elizabeth Anscombe, provided one of the great academic sideshows in the Oxford of the late 1940s. But of course, had Alexander's argument and Lewis's interpretation of it been irrefutable, had

it been the kind of thing which compelled religious certainty, then all
the philosophers in Oxford would have fallen to their knees when
they had finished reading it. They did not do so. The fact that Lewis
did is not a sign that he was illogical, merely that he was caught up
in a spiritual drama which involved more than 'paper logic'. There
were, primarily, the tugs of sympathy. His closest friend from childhood, Arthur Greeves, was religious. His closest undergraduate friend,
Owen Barfield, was also a believer. When he visited Lewis at Magdalen
(Barfield was now working as a solicitor in London), the two friends
often reverted to their 'Great War' and there was no doubt, any
longer, who was going to be the victor. Someone who occasionally
joined in these discussions was a pupil of Lewis's, Alan Griffiths, who
had also become a friend. He, like Lewis, had not yet reached a
position of religious faith, but he was dissatisfied with purely materialistic explanations for life's mysteries, and he found the conversation
of Barfield intoxicating. Once, when the three of them were sitting
in Lewis's rooms, Lewis happened to refer to philosophy as 'a subject'.
'It wasn't *a subject* to Plato,' said Barfield, 'it was a way.' 'The quiet but
fervent agreement of Griffiths and the quick glance of understanding
between those two revealed to me my own frivolity. Enough had been
thought, and said and felt and imagined. It was about time that
something should be done.'[17] Among the circle of people he found
most sympathetic, Lewis was in fact beginning to feel an odd man
out. Coghill and Tolkien were both Christians. Chesterton, always a
favourite author, was a Christian; it was at this period that Lewis read
The Everlasting Man, and it made a profound impression on him.

But there was something, or, as Lewis came to feel, someone, else.
No doubt there were many contributory external or psychological
factors in what was happening to the way he perceived his own
personality. It could be said that some sort of crisis was going to force
itself up in the life of a strongly emotional young man who was so
strictly engaged in compartmentalizing his life: a father who was never
meant to know about Janie Moore; Minto herself cut off from college;
almost all his friends kept in darkness about his emotional history,
and most of them at this period unaware of his religious interests;
pupils who were discussing with him the things he cared about most
– books – but in a fashion which prevented his strength of feeling
breaking through. Griffiths for instance, only came across Lewis's

children's stories after he had died, and he 'recognized in them a power of imaginative invention and insight of which I had no conception before. It must be remembered that Lewis always affected (I think it was deliberate) to be a plain, honest man with no nonsense about him, usually wearing, when out on a walk, an old tweed hat and coat and accompanied with a pipe and a dog.'

Beneath this exterior something was going to have to 'give' if Lewis was to survive. Shortly before he admitted what was happening to him, he re-read the *Hippolytus* of Euripides. He did so for no particular reason; it was just an impulse. The theme of the play (as Lewis somehow expects all readers of his memoirs to remember) is the rejection and suppression of erotic love. Phaedra, the all-powerful matriarch, conceives a wild passion for her stepson Hippolytus, who rejects her love with speeches hostile not just to her but to the whole erotic faculty. In her grief, she kills herself. When the father of Hippolytus, Theseus, returns from his travels, he is unable to believe that no sexual congress has taken place between his wife and his son. He banishes Hippolytus and prays for his death, which is granted when Poseidon sends a sea monster to upturn the young man's chariot. Too late, Theseus learns that his son loved and was loyal to him after all. This is a play in which the priggish young hide their emotions while their elders give themselves up to extremes of passion. It is also a play in which mortals are seen as figures of infinite pathos in a universe controlled by the whims of a cruel fate and a capricious deity.

Reading the play almost shattered Lewis. His decision, since the madness of Doc Askins, to live without the emotions, was one that he realized was impossible. 'There was a transitional moment of delicious uneasiness and then – instantaneously – the long inhibition was over, the dry desert lay behind, I was off once more into the land of longing, my heart at once broken and exalted as it had never been since the old days at Bookham.'[18]

He began to feel himself approached by God, and in the summer of 1929 went through a mystical experience. As befitted a man who had sung the pleasures of the ordinary, it occurred on a bus going up Headington Hill, on his way back to Mrs Moore's house. There were no words in the experience, but he became aware of the fact that he was keeping something at bay; or another way of looking at it would be that he was wearing some rigid outer clothing, like corsets or a suit of armour. In his moment of illumination on the bus, Lewis felt that he could either remain encased in this shell, or he could take it off. After this strange sensation he felt as if he were a snowman 'at last beginning to melt'.

Some time in that summer of 1929, in his college rooms at Magdalen, he 'gave in, and admitted that God was God, and knelt and prayed; perhaps, that night, the most dejected and reluctant convert in all England'.[19]

The 'conversion' was a recognition that God was God. It was not a conversion to Christianity. He writes about it in unforgettably dramatic terms and with the sublime egoism (to use the word purely, with no pejorative sense) of a man alone with God. He really was, at that moment, one for whom there were 'two and two only supreme and luminously self-evident beings, myself and my Creator', as Newman described his own experience. Since Lewis was to go on to become a faithful and devoted Christian, he writes rather as if the 'conversion' were a *fait accompli*, after which nothing could be the same. But men have had such experiences and done nothing further about them, either because they have decided that there was less to the experience than they at first supposed, or because they could not endure the ethical and spiritual demands which were implied in the unspoken, ineffable moment of divine knowledge.

That summer, however, events were to place a seal on what happened to Lewis in his Magdalen rooms. It is probably fanciful to cast Mrs Moore as Phaedra, or the P'daytabird as Theseus, but now Lewis was crossing the sea to see his father for the last time. A great emotional business was reaching its climax.

Lewis continued, throughout life, to be obsessed not only by his father, but also by the possibility that his life could be interpreted in a purely Freudian way. 'In those days, the new psychology was just beginning to make itself felt in the circles I most frequented in Oxford,' he told readers of the 1950 reprint of *Dymer*. Much earlier, at the time of 'the Doc's insanity' in 1923, Lewis had written to Greeves, 'Arthur, whatever you do never allow yourself to get a neurosis.' This piece of advice might suggest that his grasp of the 'new psychology' was still at the rudimentary stage, since he speaks of a neurosis as if it were something avoidable. The letter is interesting, though, for the light it casts on his rooted dread of mental imbalance, and on his horrified feeling that the unsatisfactory relations which had existed between himself and his father since early adolescence might somehow mar him for the rest of his life:

> You and I are both qualified for it [neurosis] because we were both afraid of our fathers as children. The Doctor who came to see the poor Doc (a psychoanalyst and neurological specialist) said that every neurotic case went back to the childish fear of the father. But it can be avoided. Keep clear of introspection, of brooding, of spiritualism, of everything eccentric. Keep to work and sanity and open air – to the cheerful and the matter of fact side of things.[20]

This was advice which he had been unable to follow himself. With the reading of *Hippolytus* and the cracking of the outer shell of his cheerful, hard-working, no-nonsense self, introspection was running riot and 'spiritualism' – by which he clearly meant dabbling in affairs of the spirit rather than solely a preoccupation with the dead – had, by the summer of 1929, taken a firm grip on him. No wonder, then, that when he came to write up the experience in *Surprised by Joy* he should have been so insistent that his father's last illness and death 'does not really come into the story I am telling'. He was frightened that hostile readers of his theological work would be able to say that his religion could be 'explained' in terms of the Oedipus complex (or perhaps the Hippolytus complex); and that he was only able to find peace for his heart by coming to terms with a Heavenly Father of his own projection when he had seen the last of his earthly father in Belfast. So much did he dread that his own was a case of 'redemption by parricide' that he emphasized the unwillingness with which he accepted the divine call with language which is exaggerated and almost coarse. He was a 'prodigal who is brought kicking, struggling, resentful and darting his eyes in every direction for a chance of escape'.

He crossed the Irish channel on 12 August and reached Little Lea on the morning of the thirteenth. His father had been 'under the weather' since July, and Lewis was half-aware that he might be coming home for the last time. Once he set eyes on Albert, he knew that the old man was very sick indeed. His father rejoiced to see him, and noted that Jacks was 'looking remarkably well and in great form'.

Jack fell quickly into the routine of looking out for the absurdities in his father's speech to put into a P'dayta-Pie for Warnie; but he had no heart for it. He began to write about one such P'dayta-ism, and then crossed it out. The truth was, as he wrote to Warnie, that 'P. is rather seriously ill.' It was cancer of the bowel, though the doctors were slow or unwilling to diagnose it at first. Not long after Jack came home, Albert began to run high fevers. His heart was not strong either, and by the end of the month he was confined to his bed.

Jack stayed up to nurse him. Delighted to have his boy at home, Albert was in particularly cheerful form, in spite of his pain. When the doctors broke it to him that he would need an operation, his son noted that 'he is taking it like a hero.' All of a sudden, Jack saw that his father *was* a sort of hero – a maddening, eccentric hero but a man whose decency, courage and good humour were as unshakable as his sincere piety. The two men were enjoying a condition of harmony which had been unknown in all the previous years.

The house was full of memories; but even to call them memories was to imply that Jack had put them behind him; and he had not. 'Every room is soaked with the bogeys of childhood ... The awful rows, the awful returnings to school.' He sat in the dining-room, able to enjoy a few biscuits and fruit rather than the 'gargantuan midday meal which was hitherto compulsory'.

Every day he saw Arthur Greeves, who was still living next door, having studied art at the Slade School in London and returned to Belfast with no prospects. Arthur, who had followed so much of Jack's inner journey, was the perfect companion during those strange days. Much of the time, however, Jack was alone. When his father was tucked up for the night, the son would wander out into the garden and enjoy the cool air as a contrast to the fug of the sick-room. 'My father and I are physical counterparts: and during these days more than ever I notice his resemblance to me ...' he mused.[21]

At the beginning of September, the doctors recommended an operation, and Albert was moved into a nursing home. The operation revealed the extent of the cancer, but nevertheless Jack was told that his father might live for 'a few more years'. Since he had teaching to prepare at Oxford for the following term, he said an unwilling farewell to his father and took the boat home. Four days later, on 25 September, Albert Lewis died. In the *Lewis Papers*, Warren remarked, 'With his passing we lose him who may perhaps be described as the hero of our saga . . . His age was 66 years and 33 days.'

MYTHOPOEIA

1929–1931

'I treated my own father abominably and no sin in my whole life now seems to be so serious,' Lewis blurted out to a correspondent twenty-five years after A. J. Lewis's demise.[1] His remorse was perpetual and far-reaching, and it coloured the whole of his memory. Sadness for the way he had felt about the old man blended with a sense that his childhood was irrecoverably lost, and the knowledge that the very past

> when it was in flight
> Lived, like the present, in continual death.

Moreover the death of Albert only served to emphasize the emotional burden which he was now carrying: the increasing loneliness of the ageing Janie Moore, and the total isolation of his brother. Stationed as a soldier in Shanghai, and unable to get home until the following April, Warnie was in an agony of sorrow for the old days. 'The P'daytabird is dead,' his diary solemnly records.

> All day I have been seeing pictures of him at his best; jumbled up in no chronological sequence – Saturday evening tram rides and visits to the Hippodrome with late supper afterwards in Malvern days, earlier days of 'where do you want to go to' in the study . . . the 'Well, boys this is grand' at the beginning of the holiday . . . his little drop of whiskey: his fund of wheezes.[2]

How far Warnie emulated at this stage of life his father's fondness for a little drop of whiskey, and at what point he began his calamitous descent into alcoholism is not easy to determine. He was not actually dismissed from the service, though it was because of alcohol that he was asked to volunteer his own early resignation. One thing was certain. The death of his father made him homeless. 'Worst of all, being pulled up by the roots – worse for me than for J[ack] for Leeborough has always been my base whereas his real home has been Hillsboro [Mrs Moore's rented house in Headington, Oxford] for some years now. The thought that there will never be any going home is hard to bear.'

That the other person in Jack's life, Mrs Moore, was also profoundly lonely is made clear by a generous, and at the same time comically self-revealing, letter which she wrote to Warnie on 29 October. She urged Warnie to treat Hillsboro as a home, and confessed:

> I should have been very glad of your society this last year, Maureen has been at the Royal College of Music, and I have been much alone, only for the animal's company I don't know what I should have done and poor Mr. Papworth [a dog] has been so ill we had to telephone a vet up at 2 a.m. one morning it was a funny night, Jack and I in our dressing gowns in the kitchen trying to comfort Mr. Papworth. Jack and the vet (who turned out to be an Irishman too) drinking whiskey which they thought was brandy because I'd put it into a brandy bottle . . .

All this was kindly meant, and the suggestion that Warnie was welcome with Jack and Minto was some comfort. But the exiled soldier wanted more than a place to stay: he wanted, to a Peter Pan-ish degree, everything as it had been in his childhood home. In one of his lengthy letters to Jack from Shanghai, he suggested that they 'yield to sentiment and construct the Little End Room in your sitting room at Magdalen'.[3] In another letter he suggested constructing the 'Little End Room' in a spare bedroom at Headington, 'a place where we can always meet on the common ground of the past and ipso facto a museum of the Leeborough which we want to preserve'.[4] Further- more, this 36-year-old officer was in desperation about the fate of their boyhood toys, locked up in a trunk in the attic at Leeborough. He found it 'intolerable' to think of the toys falling into the hands of other children – 'The idea of a crowd of embryo "right wee fellas" getting hold of them and Bolshevising and applying to their own base purposes that well-ordered world in which we spent so many happy hours'.[5]

Jack felt the need to treat these outbursts by Warnie with firmness as well as with gentleness, not least because his brother was giving voice to feelings which he shared quite passionately himself. He rejected the idea of a Little End Room museum, not least because 'a museum is preciously like a mausoleum'. He said it would be a mistake, 'a mistake in sentiment; for it could only mean that we were embalming the corpse of something that isn't really dead and needn't die at all – an aesthetic mistake – because we don't really want to have the taste of our schooldays established as a boundary for our whole lives'.[6] To anyone who knew Lewis in the second half of his life, and remarked his preference for boys' books such as R. M. Ballantyne or Captain Marryat over the so-called 'moderns', there can be no doubt that he was here addressing a warning not just to his brother but to himself.

Within a very few weeks of his father's death, Lewis found himself obliged once more to take up the routines of an Oxford term: weekly tutorials, college meetings and lectures. Any thought of what was to happen to his family home in Belfast had to be shelved until a joint decision could be reached with his brother when he next came home on leave.

The most marked feature of Lewis's own emotional and intellectual life as the autumn days grew shorter and the year 1929 drew to its close was the development of his friendship with J. R. R. Tolkien. It is only now, decades after they were first written down, that the reading public can begin to have any sense of the extent and range of Tolkien's mythological writings. From his early years, he had been engaged in the creation of a whole world, comparable in scale with the world of Greek mythology, with a pantheon of gods, a hierarchy of elvish immortals, and a vast cycle of stories, some of them 'forgotten', or not yet formulated, in his imagination; some surviving in fragmentary form; some planned as long prose narratives; some conceived as great poems, longer than *Beowulf*. The sheer volume of all this, much of it composed before his fortieth birthday, bears testimony to a rare artistic self-confidence. One receives the strong impression that Tolkien would have continued to write his gnomish grammars, his elvish etymologies, his histories of mythological lost ages, his compilations of names, battles and magic tales, whether anyone wanted to read them or not. And indeed, the very extent to which they would be readable was called in question by their range and bulk. For how could a reader who knew nothing of the original matter – the origin of the Silmarils, the rise and fall of Numenor, the triumphs and ultimate ruin of Gondolin, etc. – find a way *in*? There exists no easy guide to the Tolkien mythology, and the existing materials, when published, have required the extensive annotation of Tolkien's son.

Nevertheless, no writer, however self-sufficient, writes without a thought of an audience, and Tolkien was happy to discover anyone who could appreciate what he was up to. It was evident, from conversations with him at the Kolbitar, that Lewis was such a man, and in the autumn of 1929 Tolkien made bold to show him an unfinished version of his *Lay of Leithian*, the story of how the mortal Beren, returning from the wars, through the forests of Neldoreth, encounters the elfish maiden Luthien and falls in love with her. Thingol, Luthien's father, is so enraged that a mortal should dare to woo his daughter that he says he will only give her hand to Beren if he will wrest one of the Silmarils, or enchanted jewels, from the iron crown of the dark lord Margoth. This impossible quest, which indirectly leads to the undoing of Thingol's own elvish kingdom, is only possible because Luthien accompanies Beren on his journey. He manages to penetrate the fastness of the dark lord disguised in a wolfskin, while she is hidden in the garment of a bat; but it is her own enchantments, her beauty and her songs, which ultimately defeat the evil one.

Tolkien never finished the *Lay of Leithian*, though he worked at it on and off for seven years, composing at least two versions of the poem in more than four thousand lines of octosyllabic couplets. Though at times the verse is technically imperfect, it is full of passages of quite stunning beauty; and the overall conception must make it, though unfinished, one of the most remarkable poems written in English in the twentieth century.

It is worth describing it at such length so that readers who have *not* read Tolkien's 'minor' works might develop some idea of Lewis's importance as Tolkien's 'onlie begetter' or 'miglior fabbro', for there can be very little doubt that it was Lewis's friendship and encouragement which led Tolkien to write the works which made his name with the public; just as it was Tolkien's friendship which released in Lewis wells of creativity which had remained (though he was so naturally fluent) mysteriously dry.

It was therefore an important moment when Tolkien gave Lewis the *Lay of Leithian* to read in manuscript.[7] It has been said that Lewis's expressed distaste for the poetry of his contemporaries, such as MacNeice and Eliot, was based on jealousy. Tolkien, when he read this suggestion after Lewis's death – and after his own relationship with Lewis had become less than happy – rejected it as entirely unworthy. He knew that Lewis was a greater man than that. From personal experience, he knew that Lewis could be a generous, though by no means an uncritical, reader of contemporary poetry. Lewis wrote to Tolkien:

> I sat up late last night and read the *Geste* as far as to where Beren and his gnomish allies defeat the patrol of orcs above the sources of the Narog and disguise themselves in the *reaf* [Old English: 'garments, weapons taken from the slain']. I can quite honestly say that it is ages since I have had an evening of such delight; and the personal interest of reading a friend's work had very little to do with it. I should have enjoyed it just as well if I'd picked it up in a bookshop, by an unknown author. The two things that come out clearly are the sense of reality in the background and the mythical value.[8]

Lewis had seen, almost more clearly, one suspects, than the author himself saw, what was the essence of Tolkien. In order to draw this out of him, he wrote a vastly elaborate commentary on the *Lay*, softening the blow of his harsher criticisms by inventing the personae of a whole group of scholarly editors who are debating the text in the way that scholars have disputed over Homer or *Beowulf*. It would seem that Tolkien took a great deal of notice of Lewis's invented editors, for he rewrote his *Lay* and incorporated a high proportion of their emendations. The device was a clever one on Lewis's part, for since he was seven years younger than Tolkien and a relatively junior member of a faculty in which 'Tollers' was a professor, there was the need to tread carefully. It was not simply a question of age and hierarchy. Tolkien was by temperament a very different man from Lewis. He could be touchy and irritable; Lewis could be brash and tactless. There was a touch of elfish melancholy, as well as of delicacy, in Tolkien which would never respond to the broader outlines of Lewis's essentially sunny disposition. Lewis would not have guessed that Tolkien's *Lay* would remain unfinished. It must have seemed clear to him at once that Tolkien was a man of literary genius, and this fact only brought home to him his own sense of failure as a writer. 'From the age of sixteen onwards, I had one single ambition, from which I never wavered, in the prosecution of which I spent every ounce I could, on which I really and deliberately staked my whole contentment; and I recognise myself as having unmistakeably failed in it.'[9] He knew that as yet the appropriate *style* eluded him. He knew neither what to write nor how to write it. In Tolkien, by huge contrast, he met a man whose style had been with him from the beginning.

Lewis responded so warmly to Tolkien's imagined world because, as he wrote to Arthur Greeves, 'he is, in one part of him, what we were.'[10] That is to say, Tolkien's stories could be said to be an embodiment of that Northernness with which Lewis and Greeves had been in love since early adolescence. Lewis was subtle enough to see that this was at best a half-truth, and perhaps he was beginning to sense that what Tolkien's friendship had to offer him was something rather more important than a regress to the nursery. For Tolkien, whose literary pilgrimage was to be so lonely, and whose return to Oxford had not been marked by great domestic happiness, there was something very cheering in the company of this clever, widely read, humorous and spontaneously affectionate Irishman. When he reflected with sadness on the unhappiness of his marriage towards the end of 1929, he noted, 'Friendship with Lewis compensates for much.'[11]

The death of Albert Lewis inevitably involved his two sons in practical decisions. What was to be the future of their house in Belfast? Where would Warnie live? How much money would be available to them when the probate of the estate had been completed?

The decision to sell Little Lea more or less made itself. Jack could not possibly run the house from Oxford, and Warnie was still a serving officer in the Army. When he came home on leave in April 1930, they both returned to their childhood home and made all the necessary arrangements for its sale. It was 'perfectly beastly', as Warnie said in his diary, to see 'P's grave with its fresh turned earth and a handful of withered daffodils at its head alongside Mamy's'.[12] It was also a shock to discover that their father's investments only yielded an income of some £190 per annum net, considerably less than Warnie (desperate to leave the Army and live on his pension) had been hoping. The house, thought to be worth about £3,000 by the lawyers, in fact went for less.

Not the least of their tasks was the disposal of the toys. They decided in the end to bury the trunk of 'characters' from Animal-land unopened. A huge hole was dug in the vegetable patch for the purpose. After several days of dividing their possessions into things they wished to keep and things which could be given away or sold, they were ready to leave the house for the last time. It was a tremendous wrench, one from which Warnie never truly recovered. One of his last acts was to heave the contents of the wine cellar (some bottles of whiskey) into the back of a relative's car. Clearly the whereabouts of those bottles, and the number of them, had been one of the P'dayta-bird's little secrets, for Warnie writes, 'Nothing brought home to me the finality of the old life as did the carrying out of those bottles and putting them into [the] car – to see the mysteries of that jealously guarded secret room emerge as plain matter of fact bottles, and the cellar stand revealed as an ordinary empty cupboard was an unpleasant feeling.'[13]

Jack wrote a poem to Warnie, urging him not to look back out of the car window as it hurtled away, leaving their childhood behind them.

> Yet look not out. Think rather, 'When from France
> And those old German wars we came back here
> Already it was the mind's swift haunting glance
> Towards the further past, that made time dear.'
>
> Then to that further past, still up the stream
> Ascend and think of some divine first day
> In holidays from school. Even there the gleam
> Of earlier memory like enchantment lay.

Already, the germ is present which was to flower most fully in *The Last Battle*: the idea of school holidays being a mere Platonic shadow of our permanent refreshment in Paradise, of our earthly homes being but a reflection of heaven.

But in the immediate future, it was the search for an earthly home which preoccupied them. Jack had very decided misgivings about Minto's impulsive suggestion that Warnie should live with them. To Warnie, he had written a letter full of the gravest admonitions, designed to make him think carefully about what he was committing himself to.

Can you stand as a permanency our cuisine – Maureen's practising – Maureen's sulks – Minto's burnettodesmondism – Minto's mare's nests – the perpetual interruptions of family life – the partial loss of liberty? This sounds as if I were either sick of it myself or else trying to make you sick of it; but neither is the case. I have definitely chosen and I don't regret the choice. What I hope – very much hope – is that you, after consideration, may make the same choice.[14]

But the thought of sharing his Minto-life with Warnie was not without its complications for Jack himself. In a letter to Arthur Greeves, he said that Warnie and Mrs Moore liked each other, 'and, I hope, as W. gets broken into domestic life, they may come to do so still more: but in the interval there is a ticklish time ahead and in any case it is a big sacrifice of our . . .' At this point the manuscript breaks off. Greeves, in pencil, has written 'very private' and 'to be burnt' at the top of the letter and the following pages of it are missing. The letter concludes, 'You are my only real Father Confessor.'

Warnie, no sophisticate in emotional matters, found Jack's relationship with Janie Moore incomprehensible. Jack 'commonly referred to Mrs Moore as "my mother"'. On the only occasion when Warnie tried to probe Jack on the origin or true nature of his relationship with Minto he was shut up with great vehemence.[15]

There is enough recorded in Warnie's diaries over the next twenty years of friction and domestic misery to make us see why Jack had misgivings about the advisability of their all attempting to live together. The factor which clinched their decision was the discovery of a house which they could only afford to buy if all three pooled their resources.

After long years of living in unsatisfactory rented accommodation, it now looked as if Jack and Minto could afford a place of their own. They first set eyes on the house which was to be 'home' for the rest of Jack's life on 7 July 1930. Minto was 'more excited' than Warnie had ever seen her when he returned from Aldershot for week-end leave, happy to leave behind him his fellow-officers, whom he nicknamed the Aldershits. When Jack took him to see the house, Warnie was just as enthusiastic. 'I instantly caught the infection.'[16] The house itself was unimpressive, little more than a low-lying cottage of modern design which would not easily accommodate four grown-up people. In order to make it suitable, Minto believed that it would be necessary to build on at least two extra rooms. What made it so enchanting was the setting. The gardens and grounds covered eight acres, nestling at the northern foot of Shotover Hill. The house took its name – The Kilns – from the two old brick kilns which stood by its side. Further in, towards the base of the hill, was a wood, within which were one large pool and several smaller ones, formed by the hollowing-out of the old stone quarries in a previous century. It was said that the poet Shelley had been here to sail paper boats. 'Many a £10,000 house is worse situated and has a much poorer garden,' Warnie observed. The asking price was £3,500.

This was a considerable sum of money. The sort of modest suburban house which Mrs Moore was renting at the time could be purchased in those days for £850 or £1,000. The Lewises' substantial house in Belfast was finally sold for £2,300, seven months after their purchase of The Kilns. Minto airily spoke of being worth £1,000 and able to raise a further £2,000 as a mortgage, but this was not the case. Upon investigation, it was discovered that her Askins inheritance, held in trust, enabled her to have a mortgage of just £1,500.

Dons, in those days, did not reckon on buying houses, still less on having mortgages. The huge majority of them lived in rented houses in North Oxford. The Kilns venture was highly unusual, and the Lewis brothers knew that they could only afford it by taking the great risk of throwing in their lot together; in the event the purchase price was lowered to £3,300. Warnie paid the cash deposit of £300, and raised a mortgage of £500, Minto's trustees put up a mortgage of £1,500, and Jack raised a mortgage of £1,000.[17] On this precarious basis, life at The Kilns began – and the distinctive Lewisian habitat had been established.

Surprised by Joy, limited by the necessarily artificial conventions of autobiography, gives an impression that the development of Lewis's religious opinions was much more cut and dried than was really the case. He gives us a picture of a firm conversion to theism in the summer of 1929, followed by a period in which he believed in God, but not in the doctrines of Christianity. Then, in the late summer of 1931, he writes that he passed definitely from this position of 'rational theism' into a full acceptance of the Christian dispensation.

While not exactly false, this simple version of his spiritual growth gives no picture of the tremendous vacillations in his faith which he confided to Arthur Greeves during this period. For example, in his attempt to lead a new life, he attributes any success he may have had in conquering lust, anger or pride to God's *grace*, a very specifically Christian idea; and this is a full fifteen months before his conversion to Christianity. Anything which smacks of an incarnational theology, he eschews. That is to say he is not in the least drawn to the idea that Christ came in the flesh, and he finds the simplicity and literalism of what might be termed 'mere Christianity' frankly unacceptable. To Greeves, the orthodox believer, he wrote in January 1930, 'In spite of all my recent changes of view I am still inclined to think that you can only get what *you* call Christ out of the Gospels by picking and choosing and slurring over a good deal.'[18] The authors he found most helpful in this 'interim' period were all mystics, or figures who emphasized spirit over matter – MacDonald, William Ralph Inge, Jacob Boehme, whose quasi-theosophical, semi-astrological *De Signatura Rerum* (*The Signature of Things*) gave him 'about the biggest shaking up I've got from a book, since I first read *Phantastes*'.[19] But such moments of uplift as were provided by the mystics could not prevent Lewis's common-sense humility from seeing 'how much of one's philosophy and religion are mere talk'.[20] When in college, he had begun to attend chapel (i.e. the prayer-book office of morning prayer) each day. It could not prevent him from having doubts. 'I have no rational ground for going back on the arguments that convinced me of God's existence: but the irrational deadweight of my old sceptical habits, and the spirit of the age, and the cares of the day, steal away all my lively feeling of the truth, and often when I pray I wonder if I am not posting letters to a non-existent address.'[21]

For those who are familiar with Lewis's literary persona, as for the much smaller number of people who knew him in life, his acceptance of an orthodox Christian position seems in an almost literal sense fitting. There are certain clothes we feel comfortable in and which we would wear in preference to all others. On this level of mere temperamental affinity (not considering its truth or falsehood) we feel Lewis to be a man who would be most happy in Christian garb. There is no doubt that until he discovered this clothing (be it artificial carapace or 'the whole armour of God'), Lewis was only half-formed as a writer, as a literary imagination, perhaps as a person. Many readers of his apologetics must have been disconcerted by the fact that his chapter about conversion in *Beyond Personality* is entitled 'Let's Pretend'. He suggests that the moment you 'make a shot at saying your prayers' and say 'Our Father' you are 'dressing up as Christ . . . That is why children's games are so important. They are always pretending to be grown-ups playing soldiers, playing shop. But all the time they are hardening their muscles and sharpening their wits, so that the pretence of being grown-up helps them to grow up in earnest.'[22]

This process of 'let's pretend' took an irreversible step forward one September night in 1931, when Lewis was entertaining J. R. R. Tolkien to dinner at Magdalen. He had also asked Henry Victor Dyson, a lecturer at Reading University who had been an exact contemporary of Tolkien's as an undergraduate at Exeter College. Like Tolkien, Dyson (known to all his friends as Hugo) was a Christian – though he was a High Anglican while Tolkien was Roman Catholic. Lewis had got to know him because he was a frequent visitor to Oxford, anxious to get a job in the Oxford English Faculty, and a friend not only of Tolkien but also of Nevill Coghill. Dyson was a beguilingly witty man, handsome and bright-eyed, whose talk was a flow of fantasy, keen literary appreciation and occasional learning. Like many Oxford men, he belonged to the strong Socratic tradition in which dialogue was esteemed as highly as the written word. As the years went by, and some of his friends became prolific writers, Dyson came to be jealous of their reputations and to scorn what they wrote. He himself published almost nothing. In 1931, however, they were all still comparatively innocent as far as publication was concerned. Lewis had his two slender volumes of verse, and Tolkien his learned edition of *Sir Gawain and the Green Knight* and his article on *Ancrene Wisse and Hali Meith-had* (which combines deep linguistic learning with a justly famous account of the world of this West Midland prose writer which we can recognize as a foretaste of the Hobbit's native Shire). These were hardly a threat to Dyson's rhetorical skills. Dyson, besides, though unpublished and 'a don at Reading' (as he always half-ironically described himself) rather than at Oxford, was more a man of the world than either Tolkien or Lewis. He had been a friend of Lawrence of Arabia; he knew Ottoline Morrell, at whose house Garsington Manor he had met Virginia Woolf, Bertrand Russell and D. H. Lawrence, among others. The combination of Tolkien and Dyson was therefore a formidable one. After dinner the talk fell to the great question which was uppermost in Lewis's mind: that question being, in the words of his pupil Betjeman, 'and is it true, and is it true, this most amazing tale of all?'

Owen Barfield, both in conversation and in writing, had already gone a long way in revealing to Lewis the fallacy of making sharp distinctions between 'myth' and 'fact'. In his book *Poetic Diction* he had pointed out that in earlier times, those who first used language did not necessarily distinguish between 'metaphorical' and 'literal' uses of words. The Latin *spiritus*, for example, means *breath*. Modern rationalists might wish to distinguish between the 'meaning' of 'spirit in some elevated sense' and that of 'merely breath'. But early users of the language would not have made such a distinction. When the wind blew it was not 'like' someone breathing. It was the breath of a divinity.

This powerfully confirmed the way in which Tolkien had been accustoming himself to think about the world ever since he grew to manhood. One of the great distinctions in his mythology is made between the Elves, who are 'animist' and 'pagan', and the Men, who are destined to move beyond this. The Elves, who will never leave the material universe and do not know what happens to Men when they die, are embodiments of language-users for whom the breath–wind–spirit distinction would be meaningless. By contrast, God willed that 'the hearts of Men should seek beyond the world and should find no rest therein'.[23]

In his dialogue with Lewis that September night, Tolkien was really arguing for a less human and more 'elven' approach to the Gospel story. Lewis complained that he could not see any personal relevance for himself in the story of Christ. 'What I couldn't see was how the life and death of Someone Else (whoever he was) 2000 years ago could

help us here and now – except in so far as his *example* helped us.'
Tolkien pointed out that this was, as much as anything, an imaginative
failure on Lewis's part. When Lewis came across *myths* of dying and
reviving gods, he was moved. When he read stories about Balder,
Adonis and Bacchus, he was prepared to 'feel the myth as profound
and suggestive of meanings beyond my grasp even tho' I could not
say in cold prose "what it meant"'. He stopped short of understanding
Christianity because when he thought about that, he laid aside the
receptive imagination with which he allowed himself to appreciate
myth and became rigidly narrow and empiricist. He should understand
that 'the story of Christ is simply a true myth: a myth working on us
in the same way as the others, but with this tremendous difference
that it *really happened*: and one must be content to accept it in the
same way.'[24]

To this extent, Tolkien argued, 'doctrines' which are extracted
from the 'myth' are less true than the 'myth' itself. The ideas are too
large and too all-embracing for the finite mind to absorb them. That
is why the divine providence revealed himself in story. Lewis claimed
that this was tantamount to 'breathing a lie through silver', a riposte
which Tolkien felt sufficiently challenging to require a written reply.
The result was the verse known as 'Mythopoeia', some of which he
quoted in his essay. Its 'argument' repeated the discussion which
he and Lewis shared with Dyson on that memorable September night.
Myth was the exact opposite of a 'lie breathed through silver'. Man's
capacity to mythologize was a remnant of his pre-lapsarian capacity
to see into the life of things:

> Disgraced he may be, yet is not dethroned,
> And keeps the rags of Lordship once he owned.

It was a completely still, warm evening, and the three friends walked
round and round the mile-long circuit of Addison's Walk beneath
the avenues of beeches. Quite suddenly, at a crucial point in the
conversation, there was a rush of wind, causing the first fall of leaves
in the season. They stood in the dark and listened. At first the pattering
leaves sounded like rain.

It was at this point that Tolkien reiterated the argument already
made familiar to Lewis by Barfield. We speak of 'stars' and 'trees' as

Above: Jack Lewis as a child, 1907 or earlier

Inset: Jack's mother, Flora Lewis

Right: Watercolour drawing of the Little Master (Lord Big) from *Leborough Studies, 1905-16* by Jack Lewis

Left: Albert Lewis in around 1881. 'My father and I were physical counterparts.'

Below: Jack with his father, 1918

Opposite: Jack Lewis in the Little End Room, 1919 (*photograph by W. H. Lewis*)

Inset: W. T. Kirkpatrick, Jack's former teacher, with his wife at Gastons, 1920 (*photograph by W. H. Lewis*)

Jack Lewis with Paddy Moore (foreground, left and right) 1917

Jack with Maureen and Mrs Moore on holiday in Cornwall, 1927

though they were entities which we had mastered in our post-Newtonian, materialist fashion. But for those who formed the words *star* and *tree* they were very different. For them, stars were a living silver, bursting into flame in answer to an eternal music in the mind of God. All creation was 'myth-woven and elf-patterned'. It was late; the clock in Magdalen Tower had struck three in the morning before Lewis let Tolkien out by the little postern on Magdalen Bridge. Dyson lingered, and he and Lewis found still more to say to one another, strolling up and down the cloister of New Buildings. They did not part until four a.m.

Nine days later, on 28 September, there was an outing from The Kilns to Whipsnade Zoo. Minto and Maureen, accompanied by an Irish friend called Vera Henry and the dog Mr Papworth, who had recovered his strength before going hence and being no more seen, were to travel by car. Jack and Warnie were to go by motorcycle – Daudel as Warnie called it – with Warnie in the saddle and Jack in a low-slung sidecar. It was a thick, misty day, but when the two brothers got beyond the small market town of Thame, the fog gave way to bright sunshine. They stopped for beer and then waited anxiously at an agreed spot for Minto and the others. They had still not turned up by two o'clock, and since their sandwich lunch was in the car, Jack and Warnie were feeling 'uncommonly peckish'. At two-twenty Minto's party appeared, saying that the reason for their delay was that Liddiat, the handyman employed by Minto at The Kilns, had pumped up the tyres of the car so hard that it was impossible to drive at more than fifteen miles per hour. In spite of the frayed tempers caused by this, it was an enjoyable expedition. Everyone, but especially the two Lewises, loved the zoo, and Jack made friends with a bear whom he nicknamed Bultitude. He said how much he would like to adopt the bear – which, in a sense, he was to do, for Bultitude appears as one of the characters in the final volume of his space trilogy *That Hideous Strength*.[25]

To all appearances, it had been a completely normal day. Only, as Lewis tells us in *Surprised by Joy*, 'when we set out I did not believe that Jesus Christ is the Son of God, and when we reached the zoo I did.'[26] When confiding the news to Greeves, he said, 'My long night talk with Dyson and Tolkien had a good deal to do with it.'[27]

We are told that Janie Moore bitterly resented the final stages of

Lewis's conversion, chiding him when he resumed the practice of Holy Communion for attending 'blood feasts'.[28] There is something puzzling here, since Mrs Moore, though an unbeliever, had been happy to have her own daughter confirmed, and there is a steady succession of references in Jack's letters and diaries, during the years 1919–1931, of attendance at church with Minto. We must assume either that Warnie's memory exaggerated the virulence of her hostility to Jack's conversion, or that there was some particular thing about it which affected her more than anyone else.

We cannot know – and she was by this time fifty-eight years old to Jack's thirty-three – whether she felt personally slighted by the change. We do know what Jack's views were of the Christian and sexual morality: 'There is no getting away from it: the Christian rule is "Either marriage, with complete faithfulness to your partner, or else total abstinence." '[29] In later years, offered the objection that celibacy is not always possible, Lewis the radio evangelist was to be quite unambiguous: 'Faced with an optional question in an examination paper, one considers whether one can do it or not; faced with a compulsory question, one must do the best one can . . . It is wonderful what you can do when you have to.'[30] The letters to Greeves suggest that he did not find this part of a Christian's duty very easy ('Daily Castration Prevents Master Bation').[31] But he was not a man to say one thing and do another. He meant his Christian commitment to be total.

This commitment grew out of profound emotional changes over which he had no control, and of which he himself perhaps had only an imperfect knowledge. The first change, the move to theism, happened in 1929 and coincided more or less directly with the death of his father. It would be far too glib to suggest that he consciously made the second change, to adopt Christianity, merely to give himself an excuse to abandon sexual relations with Mrs Moore, whatever the nature of those relations had been.

There are some men who pay prostitutes not for overtly sexual favours, but for humiliation of the most humdrum kind. Such people, caught in a strange web of masochism, find their emotional fulfilment not in acts of love but in being made to scrub kitchen floors or scour out pans. 'He was as good as an extra maid,' said Minto.

Certainly, as his mind prepared itself for the acceptance of the

Christian orthodoxies, he was making dogged attempts to come to terms with his sado-masochistic tendencies. In February of 1931, he and Warnie had attended a production of James Elroy Flecker's *Hassan* at the Oxford Playhouse.

> It was not very well done, but well enough for me: indeed to see it really well acted would be too much for me. In reading it the cruelty is just about balanced by the extreme beauty of the lyrics and much of the dialogue, so that the total effect, tho' sinister, like a too bright dream which is sure to turn into nightmare before the end, yet is bearable. On the stage, where one has less time to dwell on the cadence or suggestion of the individual words, the cruelty is unendurable. Warnie went out half way through. I felt quite sick but thought it almost a duty for one afflicted in my way to remain, saying to myself, 'Oh, you like cruelty, do you? Well now stew in it' – the same principle on which one trains a puppy to be clean – 'rub their noses in it'. It has haunted me ever since.

The disturbing thing about this letter to Arthur Greeves is the extent to which he does not see that the remedy proposed sounds all too like the disorder he wishes to eliminate. For the shaming pleasure of voyeuristic torture, he has substituted the pleasure of having his nose rubbed in it. Like many sexually naïve people, Lewis supposed that if he eliminated the consciously erotic elements of his sexuality from the surface of life, he would be able to dispel the habits and character-istics of which these particular tastes were a mere symptom. Perhaps if he had worried less about them, and taken a less self-reproachful line, the outlines of his personality would have softened with the years. Perhaps, too, if they had known about his 'tastes', his friends would have been less puzzled by two of his most mysterious personality traits: his delight in verbal bullying, of students or intellectual op-ponents, and his apparently cheerful domestic enslavement to Mrs Moore.

The college grind of meetings and tutorials went on. Lewis had by now settled into the role of tutor, but he did not relax in it. His pupils nearly all felt (particularly the first pupil of the morning, at ten a.m., who watched him lay down his steel-nibbed pen with an air of resignation) that tutorials were an interruption to what he considered his real work. And he had a notorious asperity for which he was afterwards sometimes penitent. Treating his pupils to the compliment of rational disagreement sometimes spilled over into a verbal contest so fierce that the young person concerned was abashed or even frightened. The feelings may be imagined of the pupil who rashly let fall a slighting reference to *Sohrab and Rustum*, to be answered by Lewis's brandishing an old regimental sword of his brother's which stood in the corner of his room and shouting, 'The sword must settle this!' The experience of the others was probably less dramatic, but they all knew the sharp edge of Lewis's tongue. 'As to yesterday morning, I was a bit "short". If you take into account the fact that I have been up till after midnight every night since Monday, that I have a cold, and that that morning I had been talking on a sore throat from 9.30 to 1 o'clock, perhaps you will understand.' Quite as remarkable as the original display of ill temper was the graciousness which prompted him to apologize for it. 'The truth is,' he admitted to Alan Griffiths, 'I have a constant temptation to over asperity . . . even when there is no subjective anger to prompt me: it comes, I think, from the pleasure of using the English language forcibly – i.e. it is not a species of *Ira* but of *Superbia*.'[32]

Some pupils came in time to like it; not simply because the outbursts were part of the Lewis 'act', but because he was a conscientious teacher, who was concerned, as the Great Knock had been, to wage war on sloppy language and sloppy thinking. John Lawlor, a pupil from 1936 onwards, said of himself that he 'passed from dislike and hostility to stubborn affection, and then to gratitude for the weekly bout in which no quarter was asked or given'.[33] In this he almost certainly spoke for the majority of Lewis's pupils. As a pupil of slightly later vintage, Derek Brewer, remarked, 'Many of his pupils became teachers of one sort or another and all, or most of them, became his friends.'[34] That is pretty high praise; and though there are some obvious exceptions, they were fewer as the years went by. A tutor who could command the unhesitating affection and intellectual respect of so miscellaneous a collection of men as Derek Brewer (later Master of Emmanuel College, Cambridge), the drama critic Kenneth Tynan, the publisher Charles Monteith and the poet John Wain was clearly doing his job.

One aspect of the Lewis regime about which the majority of his pupils had some misgivings, however, was the termly dinner he gave for them. He called it the 'English binge'. It was a dinner held at his own expense in a private room at Magdalen, and it was a symptom of his great generosity. But it was also a throwback to a form of behaviour which, however natural it might have seemed to officer cadets in the First World War, was excruciatingly embarrassing to succeeding generations of Magdalen men. The idea of the evening was primarily to get drunk, and this was a matter about which Lewis was exuberantly insistent. The conversation had to be what he called 'bawdry'. 'Nothing above the belly or below the knee tonight!' he exclaimed on one of these evenings, savouring the rowdy songs and bawdy rhymes which resulted. One of his pupils, Roger Lancelyn Green, has commented on a letter which Lewis wrote to Warnie describing the 'English binge' at Christmas 1931. 'Bawdy ought to be outrageous and extravagant,' Lewis had written; and Green tells us, 'he proceeds to give a very mild example.'[35] It is a remnant which 'dates' Green and reveals our later generation as less innocent and more acquiescent. Green does not *quote* the example, which is a song about an angry father who suspects that his daughter has been ravished by the protagonist of the ballad. What Lewis calls 'the good part' goes as follows:

> Hark! I hear a step on the stair!
> Sounds to me like an angry father,
> With a pistol in either hand,
> Looking for the man that screwed his daughter
> (Rum ti-iddle-ey etc).
>
> I have seized him by the hair of his head
> And shoved it into a bucket of water
> And I screwed his pistols up his arse
> A dam sight harder than I screwed his daughter
> (Rum ti-iddle-ey etc).

Lewis spent Christmas Day 1931 transcribing this ditty for Warnie, who had returned for his last spell of service in Shanghai. With the role of the heavy father properly cast – stumping up the stairs with a desperate expression and his two pistols, he wrote, 'this anticlimax, this adding of injury to insult, seems to me irresistible'. He regretted that bawdry of this kind was the 'only living folk-art left to us. If our English binge had been held in a medieval university we should have had, mixed with the bawdy songs, tragical and even devotional pieces, equally authorless and handed on from mouth to mouth in the same way, with the same individual variations.'[36] One somehow thinks that only Lewis could have stepped, with a few vigorous steps, from a defence of drunken all-male 'stag' evenings to a vivid illustration of the life and literature of the Middle Ages.

ELEVEN

REGRESS
1931–1936

Lewis was by now thirty-three years old. By the age of thirty-three Keats and Shelley were dead; Byron had finished two-thirds of his major work. Even a figure more comparable with Lewis, G. K. Chesterton, had at this age published five of his most distinguished books, and discovered his own voice. With Lewis this was not so, and it is probably vain to look for reasons. We can account for what he was doing with his time, but this is not the same thing as explaining how or why the tone of voice – that vigour, that distinctively Lewisian freshness and vitality – was so long in coming.

What we do know is that his full conversion to Christianity released in him a literary flow which only ceased with death. From then on, works of scholarship, fantasy, literary appreciation, and apologetics poured from his ever-fertile brain. The poetry got much better too. The angel's song at the end of *The Pilgrim's Regress* is in a different league from the unhappier patches of *Spirits in Bondage* or *Dymer*. Terse, poignant, and well made, it says what could only be said in poetry. The thought, perhaps, is borrowed from Tolkien, whose immortals cannot see why men dread death. ('We who bear the ever-mounting burden of the years do not clearly understand this.')[1] But the perspective is very distinctly that of Lewis, who was to spend nearly all his literary energies imagining what the world would look like if seen from heaven.

Lewis began to write *The Pilgrim's Regress*, appropriately enough, on a return visit to Northern Ireland to stay with Arthur Greeves in the spring of 1932. 'We have come to Puritania,' he said, 'and that was my father's house. I see that my father and mother are gone already beyond the brook. I had much I would have said to them. But it is no matter.'[2]

The book owes its title and framework to Bunyan, but it is much more satirical in tone and purpose than *The Pilgrim's Progress*. Read today, its contemporary references seem crude and dead as mutton. Anyone can work out who the 'subspecies' Marxomanni, Mussolimini and Swastici are meant to represent, but they do not really play an important part in the story, since we can feel that John, the Pilgrim, is not really tempted or overwhelmed by them, any more than Lewis ever felt the slightest inclination to become a Marxist or a Fascist. Similarly, the pre-First World War diction now creates moments of unintentional comedy, as when the figure of Christ says to John, 'You must play fair,'[3] or when John's plunge into the pool of faith is described as 'he took a header'.[4] (Lewis, incidentally, had been taught to dive only very lately, by Owen Barfield, an event which he considered full of religious significance.)

Any fair-minded critic of *The Pilgrim's Regress* must also admit that some of its conceits are unfortunate. The identification of lust with 'brown girls' probably had no racial connotations in that innocently discriminatory age; but the scenes towards the end where the Witch tries to capture John with her wiles do leave the disconcerting impression that Lewis thought of Christianity as little more than a good 'cure' for lust.

All that must be conceded, and yet the book's virtues greatly outweigh its faults. Some of the contemporary satire – John Betjeman as 'Victoriana', Edith Sitwell as 'Glugly' – is still quite funny. ('She was very tall and lean as a post . . . She waddled to and fro with her toes pointing in . . . Finally she made some grunts and said: "Globol obol ookle ogle globol gloogle gloo."') The assaults on the neo-Thomist revival of the period are also well made. There are sentences in 'Neo-Angular's' speeches which are echoed almost word for word in the essays of T. S. Eliot and the letters of Evelyn Waugh.

So you have met Mother Kirk? No wonder that you are confused. You had no business to talk to her except through a qualified Steward . . . Reason is divine. But how should you understand her? You are a beginner. For you, the only safe commerce with reason is to learn from your superiors the dogmata in which her deliverances have been codified for general use.[5]

The book has the unmistakable stamp of Lewis upon it. There is the tremendous narrative verve; there are the flights of true sublimity side by side with the knockabout of comedy and debate; there is, above all, the sense which informs nearly all his religious writing, that a human being's relationship with God is the great Romance of life. The subtitle is *An Allegorical Apology for Christianity, Reason and Romanticism*, and it is important to remember that for Lewis the three things went together. Tolkien had taught him that the inability to believe in Christianity was primarily a failure of the *imagination*. This insight had enabled Lewis to recover all the things in art and in life which he had been enjoying since imaginative awareness dawned. In Puritania, religion had been the stuff of cant, of laws, of promised punishments for behaviour which the Pilgrim's inner conscience could not condemn. But there had also been this other vision – of the 'green wood full of primroses' – which he had glimpsed through a hole in the wall, and which promised all the things which Lewis and Greeves had come to label 'It' or 'Joy'. These were the pleasures he got from the beauties of nature, from the music of Wagner, from the watercolours of Beatrix Potter, from the books of William Morris, George MacDonald and Wordsworth. What he discovered in his 'regress' was that all these things were echoes of the heavenly places. In the allegory, it is not easy to work out the extent to which the regress is a return to Puritanian values. The double values of the stewards, and the ethics based on fear of punishment are rejected. But Mother Kirk – a sort of Anglican version of Langland's Mother Church – is certainly John's guide in the final stages of his journey.

J. R. R. Tolkien, to whom Lewis read aloud *The Pilgrim's Regress*, liked the book. Thirty years later, however, Tolkien saw that there was more in the word 'regress' than had immediately met his ear. He saw that Lewis

would not re-enter Christianity by a new door but by the old one: at least in the sense that in taking it up again he would also take up again or reawaken the prejudices so sedulously planted in childhood and boyhood. He would become again a Northern Ireland Prot-estant – though with a difference, certainly: he was no longer a resident; he was learned; he had the wonderful gifts both of imagin-ation and a clear and analytical mind; and above all his faith came of Grace to which he responded heroically, in patience and self-sacrifice – when he was aware of himself.[6]

Tolkien's contention was that something he called 'the ulsterior motive' – the bogey of Lewis's Ulster background – lurked beneath the surface of his imagination, and rose when he was off his guard to make him brutal in manners, crude or illogical in thought. Anyone who has studied Lewis's work must know what Tolkien meant, though the 'ulsterior motive' is much more apparent in Lewis's reported speech (particularly in speech lubricated by the wine of High Table or the beer of Oxfordshire pubs) than on the printed page. But Tolkien's censure, written from the standpoint of one who had himself hardened in a sentimental devotion to the religion of his boyhood, must not be accepted without qualifications.

With his conscious self, Lewis had a very distinct loathing of Ulster Protestantism. When he attended St Mark's, Dundela, for the first time after his conversion, he was repelled by the sense that 'these good Produsdands' went there to express party solidarity rather than religious feeling; and he found his Irish relations almost universally repulsive. He and Warnie, for example, had decided that they would erect a memorial window to their parents in St Mark's, but it was a decision they quickly came to regret when the Lewis, Hamilton and Ewart cousins all weighed in with suggestions of what should go into the window. The incumbent of St Mark's, the Rev. Claude Lionel Chavasse, suggested that the window might contain a view of St Mark's itself in the background. Lewis immediately guessed that this suggestion came not from Chavasse but from his Aunt Lily, and in the irrational way that such family meddling irritates, this prompted an extraordinary flow of anger. He described the case to Warnie:

It just occurs to me as I write that Chavasse in this matter is probably the unwilling mouthpiece of the Select Vestry: I daresay even that monstrous regiment of women, incarnated in Lily Ewart, is really at the bottom of it. Zounds! – I'd like a few minutes at the bottom of her! No 'thought inform' would there 'stain my cheek': a firm hand rather would stain both hers.[7]

He disliked the ethos of Irish Protestantism and he did not believe in its doctrines. If the mark of a reborn evangelical is a devotion to the Epistles of St Paul and in particular to the doctrine of Justification by Faith, then there can have been few Christian converts less evangelical than Lewis. When he has been a Christian for three years, we find him, in the pages of his brother's diary, reading The Epistle to the Romans, the greatest exposition in Scripture of the themes of Original Sin, Grace and Justification by Faith. 'Jack', we discover, 'has been reading this epistle with a commentary but could get no help from it.'[8]

In later years, when Lewis showed *Mere Christianity* to four clergymen, of four different denominations, for their criticisms, he received hostile comments from two of the four. One of these two, inevitably, was his old pupil and sparring partner Alan Griffiths (by then a Roman Catholic monk, Dom Bede Griffiths), who claimed that Lewis undervalued the doctrine of the Atonement. Perhaps more fundamental than this was the criticism he received from a Methodist minister that the book does not really mention, let alone do justice to, the central Christian doctrine of Justification by Faith.

Lewis came to the faith by means of what one could loosely term Neo-Platonism. It was the sense of another world which drew him; the sense he got from MacDonald (a convert to Broad Church Anglicanism from Congregationalism) of Heaven being penetrable through dreams and the subconscious and the exercise of the imagination. It was the conviction of Tolkien (a Roman Catholic) that truth is best discerned through myth which finally tipped the balance. In all this period he was influenced by Barfield (a disciple of Rudolph Steiner) and by rereading Plato himself, as well as by Neo-Platonist writers such as Dean Inge (Broad Church). It is therefore a mistake to make too much of 'the ulsterior motive'.

In actual devotional practice, Lewis was greatly guided by reading the *Imitatio Christi* of Thomas à Kempis. The hallmarks of Thomas à Kempis's approach to the religious life are a rigorous inner self-discipline and a conformity, for reasons of humility, to the existing forms of Christianity as met from day to day wherever you happen to be. As to the outward forms of religion, Lewis decided from the moment that he became a Christian that he should attend his college chapel on weekday mornings and his parish church on Sundays. As it happened, the ritual of Magdalen chapel was 'Low Church' and that of the Headington Quarry church was 'High'. With his background in Ulster, where he had seen the blasphemous absurdity of Christians hating one another on the grounds of historical or ritual difference, he was always rigorously 'non-party' in his Anglicanism. His non-ritualism was still, in the early 1930s, perfectly normal and there were many Anglicans who would have shared it, though perhaps not all would have been quite so dogged about it as he. On Palm Sunday, 1934, for example, Lewis and his brother attended the liturgy at the parish church in Headington Quarry. The vicar 'came down to the steps at the top of the nave, accompanied by a server with a basket of palms and we all went up and got one except J[ack].'[9] This might be thought to be the ulsterior motive surfacing; but if so, it has to be balanced by Lewis's unconquerable distaste for hymns (not a markedly Protestant trait). At the Quarry church, if he attended a choral service, it was his invariable custom to leave during the singing of the last hymn.[10] He had, in fact, an almost Tridentine attitude to the liturgy. In spite of his distaste for 'frills', he saw church-going as something one did out of obedience; something which shaped the life of prayer and reminded each individual that he or she was a 'member incorporate in the blessed company of all faithful people'; but not something which needed to be added to, still less enjoyed as a hobby.

Warnie, incidentally, was less brave than Jack, and dutifully went up to fetch his palm, in an agony of embarrassment. 'I think that there is a real risk that an imaginative child may get the impression that a bit of palm is in some way a magical charm,' he considered. To be on the safe side, he burnt his when he got home, presumably unaware that this was, liturgically, the 'correct' and Catholic thing to do, though some forty-six weeks too early.

By now, the household of The Kilns had taken on the shape which it was to maintain until well after the Second World War. Warnie had retired from the Army at the earliest possible opportunity, in December 1932, and moved in with Jack and Minto as a permanent fixture. He was thirty-seven years old. The question of what he was to do with himself for the rest of his life was never properly resolved in his mind or anyone else's, which perhaps accounts for his periodic assaults on the whiskey bottle – what Minto called 'Warnie's benders'.

Being Irish herself, and the sister of a man who had gone mad with syphilis, she was rather more tolerant of Warnie's foibles than he was of hers.

Among the innumerable items which they brought away from Little Lea – a lumpish wardrobe to which Jack had a sentimental attachment, for instance – there were countless letters, diaries and family papers stretching back to the lifetime of their Lewis and Hamilton grandparents. Warnie was a natural historian, and he set himself the task of putting all these documents into chronological order. The real interest of the past, he wrote, 'lies in the answer to the question, How did the ordinary undistinguished man live? ... and it is with a view to providing posterity with an addition to such all too scanty materials that the papers ... have been embodied in permanent form.'[11] Undergraduate pupils of Jack's throughout the middle years of the 1930s got used to passing through the outer drawing-room of his rooms at Magdalen where sat the mysterious figure of Captain Lewis, typing with two fingers on an ancient black portable. The finished result, eleven bound volumes of single-spaced pages, is a testimony to Warnie's extraordinary patience, as well as to his seemingly inexhaustible appetite for contemplating his own immediate past. Every note, every school report, every passing wheeze of the P'daytabird is here; and since, by a strange series of chances, the *Lewis Papers* now reside in an air-conditioned cavern in the suburbs of Chicago, we may suppose that they will survive for ever, perhaps long after Oxford and Ulster have been lost to sight.

Jack never seems to have regarded the proximity of his brother, even while doing his teaching, as a burden; if anything, it was the reverse. But the possibilities of domestic tension were increased by Warnie's presence a hundredfold. Both Warnie and Minto were jealous of anyone who claimed Jack's love; this meant that they were bound to be jealous of one another, since for both of them Jack was the most important person in the universe.

Shortly after moving into The Kilns, Minto had engaged a gardener to help her with the eight acres of ground. His name was Fred Paxford, and he lived in a small wooden bungalow on the other side of the brick kilns. Paxford was a 'character', given to looking on the black side of every passing scene, and to lugubrious murmurings of 'Abide with Me' and other hymns while he toiled. His pessimistic character was fairly faithfully reproduced in Puddleglum, the Marshwiggle in *The Silver Chair*. In spite of Paxford's strong left-wing views, Minto idolized him and allowed him to occupy the same sort of position in her household as John Brown had occupied at the court of Queen Victoria. He was consulted as an oracle on all occasions, however inappropriate, and this was something which Warnie found insufferably annoying. His diaries chronicle each phase of irritation with novelistic detail.

I quite suddenly got very bored with M's conversation tonight. She has lately developed a tiresome habit of becoming a mere compendium of Paxford's views; every conceivable topic is met with a reply beginning 'Paxford says'. I am resigned to being addressed by the new name of Pax-Warnie, but if she is to become a mere conduit of the Paxford philosophy it will be a very great bore. Further, it makes me angry with myself to find that the perfectly natural and utterly unfair result is that I begin to dislike Paxford, no exercise of the will convincing me that it is not the unfortunate P. who is boring me with his views on everything under the sun.

A magnificent example of the 'Paxford says' routine is provided when Maureen and Minto have been into Oxford to get two wireless sets on approval. The scene is the kitchen at The Kilns and both sets are plugged in.

MAUREEN: Well the A set certainly has the better tone.

MINTO: Oh no, dear, Paxford says the B set has a lovely tone; he says the A set is tinny.

MAUREEN: Well, it blurs the sound: you can't hear the 'Underneath' of any music.

MINTO: Paxford and I were saying it was so clear.

MAUREEN: Then it's easier to find stations on the A set.

MINTO: Paxford says the B set is easier; Paxford says he got forty stations on it: he made it work beautifully.

MAUREEN (trying the B set which emits a series of siren-like whoops and then a muffled jazz band): It doesn't seem particularly easy to get ANY station on the B.

MINTO: Ask Paxford, dear: he'll show you how to work it in the morning.

MYSELF (Internally): Bugger Paxford. (Aloud): Well, goodnight, I'm off to bed.

MINTO: Goodnight Pax-Warnie. Paxford says — (I close the door and go to bed).[12]

Jack avoided being a witness to these scenes much of the time by residing in college. For half the year, he would sleep at The Kilns. But during the three eight-week terms his routine was to sleep in college, at least for the days in the middle of the week. If Maureen was at home, she would drive into Oxford to fetch him home for lunch. Sometimes Paxford fulfilled this office. And if neither of them was at home Lewis would return to The Kilns by bus; so Minto was visited each day. There was, indeed, never a day, except when he was away on short holidays, during which he did not spend some time in her company, from the time of their first association in 1919 until her death in 1951. This has been represented as some kind of martyrdom on Lewis's part; and doubtless, like any long-term relationship, it called for reserves of patience and good humour on both sides. But it is absurd to suppose that Lewis had nothing to gain from Minto's company, or that all their time was spent discussing domestic trivia (much as she and Lewis both *enjoyed* such discussions). A recent pen has asserted that Mrs Moore was never seen with a book in her hands. It is true that she was not academic; this was part of her charm for Lewis. But even the most rudimentary reading of his many surviving letters will reveal passages which speak of the pleasures of reading with or to Mrs Moore. In 1936, for example, we find them reading Virginia Woolf's *Orlando* together; and in 1943, Lewis wrote to a friend that Minto was reading *Jane Eyre*.

She, for her part, accepted the fact that he was gregarious and, like the great majority of men in those days, tended to congregate with members of his own sex. Our social mores have changed so much that it is easy to single out as personal characteristics those which were actually held in common by nearly everyone. Lewis, for instance, is frequently spoken of as a man who enjoyed male coteries, as though, in the 1930s, the regiments, the London clubs, the Oxford and

Cambridge colleges and the City companies were all overflowing with 'mixed' company. This simply was not so, and the fact that Lewis spent evenings in the company of male friends was not what distinguished him.

Even to speak of those by-now famous evenings as a coterie is to imply that they were both more formal and more enclosed than was the case. For example, one day in 1934 or 1935, Lewis had influenza. In those days, if you were ill in England, the doctor visited you, rather than expecting you to stagger to the surgery. Minto summoned the man who had recently taken over the Headington practice from the household's former practitioner, Dr Wood. The doctor who appeared was R. E. Havard, and after five minutes of talk about influenza (Lewis had rather a fondness for discussing symptoms man to man), they fell to some ethical or philosophical talk. Lewis, it struck Havard, a recent convert to Roman Catholicism and a devotee of Thomas Aquinas, took a remarkably idealistic, Berkeleyan view of things.

On the strength of this exchange, Lewis realized that Havard would be a man who would enjoy meeting some of the people who had taken to dropping into his rooms at Magdalen on Thursday evenings. Not long afterwards, therefore, Havard was invited to call at Magdalen. Warnie was there to welcome him and to dispense drinks. Others present included Lord David Cecil, who had lately come back to Oxford to teach English Literature at New College, and Adam Fox, the college chaplain. Dyson and Tolkien were also there. Lewis was the presiding genius; the meeting took place in his rooms and it was he who chose the moment to ask if anyone present had any work in progress which they wanted to read aloud. It was in this way that Havard first came to hear many of Tolkien's tales, David Cecil's *Two Quiet Lives*, and reflections on Dante by Colin Hardie (who taught Classics at Magdalen and was also a regular member of the circle), as well as many of Lewis's own works. This was no ordinary gathering of men. The level of wit and comment, sometimes abusive, sometimes adulatory, about what was read was consistently high. How many 'literary' men, happily ensconced in a coterie, would ask along their doctors? Can we imagine a GP being made to feel welcome in the Bloomsbury set? But one also sees in the adoption of Havard the vivid contrast which existed between the clubbable Lewis liked by his friends and the figure he presented on the domestic scene. It is easy to get the impression that he was the only one to suffer in this area, constantly put upon by Mrs Moore or bored by her daughter. Seen from the women's angle, things could sometimes appear differently.

No sooner had Havard become a friend than Lewis casually asked one day why Minto and Maureen did not entertain the doctor's family; have his wife to tea and allow his children to swim in the quarry pond. Minto was always happy to entertain young people, and the invitation was issued. The Havards arrived at The Kilns, Maureen played tennis with them, swam with them and provided them with the sandwiches and cakes which she and her mother had been preparing all day. They liked the Havards, and were pleased to have met them. Not so Jack, who appeared to have forgotten that it was his idea to invite them in the first place. 'Really, Maureen,' he bellowed at her, 'the friends you insist on inviting round become uglier and uglier. I never saw such an *ugly* family as the Havards.'

Meanwhile, the doctor continued to be a friend whom he enjoyed meeting in the evenings. The roughness and sheer wild irrationality of Lewis's domestic persona were matched by the genuinely warm-hearted impulse which had led him to befriend Havard in the first place.

Havard, who came to be nicknamed 'Humphrey' (because this was what one member of the group thought was his name) and sometimes the UQ or Useless Quack, came to be a much loved friend of them all. His presence among them was highly symptomatic. There was nothing of 'the ivory tower', nothing 'donnish', about Lewis's intelligence. In all his talk, and in his writings, he addressed the sympathetic, lively minded 'general reader' or 'average man'. Even his learned writings have the readability and freshness of appeal of 'popular' work; indeed, the distinction between 'learned' and 'popular' is one which seems in reading Lewis to be quite false. And one feels this even when he is at his most learned.

In all available time not devoted to teaching, to domestic life or to friendship, Lewis had been hard at work, ever since the late 1920s, on the book which was to become *The Allegory of Love*. Letters to his father in 1928 revealed how he had grown to love the oldest part of the Bodleian – Duke Humfrey's Library. 'If only one could smoke and if only there were upholstered chairs, this would be one of the most delightful places in the world.' Others who have appreciated the painted ceilings, mullioned windows and carved bays of that supremely beautiful room must have felt that one of its great charms resided in the absence of modern furniture and tobacco smoke. Be that as it may, it was here that Lewis began to build up his encyclopaedic knowledge of late medieval literature. As far back as 1925, he had dreamed of a complete history of the love allegory from Ovid to Spenser, and by 1928 two chapters of a more modest scheme, starting with the Provençal troubadours, were finished. But Lewis's conception of the book changed as he himself changed, and nothing much more got written until 1931.

The substance of his book – the history of allegorical love literature from the early Middle Ages to the late sixteenth century – was worked out in lectures to undergraduates. Lewis had a distinctive manner of lecturing, which was not greatly altered over the years. He began speaking as soon as he entered the lecture-room, which he generally did five minutes after the hour. He finished five minutes before the hour. He spoke slowly, sometimes at dictation speed, if quoting an author whom he thought his audience should not miss. The lectures were delivered in a full, deep, slightly Irish version of the Oxford voice ('Lat'n' for Latin, and rolled Rs), enlivened with amusing analogies and examples from modern life and literature. He had his father's gift for sensing what sort of an audience he was addressing, and adapting his matter accordingly. He told jokes well. His lectures were above all popular because he packed them with information. Clever undergraduates liked them because of their enormous range. Lazy undergraduates liked them because Lewis did half their work for them – providing summaries of books they would never get around to reading themselves, and lightening his commentaries with entertaining asides. But it was not until the early 1930s that *The Allegory of Love* began to take shape as a book, and it was not finished until 1935. It is a phenomenal compendium of lightly worn, deeply read learning, and in every page we see why Lewis was such an inspired teacher. He unselfconsciously expects the reader to be as interested as he is in Jean de Meung or Alanus. In consequence we are, or wish that we were. What is more, it is a big-hearted, generous book. Lewis does not set out to make himself cleverer than the reader, still less cleverer than the authors whom he is discussing. Like an enthusiastic guide in a foreign country, he is anxious to share with us the unexpected treasures he has found and which we might, without his help, have missed. Indeed, if he has a fault as a critic it is in his boyishly enthusiastic generosity towards authors – Thomas Usk, Lydgate – who are not really as interesting as he makes them sound. It is not that he *lies* about them, rather that only a patient and omnivorous prospector would have found the particular treasures which he quotes. The treasures are real enough. But who would guess, for example, having read some of the Lydgate he quotes –

And as I stoode myself alloone upon the Nuwe Yeare night,
I prayed unto the frosty moone, with her pale light

– what a dull time we should have if we tried to read our way through *The Fall of Princes*? Supremely, however, this generous desire to show us the best in an author is manifested in his long chapter about Spenser, and there he marks himself out not as a kindly eccentric, but as a pioneer of modern taste. Thanks very largely to Lewis, Spenser is now once more regarded as one of the greatest English poets, having sunk into almost total obscurity before *The Allegory of Love* was written.

Moreover, in showing us what he loves about *The Faerie Queene*, he shows us in embryo what he hardly knows at this point himself: the sort of books which he himself will excel at. In his descriptions of Spenser's Christian purpose, his blending of allegory with adventure, his use of homely familiar figures, like St George, side by side with figures from a much older mythology and figures from his own imagination, Lewis is actually writing a recipe for how to construct the Narnia chronicles.

There is never a moment's dullness in *The Allegory of Love*. Its readability partly consists in the enthusiasm which has already been mentioned, and in the liveliness and unexpectedness of the examples: the comparison of Boiardo's fantasies with Mickey Mouse; the likening of Spenser's Radigund to Simla memsahibs in Kipling.[13] But the essential and unifying feature of the book is the voice of the author. One could say very certainly, therefore, that the book could not be complete until Lewis as a 'character' was complete. He is not afraid to come before us in this book as a full-blown figure, someone who is quite recognizable (from earliest school letters and the accounts of Kirkpatrick) as 'the real Lewis' but who is also, for the first time, 'found' as an artistic voice.

> Johnson once described the ideal happiness which he would choose, if he were regardless of futurity. My own choice, with the same reservation, would be to read the Italian epic – to be always convalescent from some small illness and always seated in a window that overlooked the sea, there to read these poems eight hours of each happy day.[14]

Part of the pleasure of reading Lewis, when it is a pleasure, is meeting with this figure. Few academics would think it proper to bring themselves before the reader in this way, particularly in a work of learning. But the important point is not that they would hesitate to do it, but that we would not be interested if they did. Part of Lewis's discovery of himself as a writer was the discovery of a means of presenting himself to the reader. It is the rhetoric of Romanticism – 'the egotistical sublime' – and not everyone liked or likes it.

Barfield, to whom he dedicated *The Allegory of Love*, describes a moment when he read Lewis's 'Open Letter to Dr Tillyard'. Tillyard, one of the foremost Milton scholars of his day, had suggested that we can only fully understand *Paradise Lost* when we understand the man who wrote it. For Lewis, this was 'the personal heresy', a vivid example of which would be the present biography, which seeks to shed light on a man's work by researching into the recesses of his mind and the outward events of his life. It is typical of Lewis's later self that he should have seen no virtue at all in Tillyard's approach, and that furthermore he should have labelled it 'heresy'. What struck Barfield, however, was the manner in which this slightly absurd debate was conducted. 'We have both learnt our dialectic in the academic arena where knocks that would frighten the London literary coteries are given and taken in good part; and even where you think me sometimes too pert you will not suspect me of malice. If you honour me with a reply it will be in kind; and then, God defend the right!'

Barfield describes how he read this sentence, slapped down the book and shouted: 'I don't believe it! It's pastiche!'[15] While such thoughts were inevitable for those who knew Lewis before the great change came upon his life, it was not quite right to speak of 'pastiche'. It was all a bit odder than that. After he became a Christian, Lewis did completely change his view not only of his own personality but of human personality in general. 'My own empirical self is becoming more important,' he wrote to Barfield, 'and this is exactly the opposite of self-love.'

It is said that when he heard his own voice on the radio, some seven years after writing this letter, Lewis was surprised and in some measure disconcerted. In a similar way he might have been surprised by the figure he cut in prose or come to that in life. But he was in no sense putting on an act. The strange locutions, the shabby clothes, the combination of kindliness and brusqueness, the strong 'personality' but increasing *impersonality* of his conversation and interests, were all part of the same process. It is comparable with the oddness which might visit all our outward appearances if we stopped looking in mirrors. The only contrived thing about it was the initial impulse, which interpreted the New Testament injunction to deny self as to 'live without an image of the self'. The 'image' of C. S. Lewis, which many were to find rebarbative, was not, as they imagined, stage-managed or rehearsed, but it was none the less odd for that.

The Allegory of Love was sent in manuscript to the offices of the Oxford University Press in London. As with much else in Lewis's life, it seems as though there was a Providence in its journey, for it landed on the desk of a man called Charles Williams.

TWELVE

THE INKLINGS
1936–1939

W. H. Auden, the rising star of the English poetic firmament, met Charles Williams about a year after Lewis did. Auden had been asked by the Oxford University Press to prepare *The Oxford Book of Light Verse*, and he went along to discuss this with Williams at his office in Amen House. At this period in his life, Auden was still a subscriber to the bundle of ideologies – leftist in politics, atheist in religion, Freudian in psychology – which went with being a 1930s intellectual. Yet, in the presence of Williams, he felt 'for the first time in my life . . . in the presence of personal sanctity . . . I had met many good people before who made me feel ashamed of my own shortcomings, but in the presence of this man – we never discussed anything but literary business – I did not feel ashamed. I felt transformed into a person who was incapable of doing anything base or unloving.'[1] T. S. Eliot, who published many of Williams's books, felt the same. Eliot had first met Williams – of all unlikely settings – at a tea-party given in London by Lady Ottoline Morrell, and felt 'a kind of benediction' emanating from this curious bespectacled creature who 'appeared to combine frail physique with exceptional vitality'.[2]

Williams was a man who was able to hold many apparently contradictory ideas in harmony. For example, he was able to reconcile membership of the Church of England (rather High) with belonging to such occult groups as the Order of the Golden Dawn. Thomas Cranmer and Aleister Crowley were held in uneasy balance in his sympathies. A rather unsatisfactory marriage was glorified in his imagination by high-sounding comparisons between himself and Dante, while his largely innocent office romances – which do not appear to have gone much beyond crushes on secretaries – were seen in terms of Launcelot's devotion to Guinevere and the threatened breaking of the Round Table. Entirely self-educated and cockney in speech, Williams (rather like Blake in an earlier generation of London mystics) had an almost matter-of-fact awareness of the other world. Angels – or 'angelicals' as he would have preferred to call them in his strange idiolect – were as real to him as omnibuses or mortgage repayments – and far more likely to obtrude into his consciousness. In his theological writings, it is not always easy to see at what point he steps over the borderline between magic and religion. In his fiction, there is an analogous blurring of distinctions, shocking or thrilling depending on the reader's taste. Once Oxford University Press had accepted *The Allegory of Love* for publication, it was sent to Charles Williams, who worked on their editorial desk in London. It so happened, entirely by coincidence, that Coghill lent Lewis a copy of Williams's novel *The Place of the Lion* at precisely this moment.

The merits contained in any Williams novel – and this one has many – are not purely literary. Indeed, none of his novels is well shaped or well written. The characters have improbable names and say improbable things. The excitement of *The Place of the Lion* is in its power to shake the reader up – to make us feel that the world is not the place we thought it was. Here, for example, we meet a very ordinary young woman with the very extraordinary name of Damaris Tighe. She is the sort of girl we might meet in the pages of a Barbara Pym – a bit of a scholar, leading a spinsterly existence in a middle-class house in an English country village. But she is in fact in grave theological and spiritual error. Her 'subject' is the relationship between the angels of medieval philosophers and the Ideas and Forms in Plato. Her paper *The Eidoli and the Angeli* is not a suitable one to read to the little study group which meets in a neighbour's house: the group, it transpires, is actually in touch with the world of spirits. These people are not, like Damaris, dry-as-dust, unbelieving intellectuals. They are magicians and hierophants. The Eidoli and the Angeli have power to invade even dull suburban English houses. Damaris discovers that she has been guilty of intellectual sin in failing to believe, to realize imaginatively, the nature of the material she is studying. This is rather like the moment in Lewis's life when he described philosophy as a subject and Barfield replied that to Plato, philosophy was not a subject but a way. In *The Place of the Lion*, the Platonic archetypes of which objects and creatures in the world are but reflections or repetitions actually appear. A lion which at the beginning of the book seems as though it might just be an escaped animal from a nearby zoo turns out to be the great Lion of Strength. Perhaps the most extraordinary moment in the story is when the Butterfly appears and all the butterflies in the world, in a great swarm, are absorbed back into his essence.

Lewis was overwhelmed by reading this book. In the course of time, we begin to read Williams's influence in Lewis's own work – the Lion of Strength will reappear as Aslan, Judah's Lion, crushing the Serpent's Head in the Chronicles of Narnia, for example. The immediate impact in February 1936 was inner and self-disciplinary. 'The reading of it has been a good preparation for Lent as far as I am concerned: for it shows me (through the heroine) the special sin of abuse of intellect to which all my profession are liable, more clearly than I ever saw before. I have learned more than I ever knew about humility. In fact, it has been a big experience.'[3]

If Lewis had been learning more than he knew before about humility, Williams had been learning more than he knew before about medieval literature. At the very moment Lewis was finishing *The Place of the Lion*, Williams was reading *The Allegory of Love* with great admiration. 'I regard your book as practically the only one that I have ever come across, since Dante, that shows the slightest under-standing of what this very peculiar identity of love and religion means,' Williams wrote, signing himself 'Very gratefully yours'. The bulk of Lewis's book is pure literary history, though its earlier chapters refer to the strange pseudo-religion of Love which appears to have originated in twelfth-century Provence. But it is entirely characteristic of Williams, whose head was always buzzing with Dante, and with the dangerous borderlines between sacred and profane love, that he should have read *The Allegory* in that way.

Not long after this, Lewis and Williams met in London, as they continued to do at irregular intervals for the next three years. They really were very different types. Williams was emotionally exuberant, Lewis was profoundly buttoned up. Lewis was plump, and rather coarse in appearance; Williams, who has been unkindly likened to a monkey, was actually rather ethereal in manner, with his long fingers and piercing eyes. The ugly voice was not merely ugly; it was, by many accounts, half-hypnotic. But different as they were in appearance, temperament and background, they discovered in common a strong belief in the absolute reality of the supernatural world. It had been latent in Lewis ever since his encounter with God in Magdalen in the summer of 1929. But to meet Williams was to make the belief yet more inescapable.

Many readers of *The Place of the Lion* would be unable to convict the heroine of 'sin' at all. She is a modern woman, with a modern consciousness. How can we expect her to adopt the thought patterns of an earlier age? This problem of historical relativism is one of the most besetting for anyone who wishes to read an old book without either getting it hopelessly wrong or, worse, assuming that the fact that we are modern and the author of the book 'medieval' or 'old' implies the superiority of one or the other. Quite apart from the problem of the factual reliability of old books (is it so, for example, that there really *are* such *eidoli* and *angeli* as Williams, Abelard, Pseudo-Dionysus and Plato believed?), we meet, much earlier, the simple difficulty of adjusting to old meanings. Learning an old language – Middle English, Old French, Latin – is more than an exercise in matching modern word for old word. It often involves the modern mind's entering into old concepts for which there is no modern equivalent. What writers from past centuries believed about the world, the sky, themselves is often untranslatable, and we will never quite master it without the help of a guide. This was the task Lewis set himself. The Oxford lectures which he gave at this time were eventually to be published as *The Discarded Image*, perhaps the most completely satisfying and impressive book he ever published. One could wish it eight times as long, a great compendium like Burton's *Anatomy of Melancholy*. The subtitle of the book is *An Introduction to Medieval and Renaissance Literature*. But this is not a work of criticism, nor an attempt to make you like *The Faerie Queene* or the *Confessio Amantis*. It is a wide-ranging analysis of the world picture which almost all the old writers would have taken for granted but which we, our minds fed with different mythologies and sciences, would very easily mistake. How, for instance, did a medieval man look at the sky? Having early disposed of the false idea that in the Middle Ages people believed in a flat earth, Lewis tells us to look at the sky itself.

You must go out on a starry night and walk about for half an hour trying to see the sky in terms of the old (Ptolemaic) cosmology. Remember that you now have an absolute Up and Down. The Earth is really the centre, really the lowest place; movement to it from whatever direction is downward movement. As a modern, you located the stars at a great distance. For distance you must now substitute that very special, and far less abstract, sort of distance which we call height: height which speaks immediately to our muscles and nerves. The Medieval Model is vertiginous. And the fact that the height of the stars in medieval astronomy is very small compared with their distance in modern, will turn out not to have the kind of importance you anticipated ... To look out on the night sky with modern eyes is like looking about one in a trackless forest – trees forever and no horizon. To look up at the towering medieval universe is much more like looking at a great building. The 'space' of modern astronomy may arouse terror, or bewilderment or vague reverie; the spheres of the old writers present us with an object in which the mind can rest, overwhelming in its greatness but satisfying in its harmony. That is the sense in which our universe is romantic and theirs was classical.[4]

By the time we have finished his chapter called 'The Heavens', we have not only been informed about what the shape of the Ptolemaic universe was like, and how the belief in astrology worked, and how much knowledge was in our sense 'scientific' and how much 'poetic' or 'mythological'. We have actually had our picture of the universe changed for ever. By this, I do not mean that Lewis has represented the medieval picture as 'better' than the modern; but he has shown us that both are merely pictures. And in understanding the old picture so vividly, he has prepared us to appreciate, and to understand, many things which we either could not previously have hoped to understand, or which we had been looking at with half-open eyes. He enhances our sense not only of the poets' universe – the cosmology of Dante and Milton, for example – but also of the symbolism used by painters and architects. The past is still a foreign country, but we have been shown round it by the most genial and expert of guides. Such basic matters as what people believed about their own bodies – made up of humours – or their pasts are juxtaposed with fascinating excursions into such areas of belief as the fairies and mythical beasts. The range of reading and reference is prodigious. Almost the most enjoyable thing of all is Lewis's ability to find traces of the 'old world' – beliefs which go back to Isadore of Seville or Macrobius or even as far as Plato – surviving in the pages of Fielding, Johnson or Wordsworth. In *The Discarded Image* his omnivorous reading taste is best synthesized.

If 1936 was a sort of *annus mirabilis* for Jack, it was one of mixed happiness for Warnie. The more Jack was in demand, as a lecturer, teacher, and man of letters, the more danger there was that Warnie would be thrown back on his own society or, worse, on that of Mrs Moore. They really were not compatible, in spite of the affections they held in common. There were other loves besides the love of Jack which bound them together. At the end of January, for example, Warnie took Minto and Maureen to the Electra cinema to see the funeral of George V, and it was obvious that they were all much affected by it. A fortnight later came the emotionally more disturbing death of Minto's dog, Mr Papworth. He was fourteen years old, blind and hardly able to walk, but they had grown much attached to him and could hardly endure the thought of his death. In the last four days of his life, he could take nothing but whisky, administered to him by Warnie. Jack too felt a painful void – 'one remembers his old happy days, especially his puppyhood, with an ache', and for Minto it was grief 'as if for a human being'.[5] (They were eventually to get another dog – a very lively golden retriever, but before that Warnie had bought himself a boat.)

For J. R. R. Tolkien, the 1930s were a decade of continuous literary activity. Unlike Lewis, who tended to write out his stories or essays once, and only lightly revise them, Tolkien was a cautious and hesitant 'maker'. He was in a continual process of rewriting his material and revising his mythology. It would seem as though *The Hobbit*, for instance, the story which was to make him famous when it was published in 1937, had existed in embryonic form as early as about 1930. Lewis was shown a version in 1932 and admired it enormously. It was probably in 1937 that he and Tolkien had a conversation about their distaste for much of what was being published at that time. 'Tollers,' said Lewis, 'there is too little of what we really like in stories. I am afraid we shall have to try and write some ourselves.'[6]

It was agreed that Tolkien should write a story about time-travel, and Lewis one about space-travel. Tolkien's story, *The Lost Road*, seems to be the only example of his attempting to depict the twentieth century. It is the tale of a father and son, academics, both interested in legends and lost tales of the old world, Alboin and Audoin by name. In only a very few pages, we have left the twentieth century far behind and discovered that these two descend from the Lombardic heroes mentioned in the Old English poem *Widsith* (Aelfwin and Eadwin); and since Aelfwin means 'Elf-friend', we are not surprised to find ourselves drifting further back to the times when elves still walked the earth, before Numenor (the Atlantis of the Tolkien mythology) had sunk beneath the waves.

Sadly, *The Lost Road* only survives as a fragment, and its story line is at a rudimentary stage of evolution. There could be no greater indication of the contrast between the two friends' approach to their craft than a comparison between *The Lost Road*, tentatively built up stage by stage, with an infinite number of backward glances at the whole mythology that has gone before, and Lewis's self-confident brush strokes as he dashed off *Out of the Silent Planet*. The latter is a book in which the author is firing on all cylinders. It brings together Lewis the scholar, Lewis the voracious reader of anything from medieval schoolmen or Italian epic to modern science fiction, Lewis the Christian apologist, Lewis the Irish satirist in the savage tradition of Swift, Lewis the failed Romantic poet. 'Thus skidding violently from one side to the other, his youth approached the moment at which he would begin to be a person.'

It is the story of a philologist (said to be loosely based on Tolkien, but in fact fairly unlike him: Tolkien recognized some of his own opinions and ideas Lewisified in the character) who, by a series of mishaps on a walking tour, comes to a house where two sinister scientists, Weston and Devine, are planning a visit to outer space. They have everything ready except a human being to accompany them on their voyage. They are going to a planet called Malecandra (which turns out to be Mars) and, having made a previous recce there, they are under the impression that the inhabitants are fierce and eat men. Hence their need for a human companion to placate the natives on their arrival.

Out of the Silent Planet is a book which is quite un-put-downable.

The freshness of the writing reflects the boyish excitement with which Lewis wrote it and read it aloud, chapter by chapter, to his circle of friends. Into the excitement is woven a tragic sense of the Fall, both as something Romantically conceived (the ruin of the earth, of Man's relationship with the beasts, of the erotic life) and as straight Christian theology. The theology does not wage war on the story. The *eldils*, the angelic beings who are at first invisible to Ransom, and their hierarchic sense of obedience are introduced gently. And the sheer incidentals, the imagined languages of the Martian creatures, the poetic *hrossi*, the intellectual *sorns* and the practical and commercially minded *pfifltriggs* have a playful quality which, while being purely enjoyable, is not without satiric edge.

Many of the linguistic elements are borrowed from Tolkien and – which must have been more exasperating for their originator – changed and got 'wrong'. Lewis's *eldils*, for instance, are little more than the angels of Judaeo-Christian tradition; but by confusing them linguistically with Tolkien's *eldalie* (in *The Silmarillion*), he implies that the elves of that mythology are angelic, which they are not – they are simply elves. Any irritation Tolkien felt at this appropriation of his own imaginative world did not prevent him from doing his best for the book. Since it had been a great success when read aloud to 'our local club',[7] Tolkien had absolute confidence in submitting it to the publisher of *The Hobbit*, Stanley Unwin. Tolkien's letter reveals that in the original draft of the story the hero is called not Ransom but Unwin ('The latter detail could I am sure be altered'). Ransom, the name finally arrived at, develops its own significance in the sequels to *Out of the Silent Planet*.

Stanley Unwin turned the book down. It had already been shown by Lewis to Dent, publisher of *Dymer*, who rejected it. Unwin did, however, pass the typescript to a small publishing company called The Bodley Head. They accepted it and it was swiftly published, appearing before the end of 1938.

It received high praise, often from surprising quarters. 'Here is a very good book,' declared that sentimental realist Hugh Walpole. 'It is of thrilling interest as a story, but it is more than that; it is a kind of poem, and it has the great virtue of improving as it goes on. It is a unique thing, full of stars, cold and heat, flowers of the planets and a sharp sardonic humour.' Walpole himself, after a spell of agnosticism, had returned to Christian belief in middle age. The Lewisian thing about the first of his space stories is precisely its blend of literary originality and religious truth; it is not 'theology' dressed up as 'literature'; rather it makes its best literary effects when it is at its most religious because the religious matter is what most engages the author's imagination. In this, Lewis resembles two of his favourite authors, Edmund Spenser and George MacDonald. The Muses have been traditionally at war with Christ, ever since the period of late classical antiquity, when Jerome and Augustine both viewed literary excellence with the gravest suspicion. Lewis is one of those very rare writers whose Muse appears to be an *anima naturaliter Christiana*. There have been plenty of good writers who were also Christians. Plenty of Christians have tried their hand at putting their beliefs into prose or poetry, usually with calamitous aesthetic results. There have been very few with the gift of Dante or John Milton, who have written at their best when being most Christian. It was to this great tradition, though as a self-confessedly very junior follower, that Lewis quite easily and naturally belonged. This did not mean that he was above sacrificing aesthetic principle – if there is such a thing, and if he had it – to the purely partisan pleasures of *Morte aux païens*.

Dante could turn aside from his most sublime passages of religious contemplation to hone a gratuitous insult for the benefit of Florentine families whom he happened to dislike. Milton, who sang of God and his angels, was equally happy slinging mud at bishops. Tolkien and Lewis, in some of the same spirit, decided to make a party issue out of the election to the Oxford Chair of Poetry in 1938.

Unlike other professors at Oxford, the Professor of Poetry is elected by the MAs of the University: that is to say, not only by the dons, but also by all the old members of the University who have paid the appropriate fees and undergone, either in person or *in absentia*, a short ceremony in the Sheldonian Theatre. Although there have been some famous poets who occupied this chair (for example Matthew Arnold and W. H. Auden), it has much more commonly been occupied by dons; and the point at issue when choosing candidates for the Chair of Poetry has very seldom been their views about the subject on which they are supposed to lecture, still less their competence to do so. One day over breakfast, the chaplain of Magdalen, Adam Fox, opened his newspaper and saw that Sir Edmund Chambers was being put up as a candidate for the Chair of Poetry. He described him as 'a retired civil servant who has made Shakespeare his hobby'.[8] In this Fox was simply showing his ignorance. Though indeed he had been a civil servant, Chambers was one of the foremost literary scholars in England. His books *The Medieval Stage* and *The Elizabethan Stage* remain classics of literary history, and in their range and period there are few better anthologies of verse than his *Early English Lyrics* and *Oxford Book of Sixteenth Century Verse*. He had lately come to live in a village called Eynsham, near Oxford, he was a D.Litt. of his old university, and all this Lewis must have known. Nevertheless, when Fox made the preposterous statement that 'This is simply shocking, they might as well make me Professor of Poetry,' Lewis responded, 'Well, we will.'

It is hard, at this distance of time, to see what his motives were, apart from the mere love of a fight for its own sake, and the desire to promote one of his friends. If E. K. Chambers could be suspected of being dull and pedantic, what were Fox's qualities? He had published one 'long and childlike' (his own words) poem called *Old King Cole* and he had won the sacred poem prize (in another competition open to all MAs of the University). He was no orator. He had nothing much to say about poetry. He was a grotesquely inappropriate choice. Nevertheless, Lewis put up Fox to stand against Chambers, and his gang of friends rallied to Fox's support. This had its (presumably) desired effect of annoying a lot of other dons. They, guided by the strong impression in 'literary' circles that Chambers was an old bore and Fox was a non-starter, put up their own candidate, Lord David Cecil, a friend of Lewis's, as it happened, and the English tutor at New College.

But no quarrel in England is ever about what it seems to be about. Although David Cecil was and always had been a devout Christian, he became the favourite candidate of those who resented the 'clerical candidate', the man who had been put up by Lewis, just because he was a Christian. So the literary set, many of them agnostic or hostile to religion, ranged behind Lord David, while those who had already committed themselves, together with those who esteemed him as a scholar, voted for E. K. Chambers. This was a situation which the Ulsterman in Lewis relished. For the time being, he ceased to be a cloistered academic and became once more the son of the police-court solicitor in Belfast, the city where the most popular political slogan at election times was 'Vote early, vote often'. Lewis knew well that most of the dons would vote for David Cecil or E. K. Chambers. They would thereby split the opposition. All he needed to do was to collect the votes of the majority of MAs who had left the University. By putting up a clergyman as a candidate, he could rely on the vote of hundreds of MAs who, sitting in their country rectories, could easily be persuaded by a judiciously worded letter that their old University was falling into the hands of infidels. A vote for Fox became, absurdly, a vote for the Church, a vote for Orthodoxy, a vote for all the things which Lewis now 'stood for'. In staunch Irish fashion, he laid on transport for Fox's supporters to be 'bused' into Oxford on the appropriate days and rewarded them for their votes with meals and refreshments at Magdalen. Fox was a nice man, much liked among a wide circle of his fellow-clergy. He romped home.

The election did much to harm Lewis's reputation in Oxford. The dons felt that he could not be trusted: that he was populist, bullying, showy, and hostile to them. By his campaign for Fox, Lewis probably destroyed his own chances of promotion in the University, even though he was very obviously the most distinguished member of the English Faculty.

It is certainly easy for those who did not belong to Lewis's group of friends, and who merely come upon the record of it in after days, to see its faults. Chief among them, and born of the group's increasing feeling that they stood for something, embattled against a hostile world, was their tendency not only to see merit where none existed (in the poetry of Fox, for example), but actually to think that belonging to the group – which began at around this period to be known as the Inklings – was in itself a sort of merit. One gets the feeling from Warnie's diary, for example, that it was better to be a good Inkling than a good poet, or even a good man. The most exaggerated example of this (it was the dangerous tendency which Jack himself labelled the 'Inner Ring') was when they attended a production of *Hamlet* at the New Theatre in Oxford, produced – as were so many great Oxford University Dramatic Society productions in the middle years of this century – by Nevill Coghill. 'What dramatic merit the play had', Warnie noted afterwards, 'seemed to have been supplied by Coghill and not by Shakespeare.' Shakespeare, one realizes, had the supreme misfortune not to be an Inkling. One gets the strong feeling that he would not (in the unlikely event of his standing as a candidate) have stood much chance of becoming Professor of Poetry at Oxford if Lewis and Tolkien had had anything to do with it. Though Fox was never to give a distinguished lecture, his friends were triumphant. He had defeated, as Tolkien boasted to his publisher, 'a Knight and a noble Lord. He was nominated by Lewis and myself, and miraculously elected: our first public victory over established privilege. For Fox is a member of our literary club of *practising poets* before whom *The Hobbit*, and other works (such as *the Silent Planet*) have been read.'[9] That was certainly one way of looking at things.

The original Inklings club had been started by an undergraduate at University College, and broke up in 1933. This was a literary dining club, to which Tolkien and Lewis had both, on different occasions, been invited as guests. Little by little, Lewis, with his passion for nicknames, adopted this one to describe his own circle of friends. It was never a formal club with minutes, or apologies for absence, or any 'business' or recognizable membership. Yet, as Tolkien remarked, 'it was a pleasantly ingenious pun in its way, suggesting people with vague or half-formed intimations and ideas plus those who dabble in ink.'[10]

In this way, another Oxford legend was born. It would be a mistake, however, even when the intimacy between Lewis and Tolkien was at its strongest, to believe that this was the only thing in both their lives. Tolkien always had close family ties in which Lewis had no wish to be involved. Knowing Tolkien to have his difficulties, maritally speaking, the two Lewis brothers stayed away; and Lewis, who disliked sharing spoken intimacies with friends, never allowed the conversation to develop if Tolkien tried to speak of his troubles. On one occasion when Tolkien tore a ligament playing squash, and was told that he would be confined to his bed for ten weeks, Lewis went to see him – but, as Warnie recorded, he 'found Madame [i.e. Tolkien's wife] there, so could not have much conversation with him'. The Tolkien children were invited to swim and punt on Lewis's lake at The Kilns, but there was nothing in the way of a 'family friendship' between the two. Indeed, Lewis was always impatient with 'Tollers' if he pleaded family commitments as a reason for not attending an Inklings evening.

Lewis, for his part, had *his* own private world which he did not share with the Inklings. There was the whole, and very important, world of his friendship with animals. A large part of his pleasure derived from walking holidays, when he could put Oxford, college politics and the routines of work behind him. There were many such tours in the pre-war years, often taken with Barfield, sometimes with Warnie, sometimes both. Between 2 January and 6 January 1939, for example, the brothers walked forty-two miles in the Welsh Marches (i.e. borders – from the Old English *mearc*), and rounded them off with a stay in Great Malvern. The trip awakened many boyhood memories, and Warnie remarked that they might do worse than spend their declining years there. Jack readily agreed. It was a peculiar exchange to take place between men in full vigour, aged forty and forty-four respectively. It is as though they could not wait to sink into a dotage spent in permanent contemplation of their childhood. The in-between bits – what some call life – seemed by such standards to be so much waste of time, which they could not be done with fast enough. To beguile some of the time in Malvern, they went to the cinema. The Lewis brothers were not great cinema-goers, and there were few films in the 1930s which they viewed with enjoyment. Noël Coward's *Cavalcade*, for example, though Jack could see its merit, struck him as fundamentally cheap, 'a mere brutal assault on one's emotions, using material which one can't help feeling intensely. It appeals entirely to that part of you which lives in the throat and chest, leaving the spirit untouched.' A film which apparently did touch the spirit was *King Kong*, though we do not know whether Jack found it quite as exciting as Warnie did: 'There were astounding represen-tations of the various prehistoric monsters,' Warnie confided breathlessly to his diary. 'How they were done I cannot imagine . . .'

For their third cinematic adventure of the decade (unless one counts the showing of George V's funeral), they booked tickets at the cinema in Great Malvern to see Walt Disney's *Snow White and the Seven Dwarfs*. It turned out to be 'first rate . . . It was well worth going to if only for the scene of the spring cleaning of the dwarfs' house. We came out into a lovely night: the effect of the quiet town, in the moonlight, with the snowclad hills behind is one that I shan't soon forget,' wrote Warnie. It was an evening of blissful happiness for Jack's brother, a return to boyhood, those beloved 'Malvern days when it was just the two of us against the P'daytabird'.[11] This was the last walking holiday the two brothers were ever to take together.

Warnie, though he was by all accounts a most delightful and courteous companion, was a clear case of arrested development. Emotionally, he was imprisoned in his boyhood, the only difference being that the whiskey bottle was substituted for cream buns and lemon pop as the greatest imaginable treat. With Jack, however, things were less simple; we come once more to Barfield's worry that there was something affected about the younger brother's attitudes and poses. Certainly, there is no inherent virtue in having read all the latest books, nor in following intellectual fads and trends. But if, as William Empson (no ally) believed, Lewis was 'the best read man of his generation, one who read everything and remembered everything he read', there is something a little disappointing in such a man rejoicing in the limitations of his sympathy. On one level, it is quite a good joke in the decade of Brecht's *Der Gute Mensch von Sezuan* to be relishing the washing-up scene in *Snow White and the Seven Dwarfs*; in the decade of Sartre's *La Nausée* and (as far as English publication was concerned) Joyce's *Ulysses*, to be whooping with delight at the reprint of *Adventures of Tom Pippin* by Roland Zuiz.[12] Where this is born of genuine enthusiasm, well and good. But Lewis's friends sensed, from this period onwards, something which had begun half as a tease hardening into an attitude. David Cecil, an omnivorous and generous-hearted reader, was almost always unable to persuade Lewis to like books written by 'moderns'. Although Lewis had read Kafka and Virginia Woolf, the virtues of Proust or D. H. Lawrence or T. S. Eliot were virtues he delighted in being unable to see. One picks up a suggestion of this position calcifying into something more like the outlook of a crusty old gentleman in a club in a letter he wrote in June 1938 to Barfield. In one paragraph, he makes some perfectly reasonable objections to his pupils' and colleagues' remoteness from life. In the next he moves to crustiness:

They keep sheep in Magdalen grove now, and I hear the fleecy care bleating all day long: I am shocked to find that none of my pupils, though they are all acquainted with pastoral poetry, regards them as anything but a nuisance: and one of my colleagues has been heard to ask why sheep have their wool cut off.[13]

This is all splendid and we are on Lewis's side. But then he goes on:

> It frightens me, almost. And so it did the other night, when I heard two undergrads, giving a list of pleasures which were (a) Nazi, (b) leading to homosexuality. They were: feeling the wind in your hair, walking with bare feet on the grass, and bathing in the rain. Think it over: it gets worse the longer you look at it.

It is twenty-two years since I read that letter, first published in Warnie's selection of his brother's correspondence, and on and off I have been thinking it over. At no time have I been able to see anything either Nazi or necessarily homosexual in the listed pleasures, which are precisely of the kind which might occur in a George MacDonald fantasy. But the pleasures are, of course, those of youth, and Lewis at the age of forty seems to have forgotten what it was like to be young. He sees exuberant, and perhaps sensual, pleasure in the natural world, of the kind which he once described so lyrically in letters to Arthur Greeves (there is in fact a letter about bathing in the rain at Parson's Pleasure); now such stuff seems to him 'Nazi'.

If this misgiving about Lewis is at all fair (the sense of a carapace hardening upon him), then one must also view with ambivalence his excursion into the realm of religious apologetics.

Ashley Sampson was the owner of a small London publishing house, which ran a series called 'Christian Challenge'. Knowing of Lewis's philosophical training and Christian sympathy, and admiring his two published prose works, he asked if Lewis would be prepared to undertake a 40,000-word contribution to the series. The subject proposed was *The Problem of Pain*. As Lewis tells us in the preface to the published version of this book, his initial reaction was to wish for anonymity, 'since if I were to say what I really thought about pain, I should be forced to make statements of such apparent fortitude that they would become ridiculous if anyone knew who made them'. Sampson, however, insisted that Lewis should put his name to anything which was written, and in the course of 1939 he set to work. The book was finished and completed the following year. It is a book which vigorously displays, from its opening paragraphs, all Lewis's strengths and weaknesses as a religious apologist.

Most disconcerting, to those who love *The Discarded Image*, is the apparent cheerfulness with which he abandons the depth and range of his historical imagination in favour of a style of rhetoric which seems more reminiscent of the Belfast police courts. What is so troubling is that the *Discarded Image* Lewis is there beside the bullying rhetorician, and we do not know which of them is going to speak next. 'Lay down this book and reflect for five minutes on the fact that all the great religions were first preached, and long practised, in a world without Chloroform.' That is *The Discarded Image* self, usefully prodding our imaginations into seeing things from a proper perspective. And this self, in the introductory chapter, is surely right to suggest that moral sense and a sense of the numinous do not come naturally – as some anthropological dismissals of religion might suggest – from some crude pre-scientific attempt to explain the universe. The universe, viewed in those pre-chloroform days, was dark and painful and horrible, and wherever else the human race derived its image of a loving, moral creator, it was not from a simple contemplation of nature. But then comes a statement about Christ which seems to emanate not from a rational clever man trying to help us to understand things more clearly, but from a rhetorical trickster who is not thinking at all.

> There was a man born among these Jews who claimed to be, or to be the son of, or to be one with the something which is at once the awful haunter of Nature and the giver of the moral law. The claim is so shocking – a paradox and even a horror, which we may easily be lulled into taking too lightly – that only two views of this man are possible. Either he was a raving lunatic of an unusually abominable type or else He was, and is, precisely what He said. There is no middle way. If the records make the first hypothesis unacceptable, then you must submit to the second.[14]

Since a version of this argument was repeated in his broadcast talks and made a linchpin of Lewis's defence of Christianity, it may be profitable to lay down our books for five minutes as he urged us to do when thinking of a world without chloroform and meditate on what he has laid before us.

Let us keep our meditation simple by discounting various facts which do not seem to have crossed Lewis's mind at this point: the fact, for example, that most of Christ's Jewish contemporaries did not believe in His divinity or join the newly founded Christian Church or sect. Did Lewis therefore suppose that they were all very stupid, or damnably wicked? Neither alternative is particularly probable or palatable.

Let us concentrate rather on the last sentence of the paragraph quoted and work our way back through the foregoing *non sequiturs*. 'If the records make the first hypothesis unacceptable . . .'

The Discarded Image is a book which was written by a man with an unusual sensitivity to the differences between past and present. The men and women of the past saw the same physical universe that we did, but their way of seeing it was quite different; their way of describing it in written form more different still. This does not mean that the old books can provide us with no concrete evidence from the past, but it does mean that old books must be read with delicacy; with a sense that if we go blundering into them, assuming that they mean what we mean by words like *sky*, *earth*, *history* or *nature* we shall get everything wrong. If we read the book in *their* way – whether we are reading Dante, or Chaucer, or Isadore of Seville – we will get something from it. The more we soak up their way of looking at things, their method of understanding, the more we shall get. Read it in our way and we shall merely be, as Lewis says in the preface to *The Discarded Image*, like 'travellers who carry their resolute Englishry with them all over the Continent, mix only with other English tourists, enjoy all they see for its "quaintness" and have no wish to realise what those ways of life, those churches, those vineyards mean to the natives'.[15] As an apologist, he seems totally blind to the fact that the New Testament is just such a collection of old books, which require, if we are to understand them aright, patience and a willingness to listen to scholars who have meditated for a long time on the nature of the (often quite puzzling and contradictory) material which they contain.

Lewis's claim that 'the records' give us a stark choice about Christ – either he was a 'raving lunatic' or else 'He was, and is, precisely what He said' – is startling, to say the least. To what 'records' is he referring? Different books of the New Testament have different ways of describing the indescribable, that is, the nature of Christ, and the first three centuries of Christendom are a history of ceaseless dispute among the most learned doctors of the Church as to what this nature was, and how it was made manifest during the period of the Incarnation. This is not to deny the truth of orthodox Christian belief. It is to point out that there is nowhere in existence a set of 'records' which could prove that Christ was either a lunatic or 'precisely what He said' He was. The Epistles of St Paul and the Apocalyptic Book of Revelation contain many high and mystical expressions of belief about Christ but they cannot be described as 'records' of the kind which would compel rational belief. If they were, the world would simply be divided into a majority of believing Christians and a small handful of people who were either too stupid or too wicked to accept something which was obvious and clear-cut. But the nature and being of Christ are not made obvious and clear-cut even in the pages of the New Testament. Even if we accept only the four gospels as 'the records' for the purposes of Lewis's argument, we have to see that they present a differing picture. The Fourth Gospel, for example, does not *lie* when it puts into the mouth of Christ words, and whole patterns of speech, which we do not find on His lips in the first three gospels. But it does, by this convention, proclaim itself to be a book of a special kind, one designed to proclaim what the faithful believe about Christ, not necessarily a book which is straight narrative history in the modern mode. The first three gospels contain no reference to Christ's having made any such great discourses as fill chapters 13–16 of St John, and since it seems unlikely that the author of the Gospel took notes during the utterance of this sublime discourse, we have to assume them to be a literary creation. Not a lie, but a creation of what the author believed to be more true than verbatim records.

It follows that behind every statement we make about the historical Jesus there has to be a tacit qualification: 'We are told this by such-and-such an evangelist, writing in a particular literary mode, for a particular audience, in a particular place at a particular period of history.' You cannot, in isolation from church doctrine, and in isolation from the plain facts of literary history, say that Jesus said this thing or that thing. If you do, you find yourself faced with unedifying alternatives such as those which Lewis proposes. All we have is what the Gospels say that He said. Precisely what these differing accounts *mean* by such phrases as 'Son of Man', or even 'Son of God', cannot be translated into our own modern thought processes without some *Discarded Image*-style readjustments of sympathy. And besides that, we discover in the various Gospels quite differing accounts of the earthly Christ's reticence about Himself. The famous 'secrecy' of the Messiah in St Mark's Gospel, for instance ('See thou say nothing to any man'), does not really fit into either of Lewis's categories of raving lunatic or self-proclaimed Divinity.

The curious thing is that Lewis, though so very widely read in other areas, had read almost no works of biblical scholarship. The revolution in New Testament scholarship which had come about during the hundred years before he wrote *The Problem of Pain* appears to have passed him by. Perhaps in one sense it does not matter that he ignored the sometimes vandalistic assaults on the gospel texts by Form-critics and Redaction-critics; just as it could be seen not to matter that the school of philosophy in which he was reared had been rendered more or less obsolete by the man who – in the year that Lewis was writing *The Problem of Pain* – had become a professor of philosophy at Cambridge: Ludwig Wittgenstein. What is so odd, though, is that Lewis was tempted to *argue* the faith, to analyse and defend it in a manner at once so roughshod and so cerebral when it had come to him by quite other means. The philosophy of Wittgenstein did not destroy the faith – it destroyed certain methods of nineteenth-century Idealist argument. The new biblical critics did not destroy the faith: they merely forced on intelligent people the distinction between history and church doctrine. Neither philosophy nor textual criticism, however, had led Lewis to the faith. He had been led to it by his experience of the numinous, and by the exercise of his imagination. Above all, he had been led to it by the discovery that story, myth, could not only carry truth, but also *be* truth. Surely the corollary of his great 'mythopoeia' discussion with Dyson and Tolkien was that the story of Christ was much more important than any doctrine which a fallible or fallen human mind could extract from it? Trying to define, or speaking as if it were possible to define, 'precisely what He meant' by saying who He was, was a sort of profanity.

Yet of course it was not meant profanely. *The Problem of Pain* was written with the best of intentions. Lewis felt that he must put all his talents to the service of God. This led him to suppose that his capacity to argue a case was a talent which, quite as much as his imagination and his literary taste, must be consecrated. And in the context of the time, there was a sort of heroism in this. Lewis was fully aware of the fact that there was a purely irrational intellectual snobbery abroad in England at that time, more powerful than any genuine intellectual stumbling-block to faith. When one sees that it was this snobbery which he set out to attack, it is possible to understand why he set about the delicate problem of pain in so breezy a fashion. Similarly, when one reads the dedication of *The Problem of Pain* – 'to the Inklings' – one understands some of its short-cuts, as well as some of its more peculiar turns of phrase (e.g. of the Incarnation – 'It has the master touch – the rough, male taste of reality.'). This was a book which began life as chapters to be read aloud to like-minded male friends. It was brief, pithy and, like everything Lewis wrote in prose, hugely readable. None of that small band of men who sat round smoking and drinking their beer or whisky could have had any idea, as they heard Jack vigorously defending the doctrine of hell in nine pages, that the publication of these religious speculations, pieced together at a busy time between giving lectures and examining, was to change his destiny forever. They would certainly have been completely astonished to learn, as would the author, that *The Problem of Pain* would become a great commercial success. By the time it came out, in any case, all their lives had been irrevocably altered by the progress of world events.

There is one encounter worth mentioning before we bring to an end this account of Lewis in 1939. Some time during the course of that summer, Dr Havard introduced Lewis to the Roman Catholic Chaplain to the University, Monsignor Ronald Knox. One would have assumed that as two classicists, *Punch* contributors and men of letters of an old-fashioned Christian temper, Lewis and Knox would have known each other for years. But Knox, who was the most brilliant orator of his generation at Oxford – star of the Union, wit, punster in tongues ancient and modern – had left Oxford before the end of the First World War to become a Roman Catholic, and after his return there as chaplain to the Catholics, it was perhaps understandable that he should have kept a low profile. Lewis greeted him warmly with the assertion that he was possibly the wittiest man in Europe. Knox modestly demurred, but the meeting was said to be happy and humorous. Perhaps they might have developed into friends. Though Lewis was not friendly to Catholicism, the two men had much more of a playful kind in common. Both enjoyed 'bad' literature – in Knox's case, the poetry of Ella Wheeler Wilcox, in Lewis's the novels of Amanda McKittrick Ros. Both were brilliant parodists. Both liked spontaneous rhyming. Their friendship, however, was not to be. Within a few weeks of their meeting, England was at war. Knox had gone into the country to translate the Vulgate into English and Lewis was being prepared by an unseen providence for war work no less surprising.

THIRTEEN

SCREWTAPE
1939–1942

'This is a fallen world,' J. R. R. Tolkien wrote to one of his sons early in the Second World War. 'The world has been "going to the bad" all down the ages.'[1] Wars tend to prompt religious reawakening in a populace. Although, as Lewis remarked in a wartime sermon, all individuals face the ultimate realities all the time, war quickens and sharpens our awareness. When everyone in the country lives with the prospect of having their house destroyed by a bomb during the night, the Christian talk of Armageddon seems less fanciful than in the 'weak piping times of peace'. Those who in peacetime seemed brave or merely quaint for believing in all those old doctrines found themselves in wartime much in demand, some as evangelists, some as prophets, some as teachers.

The immediate consequence of the outbreak of war was that Lewis found his circle of friends broken up and changing. The Useless Quack joined the Navy and grew a gingery beard, which enabled Lewis (always anxious to invent fresh *sobriquets* for his friends) to label him the Red Admiral. Warnie, though forty-one, was recalled to active service, given the rank of major, and sent to France, where he remained until the evacuation from Dunkirk. Most of the friends were too old or too physically enfeebled to be capable of offering themselves for military glory. Dyson had a club foot; Lewis still had shrapnel in his lung. They, Tolkien and Coghill stayed in Oxford and when need arose worked as ARP wardens.

The life of the University both did and did not go on. Young men still came up to the colleges, but they reminded Lewis of his own position in 1917, when his glimpse of Oxford life was just a prelude to the horrors of battle.

The war had its compensations. Not the least of these was that the

Oxford University Press moved out of London, and took most of its remaining employees to Oxford. Among them was Charles Williams, who rather surprisingly left his wife and child behind to brave the Blitz in their Hampstead flat while he and his beloved secretary Celia came to take up their (separate) residences in Oxford. He claimed that Lewis was the only person in Oxford whom he really saw, but this was the reverse of the truth. It may have been largely thanks to Lewis that Williams became something of a cult figure, idolized by pious lady dons, aspirant mystics and others. He had real charm, which made canny figures such as Tolkien distrust him. Lewis was bowled over by him, and was anxious that as many people as possible should have the benefit of his wisdom. It was the strange circumstance of wartime which enabled Lewis to put Williams forward as a lecturer in the English Faculty. They needed teachers, and Williams was an experienced public speaker at WEA lectures and evening classes. His lectures on Milton were first given in the beautiful fifteenth-century Divinity Schools, underneath the Bodleian Library. The audience packed this room to capacity.

It was certainly not what undergraduates at Oxford had come to expect from a lecturer. Many were surprised by Williams's appearance, which was simian and scarlet-faced, slightly boozy. The cockney voice was declamatory, hierophantic. It was more like being present at a seance than at a lecture. He held a copy of Milton's works in his hands, but whenever he quoted from the poet he held the book aloft, like the Gospel at High Mass, sometimes going so far as to wave it to and fro behind his head as he chanted out the words. The first lecture was on *Comus* (subsequent talks on Milton had to move to the large lecture-room at the Taylorian Institute, the Divinity Schools being too small). *Comus* is a masque in which a young lady's chastity is tried and not vanquished. Some of those who attended the lecture have implied to me that not everyone took it particularly seriously. There were even giggles as this (as he seemed to some of them) funny little man with a funny voice urged the audience to abstain from fleshly lusts.[2] But we see what we want to see, and for Lewis this performance by Williams was a revelation.

There we elders heard what we had despaired of hearing – a lecture on *Comus* which placed its importance where the poet placed it –

and watched 'the yonge fresshe folkes he or she' who filled the benches listening first with incredulity, then with toleration, and finally with delight, to something so strange and new in their experience as the praise of chastity.[3]

The lecture, and Williams's conversation, turned Lewis's own thoughts to Milton. In the second year of the war, he was asked to deliver some lectures at Bangor – the University College, North Wales – and he chose as his theme Milton's *Paradise Lost*. The lectures, which were subsequently published as *A Preface to 'Paradise Lost'*, represent Lewis at his very best. If someone had never read Lewis before, and wished to get a taste of him, there would be no better book with which to start. In its asides – quite apart from what he tells us about Milton – we see what it was about Lewis which struck W. T. Kirkpatrick as so remarkable, and which made him such a valued teacher and friend to so many people in the course of his life. Here is evidence of a mind abundantly stocked with reading which the author has enjoyed – effortlessly, intelligently, and selflessly enjoyed – and he wishes to communicate this enjoyment to us. The range is so impressive – everything from Lucretius to *Tristram Shandy*, from Virgil to Kinglake, from Beowulf to T. S. Eliot has been absorbed, not for the sake of being bookish but always – one feels – in an outward-looking manner. There is a great moral self-confidence and a common sense in the writing – as when he offers one possible explanation for why so many people, reading *Paradise Lost*, have supposed Satan to be the 'hero'.

> To make a character worse than oneself it is only necessary to release imaginatively from control some of the bad passions which, in real life, are always straining at the leash; the Satan, the Iago, the Becky Sharp, within each of us, is always there and only too ready, the moment the leash is slipped, to come out and have in our books that holiday we try to deny them in life.[4]

There is, too, a constantly intelligent conversational quality about the writing which makes one see how very good his talk must have been. One thinks of him saying, of the *Odyssey*, 'The poem is an adventure story. As far as greatness of subject goes, it is much closer to *Tom*

Jones or *Ivanhoe* than to the *Aeneid* or the *Gierusalemme Liberata*.' Or, apropos of the necessity of having a good historical imagination when reading, 'I had much rather know what I should feel like if I adopted the beliefs of Lucretius than how Lucretius would have felt if he had never entertained them.' On a purely aesthetic level, one is frequently haunted by his (at first sight paradoxical) defence of Milton's preference for Hebrew over Greek lyrics. 'But if any man will read aloud on alternate mornings for a single month a page of Pindar and a page of the Psalms in any translation he chooses, I think I can guess which he will first grow tired of.'[5]

So much for the asides – but how good is Lewis on the subject he sets himself – on Milton? I think I have read most of what was written by or about him in English between the seventeenth century and, say, 1975. There are not many better books than Lewis's. The passages on Milton and St Augustine, Milton and angels, Milton's theology, are all first-rate. He has done more theological 'homework' here than he did for some of his own religious books, and it shows, even though learning was never more lightly worn. Moreover the basic picture of Milton himself, though only sketched in very lightly, is completely authentic:

> He is a neat, dainty man, 'the lady of Christ's'; a fastidious man, pacing in *trim* gardens. He is a grammarian, a swordsman, a musician with a predilection for the fugue. Everything that he greatly cares about demands order, proportion, measure and control. In poetry he considers decorum the grand masterpiece. In politics he is that which of all things least resembles a democrat – an aristocratic republican who thinks 'nothing more agreeable to the order of nature or more for the interest of mankind than that the less should yield to the greater, not in numbers but in wisdom and virtue'.[6]

An extraordinarily high proportion of Milton scholars have chosen to disregard these truths about their subject, and have decided that because Milton was on the side of the regicides this made him a revolutionary and, because a revolutionary, therefore a man of the Left, perhaps even an agonized Marxist, or at least a sympathizer with the Diggers and Levellers of his own day. The less biographical or historical evidence there is for this view of Milton, the more the scholars believe it, producing readings of *Paradise Lost* which ignore Lewis's golden rule, 'You must, so far as in you lies, become an Achaean chief while reading Homer, a medieval knight while reading Malory, and an Eighteenth Century Londoner while reading Johnson. Only thus will you be able to judge the work "in the same spirit that its author writ".'[7] Lewis does present in his *Preface to 'Paradise Lost'* a very convincing impression of having read the poem which John Milton set out to write and meant us to read. If that seems like faint praise, you should read the dozen most recent books on *Paradise Lost*.

Very little *criticism* as such survives the generation in which it is written. The same is true, incidentally, of most philosophy and theology. Those who practise these branches of study often mistake them for spheres of knowledge when they are more accurately seen as examples of dialectic or rhetoric – ideas which may be better aired in talk. All critics, however dispassionate, bring to their subject thick encrustations of personal prejudice and, which they are probably even less well equipped to notice, assumptions which are attributable to the spirit of the age. Lewis's debate in the *Preface* with other Milton critics – with Saurat, Eliot, I. A. Richards or Leavis – all seems pretty dead to us now, since not many people would read any of the aforementioned critics nowadays as *critics* unless they were interested in the history of criticism for its own sake. What makes Lewis's criticism rather different is a combination of two very rare qualities. One is contained in the sentence which is most often mocked in the *Preface to 'Paradise Lost'*: 'A schoolboy who reads a page of Milton by chance, for the first time, and then looks up and says "By Gum", not in the least knowing how the thing has worked, but only that new strength and width and brightness and zest have transformed his world, is nearer to the truth [than the critics].'[8] Lewis never lost his schoolboyish sense of wonder and enjoyment. It is what makes him such a refreshing literary historian. He was not ashamed of the 'By Gum' school of reading. What we also notice in the chapters dealing with the Fall, and in particular with Adam and Eve, is that this is not just a book by a scholar in a library. It is also a reading of Milton by a creative intelligence. In stories of great temptation, of interplanetary flights, wrestlings with the powers of good and evil, Lewis found something which had already engaged his own pen, and would continue to do so.

Not least among the new friendships which Lewis formed during the war was his friendship with an Anglican nun called Sister Penelope (Lawson) of the Community of St Mary the Virgin at Wantage. She was eight years Lewis's senior, and a woman of high intellectual abilities. Richard Hunt, former Keeper of Western Manuscripts at the Bodleian Library and a considerable Medieval Latinist himself, once told me that he thought Sister Penelope the best translator from Latin in her generation. It was not, however, of learned matters that she first wrote to Lewis but of science fiction. She had enjoyed *Out of the Silent Planet*. 'At ordinary times we do not read novels at all, as you may imagine, but the right novel at the right moment can have a real spiritual value.' In return for a book of her own – *God Persists* – Lewis sent Sister Penelope *The Pilgrim's Regress*, and she noted his acerbic satire on High Anglicans. He admitted to her, 'I'm not . . . what you call high. To me the real distinction is not high and low, but between religion with a real supernaturalism and salvationism on the one hand and all watered-down modernist versions on the other.'

This sounds like a true distinction, but in real life things are a little different. An Anglican may not wish to be seduced into all the absurdities of church politics, still less into the hobby of church ceremonial. But the distinctions between 'high' and 'low' in so far as they are doctrinal do of necessity affect devotional practice. An instance had arisen on a walking tour Jack and Warnie took in Derbyshire in 1936. Coming to the parish church at Taddington, they found a notice to say that the Blessed Sacrament was reserved there and should be treated with 'special reverence'. The two brothers later had an argument about it over their lunch. Warnie 'said that there was room only for a clear cut division of opinion – if one is a Catholic, the aumbry contains Our Lord and of course even prostration is hardly reverence enough: but if one is Church of England, it contains but a wafer and a little wine, and why in front of that should one show any greater reverence than in any other part of the church? . . . Jack was not satisfied and seemed to think that there was a middle view between the two.'[9] Seven or eight years later, by the time he preached his remarkable sermon 'The Weight of Glory', C. S. Lewis clearly had a full belief in the Eucharistic Presence, or there would be no force in the rhetoric of his 'Next to the Blessed Sacrament itself, your neighbour is the holiest object presented to your senses.'

It might be imagined by those who are not themselves Anglican that the habit of 'going to confession' is limited only to markedly 'High' churches, but this is not necessarily the case. The practice does take place in the Church of Ireland, though as it happened, it did not seem to have come Lewis's way at St Mark's, Dundela. In Oxford, after his conversion, things were different. Among his Anglican friends, Coghill probably went to confession. Dyson certainly did. It was very much the custom of most churches in central Oxford, even though it has never been obligatory in the Anglican Communion. 'All may; some should; none must' is the Church of England rule. Lewis undoubtedly felt that he should, but was nervous about taking the plunge. His friendship with Sister Penelope somehow made it easier. 'The decision to do so was one of the hardest I have ever made: but now that I am committed (by dint of posting the letter before I had time to change my mind) I began to be afraid of opposite extremes – afraid that I am merely indulging in an orgy of egoism.' He had written to Father Walter Adams, who had a strong reputation as a confessor and spiritual director. He was a member of the Society of St John the Evangelist, an Anglican religious order popularly called the Cowley Fathers and based in Oxford.

The drama of the moment was recaptured in *Perelandra*, the second in the science-fiction trilogy, where Ransom remembers the strength which was given to him in a moment requiring supreme moral courage.

It happened once while he was trying to make up his mind to do a very dangerous job in the last war. It had happened again while he was screwing his resolution to go and see a certain man in London and make to him an excessively embarrassing confession which justice demanded. In both cases, the thing had seemed a sheer impossibility; he had not thought but known that, being what he was, he was psychologically incapable of doing it; and then, without any apparent movement of the will, as objective and unemotional as the reading on a dial, there had arisen before him, with perfect certitude, the knowledge 'about this time tomorrow, you will have done the impossible'.

Having been to confession and passed through 'the wall of fire', Lewis wrote to Sister Penelope, 'the suggestion about an orgy of egoism turns out, like all the Enemy propaganda, to have just a grain of truth in it, but I have no doubt that the proper method of dealing with that is as I intend to do, to continue the practice.'*

The practice of confession brought before Lewis the drama of redemption as a perpetual game of cat and mouse with the Devil – the Enemy. The very particularity of the sacrament forces upon the penitent the sense that it is on the here and now – that row we had with the neighbours, the bad temper with which we did the washing-up, this specific uncharitable thought or unchaste deed – that salvation and damnation depend. It is in the small area of our own conscience and our own personal behaviour that the good angels and the bad angels are wrestling over our souls, an idea which is both stupendous and slightly comic. Betjeman's poem 'Original Sin on the Sussex Coast' makes a point unwillingly learnt from his old tutor when it depicts the sheer wickedness of children bullying one another, unseen by the sentimental eyes of the mother whose mind has been washed by modern advertising techniques and the vacuous optimism of the age:

> Does Mum the Persil-user still believe
> That There's no Devil and that youth is bliss?
> As certain as the sun behind the Downs
> And quite as plain to see, the Devil walks.

---

* It is categorically not the case that Lewis had 'always wanted to attack the practice' of sacramental confession 'whenever he found it'. This strange assertion (among many other inaccuracies) occurs in *Clive Staples Lewis: A Dramatic Life*, by William Griffin. Griffin quotes Lewis as saying, in a letter written to his father in March 1928, 'If you try to suppress it, you only make martyrs.' Griffin's readers are not told that Lewis was not, here, speaking about confession. The 'it' which he speaks of suppressing is the Oxford Group Movement formed by Frank Buchman and later known as Moral Rearmament. The letter (written four years before Lewis became a Christian) expresses distaste for the Groupers' reported custom of extracting *public* confessions from their devotees.

Lewis was possessed by this line of thought in the first year of the war. It was some time after making his first confession that he bumped into a pupil in Addison's Walk. The pupil had been at Magdalen for a year, and then left to join the Army. He was in uniform, very much in the situation in which Lewis had found himself as an undergraduate at Univ. Having given his news, he asked Lewis what he was writing. 'I've had this idea', said Lewis, 'of letters from a senior devil to a junior devil.'[10]

The Screwtape Letters brought into literary use qualities which Lewis had had to a highly developed degree ever since adolescence. His ability to see through human failings, his capacity to analyse other people's annoyingness, his rich sense of comedy and satire, had as yet only found their outlet in letters to Greeves, and to a lesser extent in such collections as P'dayta-Pie. In *The Screwtape Letters* his inspired malice is given creative rein. 'She's the sort of woman who lives for others – you can always tell the others by their hunted expression.'[11] Or take the old woman who is really a slave to the Gluttony of Delicacy but thinks she is the very model of abstinence:

> She is a positive terror to hostesses and servants. She is always turning from what has been offered her to say with a demure little sigh and smile, 'Oh, please, please ... *all* I want is a cup of tea, weak but not too weak, and the teeniest weeniest bit of really crisp toast.' You see? Because what she wants is smaller and less costly than what has been set before her, she never recognises as gluttony her determination to get what she wants, however troublesome it may be to others ... In a crowded restaurant she gives a little scream at the plate which some overworked waitress has set before her and says, 'Oh, that's far, far too much! Take it away and bring me about a quarter of it.'[12]

To the comedy of such pen-portraits (and *Screwtape*, it has to be admitted, is a cruel book), is added moral wisdom and a developing religious vision. Lewis is extremely good at describing the actual territory in which the moral life, for most of us, is thrashed out, and the extent to which we enable ourselves to be deluded about ourselves and other people:

When two humans have lived together for many years it usually happens that each has tones of voice and expressions of face which are almost unendurably irritating to the other. Work on that. Bring fully into the consciousness of your patient that particular lift of his mother's eyebrows which he learnt to dislike in the nursery and let him think how he dislikes it. Let him assume that she knows how annoying it is and does it to annoy – if you know your job he will not notice the immense improbability of the assumption.[13]

It is the last bit of that sentence which contains the punch. Though Lewis is said to have found the task of writing these letters morally exhausting – entailing as it did the ceaseless identification of himself with the malign and diabolical point of view – their great strength is that, rather like a dramatic monologue by Browning, they reveal the speaker *without* succumbing to his terrible outlook. Although they are the letters of instruction from an older devil to a younger, Screwtape's sense of what the Enemy (i.e. God) is preparing for his servants cannot fail to break through.

One must face the fact that all the talk about His love for man, and His service being perfect freedom is not (as one would gladly believe) mere propaganda, but an appalling truth. He really *does* want to fill the universe with a lot of loathsome little replicas of Himself – creatures whose life, on its miniature scale, will be qualitatively like His own, not because He has absorbed them but because their wills freely conform to His. We want cattle who can finally become food; He wants servants who can finally become sons. We want to suck in, He wants to give out.[14]

Or again:

He's a hedonist at heart. All those fasts and vigils and stakes and crosses are only a façade. Or only like foam on the sea shore. For at sea, out in His sea, there is pleasure, and more pleasure. He makes no secret of it; at His right hand are 'pleasures for evermore'. Ugh![15]

Once he started, Lewis appears to have written *The Screwtape Letters* very quickly. He offered them to the editor of the one periodical which, by this stage, he was in the habit of reading: a High Church weekly, since defunct, called *The Guardian*. *The Guardian* published the letters in weekly instalments from May to November 1941. Lewis was paid £2 per article, and the money was paid directly into a fund for 'Clergy Widows'.[16] Ashley Sampson, who had commissioned *The Problem of Pain*, persuaded his parent publisher to make an offer for the publication of *Screwtape* in book form. When it was published, in February 1942, the first printing of 2,000 copies was sold immediately. There were two reprintings in March, and the book has been in print ever since, selling over a million copies. What had begun as a *jeu d'esprit* of a mere 30,000 words or so made Lewis a household name.

The other factor which contributed to this effect was his decision to become a broadcaster. This came about in an equally haphazard fashion. Feeling sheepish about his ineligibility for active service, Lewis had accepted an invitation from the RAF chaplains to tramp around the country and give talks to the men in various RAF stations. Tolkien, who found the contents of these talks, when published, not especially to his taste, nevertheless admired the simple religious feeling which inspired them.

Teaching was his original object. He took it up in a Pauline spirit, as a reparation; now the least of Christians (by special grace) but once an infidel, and even if he had not persecuted the faithful, one who scorned the Faith, he would do what he could to convert men or stop them from straying away. The acceptance of the R.A.F. mission, with its hardship of travel to distant and nasty places and audiences of anything but the kind he was humanly fitted to deal with, lonely, cheerless, embarrassed journeys leaving little behind but doubt whether any seed had fallen on good soil; all this was in its way an imitation of St. Paul.[17]

The talks which Lewis gave to the RAF were on such basic issues as 'Why we think there is a Right and Wrong', and from such simple beginnings he framed, in language which was meant to be arresting to ordinary men in the ranks, an exposition first of the theist position, then of the Christian religion. In February 1941, he was approached by the Director of Religious Broadcasting at the BBC and asked if he would be prepared to give a series of broadcast talks on 'The Christian

Faith as I see it – by a Layman'; and although there was first a certain amount of debate about what the nature and title of the broadcasts should be, Lewis began to do this in the late summer of 1941, taking the train from Oxford to London every Wednesday evening, and broadcasting from 7.45 to 8.00 p.m.[18]

Sound-broadcasting is a particular skill, not necessarily related to literary ability though impossible without it. That is, one needs the literate ability to express oneself clearly; but one also needs the right voice and the ability to be concise. Lewis's broadcasts during the war were in three series, and they were written up (published more or less as spoken over the air) as *Broadcast Talks* (1942), *Christian Behaviour* (1943) and *Beyond Personality* (1944). The key to them lies in the title of the second series – *Christian Behaviour*. Lewis is better than any modern writer both at explaining what Christian behaviour should be and at analysing its difficulties.

> People often think of Christian morality as a kind of bargain in which God says, 'if you keep a lot of rules I'll reward you, and if you don't I'll do the other thing.' I do not think that is the best way of looking at it. I would much rather say that every time you make a choice you are turning the central part of you, the part of you that chooses, into something a little different from what it was before. And taking your life as a whole, with all your innumerable choices, all your life you are slowly turning this central thing into either a heavenly creature or into a hellish creature.[19]

It is unfortunate that shorthand here makes Lewis imply that the life of submission to Grace is a course of self-improvement. Indeed overall, he says surprisingly little about Grace and next to nothing about the sacramental life; for these reasons one might regret the title which he gave to the three books gathered into one – *Mere Christianity* – for it implies that he has written a sort of mini-Summa or encyclopaedia of theology. That was not his intention. His intention in the lively fifteen-minute talks was to answer such questions as 'Can an intelligent person be a Christian?' 'What should a Christian's attitude be towards war, sex or money?' 'Is there a heaven and a hell?' He answers these questions with a breeziness and a self-confidence which on an academic podium would have been totally unacceptable. And the language and idiom of the broadcasts has dated: 'There has been a great deal of soft soap talked about God for the last hundred years. That is not what I am offering. You can cut all that out . . .'[20] or 'The Christian replies [to some Aunt Sally which Lewis has conveniently erected] "Don't talk damned nonsense . . ."'[21] or 'I personally think that next to Christianity Dualism is the manliest and most sensible creed on the market.'[22] It is hard to read these sentences without a smile. Nor are all his attempts at analogy helpful. Certainly to explain the Incarnation in a quarter of an hour over the air is a tall order, but Lewis could surely have done better than to say, 'If you want to get the hang of it, think how you would like to become a slug or a crab.'[23] Apart from being offensive, this is bad theology. God made human beings in His own image and likeness. Human beings did not make slugs or crabs. Man could not 'redeem' the slugs even if slugs were in need of redemption.

Such lapses were seized upon eagerly by Lewis's jealous academic colleagues. There is nothing like worldly success on the part of one academic to make all the others hate him or her. Lewis's immediate success with the general public, and the huge popularity of his theological books, guaranteed him a rough ride with the Fellows of Magdalen, as well as with those in the Oxford Faculties of Theology and English Literature. Of course, it was not just the atheists who disliked him. It was a Christian colleague in the English Faculty who said, 'The problem of pain is quite bad enough without Lewis making it worse.' Even those one would expect to have rejoiced at the religious revival which Lewis's popularity heralded and to a certain degree inspired could only bring themselves to sneer. R. H. Lightfoot, for example, the chaplain of New College, and author of a learned commentary on St John's Gospel, remarked to a young colleague of Lewis's: 'His defection to the area of theology is a sad loss to the English Faculty. I wish it could be said to be a gain to the Faculty of Theology.' Lewis knew that they were all saying things like this, and it stung. It hurt even more that friends like Tolkien, to whom he had dedicated *The Screwtape Letters*, could not respond to Lewis's effusions as 'Everyman's Theologian'.

However little his colleagues liked Lewis's activities as a lay evangelist, there can be no doubt about his tremendous impact on the church of his day. Father Andrew, the saintly co-founder of the Society of the Divine Compassion, wrote to one of his many correspondents: 'To me it is one of the most hopeful things of this epoch that it has produced C. S. Lewis.'[24] As far as the Church of England was concerned, there were giants in those days. Perhaps they were the last days before the final eclipse. T. S. Eliot was completing the *Four Quartets*. All too briefly, until his untimely death in 1944, there was an Archbishop of Canterbury who was not only a learned philosopher and theologian but was also able, in such writings as his *Readings in St John's Gospel* to speak to people at a simple devotional level. Dorothy L. Sayers was writing her series of radio plays about the life of Christ called *Man Born to Be King*.

Lewis's popularity was part of this, and it was with more than a scent of victory in the air, victory over the agnostics and freethinkers, that he consented to be involved with the foundation of the Socratic Club in Oxford in 1941. This was an undergraduate debating society, founded with an aggressively Christian purpose by a student at Somerville College called Stella Aldwinkle. Since all undergraduate societies are meant to have one senior member, she asked Lewis to become the President of the Society, a position he held until his departure for Cambridge in 1954. 'Those who founded it do not for one moment pretend to be neutral,' Lewis confessed.[25] 'It was the Christians who constructed the arena and issued the challenge . . .' Socratic evenings took the form of two speakers facing one another over some such topic as 'Is theology poetry?' or 'If we have Christ's ethics does the rest of Christianity matter?' The ideal Socratic evening came about when one of the speakers was an out-and-out atheist, but sometimes the society could only find speakers of opposing viewpoints within the Christian fold. When Lewis himself was speaking, it was not always easy to find a tame atheist who was prepared to come along and be mauled in public debate; for on these occasions he reverted to type and became again the P'daytabird prosecuting an unlikely prisoner in the Belfast police courts. No one who witnessed these debates has ever suggested that Lewis played fair. He argued with tremendous vigour, and when he demolished his victims it was with evident relish. There were those who admired Lewis's moral courage in being thus prepared to testify for the Christian faith, but not everyone found the spectacle altogether edifying.

On top of all his other commitments, Lewis was writing the second volume of his space trilogy. 'I've got Ransom to Venus and through his first conversation with the "Eve" of that world: a difficult chapter . . . I may have embarked on the impossible,' Lewis wrote to Sister Penelope on 9 November 1941.[26] The effort shows in the writing. *Perelandra* is the most ambitious of the outer-space stories, and the one with the most single-minded theological aim: nothing less than an imagined temptation-scene between Satan and Eve in which she does *not* succumb. For the purpose of saving her, Ransom (veteran of the journey to Malecandra in *Out of the Silent Planet*) is actually made a Ransom for her, a sort of Christ figure sent to wrestle with the wicked scientist Weston who tries to bring about the Fall on the newly inhabited planet Venus.

Not even John Milton's imagination had attempted such a theme. It is no wonder that *Perelandra* is an artistic failure. How could it have succeeded? This is not to say that it does not contain many magnificent passages, some comic, some sublime. And, almost more than any of his other fiction, it reveals what Lewis as a writer was chiefly concerned to achieve. He wanted nothing less than a revival of the Romantic movement in literature, only a revival under firm Christian management. The key passage, from this point of view, is the temptation offered by Weston/Satan (the Un-Man) to which the Woman all but yields: the image of herself as a great soul. 'Greatness, tragedy, high sentiment – these were obviously what occupied her thoughts.' The new Eve momentarily wants to be a tragedy queen; for a few flickering instants, she wants to be like almost all the characters in literature whom we find most beguiling – Cleopatra, Anna Karenin, Madame Bovary, Eve herself in *Paradise Lost* – a figure who has risked everything for the sake of *une grande passion*. To set against this the prosaic virtues of humility and obedience, and to make them seem not merely right but also interesting, is – when the writer is a fallen creature writing for other fallen creatures – an impossible task. Lewis tried, and inevitably blundered this way and that, sometimes falling into appalling sentimentality, sometimes writing ridiculous masculine-minded nonsense about 'a woman's place'.

The story does, however, abound in felicities; the physical descriptions of the planet, for example, are superb. And there are scenes of great moral effectiveness, as when Ransom, plucking up his courage for the struggle with Weston, recalls that 'at that moment, far away on earth . . . men were at war, and white-faced subalterns and freckled corporals who had but lately begun to shave, stood in horrible gaps or crawled forward in deadly darkness, awakening like him to the preposterous truth that all really depended on their actions.'[27] The effectiveness of that is not just to make Ransom's struggle real, but also to demonstrate the metaphysical excitement of all moral choices, on the silent planet as well as beyond the music of the spheres.

Outwardly, the plot of *Perelandra* is borrowed from Milton's *Comus*, and its chief ideological failing stems from this. Milton never makes clear exactly how the Lady's virtue is saved. In the end, it would seem that she is not strong enough to resist Comus's wiles without the intervention of Sabrina. Likewise in the case of Lewis's Eve: if she is ransomed by Ransom's struggle with the Un-Man in the underworld, a sort of Harrowing of Hell sequence, how can she be said to have resisted the temptation on her own; and if she has not *really* resisted through her own strength – if she is to be rewarded with immortality and felicity for something she has not done herself – where is the justice in the punishment, on another planet, of Eve and her descendants, for something which again was not wholly her responsibility? Are we to suppose that human beings only exercise free will when they sin – or, worse, only sin when they exercise free will? These questions were to make John Milton abandon any discernible belief in the doctrine of Grace and become a sort of Stoic. Lewis never seems to have faced the problem, either in his imaginative writings or in his works of theology. If the woman resisted Weston's voice simply out of obedience to Maleldil, then what was the function of Ransom? This was the question, in notional form, which he had asked Tolkien and Dyson during the September night of 1931 when they talked Lewis into becoming a Christian. 'My puzzle was the whole doctrine of Redemption: in what sense the life and death of Christ "saved" or "opened salvation" to the world . . . What I couldn't see was how the life and death of Someone Else "whoever he was" 2000 years ago could help us here and now.'[28]

Perelandra shows that even on the mythopoeic level this most difficult of doctrines had not been absorbed by Lewis. Another decade was to pass before it really sank in, and he could write, 'What an ass I have been both for not knowing and for thinking I knew. I now feel that one must never say one believes or understands anything . . .'[29]

This was an admission made to Sister Penelope in 1951. In 1941 he was still very content with an unrealized, cerebral exposition of the Christian gospel which was to lead him into many distortions. Nevertheless, the sisters of the Community of St Mary the Virgin were very happy to receive the dedication to *Perelandra*: 'To some ladies in Wantage'.

FOURTEEN

SEPARATIONS
1942 – 1945

Among the many changes wrought in Oxford lives by the war, not the least was the arrival of evacuees from London. Once it had become clear that the Luftwaffe intended to bomb London flat, children in the capital were sent into the country. Many of them were separated from their families for several years, and acquired a taste for country life which in some cases made their return to the cramped conditions of city living difficult. Evelyn Waugh's novel *Put Out More Flags* describes amusingly the lengths to which some people might be prepared to go to avoid having children billeted on them. Mrs Moore's attitude to the situation was quite different. Maureen was now married and lived with her schoolmaster husband in Worksop; Jack was much of the time in college or out on his lecture tours. The Kilns was in danger of being not only lonely but also understaffed. The indispensable Paxford, for example, had been seconded for work in the Cowley motor factory, and gardening was now in the hands of a woman whom Mrs Moore did not especially like. When the possibility arose that she might be sent some convent schoolgirls from London to share her life at The Kilns, she leapt at it, and the first 'consignment' arrived in 1940, leaving in 1942. It would seem that they did not fit particularly well into The Kilns and its routines. Then, in the summer of 1942, the convent sent another girl, June Flewett, who was in her sixteenth year, to be interviewed by Mrs Moore as a possible replacement.

June Flewett was a pretty, fervently devout young Catholic girl whose favourite books were *The Screwtape Letters*, *The Problem of Pain* and *Out of the Silent Planet*. She had no idea who resided at The Kilns apart from Mrs Moore, with whom she found an instant rapport. The blonded hair, the cigarette dancing about on her lips and seldom removed, the Irish voice – all these features charmed June Flewett, as did Mrs Moore's sense of humour and the ramshackle but pleasant household – the hens, the garden, the acres of woodland, the lakes, the dogs and cats. In the background, there were two slightly peculiar overweight gentlemen, one of whom was Mrs Moore's 'son'.

One of the first questions Minto asked was about ration books. Could June please surrender her ration book as soon as possible, so that they could use it to buy chicken food? She said she would be very happy to do so, and went home to her parents, extremely excited that she had found such a pleasant 'billet'. The idea was that she should spend the term living with Mrs Moore and then take the exams to get into the Royal Academy of Dramatic Art. That summer, however, the Reverend Mother of her convent decided to move back into the London suburb of Hammersmith, and June had to write to Mrs Moore to say that she would not be coming to The Kilns after all. 'I can't tell you how disappointed I am,' Minto wrote back. 'I shall miss "my children" awfully though I know you girls naturally prefer to go to your own school at Hammersmith and to be at home as well.'[1]

Since Minto had already appropriated June's ration book, it was arranged that she should continue to supply the Flewetts with fresh eggs for the next six months. This she did throughout the winter of 1942–3, though it is not at all clear how she managed to post the eggs on their journey of fifty-five miles without them breaking. These were the days when most families in London were getting by with one powdered egg per week, so the Minto egg benefaction was received by the Flewetts with something like rapture. In response to their thank-you letters, Minto invited June to come and stay for the summer holidays before she went up to RADA. She knew they would be 'great friends. You like the country and the animals as we do.'[2] June came and stayed for three weeks.

This time, she had more chance to observe Mrs Moore's 'son' and his brother. Their routines were guarded jealously by Minto, as they both called her, and she tried to make sure that Jack – her 'son' – was never disturbed when he was working. In the course of those three weeks, June, who was just sixteen, fell in love with Jack.

The undercurrents of worry and unhappiness which were possessing the household did not reach her. 'Things are pretty bad here,' Lewis was writing to Greeves not long afterwards. 'Minto's varicose ulcer gets worse and worse, domestic help harder and harder to come by. Sometimes I am very unhappy, but less so than I have often been in what were (by external standards) better times.'[3]

As far as Minto was concerned, the domestic crisis was solved by the arrival of young June, who was so bright, so good-humoured, and who only occasionally could be seen to sit giving Jack rather soulful looks. At the end of her three-week stay, June was asked by Minto to stay on and help in the house. She accepted. For the next eighteen months she was to relieve Jack of many of his domestic worries, cleaning, scrubbing, cooking, doing out the hens, and being a general dogsbody for Minto. Of course, Minto did not always keep to her own rules, and the cries of 'Barboys' whenever she wanted something from Jack were frequent. 'The great thing,' he told himself, 'if one can, is to stop regarding all the unpleasant things as interruptions of one's "own" or "real" life. The truth is of course that what one calls the interruptions are precisely one's real life – the life God is sending one day by day.'[4]

To June's eyes, there had never been a more devoted son than Jack was to his – as she now learnt – adopted mother. In particular, she was struck by their evening routines. Minto was by now becoming very decidedly an old woman, with aching legs and persistent little bouts of illness. Jack was always kind with her, always gentle. Every evening he went to her bedroom to get it ready; then, when he had turned down the sheets and lit the light and helped her into bed, he would always sit with her, sometimes reading aloud, sometimes chatting until it was time to say good-night. June noticed how tenderly he kissed Minto and, however demanding she was, how patient and solicitous was his response.

She was also struck by his extreme kindness to the houseboy, or gardener's mate, who had been supplied to them by the social services department. This young man had the mental age of an eight-year-old child. He was illiterate and wanted to learn to read. Every evening Jack made cards showing letters and pictures and words; every evening for two months he recited the alphabet with this young man. He did not make much progress.

It was only after she had been living for a little while at The Kilns and absorbing its strange routines and atmospheres that June Flewett realized that 'Jack', with whom she had fallen so much in love, was the same person as the author and broadcaster whom she so much idolized.

June Flewett's 'crush' on Jack was one of the many realities which went, barely digested, into the third of his outer-space novels, *That Hideous Strength*, where it appears as Jane Studdock's hopeless devotion to Ransom. Twice as long as its two predecessors, *That Hideous Strength* occupied Lewis, in the midst of many other concerns, for the last two years of the war. From an aesthetic point of view, it is much the least successful book of the trilogy, and by far the most self-indulgent. All his passing concerns – affectionate memory for the Great Knock, loathing of his more 'progressive' Magdalen colleagues, dread of State Socialism, genuine fear that England was going to be 'developed' and ruined by those who did not care for its natural or historical heritage, and many things beside – were poured into its overloaded pages. It is above all a book drenched in admiration for Charles Williams. It has been called 'a Charles Williams novel written by C. S. Lewis'.[5] What could be more Williams-ish than the sudden swoop from a depiction of ordinary, provincial, middle-class English life in the first chapter to the discovery that in a wood adjacent to a twentieth-century college, Merlin's uncorrupted, undead body has been sleeping since the close of the Dark Ages? What more Williams-ish idea could be found than that when Merlin awakes, full of knowledge which has been lost to mankind, there should be a cosmic struggle between the forces of Right, led by our old friend Ransom (from the Perelandra and Malecandra voyages, now renamed Mr Fisher-King), and the mad scientists. Mr Fisher-King, of course (as all readers of Williams's Taliessin poems or listeners to Wagner's *Parsifal* would expect) is a wounded figure, sustained by a diet of bread and wine.

The trouble with *That Hideous Strength*, as with *Perelandra*, is that Lewis has attempted the impossible; in the end, the seriousness of the cosmic struggle is not something which he can put into words. This is not simply attributable to literary boldness, as it was in the case of *Perelandra*. Rather, it is that Lewis the satirist cannot resist letting his own ribald loathing of fat bossy women and atheistical science dons intrude into the high cosmic themes. The book is full of good things, but it is not a whole. And it is not made clear, either as an allegory or in terms of sheer factual narrative, how Merlin and Ransom conquer the Satanic employees of NICE.

The general thrust of the book is that science is getting out of hand:

> The physical sciences, good and innocent in themselves, had already, in Ransom's own time, begun to be warped, had been subtly manoeuvred in a certain direction . . . The very experiences of the dissecting room and the pathological laboratory were breeding a conviction that the stifling of all deep-set repugnances were the first essential for progress. And now all this had reached the stage at which its dark contrivers thought they could safely begin to bend it back so that it would meet that other and earlier kind of power [i.e. witchcraft and 'forbidden knowledge'] . . .[6]

Reading the book today, one is struck by how much Lewis, paradoxically by the very fact that he is so conservative, anticipates many of the modern 'environmentalist' objections to scientific development. Though no advocate of nut cutlets and sandals, he had a profound and immediate objection to experimentation on animals which anticipated much of the modern animal rights movement, just as there is much that the Green Party and the Friends of the Earth would find to admire in his horror at the spoiling of that wood behind the college.

But although the plots of Devine (now Lord Feverstone) to ruin England for the sake of Forbidden Knowledge and to colonize the universe for Satan are horrifically well evoked, they are but one disparate element among many in this book. There are the Charles Williams characters hovering around the figure of Fisher-King at St Anne's – a woman called Grace who really brings Grace, for example. Then there are elements from Lewis's own nursery-style fantasies, such as Mr Bultitude the bear, based on the bear he had met the day he became a Christian at Whipsnade. The tramp the scientists mistake for Merlin has strayed in from E. Nesbit, while Merlin himself is a portrait of Yeats as Lewis remembered him. (Another 'portrait' in the book is the character of McPhee, who is more or less the same as the Great Knock as he appears in Lewis's autobiography. As if these were not enough for the mixture, Lewis adds Tolkien's legend of Numenor and the True West, but spells it Numinor, obviously under the impression that this has something to do with the 'numinous'. Tolkien, who disliked the book strongly, was understandably irritated that his own mythology should have been adopted and distorted in this way.

But one cannot finish the science-fiction trilogy in a purely negative spirit. The books fail because of the size of the attempt. If *That Hideous Strength* lacks the imaginative cohesion of Lewis's later fiction, it yet remains a great achievement. There are so many moments which are not merely 'good' but which are also distinctively Lewisian and which come from the depths. Who but he could have written 'The voice . . . seemed to be sunlight and gold. Like gold not only as gold is beautiful but as it is heavy: like sunlight not only as it falls gently on English walls in autumn but as it beats down on the jungle or the desert to engender life or destroy it'?[7] Who but he – in quite another vein – could have supplied us with the particular quality of the comedy in 'While she was speaking, Miss Hardcastle was undoing her belt, and when she had finished she removed her tunic and flung it on the sofa, revealing a huge torso, uncorseted . . . rank, floppy and thinly clad; such things as Rubens might have painted in delirium'?[8] Though Lewis's cooking may be rough, you never forget its flavour.

How Lewis's colleagues responded to being guyed in *That Hideous Strength* may be readily imagined. One old don, a fellow of Magdalen in those days, once advanced to me the preposterous notion that Lewis was 'the most evil man he had ever met'. On further enquiry, it transpired that what this man meant was that he could not share Lewis's religious opinions. 'Using his cleverness to corrupt the young', he called it – a criticism which, it occurred to me, had been levelled at Socrates. Until meeting him, I had not realized the deadly accuracy of Lewis's portraits of the dons in *That Hideous Strength*. The 'examinee' is a particularly recognizable figure.

His education had been neither scientific nor classical – merely 'modern'. The severities both of abstraction and of high human tradition had passed him by: and he had neither peasant shrewdness nor aristocratic honour to help him. He was a man of straw, a glib examinee in subjects that require no exact knowledge (he had always done well on Essays and General Papers) . . .'[9]

The suggestion that such figures, as well as being men of straw, were potentially Satanic did not make him popular with those dons who were already jealous of his popular success.

But in spite of that, or perhaps in a ghastly way because of it ('It is difficult not to hail as a Friend the only other man in College who really sees the faults of the Sub Warden'),[10] the war was a period when Lewis knew much happiness. Tolkien's letters – profuse monologues to his sons serving in the armed forces – Lewis's own letters to Greeves, Warnie's diaries and the memories of those who were there, all paint a picture of wartime Oxford in which comfortable and comradely routines were all the more sweet for the contrast they presented with the surrounding fear and dreariness of the war. As Tolkien wrote to his son Christopher, then in the RAF, 'I imagine the fish out of water is the only fish to have an inkling of water.'[11]

With the increased workload caused by the absence of academic colleagues in the services, and with their own war-work, the Inklings did not meet on so regular a basis as in peacetime, but they were often together. Even something so tedious as fire-watching, staying up at night to watch for an air-raid in their capacity as Home Guard officers or ARP wardens, had a kind of comic richness when shared with clownish companions. The early part of the war, for example, had seen Lewis – 'save the mark! a Home Guard' – spending 'one night in nine mooching about the most depressing and malodorous parts of Oxford with a rifle'. Still, having to stay up until one thirty or two a.m. had its consolations if the irrepressible Dyson could be there, booming out, 'Well, masters, we hear our charge. Let us go sit here upon the Church bench till two and then all to bed.'

Dyson was a bottomless well of apt or comically misapplied Shakespearean quotations. If driving him in a car, one never approached a roundabout or considered overtaking the vehicle in front without his crying out, 'Be bloody, bold and resolute!' His most usual preface to going to the lavatory was 'Let's briefly put on manly readiness, And meet i' th' hall together.'

One of the high points in the stage-struck June Flewett's time at The Kilns was the night in June 1944 when Jack took her to Nevill Coghill's production of *Measure for Measure*, performed in the cloisters at Christ Church. Three seats were placed like thrones in the front row for June, Jack and Nevill. Roger Lancelyn Green, a pupil of

Lewis's and his future biographer, played Elbow the constable. John Wain, another pupil, and a future Professor of Poetry, novelist and poet, played Claudio. The part of Angelo was played by a young man called Richard Burton. It was a perfect, almost midsummer night; the stars were bright in a clear sky. For the first time, June Flewett saw her hero not as Jack the patient domestic drudge of The Kilns, but as an urbane, grown-up man at ease with his friends. And perhaps he was never more civilized, less inclined to shout, than when in the company of Nevill Coghill, a fellow-Irishman who valued, and had taught him to value, 'traditional sanctity and loveliness'.

Some of his other companions June Flewett did not meet at all. She was not a witness, for example, to his increasing devotion to Charles Williams, a hero-worship which some of Lewis's other friends felt to be in danger of exciting ridicule. 'He emanates more *love* than any man I have known,' Lewis told Greeves. 'As soon as he begins talking, whether in private or a lecture, he is transformed and looks like an angel.' To a younger friend, Lewis went further, saying, 'If you were going up the High in a bus and saw Charles Williams walking along a pavement among a crowd of people, you would immediately single him out because he looked godlike.' As it happened, Peter Bayley, the pupil to whom this remark was addressed, *had* seen Williams from the top of a bus. 'To my eye,' he recalled, 'he looked like a clerk or craftsman in a small line of business – perhaps a joiner, or a carpenter; but I thought there was nothing godlike or angelic about him.'[12]

Tolkien rather resented the fact that the tradition of his quiet lunchtime drink with Lewis on Mondays at the Eastgate Hotel, which went back nearly a decade, was now broken in upon by Williams. What had been a sacrosanct meeting *à deux*, when the friends mulled over their mutual loathing of fellow-members of the English Faculty, or their interest in different branches of Tolkien's mythology, now became a dose of Coinherence, the Omnipotence, Angelicals, and the whole bundle of Williams's mystical, self-educated and vaguely occult preoccupations.

For Williams himself, the time in Oxford was enormously productive. In 1943, he had published by far his best book, a thoroughly original, imaginative and yet scholarly reading of Dante called *The Figure of Beatrice*. By the end of that year, he was reading aloud to the

Inklings some draft chapters of a new novel, *All Hallows Eve*, which must have one of the most dramatic openings in fiction: the heroine is flitting about her old haunts in London, not yet realizing that she has just died. Some of the ideas for this book, and indeed the whole of the first bit of dialogue in Chapter One, came to Williams in discussion with a new member of the Oxford English Faculty, Helen Gardner, who had recently returned not only to her old college of St Hilda's, but also to the practice of the Christian faith. She and Williams used to go to the same church for mass: St Cross. She was one of the many people who would have acknowledged the truth of Lewis's words, 'Women find [Williams] so attractive that if he were a bad man he could do what he liked.'[13] Williams introduced Helen Gardner, among many others, to his idea of Substitution: that you do not merely pray for a sufferer, you ask to take their suffering upon yourself.

Another woman who fell under his spell, spiritually speaking, was Dorothy L. Sayers. So impressed was she by the Dante book that she undertook herself to produce a Penguin translation of the great poet; it is inaccurate and 'dated' in literary manner, but full of gusto. Lewis was a great admirer of her work, particularly of her series of radio plays *Man Born to Be King*. Tolkien liked the radio plays, too, which is in some ways surprising. Less surprising is the view which he confided to his son: 'I could not stand Gaudy Night. I followed P. Wimsey from his attractive beginnings so far, by which time I conceived a loathing for him (and his creatrix) not surpassed by any other character in literature known to me, unless by his Harriet. The honeymoon one (Busman's H?) was worse. I was sick.'[14]

A clash of sympathies of a more serious kind had occurred one noon at the Eagle and Child pub, at one of the Inklings' regular Tuesday meetings. The poet Roy Campbell, a Catholic who had fought on the Fascist side in the Spanish Civil War, turned up to meet the famous group of friends. Lewis, who had consumed a lot of port before Campbell's arrival, insisted on belligerently reading aloud a lampoon which he had written of Campbell in the *Oxford Magazine*. Campbell, whose idea of fun was a pub brawl, took this in good part, but the conversation then turned to the awkward question of Spanish Fascism. At that period the Dominican Order was almost alone among English Catholics in decrying Spanish Fascism. In Catholic churches all over England, Novenas of Prayer and Masses had been offered for Franco's victory over the Communists, for the very simple reason that the Communists were committed to the violent overthrow of the Church and the Fascists, in Spain, to its maintenance.

Lewis always took the line that Communism and Fascism were equally evil, and this was something which Tolkien and Campbell could not understand. 'Nothing is a greater tribute to Red Propaganda', Tolkien wrote, 'than the fact that Lewis (who knows they are in all other subjects liars and traducers) believes all that is said against Franco, and nothing that is said for him . . . But Hatred of our Church is after all the only real foundation of the C of E.'

This religious divide was to grow wider and harder to cross when the friendship between Tolkien and Lewis had cooled. During the war years, however, it was only an aggravation to what remained a harmonious and loving friendship. Tolkien, who as Rawlinson and Bosworth Professor of Anglo-Saxon was obliged to be a Fellow of Pembroke (the college to which the Professorship was attached), dreamed of becoming the Merton Professor of English Language, and of Lewis being freed from his disagreeable colleagues at Magdalen and becoming the Merton Professor of English Literature. 'It would be marvellous to be both in the same college and shake off the dust of miserable Pembroke.'

Unquestionably, the bond which united them most deeply at this period was Lewis's spontaneously generous and passionate admiration for *The Lord of the Rings*, the 'sequel' that Tolkien was writing to *The Hobbit*. It was, of course, infinitely more than a sequel. It was nothing less than a description of the war which brought an end to the 'Third Age'. What began as a small adventure story to amuse children broadened out into a book so vast in its imaginative scope that no genre-word – such as 'epic' or 'romance' – really covers it. In the journey of the Ring-bearers to the Cracks of Doom in the Land of Mordor, the reader is presented not only with one of the most exciting narratives in the English language, but also, by allusion, quotation, inference and episode, with a glimpse of Tolkien's entire imaginative world, the whole mythology of the Elves, with their ancient memories recorded in half-forgotten language and old songs; of the Dark Lords; even, in half-memory, of times stretching far back to the First and Second Ages, to the making of the Silmarils, and the Fall of Numenor.

Although Tolkien always denied that his world was meant to be an echo, still less an allegory, of what was happening in the mid-twentieth century in Europe, there can be no doubt that the high seriousness and urgency of the Ring-bearers' mission against the forces of darkness were quickened by his sense that 'there will be a "millennium", the prophesied thousand year rule of the Saints, i.e. those who have for all their imperfections never finally bowed heart and will to the world or the evil spirit (in modern but not universal terms: mechanism, "scientific" materialism, Socialism . . .).'[15]

Out of this highly distinctive blend of preoccupations grew one of the great literary masterpieces of the twentieth century. It may seem paradoxical to describe a man who composed so much as an indolent writer, but this, temperamentally, Tolkien was. That is not to say, in the days of his active creativity, that he was lazy, but that he could not stir himself to get on with the narrative. A whole year went by, for example, between his bringing the travellers to the Mines of Moria (where Gandalf apparently plunges to his doom) and getting them to resume their journey.

The greatest single goad to Tolkien's pen was Lewis. He had long since come to admire Tolkien's mythology, and had probably heard all or parts of *The Silmarillion*; he had read much of Tolkien's poetry and reviewed *The Hobbit* in generous terms. But he must have seen that *The Lord of the Rings* represented a quickening of Tolkien's style. By presenting his matter in so supremely exciting a narrative, Tolkien had transformed it. He had to be made to finish, however tiring the task in the midst of all his many other commitments, domestic and professional. Month after month, throughout the war, Lewis nagged Tolkien for more. Another incentive was that J. R. R. Tolkien's son Christopher, by now posted to South Africa, was a keen follower of the story and as anxious as Lewis that it should be completed. His father posted it to him in instalments, as it was written. A typical letter to Christopher Tolkien, from May 1944, informs the young man:

I worked very hard at my chapter – it is very exhausting work; especially as the climax approaches and one has to keep the pitch up: no easy level will do; and there are all sorts of minor problems of plot and mechanism. I wrote and tore up and rewrote most of it a good many times; but I was rewarded this morning as both C.S.L. and C.W. thought it an admirable performance and the latest chapters the best so far.[16]

It could be said with almost complete certainty that we should never have had *The Lord of the Rings* had not 'C.S.L.' been so anxious to read to the end.

If for Lewis reading the book was one of the great pleasures of the war in Oxford, together with 'laughter and the love of friends' on Thursday evenings in his Magdalen rooms, and Tuesday lunchtimes at the Eagle and Child, it should not be supposed that all his lecture commitments in other towns were penitential. In February 1943, for example, he had been asked to deliver the Riddell Lectures at the University of Durham, and this gave him and Warnie the excuse for a jaunt in the North of England. The lectures themselves were delivered on three successive evenings in Newcastle-upon-Tyne, but in the course of their time in the North they were able to explore York, as well as to stay in Durham. The beauty of the cathedral town and its stupendous setting on the banks of the Wear took both brothers by marvellous surprise.[17] (Lewis used the place as a model for his university town in *That Hideous Strength*.) The lectures themselves were published in 1944 as *The Abolition of Man*.

This is an important book: nothing less than an analysis of where and how the modern world has gone wrong. This may provoke in many readers the response, 'As we should expect, here is an affectedly old-fashioned, crusty man with a pipe and a lot of male cronies who is going to complain about any modern developments in thought, knowledge or understanding.' One has to recognize that Lewis was by temperament in danger of turning into a caricature backwoodsman. But he was also a man with a supremely workable intelligence, and in this book he deserves to command his widest audience. He is not simply addressing – as in his works of literary scholarship – those who might want to read Macrobius or Thomas Usk; nor is he, overtly at least, arguing a case for Christianity. Rather, he is analysing what has happened to society and, indeed, to our whole way of looking at the universe. This is something which affects us all, and we all need to consider the validity or otherwise of Lewis's arguments. I consider *The Abolition of Man* to be quite detached from *That Hideous Strength*.

It is true that many of the fears expressed in *The Abolition of Man* were translated into fiction in the novel, as was the insight which many readers of the lectures might deem their most fanciful strand: the observation about the close kinship which exists between what we call science and magic – 'For magic and applied science alike the problem is how to subdue reality to the wishes of men.'

But *The Abolition of Man* is concerned with something much more incontrovertible than this. And it must be remembered that it was written at a period when, abroad, Hitler and Stalin were defying all previously understood notions of decency – indeed inventing value or non-value systems of their own – while at home Lewis was finding himself, at the Socratic Club and elsewhere, with philosophers like A. J. Ayer who absolutely denied the possibility of attaching meaning to sentences which were not either verifiable through sense perception or verifiable as a priori truths. Into the latter category Ayer and the other logical positivists would only admit certain mathematical and logical formulae. Such concepts as right and wrong, good and evil, beautiful and ugly, were dismissed from their vocabulary.

Lewis's contention – which cannot, historically, be denied – was that there has been a system of values, discernible in almost all moral and religious centres, from the beginning of literature until the mid-twentieth century. To emphasize that he was not talking just about the Judaeo-Christian tradition but about something both deeper and wider than that, Lewis borrowed the Chinese word and called this the *Tao*. In an appendix quoting from sources as varied as the Old Norse *Voluspa*, the Ancient Egyptian *Confession of a Righteous Soul*, the Old Chinese Analects, Cicero and Epictetus, he makes his point. They all point to the existence of something outside individual feelings or the purely utilitarian requirements of a society, something which might be termed a generally accepted standard of right and wrong. All these sources abhor murder, dishonesty, theft, unkindness, disregard of the old, cruelty to children, ruthless 'justice' untempered by mercy.

That these should be considered abhorrent, Lewis gently points out, is no longer taken for granted. And his rhetoric is all the more effective for the fact that he does not terrify his audience at the outset with examples which might be deemed monstrous or freakish. He says nothing about Hitler, nothing about Stalin. Instead he starts off with two harmless English schoolmasters who have written a textbook for the use of older children. In this book, which Lewis calls *The Green Book*, the authors quote the well-known story of Coleridge at the waterfall. Two tourists approach, one who calls the waterfall *sublime* and the other who calls it *pretty*. Coleridge rejects the second judgement with disgust and endorses the word *sublime*. *The Green Book* tells its readers, 'When the man said *That is sublime* he appeared to be making a remark about the waterfall ... Actually ... he was not making a remark about the waterfall but a remark about his own feelings.' *The Green Book* translates the sentence as 'I have sublime feelings.'

Having dismissed the absurdity of making *That is sublime* mean *I have sublime feelings* (by this interpretation it would mean, by contrast, *I have humble feelings*), Lewis reflects on the implications of this teaching, and in the rest of his short book he sketches these implications out with nightmarish clarity. If all value judgements are *really* statements about our feelings, and if we no longer believe in the *Tao*, where does that leave us? 'It is the sole source of all value judgements. If it is rejected, all value is rejected.'[18]

He concludes that the two schoolmasters who wrote *The Green Book* were unconsciously passing on what they had absorbed from the higher reaches of the intelligentsia, a disregard of all value judgements. In answer to the question Where does that leave us?, Lewis predicts that it will leave us in the hands of unscrupulous operators who do not believe in humanity itself. The abolition of man will have occurred because there will be no reason to regard man, as the *Tao* has always regarded him, as a moral being.

Many a mild-eyed scientist in pince-nez, many a popular dramatist, many an amateur philosopher in our midst [i.e. Freud, Shaw and A. J. Ayer] means in the long run just the same as the Nazi rulers of Germany. Traditional values are to be 'debunked' and mankind to be cut out into some fresh shape at the will (which must, by hypothesis, be an arbitrary will) of some few lucky people in one lucky generation which has learned how to do it. The belief that we can invent 'ideologies' at pleasure, and the consequent treatment of mankind as specimens, mere ὕλη, preparations, begins to affect our very language – once we killed bad men: now we liquidate unsocial elements. Virtue has become 'integration' and diligence 'dynamism' and boys likely to be worthy of a commission are 'potential officer material'.

He concludes his lectures by imploring scientists to return to a sense of the *Tao*. 'The regenerate science which I have in mind would not do even to minerals and vegetables what modern science threatens to do to man himself ... It is no use trying to "see through" first principles. If you see through everything, then everything is transparent. But a wholly transparent world is an invisible world. To "see through" all things is the same as not to see.'[19]

In his short book Lewis does not elaborate on what remedies there can be which will save the world from the effects of exploitation by a comparatively few unscrupulous people. He does not claim to know the answers. Those who identify Lewis's fears purely with the Nazi 'experiments' might consider that the world has become a better place since 1944 and that he was exaggerating. But the whole growth since that period of ecology, of knowledge about the calamitous consequences of viewing the Earth merely as a thing to be exploited by man its master, gives the lie to this. Lewis's arguments cover the proliferation of nuclear arsenals; the so-called advance of medical science in the area of experimenting on human embryos; the effect on Third World countries of such fruits of enlightenment as modern baby food and aerosol sprays. His diagnosis of the disease cannot be lightly dismissed. In *The Abolition of Man* he does not advance the cure, though it is no secret where he thought it lay, if there was one.

The highly serious journey of Dante Alighieri from Hell to Paradise was entitled *The Divine Comedy* because this was a poem with a happy ending rather than an unhappy or tragic one. It was not 'a comedy' in the sense of being intended to make its readers laugh. Lewis's boldest fiction, *The Great Divorce*, is a comedy in both senses. It is a conscious echo of Dante, being a journey from Hell to Heaven. But it is also full of human vignettes which are cruelly amusing. The 'divorce' of the title is the gulf fixed between Heaven and Hell, a gulf which varies in size depending upon the perspective from which it is viewed. The journey, in a celestial bus from the dingy town of Hell up to the outer borders of the Heavenly Places, is long and steep. Just as the town itself owes much to the dingier parts of Dante's *Inferno* – particularly to his sixth circle, home of the heretics 'whom the wind leads and the rain beats' (*che mena il vento e che batte la pioggia*), so the journeying up through a vast gorge to the heights of Paradise is also modelled on Dantean geography. But viewed from the perspective of Heaven, this vast gorge is just a tiny little crack in the grass. And the infernal ghosts who seem so hellishly substantial on the bus are wraith-like and insubstantial when exposed to the bright beams of reality.

Behind the story is the idea – more generous than anything in Dante – that all may be saved if they so choose. Everyone on the bus from Hell can stay in Heaven if they wish; and they will then look back on their time in the dingy twilit town as a mere period of purgatory. But many of the ghosts on the bus are already lost souls. They prefer their own sinful obsessive selves to the loss of self which is necessary before they can be saved.

Perhaps none of Lewis's portraits is more cruel than that of the figure of Dante himself, who appears at the end as a figure so besottedly in love with his own unhappiness, and with what he calls his love for his lady, that he cannot let go. He is represented as a dwarf leading the other part of himself, the Tragedian, round on a chain, rather as a street vendor might lead a pet monkey. Lewis the narrator remonstrates with his Heavenly Guide at the cruelty of this. Surely this lady, who is enjoying the sort of heavenly beatitude of Dante's Beatrice (though here she is represented as a very ordinary woman who has lived in Golders Green, a suburb of North London), should pity the poor man who has been her husband. No, says Lewis's Guide through the Heavenly Places, 'That sounds very merciful; but see what lurks behind it . . . The demand of the loveless and the self-imprisoned that they should be allowed to blackmail the universe: that till they consent to be happy (on their own terms) no one else shall taste joy . . .'

Dante's Guide through the Other World is Virgil, who has to stop short of Heaven. With Lewis's *Commedia* it is otherwise. He makes the bus journey on his own, and only meets his Guide – none other than George MacDonald – when he reaches the Bright Land. His conversations with MacDonald include some of the finest religious writing in the whole Lewis *œuvre*.

But did I say that he travels on the bus alone? Nothing could be further from the truth. For he is surrounded by a whole collection of grotesque egotists, struggling to hold on to their damnable selves. At times one feels that it is hard (as it is in Dante himself) to distinguish between qualities which are indeed damnable, and ones which our author merely happens to find distasteful. The modernist bishop; the Lady Macbeth of the Suburbs who forced her husband to 'better himself' and, having driven him to a nervous breakdown, longs to have him with her in Hell so that she can give him another chance to be 'improved'; the old woman who is literally possessed by grumbling to the point where she has almost stopped being a woman and just become a grumble; the belligerent man who 'only wants his rights' – these are among the best and most savagely misanthropic portraits Lewis ever drew. The side of his genius which, from early childhood, enjoyed 'collecting' the infuriating absurdities of the grown-ups, and had, since prep-school days, been creating monsters such as Oldie and the P'daytabird, here comes into its own. *The Great Divorce* shows Lewis at his very best; it is something approaching a masterpiece.

Though it seems paradoxical to say so, the Second World War was one of the happiest periods of C. S. Lewis's life. It had provided a very welcome disruption to the quotidian routines of Kilns and college. It had introduced him to new audiences in RAF stations and at the Universities of Wales and Durham and, above all, to the huge audiences who heard and responded to his wireless talks. Had he wished to make a fortune, this would have brought him one. It certainly brought him fame, and a huge readership for the books which now seemed to flow abundantly from his pen. For the Inklings as a whole, it had been a fructiferous time – producing *The Figure of Beatrice*, *All Hallows Eve*, *The Lord of the Rings*, *The Screwtape Letters*, *The Abolition of Man* and *The Great Divorce*. Any group of men sitting in a pub who could boast a comparable list of books in the space of four or five years could declare themselves indeed 'a nest of singing birds'.

Above all, it had been a time of friendship. But even before the war finished it was clear that 1945 would be a year of losses, endings and partings. The first separation was at home. After any number of delays and procrastinations it was decided that the time had come for June Flewett to take up her place at the Royal Academy of Dramatic Art. Much as she loved them all, it was not her destiny to be a skivvy at The Kilns for the rest of her life. It was Minto who finally decided that June, the intensity of whose feelings for Jack was now obvious, should go. It was a sore wrench on both sides. Ever since September 1944, Jack had been steeling himself for it. 'Every argument which my mind brings against this conclusion I regard as a temptation,' he told her parents. 'And since in talking to June it is no use to appeal to selfish motives (she is, without exception, the most selfless person I have ever known) I told her that she has a duty [to her parents]. June's own view is simply and definitely that she will not leave here of her own free will.'[20]

In the event, Lewis paid for her training as an actress, giving her an allowance to cover fees and maintenance not only for the two years while she was at the Academy, but also for a year afterwards. 'No gratitude or affection or life long interest which Mrs. Moore and I can feel will ever be adequate to the extraordinary goodness she has shown.' She went on 3 January. On the fourth, Lewis wrote to June's mother:

> Oh what a sad waking up this morning when we realised that June was gone! ... Tell June that the hens were asking for her first thing this morning; that Warnie is even more depressed than usual; that the cats, under this shared calamity, sank their common differences and slept, mutually embracing, in the same box ... We are the ghost and ruin of a house [sic] ... Ichabod, Ichabod! God bless her (Indeed that is what I keep on telling him).[21]

With June gone, the domestic responsibility was now placed firmly on Jack's shoulders once again. Warnie sought periodic relief for his greater than usual depressions in the whiskey bottle; and Minto, now in some pain, was getting no easier with the passing months, either as a patient to be nursed, or as a taskmistress who dictated the chores. That did not mean that there were not occasional happy interludes, however, particularly since, with her increased inactivity, she had become much more bookish. She read the whole of *War and Peace* in 1945 and thoroughly enjoyed it.[22]

If June's departure left The Kilns 'the ruin of a house', there was to be a still more dramatic departure from the Inklings circle, which led ultimately to the breaking of the fellowship. The war ended on 9 May, and the next day Charles Williams was suddenly seized with pain. He was operated on at the Acland Nursing Home, only four hundred yards north of the regular Tuesday meeting-place, the Eagle and Child. Before going to the pub as usual, Lewis looked in at the Acland to ask how Williams had survived the operation. None of his friends had had any idea that it was serious.

The hospital staff told him that Williams was dead. 'The very streets looked different' to him as he walked away. The hospital had rung Lewis's college rooms but only managed to reach Warnie, who was sitting there working on French history and whose immediate reaction was to go out to the King's Arms, a pub which he had last visited with Williams, and the sight of which immediately quickened his own sense of loss.

As one would expect of Williams, for whom the Other Side was quite as real as this world, he did not go away immediately after he had shuffled off this mortal coil. At the funeral, in the beautiful cemetery of St Cross where so many great Oxford figures lie, Dyson remarked, 'It is not blasphemous to believe that what was true of Our Lord is, in its lesser degree, true of all who are in Him. They go away in order to be *with* us in a new way, even closer than before.'[23] Lewis discovered that 'all that talk about "feeling that he is closer to us than before" isn't just talk. It is just what it does feel like – I can't put it into words. One seems at moments to be living in a new world. Lots, lots of pain, but not a particle of depression or resentment.'[24]

It was partly in memory of Williams and partly to celebrate the ending of the war that it was decided to have a 'Victory' Inklings – a holiday at the beautiful Gloucestershire village of Fairford. They booked rooms at the Bull Inn for the second week of December, by which time it was assumed and hoped that College entrance exams would be marked and a lull in the domestic routines could be enjoyed before Christmas. Warnie and Tolkien set out for Fairford on the Tuesday morning, and Jack came the next day. He was not, as had been arranged, accompanied by Barfield, for Barfield was ill. Havard came over from Oxford by car and had lunch with them and afterwards they all walked through the hamlets of Horcott and Whelford. In the little church at Whelford, Tolkien amazed and pleased the brothers, at this period when Roman Catholics were forbidden to pray in Anglican churches, by kneeling and praying. It was a holiday which had to it the feel of something coming to an end. Coln St Aldwyn, where they walked on the Friday, seemed like a 'dream village'. There was a pub called the Pig and Whistle where they had early drinks. But the train back to Oxford was at 2.12, and they had to run to catch it. 'As if our holiday had intended to end then, the sky clouded over and the world became dim: the curtain had fallen most dramatically on our jaunt.'[25]

FIFTEEN

NARNIA

1945–1951

Peacetime Oxford was in many ways less peaceful than wartime Oxford. There were more undergraduates, and that meant more teaching. More tutorials, more college meetings; more of all the things which kept Lewis away from his three chief pleasures in life – reading, writing and seeing his friends.

At forty-seven, he was getting a bit old for the all-boys-together raucousness of the English binges which he still insisted on holding at regular intervals for his pupils: the same readings aloud from Amanda McKittrick Ros, the same roaring of bawdry, the same insistence that his pupils be drunk before the evening was over. Many of them found it embarrassing, and he was acutely aware of this. Staggering out to the urinals during one 'binge', he stood beside a pupil who had returned from the war badly shot up. Fixing the young man with an inebriated stare, Lewis remarked, 'You don't like me much, do you?' Since the remark was absolutely true, the young man did not know how to reply.[1]

But for each pupil who did not like Lewis much, there were probably ten who did like him very much indeed, and who valued not only his qualities of mind, but also his inspiration on a personal level. One such, as his friends were sometimes surprised to discover, was Kenneth Tynan, destined to be the most famous avant-garde theatre critic of his generation, the discoverer if not inventor of Angry Young Men, kitchen-sink drama, and the all-nude revue *Oh Calcutta!* Anyone less likely to be a C. S. Lewis admirer it would have been hard to find, but from the moment he came up to Magdalen in the Michaelmas Term of 1945, Tynan was devoted to his tutor. Though disconcerted by Lewis's habit of walking next door to his bedroom to relieve himself into a chamber pot, sometimes while still talking, Tynan was early aware not only of his tutor's wisdom but also of his kindness. Because Tynan had a marked stammer, Lewis used to read his essays aloud for him, and 'It became quite a test writing essays that could survive being read in that wonderfully resonant voice.'[2] When he was laid low by bronchitis and an unhappy love affair, Tynan asked if he could delay taking his final examinations, and confided in Lewis that he saw no reason to go on living. Lewis was bracing in just the right spirit. During the war, he reminded Tynan, a bomb had fallen in Birmingham narrowly missing Tynan's house. 'You have had eight years of life that you had no reason to expect. How can you be so ungrateful?' When Tynan did eventually die, in 1980, he asked for his ashes to be buried at Magdalen. The college refused, but the ashes were interred nearby in St Cross cemetery – in the same burial ground as, among many others, Kenneth Grahame, Hugo Dyson and Charles Williams. By Tynan's special request, Lewis's words were read as he was returned to the earth:

> These things – the beauty, the memory of our own past – are good images of what we really desire: but if they are mistaken for the thing itself they turn into dumb idols, breaking the hearts of their worshippers. For they are not the thing itself; they are only the scent of a flower we have not found, the echo of a tune we have not heard, news from a country we have never visited.[3]

Tynan responded, as did the majority of his pupils, to a recognizable and tangible greatness in the man.

Lord David Cecil, eventually to become the Goldsmiths' Professor of English Literature at New College and famous as a literary biographer, always seized upon this fact when he spoke of Lewis. He was a great man. You felt you were in the presence – as Samuel Johnson's friends did – of someone who made his contemporaries seem like pygmies. David Cecil would comment on the agility of Lewis's mind, its immense fund of reading and reflection, and its bedrock of common sense. Lewis was also great fun. John Buxton, who had come back to New College after the war to teach English Literature with David Cecil, always enjoyed Lewis's visits to the college, not least because of their shared interest in the sixteenth century, and shared love of Spenser and Sidney. 'He had the extraordinary gift', Buxton remembers, 'of instant parody. It was not prepared as a party piece – it came out naturally.' He could parody *any* author – 'Spenser, Kipling, anyone'.[4] But Oxford is a strange place, and dons are strange people. Brilliance in a colleague is quite as likely to excite their envy as their esteem, and, where mediocrity is the norm, it is not long before mediocrity becomes the ideal.

Tolkien in 1945 had told his son Christopher that his ambition was 'to get C.S.L. and myself into the 2 Merton Chairs'.[5] He was to achieve his own ambition of moving to Merton in 1945. But the Merton Chair of English Literature was to elude Lewis. In 1947 its occupant, David Nicholl Smith, retired, and Lewis assumed that he would be at least eligible, if not the likeliest candidate. He was weary of the repetitive round of undergraduate tutorials, and he disliked his colleagues at Magdalen. But even apart from these negative considerations, he considered himself worthy of the job. He was a popular and distinguished lecturer; and the job of an Oxford professor consisted very largely of lecturing in those days before the huge increase in graduate students needing supervisors for their doctoral dissertations. The other part of a professor's job was – as it still is – to be involved in the administration of the Faculty.

Lewis was unaware of quite how unpopular he was in the English Faculty at Oxford, and indeed in the University at large. There would have been no chance of his being elected to the Merton Chair even though *The Allegory of Love* and *A Preface to 'Paradise Lost'* (quite apart from other lectures and learned articles which he had written to date) were far more interesting and distinguished than anything which his rivals for the job had produced. They, however, were safe men, worthy dullards: and that is usually the sort of man that dons will promote. It was not Lewis but his old tutor, F. P. Wilson, who got the Merton Chair in 1947–8: a thoroughly worthy Shakespearean scholar who could be relied upon not to cause trouble, and not to embarrass his colleagues by writing books about Christianity. Even colleagues who were Christians found Lewis's career as a popularizer embarrassing, 'not quite the thing'. And they noticed that his variety of Christianity did not extend to meekness, or even necessarily to politeness, towards his colleagues.

An example of this occurred about now at a heated English Faculty meeting where syllabus reform was under discussion. Lewis's and

Tolkien's syllabus, stopping in 1832, was coming under strong attack from younger members of the Faculty. Helen Gardner, the English Fellow at St Hilda's, was among those who felt strongly that the syllabus should extend at least as far as 1900; and that there was a kind of absurdity in the idea of students who had 'read English' at Oxford going away after three years without having read Tennyson, Browning, William Morris, Dickens, Thackeray or George Eliot. Lewis, in roaring police-court style, defended 'his' syllabus with great paradox and gusto. It was precisely because he valued the nineteenth century above all others in literature that he thought it was an unsuitable subject for undergraduate study. It was too big. How could you understand it if you merely read bits of its poets, and a few novels? You needed to be aware of all the intellectual ferment of the period, to read Carlyle, Newman, Herbert Spencer, John Stewart Mill – and what undergraduate would have the time to read all these?

Not to be outdone, Helen Gardner was on her feet to respond to this. 'If Mr Lewis takes the line that it is improper to read the literature of the period without a thorough knowledge of all the intellectual background, does this argument not extend to all periods of literature? In the area of the sixteenth century, for example, which of us has pupils who have read Calvin's *Institutes of Religion*?'

Carried away by the heat of the debate, Lewis replied, 'Well, my pupils have all read Calvin.'

His eyes met Miss Gardner's. He knew that she knew that he was lying.

Lewis must have heard of her churchgoing habits from their mutual friend Charles Williams, or seen that in her criticisms she wrote overtly as a Christian. For after the meeting he came up to her and said, by way of an apology, 'In spite of our disagreements over the syllabus, I know that you and I agree about the most important things in life. Would you care to dine with me one day?'

Helen Gardner said that she would like to dine and – rather unusually – she was duly invited not to Magdalen, but to dinner at The Kilns. The squalor of the house was something which she found little to her taste. She was astonished to find that there was no object or picture at which one could gaze with pleasure, and that the furniture was bleak and uncomfortable. There was quite a party, and she was nervous, being the only woman at the table (Mrs Moore was in bed), and the only person there who was not an old friend of Lewis.

Conversation at the table turned on the interesting question of whom, after death, those present should most look forward to meeting. One person suggested he would like to meet Shakespeare; another said St Paul. 'But you, Jack,' said the friends (or, as Helen Gardner felt, the disciples), 'who would be your choice?'

'Oh, I have no difficulty in deciding,' said Lewis. 'I want to meet Adam.' He went on to explain why, very much in the terms outlined in *A Preface to 'Paradise Lost'*, where he wrote:

Adam was, from the first, a man in knowledge as well as in stature. He alone of all men 'had been in Eden, in the garden of God, he had walked up and down in the midst of the stones of fire'. He was endowed, says Athanasius, with 'a vision of God so far-reaching that he could contemplate the eternity of the Divine Essence and the coming operations of His Word'. He was 'a heavenly being' according to St. Ambrose, who breathed the aether and was accustomed to converse with God 'face to face'.

Be that as it may, Adam is not likely, if she has anything to do with it, to converse with Helen Gardner. She ventured to say so. Even, she told Lewis, if there really were, historically, someone whom we could name as 'the first man', he would be a Neanderthal ape-like figure, whose conversation she could not conceive of finding interesting.

A stony silence fell on the dinner table. Then Lewis said gruffly, 'I see we have a Darwinian in our midst.'[6]

Helen Gardner was never invited again. Another Oxford woman with whom Lewis famously crossed swords at this period was Elizabeth Anscombe, the philosopher. This was a contretemps of much graver importance in Lewis's imaginative life. It was one of those landmarks which, like other Romantic egoists before him, Lewis used as a way of punctuating or mastering experience. The death of his mother was perhaps the first of these great mythological moments, sealing off, had he but known it, a greater part of his capacity to love, and internalizing much of his capacity to suffer. The reading of *Phantastes* had suggested to the adolescent with No Way that there was the possibility of recovering some of this agonizing loss through the exercise of the imagination; that the imagination, as Plato had believed, gave to human beings the chance to penetrate other worlds, to recover earlier states of being, and ultimately to see God. All exercises of memory, all harking back, thus became voyages of not just self-discovery but discovery of the nature of things. Through the emotional ups and downs of life with the P'daytabird and later with Minto, Lewis as a young man kept these ideas at bay, until, as it seemed, the Other World intruded upon his own and would not be resisted. Then came the other great mythological moments – his submission to God in the year that his father died; his acceptance of the idea of Christ's incarnation after the visit to Whipsnade Zoo.

All these great landmarks in Lewis's emotional development were now sixteen years in the past, and there had intervened the strange, and for Lewis unlooked-for, period of his public popularity as a Christian apologist. The confrontation with Elizabeth Anscombe was to have no effect whatsoever on Lewis's popularity with the Christian public; but it had a profound effect on his career as a writer. It was the greatest single factor which drove him into the form of literature for which he is today most popular: children's stories.

It happened in this way. In 1947, he published a book called *Miracles*, which is his most carefully thought and judiciously written theological work. It is a book which implores to be taken seriously, much more than, say, *Mere Christianity*. It is not, like that earlier book, a casual collection of broadcast talks. It is an attempt to return to the matter which had interested him ever since, as an undergraduate at Univ, he had considered doing a further degree and writing a thesis on Bertrand Russell. In the simplest possible terms, the question for Lewis was whether this universe, discernible by sense perceptions, is all that there is, or whether there is another world, another universe, a supernatural order into which our universe fits or is concealed; another universe which, if we could but tune into it, would make sense of our own. Lewis felt it was essential to choose between whether you believed that there was a Total System – that everything we do, think or experience must be explicable in terms of the physical universe we inhabit – or that there was an argument, as philosophers from Plato to Hegel had been interested to explore, which suggested that in many of our judgements we step outside this closed system of thought and value and bring to bear upon it values which actually come from Somewhere Else.

Before attempting to prove that the miraculous is a perfectly possible thing to happen, and that the greatest miracle of all – the Incarnation – did happen, Lewis meditated in Chapter Three of *Miracles* on this more fundamental question – Is thought itself a supernatural act? 'Unless human reasoning is valid no science can be true. It follows that no account of the universe can be true unless that account leaves it possible for our thinking to be a real insight.' By 'real insight' Lewis appears to mean one which can be justified or explained outside itself. But he is never quite content in his argumentative writings to be a philosopher; the police-court solicitor will out. By the end of a very short chapter, Lewis has reached the conclusion that only Supernaturalists have any claim to know – or indeed be interested in – the truth. 'Unless the Naturalists* put forward Naturalism as a true theory we have of course no dispute with them. You can argue with a man who says, "Rice is unwholesome," but you neither can nor need argue with a man who says, "Rice is unwholesome but I'm not saying this is true."' In other words, those whom he calls Naturalists have no universe of value or truth outside themselves. If this world is all there is, and we are just a collection of atoms, without souls, how can we trust our 'minds' to tell us anything hard, substantial, true?

Any dispassionate reader can at once see many flaws in Lewis's arguments here. For a start, if his distinction between Naturalists and Supernaturalists held good it would have to be demonstrable that the Supernaturalists had some specific means of acquiring their superior knowledge and of explaining it to the Naturalists. Much more seriously, there is no need whatsoever to posit a dualistic theory such as Lewis's in order to 'prove' the existence of God. Theism was not a matter to which Ludwig Wittgenstein was prepared to devote thought. 'What we cannot speak about we must pass over in silence.' Nearly all the philosophers of his generation took as their starting-point the opening sentence of Wittgenstein's *Tractatus*: 'The world is that which is the case.' Like all Wittgenstein's gnomic sayings, this is open to many interpretations and much reflection, but it must include the sense that for rational conversations to take place there

---

* He uses the word to mean not students of Natural History, but those who believe that there can be no Supernatural.

must be an agreed set of terms, acceptable to both speakers. But Lewis in his careless way has failed to see this in Chapter Three of *Miracles*, and the arguments he proceeds to construct about the existence of God actually depend on a non-Christian, dualistic concept of the world in which Spirit and Matter are separate, and religious truth – this is the ultimate conclusion of such gnostic argument – only available to initiates.

When Elizabeth Anscombe chose to reply to Chapter Three of *Miracles*, she must have done so partly as a pupil and friend of Wittgenstein, partly as the ardent Catholic convert and student of Thomas Aquinas which she was. It was not Lewis's Christianity which she was attacking; it was his sheer inadequacy as a philosopher.

The debate took place early in 1948 at the Socratic Club, and instantaneously became legend. Elizabeth Anscombe was a match for Lewis not only in mind but also in personality. She shared his taste for fisticuffs, for brutality as well as finesse in argument. She is, as countless stories about her attest, deeply exhibitionistic. (Many years later, when being inaugurated as Professor of Philosophy at Cambridge, she insisted on wearing Wittgenstein's ragged old gown. Those organizing the ceremony forbade her to wear trousers. She was sworn in wearing a long black skirt which, the moment the Vice Chancellor had accepted her oath, she removed to reveal trousers beneath.) Like Lewis, she is a massive physical type. She was quite equal to the bullying and the exploitation of the audience to which Lewis resorted when he was boxed into a corner. She could employ analogous techniques herself. That evening at the Socratic Club was the first in the Society's history that Lewis was thoroughly trounced in argument. Because Anscombe was herself a Christian, the pious audience could not have the satisfaction of feeling that Lewis was a defender of the faith against the infidel. He was merely shown up as a man who had not bothered to come to terms with the way that philosophers since Wittgenstein thought.

He found this debate emotionally depleting. He told George Sayer that 'his argument for the existence of God had been demolished'.[7] A few days after the debate, dining with a group of male cronies, he was in a state of near-despair. Dyson said, 'Very well – now [he had] lost everything and come to the foot of the Cross.'

Seen from a purely academic perspective this hyperbole makes no sense. All that had happened, humiliating as it had been at the time, was that Lewis had been shown to have no competence to debate with a professional philosopher on her own terms. An exactly analogous situation would have arisen if a member of the English Faculty had challenged him to conduct a debate about James Joyce, of whom he knew next to nothing. Indeed, very similar evidences of Lewis's breezy refusal to follow what was going on outside his own imaginative world and his own range of old-fashioned reading tastes were apparent even at the Kilns dinner table. ('Last night at dinner I mentioned Tito's volte face in Yugoslavia where there is a state fostered return to Christianity. I thought J very stupid about the whole affair and we had talked for a minute or two before I found out that he was under the impression that Tito was the King of Greece.')[8]

What had happened at the Socratic Club was no mere intellectual brawl, however. It awakened all sorts of deeply seated fears in Lewis, not least his fear of women. Once the bullying hero of the hour had been cut down to size, he became a child, a little boy who was being degraded and shaken by a figure who, in his imagination, took on witch-like dimensions. He felt that he was arguing so coherently for the existence of that Other World because he had been there himself. And now here was a grown-up who was not convinced by his explanations of those inner adventures beyond the discernible surface of things. It was all a little like what had happened to his mother when, as a child in Rome, she had believed she saw a statue moving, and none of the grown-ups had credited her tale. Ever since his mother had died, Lewis had been in search of her, and the journey which had begun when he first read George MacDonald's *Phantastes*, and which had continued through his discovery of great Christian literature and wise Christian friends, now chillingly felt as if perhaps it had been a game of make-believe. Unless, unless . . . Unless, that is, Tolkien and Dyson had been right during their great conversation in Addison's Walk in 1931; unless make-believe was really another way of talking about the reality of things; unless the brutal and cerebral way in which grown-ups tried to come to conclusions about the world was not the only way; unless he could explore the way of *Phantastes* – in which another world opens up to the Dreamer through a piece of bedroom furniture. The seeds of the first Narnia story were dawning in his mind. Lewis never attempted to write another work of Christian apologetics after *Miracles*. Even though this book, and the argumentative works which precede it – *The Problem of Pain, Mere Christianity* – remain so vastly popular in the Christian world, and continue to sell in Christian bookshops, he came to feel that their method and manner were spurious. There must be another way 'further up and further in'.

Meanwhile, the routines of teaching, literary composition and domestic drudgery continued. Life at The Kilns had not been easy since the departure of June Flewett, whose career as an actress – she took the name of Jill Flewett – began to blossom. A succession of domestics were engaged. Chief of them was a maid called Vera whom Minto 'took against', and there were two others (who took it in turns) called Queenie and Flora. Minto being 'poorly' – it often took the form of crazy conspiracy theories about the maids – only exacerbated Warnie's tendency to have one of his 'turns'. When both recovered their senses, it was to open their eyes upon the bleak world of Mr Attlee's Britain – a Labour government, food shortages, austerity, and, as Jack called the Chancellor of the Exchequer Sir Stafford Cripps, 'the nursery governess of England'.[9] To Jack, the rewards of worldly success – such as being offered a Doctorate of Divinity by St Andrews University – were small consolation. 'A case of Scotch whisky might have been a kinder compliment,' he remarked.[10]

The excessive discomfort of rationing and the threatened increase in taxes united the household against the Labour Party, and this led to a certain diminution of Paxford's status in Mrs Moore's eyes. 'You should hear Warnie's views on the said Government,' Minto told June, 'and his Pessimism. The latter I fear we all share. Paxford (with whom we all keep well away on politics) says in 20 years every one will talk of the wonderful things it has done! By that time I don't think they'll have much of Britain or her possessions left.'[11]

Both brothers were large men, and in spite of their perpetual smoking they had big appetites. This meant that they watched the schemes for food rationing with eagle eyes. 'A staggering blow in the papers this morning,' Warnie recorded in November 1947.

Potatoes are put 'on rations' on a scale of 3lbs per week for the bourgeois. And so the last 'filler' food disappears from the diet, and the days of real hunger come upon us. It's extraordinary how one is conditioned by a secure past: even now I can't grasp the fact that I, WHL, will go to bed hungry and get up hungry; these, I say, are things that happen to nations one reads about in the papers, not to me.[12]

Jack felt the strain of this too. The post-war years were ones of intense unhappiness for him. In spite of now having a younger colleague, J. A. W. Bennett (a former pupil, the one he threatened with a sword for not liking *Sohrab and Rustum*), to help with the teaching of Old and Middle English, he felt overworked. The various maids and 'helps' at The Kilns were not much use. As he had said to Sister Penelope on a slightly earlier occasion, 'There is never a time when *all* three women are in a good temper. When A is in B is out; and when C has just got over her resentment at B's last rage and is ready to forgive, B is just ripe for her next and so on.' But saddest of all, a sadness which put affairs of the Government and Magdalen and The Kilns in the shade, was the fact that there was now a cooling between Lewis and his closest friends, especially Tolkien.

Various new Inklings had been recruited. A young man from St John's College whom Lewis had taught during the war, the poet and novelist John Wain, felt that the best of the Thursday evenings 'were as good as anything I shall live to see'.[13] He was intoxicated by the sense of having entered 'a circle of instigators, almost of incendiaries, meeting to urge one another on in the task of redirecting the whole current of contemporary art and life'.

But this was not how the Inklings saw themselves. Another new face in the circle after the war was J. R. R. Tolkien's son Christopher. He felt that the famous Thursdays were never without embarrassment. He developed a profound attachment to and admiration for Lewis which made the cooling between his father and Lewis all the more painful to him. The old 'cut and thrust' of conversation was beginning to cause wounds on all sides. Dyson, for example, who had been elected to a Fellowship at Merton after the war and now taught English there, felt a marked antipathy to Tolkien's writings, so that the readings of *The Lord of the Rings* – always a high point of the better evenings – were no longer a pleasure. Aware that some of his audience were unappreciative, J. R. R. Tolkien mumbled and read badly. Christopher, who was about to show himself one of the most eloquent lecturers Oxford has ever known, was brilliant at reading aloud, and took over the task. But he could not be sure that his readings would not be interrupted by Dyson, lying on the sofa with his club foot in the air and a glass of whisky in his hand, snorting, grunting and exhaling – 'Oh fuck, not another elf!' In such an atmosphere, it was not surprising that the Tolkien readings were discontinued.

Lewis read aloud some of the chapters of his work in progress on *English Literature in the Sixteenth Century Excluding Drama*; it was to be a volume of the Oxford History of English Literature, inevitably nicknamed OHEL. We do not know which passage particularly annoyed Tolkien *père*, but it could have been any of the moments where Lewis reflects upon the religion of the period – his provocative use of the word 'papist' for 'Roman Catholic', his praise of Calvin, his claim that Tyndale was superior to Thomas More as a stylist, or perhaps even his enthusiasm for Spenser, in whose work Tolkien, when in the mood, was capable of nosing out 'anti-Catholic mythology'.[14]

Clearly, Tolkien's fierce reaction to whichever section it was stunned Lewis. In the early spring of 1948, Tolkien wrote at immense length to his old friend to apologize.

> I write only because I find it easier so to say such things as I really want to say. If they are foolish or seem so, I am not present when they fall flat. (My whispering asides are most often due to sheer pusillanimity, and a fear of being laughed at by the general company.)
>
> This requires no answer. But as for yourself: rest in peace, as far as I am any 'critic' of behaviour. At least you are the fautlest freke that I know. 'Loudness' did you say? Nay! That is largely a self-defensive rumour put about by Hugo. If it has any basis (for him) it is but that noise begets noise. We are safe in your presence and presidency from contention, ill will, detraction, or accusations without evidence. Doubtless, as you say, I have as a member of the brotherhood a right to criticize an I please. But I shall not lightly forget my vision of the wounds; and I shall be deterred from rash dispraise, for myself . . . And let me beg of you to bring out OHEL with no coyness.[15]

All this sounds very much as if Tolkien's harsh judgement of what was to grow into Lewis's biggest book had reduced its author to visible signs of grief – perhaps to tears. Although the long letter of apology expresses such devotion, and although Tolkien's admiration, and in a way fondness, for Lewis was never to die, the friendship itself was dying. This letter was a kind of obituary for it, though neither man quite realized that. The strange, and greater than usual, intrusion of archaisms – 'an I please', 'fautlest freke' and so forth – betrays an agonizing awkwardness.

Perhaps it was precisely because this period of his life was so difficult that Lewis plunged, with such a depth of concentration, into imaginative composition. Perhaps the feeling that he was estranged from Tolkien inspired Lewis to remember that great conversation – about myth – which could be said to have changed his life. Certainly the disputation with Miss Anscombe, combined with the memory of what Tolkien had said about myth – made Lewis feel that there were other, and better, ways of telling the truth than by means of argument. As an apologist, in any case, how successful had he been? True, he had the St Andrews DD and a huge mail-bag from American admirers. But to those most close to him, he did not seem to have been a very convincing apologist. He told Warnie that he thought Minto had 'never come in contact with anything approaching Christianity',[16] an extraordinary confession for the author of *The Screwtape Letters* and *Mere Christianity*. Arthur Greeves, his oldest friend, had been a Christian when they began their correspondence all those years ago. Now he had left the Church of Ireland, dallied with the Unitarians, and thought of joining the Baha'i faith. It was a pattern which was to repeat itself throughout life. June Flewett, when she grew older and had been married for some years to Clement Freud, the wit and Member of Parliament, abandoned the practice of Christianity. The figure who, on the page, appears to have persuaded so many of the truth of the gospel was evidently a prophet without honour in his own country.

One reason for this must be that mere force of argument is never enough to convert another human being to Christianity, any more than mere acceptance of the creeds, as an intellectual proposition, is identical with faith. The whole person, the whole imagination, must be consecrated. This was something which Lewis only learnt through great suffering, and his best art came out of it.

In 1947, for example, he published in *Punch*, anonymously, a poem called 'The Late Passenger'. It is one of his finest, written in a sub-Chestertonian manner. Not only does it have an ingenious and pleasing metre, but the point of the poem is buried in its myth. It is a good example of what he wrote to a fellow-poet, Kathleen Raine: 'What flows into you from the myth is not truth but reality (truth is always about something but reality is about which truth is) and therefore every myth becomes the father of innumerable truths on the abstract level.'[17] The Late Passenger is an animal who canters up and is too late to get into Noah's Ark. Ham, the idle son of Noah, cannot be bothered to unlock the door of the Ark to let in this creature; in any case, the Ark is already full. But Noah, seeing it turn away in flight, addresses it:

Oh noble and unmated beast, my sons were all unkind:
In such a night what stable and what manger will you find?
Oh golden hoofs, oh cataracts of mane, oh nostrils wide
With indignation! Oh neck wave-arched, the lovely pride!
Oh long shall be the furrows ploughed across the hearts of men
Before it comes to stable and to manger once again.

The creature, of course, is the Unicorn, a mythological beast always associated in medieval bestiaries and heraldry with Christ Himself. His rejection from the Ark is 'myth' on just the level Lewis expounded to Kathleen Raine, a *story* to set forth the reality that Christ came to His own, and His own received Him not. Surprisingly, Roger Lancelyn Green, a rich man who had cultivated Lewis ever since he had heard his lectures before the war and was now by way of being a friend, wrote to congratulate Lewis on having written a comic poem. Presumably the confusion arose in Green's mind because the poem appeared in *Punch*, a supposedly comic paper (then under the editorship of Malcolm Muggeridge). Lewis was obliged to write back and correct him.

Green's chief area of literary interest was children's literature, and he was himself the author of several charming stories for children. In the biography of Lewis that he later wrote with Walter Hooper, he has left a slightly confused account of the chronology of the Narnia stories, and it may well be the case that no one knows exactly when they were written.[18] The first of them, *The Lion, the Witch and the Wardrobe*, was begun at the end of 1939 but not resumed and finished until 1948 or 1949. We know it was complete then, in more or less the form we have it today, because he read it to Green in March 1949. *The Voyage of the Dawn Treader* was finished by February 1950; *The Horse and His Boy* seems to have been written by the middle of 1950. Lewis once told Jill Freud that he had written all the children's stories in the space of a single year. This must have been an exaggeration, but it was not necessarily much of one. By March 1953, Lewis had told his publisher that he had finished the seventh story in the series, *The Last Battle*. The books were published at more or less annual intervals throughout the 1950s, and they remain hugely popular with the reading public today. Now a whole generation has grown up of people who read the Narnia stories in childhood, and have passed on the secret to their own children in turn. Whatever Lewis's future reputation as a theologian or literary critic, he is certain of a place among the classic authors of children's books, together with his own favourites, E. Nesbit, Beatrix Potter and Kenneth Grahame.

The Lion, the Witch and the Wardrobe grew out of Lewis's experience of being stung back into childhood by his defeat at the hands of Elizabeth Anscombe at the Socratic Club. It tells the story of how four children, staying with an old professor in the heart of the country, find a wardrobe in a remote part of his house which leads to another world, a world called Narnia. To write an outline of the story, which turns out to be the redemption of Narnia by a great lion called Aslan, who gives himself up for the sins of the children and rises again from the dead, would be to present as an 'idea' – what Lewis himself would have called 'a truth about something' – a story which is felt, in reading, to be reality itself. This story is delightful, a wholly absorbing narrative in its own right. It is as though Lewis, in all his tiredness and despondency in the late 1940s, has managed to get through the wardrobe door himself; to leave behind the world of squabbles and grown-ups and to re-enter the world which with the deepest part of himself he never left, that of childhood reading. In a very few pages, there is a rich concentration of all that he has most intensely felt and enjoyed as a reader – the talking animals of his own early stories, the fauna of classical mythology, the cold Wagnerian gusts of Northern-ness brought by the witch, the drama of religious confrontation, when the children witness 'deeper magic from before the dawn of time'. They are E. Nesbit children; they 'jaw' rather than talk; they say 'by gum!' and 'Crikey!' They seem no more to belong to the mid or late twentieth century than Lewis did himself. But generations of children can now testify to the irresistible *readability* of the Narnia stories. This must derive – at the risk of voicing once more the 'personal heresy' – from the fact that Lewis wrote them for the child who was within himself. It is not whimsical to say that Narnia *is* the inside of Lewis's mind, peopled with a rich enjoyment of old books and old stories and the beauties of nature, but always threatened by a terrible sense of loss, of love's frailty. Its method, of a heterodox absorption of so many different influences into one Christian allegory – MacDonald, Malory, Nesbit, Ovid, all have their deliberate echoes here – is one borrowed from Spenser; or perhaps it would be truer to say that it is at one with Lewis's own reading of that poet. The unifying element in *The Faerie Queene* is the place – 'Faerie Land itself provides the unity.'[19] Narnia provides a precisely similar unity for all the disparate elements which Lewis chooses to pour into his allegory. Green remonstrated with Lewis about the inclusion of Father Christmas in *The Lion, the Witch and the Wardrobe* but, guided by Spenser, Lewis rejected his advice. The appearance of a familiar figure like Father Christmas among so much that was new and strange is precisely the effect which Spenser achieved by juxtaposing old friends like St George with new monsters of his own invention.

Indeed, whenever Lewis writes about Spenser, we find it difficult not to think that the words apply equally well to himself. 'He is sure that popery is not "the pure springe of lyfe" but "nothing doubtes" the salvation of many Papists. He loves Ireland strongly, in his own way, pronouncing Ulster "a most bewtifull and sweete countrie as any is vnder heauen".' But we feel most of all that Lewis is, consciously or unconsciously, describing himself when he contrasts the Christian Platonism of the poet with the modern existentialists.

The Existentialist feels *Angst* because he thinks that man's nature (and therefore his relation to all things) has to be created or invented, without guidance, at each moment of decision. Spenser thought that man's nature was given, discoverable, and discovered; he did not feel *Angst*. He was often sad: but not, at bottom worried . . . His tranquillity is a robust tranquillity that 'tolerates the indignities of time', refusing (if we may put the matter in his terms) to be deceived by them, recognising them as truths, indeed, but only the truths of 'a foolish world'. He would not have called himself 'the poet of our waking dreams': rather 'the poet of our waking'.[20]

This is the figure who comes before us as the author of the Narnia stories. Not all his friends liked them. Tolkien hated *The Lion, the Witch and the Wardrobe*. He regarded it as scrappily put together, and not in his sense a 'sub-creation'; that is, a coherently made imaginative world. Moreover it was an allegory, a literary form which he never enjoyed. But presumably, since he was only human, he also felt an element of resentment at Lewis's fluency, his ability to get a thing done, and his increasing attractiveness to publishers. Tolkien himself managed to finish *The Lord of the Rings* in 1949, after twelve difficult years' work. It had first been submitted, together with *The Silmarillion*, to the publishers Collins, and whether or not it would be published still remained a matter of great uncertainty. He showed the completed typescript to Lewis, who, undeterred by Tolkien's view that Narnia 'just won't do', happily reabsorbed himself in his friend's great work. When he had finished it, he was effusive in his genuinely felt praise.

But as far as the Thursday evenings went, it was the end of the story. By October 1949, Warnie's diary was recording 'No one turned up after dinner.' There was still a regular assembly of Lewis's friends on Tuesdays at the Eagle and Child in St Giles's, but the high old days of the Inklings were over.

Even if the fellowship had not been broken for various other reasons, it is doubtful whether Lewis would have had the time or the energy for his salon in 1949 and 1950. He was writing, and teaching a great deal, and the strains at home were building up to a crisis point. All his weekends were devoted to nursing and caring for Minto, who was declining with greater and greater speed into a malign senility. In the middle of June 1949, Lewis himself collapsed under the burden of it all. Havard moved him into the Acland nursing home. He had a high fever and swollen glands, and Havard believed his condition to be 'serious . . . for a man of fifty'. Warnie, terrified by this development, went straight back to The Kilns 'and let her ladyship have a blunt statement of facts: stressing the exhaustion motif and its causes. I ultimately frightened her into agreeing to grant J a month's leave.'[21] When Miss Griggs, the daily help, arrived, he records that she entered Minto's room and 'forestalled any possible Mintonic opening with the words, "No, I don't want to hear anything about Bruce's health, I want to hear about Dr. Lewis's health."' Bruce was Minto's fifteen-year-old dog, ailing in health and much preying on her poor tormented mind. Warnie's next contribution to the family happiness was, while Jack was still languishing in the Acland, to go on one of his 'benders'. He was himself taken by force to the Acland to join his brother, but was eventually transferred for a brief period to the mental hospital in Headington, the Warneford. 'I am a man in chains,' Jack wrote.

The hellish responsibility of looking after an alcoholic brother and a furiously senile old woman were to remain with him for another ten months; but there were intervals of happiness. There were long periods when Warnie appeared to have got the drinking under control, though what made it all so frightening was the fact that it was precisely in moments of crisis, when Jack needed him most, that he was most likely to take once again to the bottle.

Events gradually took their course and eased the burdens on Lewis's shoulders. The unfortunate Bruce died on 17 January 1950. ('Joyful news,' Warnie recorded. 'As Minto's brain began to give way, his "little walks" became an obsession with her. I have known him taken out three times an hour.'[22] In April, 'Once again the axe has fallen.' Minto fell out of bed, and the doctor ordered her to be transferred to an old people's nursing home, Restholme, on the Woodstock Road, Oxford. The expense was crushing – well over £500 per annum – and Lewis began to wonder gloomily how he could possibly afford it if she were to live beyond his retirement. 'I hardly know how I feel,' he told Arthur Greeves, writing to his old friend to cancel his annual Irish holiday for lack of funds. 'Relief, pity, hope, terror, and bewilderment have me in a whirl. I have the jitters!'

Although it was a relief not to have to live with Minto in her present condition, it was also a wrench. Lewis's excruciatingly painful visits to Restholme, which he kept up every day that she was there, were a preparation for the final parting – a parting which Warnie could view with the cheerful emotional greed of a schoolboy waiting for the end of term, but which excited in Jack very different emotions. For the approaching loss of his 'adopted mother' threatened to reawake the trauma of his life, the loss of his real mother.

The New Year, 1951, brought with it a particularly virulent strain of influenza – 'the old man's friend', as it used to be called. In this case, it was the old woman's friend, since Janie Moore went down with it. She had long been addled in her wits, a figure of pathos to those who cared for her at Restholme. On 12 January, at five o'clock in the afternoon, she died. Lewis was with her. 'And so ends the mysterious self imposed slavery in which J has lived for at least thirty years,' Warnie wrote in his diary. 'How it began I suppose I shall never know.'

Warnie, who had come to hate and resent Mrs Moore, went down with a bout of influenza himself, and devoted an extended passage in his diary to a final vilification of Minto's memory. He described her association with his brother as 'the rape of J's life . . . I wonder how much of his time she did waste? It was some years before her break-down that I calculated that merely taking her dogs for unneeded "little walks" she had had *five months* of my life.' But this was a very strange way of regarding things. When all allowance has been made for the fact that Mrs Moore was, by any standards, a 'difficult' woman, it is perverse to blame her for the fact that life itself is humdrum. Most time *is* taken up, on this side of the grave, in trivia – in walks, in domestic conversations, in chores. To describe this as *waste* might have been just if it had made it impossible for Lewis to write his books. But very plainly it had not. He wrote at least twenty-five books during the time of his association with Minto.

As he followed her coffin to the churchyard at Headington Quarry, Jack Lewis would have had very different memories from those of his brother: 'Most infuriating to the onlooker was the fact that Minto never gave the faintest hint of gratitude; indeed regarded herself as Jack's benefactor . . .' Jack would remember a time when he had wired home that he was on 48-hour leave before being sent to the Western Front. His father did not even come to say goodbye. It was Minto who gave him a home during those momentous two days. When he came back from France, wounded with shrapnel and confined to various hospitals for five months, it was Minto who had stayed with him while the P'daytabird mysteriously refused to stray from Belfast.

Unlike Warnie, Jack would have remembered the early days with Minto – their struggles together in poor lodgings while he was a student; their shared grief and horror at her brother's madness; the joy of holidays in Somerset or by the sea in Cornwall; her pride in his work and success; her warmth and her affectionate, generous nature which had been with him throughout his adult life. Though in the end she had become a monster to Warnie, Jack always remained completely true to his commitment to her – 'I have definitely chosen and I don't regret the choice.' Some months later, 'the Beast' followed her to another world. Her husband, that is to say Courtenay Edward Moore, died somewhere in Ireland.

If the Anscombe debate about Supernaturalism had stung Lewis into a quite different sort of writing, the decline of Minto had also helped to drive him back imaginatively into childhood worlds. There can be little doubt that the energy and passion of the Narnia stories spring from the intensely unhappy and physically depleted state through which he had been passing. With the cooling of male friendships, with the sense that his intellectual defence of himself as a Christian was, at best, flawed, and with the gradual removal of his mother-substitute, he needed more than ever the comradeship which he had only ever found with Warnie in the Little End Room. And Warnie, much of the time, was blind drunk. This is what necessitated the escape not merely to the Little End Room, but beyond the wardrobe into imagined lands.

Tolkien's aesthetic objection to the Narnia stories is a perfectly valid one if we attempt to judge Narnia by the standards of *The Silmarillion*. Lewis's books for children show signs of extraordinary haste in composition; they are full of inconsistencies, and by his standards they are not even particularly well written. He frequently repeats epithets, and if the series is read entire by an adult reader the tone of voice can become wearisome. But it is a mistake to judge the Narnia stories as if they were a sort of slapdash *Lord of the Rings*. They are a quite different sort of book, and their readability and fascination stem from wholly individual qualities. The fascination of Tolkien is that his was a finished and enclosed imagination. His world, with its creatures, gods, angels, languages, lost tales and civilizations, is as complete as the 'real' world; perhaps more so. There is never an intrusive moment in Tolkien of two worlds jarring together; no hint, for example, that the creation story in *The Silmarillion* might relate to anything we have read in the Bible, or that the legendary figures and dynasties might interconnect with other cycles, such as those of the Edda or Homer. Lewis's Narnia books are quite different. Their whole theme is the interpenetration of worlds, and he poured into them a whole jumble of elements, drawn from his reading, and the world he was inhabiting when he wrote the books. *The Magician's Nephew* consciously locks itself into the worlds of other books.

This is a story about something that happened long ago when your grandfather was a child. It is a very important story because it shows how all the comings and goings between our own world and the land of Narnia first began.

In those days Mr Sherlock Holmes was still living in Baker Street and the Bastables were looking for treasure in the Lewisham Road . . .[23]

The Bastables are the children in E. Nesbit's books, such as *The Story of the Treasure Seekers*. Lewis was a devoted reader of Nesbit and borrowed elements of her stories for his Narnia plots. The Cabby and his wife who become the first King and Queen of Narnia in *The Magician's Nephew* are a direct copy of Nesbit's idea in *The Phoenix and the Carpet*, where the cook is transported by magic to a desert island and made Queen of the Savages. At the same time, there are many elements in the hotch-potch which are seized from the immediate present. In *The Silver Chair*, Puddleglum, the heroically melancholy Marshwiggle, is a direct portrait, as Lewis acknowledged, of his gardener at The Kilns, Paxford. The moment when the Witch 'in a loud terrible voice' traps the children underground and tries to persuade them that there is no world above the ground as they supposed, is a nursery nightmare version of Lewis's debate with Miss Anscombe. Characteristically, Lewis places the best speech of reply on the lips of Puddleglum himself:

One word, ma'am . . . one word. All you've been saying is quite right, I shouldn't wonder. I'm a chap who always likes to know the worst and then put the best face I can on it. So I won't deny any of what you said. But there's one thing more to be said, even so. Suppose we *have* only dreamed, or made up all those things – trees and grass and sun and moon and stars and Aslan himself. Suppose we have. Then all I can say is that, in that case, the made-up things seem a good deal more important than the real ones. Suppose this black pit of a kingdom of yours *is* the only world. Well, it strikes me as a pretty poor one. And that's a funny thing, when you come to think of it. We're just babies making up a game if you're right. But four babies playing a game can make a play-world which licks your real world hollow. That's why I'm going to stand by the play-world. I'm on Aslan's side even if there isn't any Aslan to lead it. I'm going to live as like a Narnian as I can even if there isn't any Narnia . . .[24]

If that is Lewis the wounded Christian, unable to think out his position but determined, in a moving and dogged way, to be loyal to it, then there are many other passages in the Narnia books where we meet Lewis the despondent conservative man living in the post-war Britain of austerity and Clement Attlee. Puzzle the Donkey, who is sent on errands to the market by the Ape in *The Last Battle* and is unable to find oranges or bananas to satisfy his taskmaster, is treading the same road that Lewis trod at the behest of Minto. The Ape's interfering desire to dupe the populace owes something to the Labour Government's treatment, as Lewis saw it, of the people of Britain, though it also draws upon a much deeper and more atavistic instinct in Lewis's imagination. The Ape's pretence that the people can only speak to Aslan through him reflects the Ulster author's view of the papacy. 'I'm a Man. If I look like an Ape, that's because I'm so very old: hundreds and hundreds of years old. And it's because I'm so old that I'm so wise. And it's because I'm so wise that I'm the only one Aslan is ever going to speak to . . . He'll tell me what to do and I'll tell the rest of you . . .' The 'progressive' school in *The Silver Chair* – 'Experiment House' – is a similarly crude piece of satire. 'It was Co-Educational, a school for both boys and girls, what used to be called a "mixed" school; some said it was not nearly so mixed as the minds of the people who ran it.'

The fact that Lewis threw into the mixture all the things which immediately concerned him certainly makes for a most imperfect 'sub-creation' by Tolkien's strict standards; but it is symptomatic of the much more important fact that in the Narnia stories Lewis is deeply and unselfconsciously engaged in the stories he is creating. He has abandoned here a cerebral and superficial defence of religion of the kind attempted at the Socratic Club. He has launched back deep into the recesses of his own emotional history, his own most deeply felt psychological needs and vulnerabilities. It is this, surely, which gives the books their extraordinary power. They are written white-hot. The time when the comings and goings between our world and Narnia began is not as you might guess remote in history. It was when Sherlock Holmes was still living in Baker Street and the Bastables were looking for treasure in the Lewisham Road; in other words, at the time when a certain Belfast solicitor called Albert Lewis was wooing a girl called Flora Hamilton. The penetration between the worlds began with his parents' marriage, and this is made clear at the end of the series, even if one rejects any Freudian explanation for its beginning. That is to say, we hardly need to dwell on the psychological significance of the wardrobe in the first story; we do not need, though some will be tempted to do so, to see in this tale of a world which is reached through a dark hole surrounded by fur coats any unconscious image of the passage through which Lewis first entered the world from his mother's body. We do not need to be ingenious because, by the end of *The Last Battle*, it is all spelt out for us. If *The Lion, the Witch and the Wardrobe* is a story which hangs on the gospel narrative of the Resurrection, then *The Last Battle* is the Apocalypse in which there is a final conflict with the forces of evil. The old heaven and the old earth pass away, Narnia is destroyed, and then remade for eternity. The children all come together because they and their parents have now entered Narnia for ever, not by the magic of stepping through a wardrobe, but through an actual railway accident, a real death. Only one of the children from the original quartet is excluded from heaven. This is Susan. She has committed the unforgivable sin of growing up.

'Yes,' said Eustace, 'and whenever you've tried to get her to come and talk about Narnia or do anything about Narnia, she says, "What wonderful memories you have! Fancy you still thinking about all those funny games we used to play when we were children."'

'Oh, Susan!' said Jill, 'She's interested in nothing nowadays except nylons and lipstick and invitations. She always was a jolly sight too keen on being grown-up.'[25]

For the magic of Narnia to work, you have to be devoid of any such desire; you have to be as Warnie was when he left the Army, wanting to re-create the world of the Little End Room and live in it for ever and ever. Lewis had tried to resist Warnie's idea at the time, but his children's writings show that he found it all but irresistible. For what the children discover when Aslan/Christ has made all things new is that the old things have not passed away at all. They find that not only has the old Narnia been preserved and refashioned, but that England has been too, and some people who are more important even than the many strange characters, fauns, centaurs, talking animals, whom they have met in their imaginative adventures.

'Why!' exclaimed Peter. 'It's England. And that's the house itself – Professor Kirk's old home in the country where all our adventures began!'

'I thought that house had been destroyed,' said Edmund.

'So it was,' said the Faun. 'But you are now looking at the England within England, the real England just as this is the real Narnia. And in that inner England no good thing is destroyed.'

Suddenly they shifted their eyes to another spot, and then Peter and Edmund and Lucy gasped with amazement and shouted out and began waving: for they saw their own father and mother, waving back at them across the great, deep valley. It was like when you see people waving at you from the deck of a big ship when you are waiting on the quay to meet them.[26]

It was on the quayside that Lewis and Warnie parted from their father only two weeks after their mother had been taken from them. That terrible severance, which took them away from Ireland and childhood and all that had made them comfortable, is here longingly stitched up. *The Last Battle* is the story which Lewis, when he came to write his autobiography for grown-ups, was incapable of telling. It is an exploration on a level which George MacDonald would have understood of the unplumbed psychological depths where regret and longing and unhealed heartbreak find their consolation in old Christian story.

SIXTEEN

THE SILVER CHAIR
1951–1954

Three weeks after the demise of Mrs Moore, Oxford found itself once again in the throes of an election for the Chair of Poetry, an event which takes place every five years. Lewis's own candidate in 1938, the Reverend Adam Fox, had been a disgracefully tedious occupant of the post. In 1943, he had been succeeded by the Dean (later Warden) of Wadham College, Maurice Bowra. Bowra was a famously witty man, whose *mots* – 'I am a man more dined against than dining,' or, on becoming engaged to a rather 'difficult' woman, 'Buggers can't be choosers' – were hawked around and repeated by his admirers and friends. Strangely enough, he was a crashing bore on the subject of literature. His books are flat as pancakes, and so were his lectures as Professor of Poetry. This time, in 1951, the old cry went up that the University deserved something a little more exciting. C. S. Lewis was persuaded to stand. He had two rivals, supported by those who echoed Lewis's own view of 1938 that 'we must have a practising poet': they were Edmund Blunden and C. Day-Lewis.

Jack Lewis's campaign manager was Dyson, who hobbled round the colleges on his club foot, canvassing for votes. One don informed him that he would not be voting for Lewis on the grounds that he had written *The Screwtape Letters*. 'If they offer you sherry, you're done,' was Dyson's rule of thumb. 'I had lots of sherry.'

C. Day-Lewis's campaign manager was the diminutive French scholar Enid Starkie, a peculiar little Irish woman who wrote books about Flaubert and Baudelaire, and would often be seen weaving her way from Somerville College to her house in St Giles in bright variations of a *matelot*'s uniform. ('All the colours of the Rimbaud,' as Bowra inevitably remarked.) She was one of those self-created Oxford 'characters', with her strongly Irish-French accent, her hints at a raffish past and her acquaintance with modern French intellectuals. She once boasted to Gide that in order to pay for her years of study in Paris she had been reduced to selling her body, a transaction which makes one wish, if it ever took place, that the pen of Osbert Lancaster had depicted it. The Chair of Poetry was one of her obsessions. Indeed, when she stood for it herself, in a later contest, it could be said to have driven her rather mad. On this occasion, she backed C. Day-Lewis and she was an efficient operator. She persuaded Edmund Blunden to retire from the contest and stand again next time. C. S. Lewis's opponents were thus united in a single band.

C. Day-Lewis, who had best exercised his talents in life as a publisher (at Chatto & Windus in London) and as the author of a fine series of detective stories under the pseudonym Nicholas Blake, was put up as the 'practising poet'. In reality, there was probably little to choose between C. Day-Lewis and C. S. Lewis as poets. Both were men who passionately wanted to be poets, and who wrote a few good poems, but who will never rank very high in any history of English poetry.

Warnie, and perhaps other members of Jack's circle, saw it as a contest between the 'atheist–communist bloc' and the forces of sweetness and light. This was pretty largely nonsense. It could equally well have been seen as a contest between a man whom there was already every opportunity of hearing lecture in Oxford and an outsider – a man of letters from London, who might have things to say which Oxford had not heard. In the event it was an election which did not excite much interest among the thousands of people who, as MAs, were entitled to vote. Only 367 votes were cast: 173 of them were for C. S. Lewis, which left 194 for C. Day-Lewis, scraping home by 21 votes. Since the names on the voting slips were given merely as LEWIS C.D., and LEWIS C.S., it is even possible that some of the country clergy, after good luncheons at their old colleges, unintentionally allied themselves to the so-called atheist–communist bloc.

A dinner had been arranged that night at a large ugly hotel near the railway station to which the Lewis brothers were for some reason devoted: the Royal Oxford. Barfield, Havard, David Cecil, J. A. W. Bennett and Warnie were there. When the news came that Jack had been defeated, the supporters were more dashed than their candidate.

Warnie, who had been going through the names of those who 'backed' C. Day-Lewis, had begun the dangerous game of finding their surnames a little suspect ('Pentacostal [sic] sweepings bearing all sorts of Slav and Balkan names').[1] Jack 'took it astonishingly well', almost certainly because he did not really care. The fact that his life was no longer circumscribed by depressing visits to Restholme, by the dread of domestic quarrels, by the sheer financial drain on his purse involved in nursing Minto, brought with it a deep inner peace.

The real strain of living with Minto had not been what Warnie or Lewis's friends thought it was. Dyson quoted the line from *Othello* – 'O cursed fate that gave thee to the Moor(e),' and Warnie considered this 'poor Jack's whole catastrophe epitomised in nine words'. Jack himself stopped speaking to Dyson for about a month when he heard this quip (and Dyson was never one to make a quip just the once). It was both deeply true and deeply untrue. The 'cursed fate' was that his relationship with Minto forced him into the position, from the very beginning, of living a lie. As an undergraduate he had had to conceal his actual living arrangements from his college, or he would certainly have been sent down from the University. He also felt he had to lie to his father, and pretend that he was not living with Mrs Moore. It was during these years that the formula emerged of her being his 'mother' or 'adopted mother'. But this in itself was artificial, because she was *not* his mother, and the relations he had with her were far more intense than those which most men have with their mothers. Whatever the relationship was, it was a closed book to Warnie.

Now that she was dead, Jack was ready to start his life all over again. The children's books written at this period were more than an imaginative return to his own childhood. They were a sort of sluicing of the system which, together with his regular confessions and communions, represented a conversion every bit as deep as the conversion to a belief in the supernatural and the divinity of Jesus Christ which occurred in 1929–1931. Then, it will be remembered, he had no real interest in the traditional teachings or concerns of Christianity. The teachings of St Paul, about the Cross, about grace, about the forgiveness of sins, meant nothing to him: he could 'get nothing out of them'. The only doctrine of St Paul's which seemed to have 'stuck' at this period was the rather esoteric one that a man and a woman, having once made love, whether or not they are married, have become one flesh, and are therefore bound to one another forever afterwards, through thick or thin. After he had 'become a Christian', the tension of his life with Minto therefore became all the more pronounced. He was having to live with her in a way which would conceal, even from Warnie, whatever had once been 'sinful' in the relationship. No wonder all his friends found that relationship totally baffling. No wonder, too, that he developed the habit of never discussing personal matters, never seeming, when in the company of male friends, even to have a personal life.

Shuffling off the guilt and relief which came at the time of his father's death, Lewis had felt (in his mystical experience on the bus on Headington Hill) as though 'some stiff clothing, like corsets, or even a suit of armour, as if I were a lobster'[2] were being removed from him. In his second, and more radical, phase of conversion, twenty and more years after the first, Lewis began to feel for the first time that he knew what was meant by the grace and forgiveness of God. In June 1951, he wrote to Sister Penelope at Wantage:

> I specially need your prayers because I am (like the pilgrim in Bunyan) travelling across 'a plain called Ease'. Everything without, and many things within, are marvellously well at present. Indeed (I do not know whether to be more ashamed or joyful in confessing it) I realise that until about a month ago I never really believed (tho' I thought I did) in God's forgiveness.[3]

It was in this frame of mind that he finished the Narnia stories, which probably contain his finest passages of religious writing. One of the great paradoxes inherent in the process I have been describing in this chapter is that his intimates were the last people to know what was going on, as it were, *inside* Lewis. The softening process did not change his lifelong habit of keeping 'talk' rigidly to a level in which anyone could join. There was never any intimate chat with Lewis. Christopher Tolkien has often remarked to me not only that Lewis repelled any attempt to gossip in his presence, but that he would display no interest whatsoever in a friend's private life. Sessions at the pub would not begin with routine enquiries about one's wife, health, family. For all Lewis knew by the end of the conversation, one could just have got divorced or been told that one had cancer. All that would have been discussed would have been the merits of Layamon as a poet, or the rights and wrongs of cannibalism. It was this inability to be personal – to be, in one sense, natural – which led so many of his friends to be surprised by sides of Lewis which emerged in his work: mention has already been made of Dom Bede Griffiths' astonishment at the imaginative force and sheer emotion of the children's stories; neither were apparent in the conversations he had, over many years, with Lewis himself.

As someone of so passionate a nature, and so good at articulating emotion on the page, it was natural that Lewis should have built up a large correspondence. From the moment he came to prominence as a writer on religious subjects, Lewis had correspondents from both sides of the Atlantic, who wrote to him as to a spiritual director about their problems – their marriages, their difficulties in prayer, their sexual and emotional troubles, their struggles with drink. Since they seemed like souls crying out for comfort, he answered them. It could be said that a man who was better-adjusted, less buttoned-up with his friends, might have seen the dangers of such correspondences. They quickly develop into fantasies, in which an 'intimacy' of a completely false kind grows up between two people who do not actually know one another at all. One of his correspondents always signed herself 'Jehovah'. But from the first, Lewis was addicted to the custom of answering all the letters which were sent to him, often rising a good while before daybreak to complete the task. This accounts for the huge number of his letters which survive, many of them in American libraries.

Even more astonishing than the fact that he was prepared to read the letters was his willingness on occasion to meet the people who wrote them. One can interpret this in any number of ways. On one level, it can be said that Lewis merely felt that he was doing his duty. He had written a book on a subject close to everyone's heart, *The Problem of Pain*. So when a clergyman wrote to him to say that he was finding it impossible to reconcile a belief in God's omnipotence with a belief in his love, Lewis consented to spend an afternoon talking to this man about the problem. He was patient, friendly, helpful. The priest, who had expected the author of *The Problem of Pain* to look pale and ethereal, was astonished by the red-faced pork butcher in shabby tweeds whom he actually encountered. Since this was a case of a devoted parish priest in danger of losing his faith, one can see why Lewis consented to meet him. But what of the case of Kathryn Stillwell,* an admirer of Lewis's from the United States who had made a fascinating connection with the master? Lewis's mother was forty-six years old when she died on 23 August 1908. Exactly forty-six years later (and she does not explain in her account of the matter what was so magical about the number forty-six), a friend of hers borrowed one of Lewis's books from a public library. 'You could say that I was mentally "married" to Lewis that very day,' she wrote. You could. But then again, you couldn't. It is surely very interesting that when she wrote to Lewis from a London hotel, he should have invited her to tea with him at his beloved Royal Oxford Hotel. Finding herself sitting next to him on a sofa she was – not surprisingly after her mystical marriage in the public library – 'giddy with awe'.[4]

In the event, this devotee married Mr Lindskoog. Not that being married necessarily deterred Lewis's penfriends from hope. A case in point was the experience of Mrs Joy Gresham of Westchester, New York State, who had been converted to Christianity in 1946, and began corresponding with Lewis on 10 January 1950. 'Just got a letter from Lewis in the mail,' Mrs Gresham remarked to her cousin Renée Pierce at the time. 'I think I told you I'd raised an argument or two on some points? Lord, he knocked my props from under me unerringly; one shot to a pigeon.'[5] Evidently, she derived some emotional satisfaction from having the sheer illogicality of her letters exploded by the great man himself. 'Being disposed of so neatly by a master of debate, all fair and square – it seems to be one of the great pleasures of life.' Since this was precisely the period in Oxford when Lewis was beginning to have his doubts about the value of verbal fisticuffs, and when he was still licking the wounds inflicted by Miss Anscombe at the Socratic Club, it was reassuring to be able to provide such satisfaction as he could to these unseen ladies across the water.

But whereas in books it does not really matter where fantasy

---

* Later Kathryn Lindskoog. She went on to write several books about Lewis, one of which, *The C. S. Lewis Hoax*, is discussed in the Preface.

ends and reality begins, in the dangerous game of letter-writing to strangers, the reader can actually hit back at the artist, or involve herself – if she chooses and he lets her – in his fantasy. Renée Pierce became convinced, the more she saw of Joy Gresham at this period, that her cousin was falling in love with Lewis, even though she had never seen him.[6]

Joy Gresham was thirty-five when she started writing to Lewis. She was small – five foot two inches in height – highly animated and emotional, and trying to make her way in the world as a poet and novelist. One of her earliest literary triumphs was to win the Bernard Cohen Short Story Prize at Hunter College, New York City, where she was a student in 1934.[7] At Hunter, her closest friend was the future novelist Bel Kaufman, who recalled that 'Joy seldom dated. When she did go out, her escorts were older men seriously interested in literature.'[8] This taste for literary old gentlemen was to take a long while to satisfy, and her life's journey took some wild swoops before she arrived in this story. Leaving Hunter in the Depression years Joy (née Davidman), like many East Coast would-be intellectuals of the period, was drawn to Communism and eventually joined the party. Equally of its period was her desire to get involved with writing for the movies. When she was twenty-seven, she married a handsome man called Bill Gresham, whose first novel *Nightmare Alley* was sold for $60,000 to Hollywood, instantly lifting them from the pauperism of life in a cramped little apartment in East 22nd Street, New York City, to the gracious lifestyle of country dwellers at Pleasant Plains, near Staatsburg.

But in spite of having two children in swift succession – David born in 1944 and Douglas in 1945 – all was not well with the Gresham marriage. Bill Gresham was an alcoholic and a compulsive womanizer. Devastated by the discovery of yet another of her husband's infidelities six months after Douglas was born, Joy had a religious experience. 'All my defences – the walls of arrogance and cocksureness and self-love behind which I had hid from God – went down momentarily – and God came in.'[9]

For a time, Bill Gresham went along with the new religious phase: but for him, Christianity was only a phase. It was not long before he had admitted to her that 'I am not a Christian and will probably never be one since I cannot understand the basic doctrines nor accept them.'

He also admitted to her that, yet again, he had been unfaithful. As Joy's biographer remarks, 'Bill Gresham's growing away from Christianity is a real-life example of Christ's parable of the seed falling on rocky soil.' By February 1951, Joy had brought an end to the physical side of her relationship with Bill Gresham,[10] and the correspondence with Lewis – who could, at this stage, have had no conception of the amount of emotional capital Joy was investing in it – continued to flourish.

In September 1952, she crossed the Atlantic.

The death of Minto in January 1951 had provided necessary emotional punctuation in Lewis's life, an opportunity to start again from childhood. In May 1952, there was another death, obviously less momentous, but not without significance in the story that follows. Father Walter Adams SSJE died while saying Mass on 17 May. His last words as he fell backwards on the altar steps were 'I am coming, Lord Jesus.'

For ten years, he had been what Lewis called 'my old *directeur*'. For those not acquainted with the ways of Anglican piety, it is worth dwelling on the phrase. Not all Anglicans go to confession and, of those who do, not all have a regular confessor, still less anyone they would describe as their spiritual director. The majority, probably, simply go to confession at a time when there happens to be a priest available in church, and the whole transaction is totally impersonal. The priest would not necessarily know who his penitents were, let alone anything about their past lives. In such a case, he would merely be pronouncing God's forgiveness for the itemized sins committed since the penitent's last confession.

For those who choose to have a spiritual director, it is all a bit different. The director is not necessarily the same person as the confessor, though in Lewis's case he was. The director is a man (or woman) who gets to know the 'client' personally, and advises him not only about his life of prayer, but also about his conduct of life in general, including how often, if ever, he should go to confession. (Baron von Hügel, the great Roman Catholic lay theologian, who was the spiritual director to the Anglican mystic Evelyn Underhill, used to advise her *never* to go to confession. I mention the example to establish the difference between a director and a confessor.)

Though Lewis was to continue, for the rest of his life, to go to confession, he was deprived in 1952 of his spiritual director, and he never, properly speaking, took up with another, though Austin Farrer was evidently a close spiritual friend with whom it was possible to discuss some matters. Had Father Adams lived until, say, 1960, we do not know whether the following story would have been different. But without his presence to admonish and guide, Lewis must have felt both a little bereft and, in a sense, liberated. The Cowley Fathers at this period were all noted for the extreme strictness of their spiritual direction. 'I owed him a great deal,' Lewis said. 'Everything he ever said to me was so simple that you might have thought it childish, but it was always what was needed.'[11]

Not much imagination is needed to guess what Father Adams would have said about the arrival in Oxford of a 37-year-old married woman from New York who invited Lewis and his brother to luncheon at the Eastgate Hotel, just opposite Magdalen. Lewis clearly liked her, and asked her, in return, to lunch at Magdalen. This time, Warnie backed out of the meal, and Lewis asked along an old pupil, now a master at his old school Malvern, called George Sayer. Evidently, he was aware from the first that there was some inherent 'danger' in the situation, or he would not have gone out of his way to provide a chaperon on each occasion he saw Mrs Gresham. (It was very different from tea with Kathryn Stillwell, giddy with awe at the Royal Oxford Hotel; he knew he was safe with her.)

Mrs Gresham returned to London, where she was staying, but some weeks later Lewis invited her to a slightly larger lunch party at Magdalen to meet his friends. Warnie's verdict on this party, recorded some years later, was as follows:

I was some little time in making up my mind about her: she proved to be a Jewess, or rather a Christian convert of Jewish race, medium height, good figure, horn rimmed specs, quite extraordinarily un-inhibited. Our first meeting was at lunch in Magdalen, where she turned to me in the presence of three or four men, and asked in the most natural tone in the world, 'Is there anywhere in this monastic establishment where a lady can relieve herself?' But her visit was a great success . . .[12]

Warnie's diaries were written, it will be remembered, for the record; he knew that there was always the possibility that one day he would die and Jack would read them. And by the time he wrote these words he was genuinely fond of Joy. Her five foot two inches had become 'medium' height, though it is what some would call short. He had forgotten that he first met her not with Dyson and the others at Magdalen, but with just Jack at the Eastgate Hotel. And, being a gentleman, he had considerably toned down the way she asked for the whereabouts of the lavatory. Others were present at the luncheon and noted her 'lack of inhibition', and found it embarrassing. She spoke habitually in language that most of those present associated more with their days in the Army than with a lunch in pleasant civilian surroundings in peacetime. There seemed something strident about her, as though – either from nerves, or extreme self-conceit, or both – she had to justify herself. Part of the point of saying 'bloody' and 'fuck' so often appeared to be in order to suggest that with Jack she was so much at ease that she could be herself. Or perhaps – 'monastic establishment' – she was genuinely under the impression that these were words her company did not know, or that she had a duty to shake them up a bit. She habitually spoke and wrote as if she were the first American, let alone the first Jewish American, to pene-trate the hallowed cloisters of Oxford, and some of those who have written about Lewis seem to share this view, unaware of the fact that, since the time persecutions in Continental universities began in the 1930s, Oxford was fuller than most towns in the world of Jewish intellectuals, many of them holding fellowships of colleges including Magdalen. If Lewis's friends at first took against Joy Gresham, and if their feelings of initial suspicion deepened into something like loath-ing, one needs to look about for reasons other than her sex, race or place of birth.

Whatever the others thought, Lewis was charmed. Far from finding her, as his friends did, foul-mouthed, bad-tempered and self-assertive, he found himself roaring with laughter at everything she said. He asked her to stay at The Kilns for Christmas, and she stayed a fortnight.

She had now been away from her husband and children for four months, and while staying at The Kilns during that Christmas of 1952 she produced a letter from Bill informing her that he was in love with her cousin Renée. The optimum solution, he told her, would be for her, Joy, to be 'married to some real swell guy, Renée and I to be married' and 'somehow arrange things so that the Gresham kids could have Mommy and Daddy on hand'. There is absolutely no way of knowing whether Joy had known about this 'bombshell' for some time. Her motives in apprising Lewis of the situation, during their Christmas together, would seem fairly clear. One of the last things he did before she sailed back to the United States was to take her to the pantomime. They laughed at 'the oldest jokes' and joined in the songs. 'I'll never forget Jack', she recalled, 'coming in loudly on something that went like this:

> Am I going to be a bad boy? No! no! no!
> Am I going to be awful? No! no! no!'

There is something hugely touching about the idea of this large, red-faced man fifty-four years old shouting out a pantomime song designed for little boys. His second childhood had raced past while he wrote the Narnia books. Now he was on the threshold of an adventure which many people experience in their teens – a boy–girl relationship with a woman of his own age or younger. He could shout No, no, no! as loud as he liked. Mrs Gresham's answer to the question of whether he was going to be 'awful' would have been very different, as she took the boat back to New York.

As far as Lewis's professional life was concerned, 1953 was dominated by his monumental literary history of *English Literature in the Sixteenth Century*. He had been commissioned to write it by the Oxford University Press (at F. P. Wilson's suggestion) over twelve years before, and – at almost 700 pages by far his longest work – it had been a tremendous effort. Some of it had been completed in 1944, when he read a few chapters as the Clark Lectures at Cambridge. But interruptions had been constant, not least the great emotional interruption of Tolkien's distaste for the book, and the whole imaginative excitement of writing Narnia. At last it was done. In sheer magnitude, it is his biggest achievement, and it must rank as about the most entertaining work of criticism ever written. When he wrote to Sister Penelope in 1951 that he was 'travelling across a Plain called Ease', he could have been putting his finger on what makes the book so immensely attractive. It reads like a very clever and wise person talking about the things which concern him most. To this extent, it is one of the most truly Christian books he ever wrote: it gives us more of what is best in Lewis's Christianity than do those where he has mounted the pulpit steps to proclaim the word. I am thinking of such sections as his description of *The Book of Common Prayer*, which reveals so much not only of the treasures of that book, but also of Lewis's own piety.

> In the Prayer Book, that earnest age, not itself rich either in passion or in beauty, is matched in a most fruitful opposition with overwhelming material and with originals all but over-ripe in their artistry. It arrests them, binds them in strong syllables, strengthens them even by limitation as they in return erect and transfigure it. Out of that conflict the perfection springs. There are of course many good, and different, ways of praying. Its temper may seem cold to those reared in other traditions but no one will deny that it is strong. It offers little and concedes little to merely natural feelings: even religious feelings it will not heighten till it has first sobered them; but at its greatest it shines with a white light hardly surpassed outside the pages of the New Testament itself.[13]

The chapters on 'The Close of the Middle Ages in Scotland' and on 'Sidney and Spenser' are perhaps the best. Of course, what makes the book *unboring* is what makes it, in the judgement of bores, unreliable. It offers the stimulation of good talk, and it is frequently opinioned. The idea that the 'humanists' of the late fifteenth and early sixteenth century – More, Erasmus and Colet – were far less interesting than the late medieval thinkers whom they hoped to displace; the idea, indeed, that the Renaissance in England either did not happen or, if it did, that it was a Bad Thing, could not pass without other scholars attacking it. The discovery that 'drab' in this book means 'good' tells us much about Lewis and his aesthetic, but it is perverse. And there are, as readers of his life would expect, some very strange emotional lacunae. His bluff, Johnsonian 'What man in the whole world, except a father or a potential father-in-law, cares whether any other man gets married?' is a rhetorical question which invites the opposite answer to the one he wants. (He was writing of Shakespeare's Sonnets to the Young Man; he was about to discover that, quite apart from extraordinary emotional entanglements such as the one chronicled in the Sonnets, a man's friends can mind very much whether he gets married, and to whom.)

In his autobiography, Lewis enunciates the great truth:

> Tea should be taken in solitude . . . for eating and reading are two pleasures that combine admirably. Of course not all books are suitable for meal-time reading. It would be a kind of blasphemy to read poetry at table. What one wants is a gossipy formless book which can be opened anywhere . . . Boswell . . . Tristram Shandy, Elia and the *Anatomy of Melancholy* are all good for the same purpose.[14]

To this illustrious list one would want to add his own *English Literature in the Sixteenth Century Excluding Drama*. Whether in its abundant (and often enjoyably questionable) epigrams, its golden or almost purple passages, its passionate enthusiasms, its magnificent unfairnesses, its gusto, or its overall common sense, it never fails as a book to read alone over a large cup of tea. It probably deserves much more learned appreciation than that but, in so far as a book can increase the sum of human pleasure, there are not many higher terms of praise. How many works of academic criticism or literary history would we look at twice, except for the purpose of checking a reference? Here is one which repays any number of enjoyable rereadings.

In spite of those who cavilled at the peculiarity of its judgements, the book got a very good reception from the critics. One who reviewed it was A. L. Rowse, the Cornish fellow of All Souls who had achieved a name for himself as a leading authority on the sixteenth century and biographer of the Churchill family, and was still at that date a supporter of – and Parliamentary candidate for – the Labour Party. Rowse and Lewis had known each other since 1926, when Lewis had Rowse to dinner at Magdalen. They had never been much one another's 'type', and over the years their views had diverged. Indeed, during a public debate with Rowse over historical relativism, held in the University church, Lewis had walked out, leaving a very poor impression on the audience. He failed to stay to hear, let alone contest,

Rowse's argument that a modern man's view of the universe was so different from, say, that obtaining in the first century AD that this *must* affect our reading of historical documents. If we no longer think that epileptics are people who are possessed by devils or that heaven is a place located directly above us in the clouds and penetrable by direct take-off from Galilean hillsides, this must change our reading of the Gospels. Lewis would have none of it, and went so far as to put this line of argument on Screwtape's favourite list of intellectual fads, thereby assigning Rowse (at least by implication) to hell. Rowse, who is capable of taking great offence over smaller matters than this, always admires and recognizes greatness and genius in others; and he could see Lewis's greatness and genius, though finding him personally uncongenial. Lewis was touched by Rowse's kind review and came up to him in a train to thank him. As they sat down together in the compartment, Rowse said, 'I did enjoy the book *very* much, and I think it was a good book. But now that I have got you in person, let me tell you some of the things which were wrong with it.' He went on to say, as many others had said, that it was silly to disparage the growth of New Learning, and the arrival in England of the Latin and Greek classics. Had not Lewis himself enormously benefited from the work begun by More and Erasmus, Sir John Cheke and others? Lewis conceded the point.

'Now, as for the prose writers of the period,' said Rowse, 'I cannot agree with all that you write. You praise Cardinal Allen, who is really negligible and wrote very little, but you do not even mention Robert Parsons, the Jesuit who wrote over thirty books and was one of the most considerable prose writers of the Elizabethan period. Why?' If the question had been put to a candidate at a viva voce examination it would have bowled him full stump. Rowse could tell from his companion's face that Lewis realized, in that moment, that he had simply missed Parsons out by an oversight – probably because he had not read him. But the police-court lawyer suddenly appeared in the carriage – the same man who had told Helen Gardner on a reflex that all his pupils read Calvin. 'I did not think he was sufficiently important to be included,' said Lewis. But it was a bluster, and both men knew it, and they passed the rest of the journey in silence.[15]

In spite of its lacunae and eccentricities, the OHEL volume established Lewis beyond question as a giant among the pygmies of the

Oxford English Faculty, which made their failure to promote him to a professorship all the more surprising.*

It was to be another university – Cambridge – which recognized his merits and rewarded them. In the summer of 1954, Cambridge established a new Chair of English specializing in the literature of the medieval and Renaissance periods. It was fairly obvious who should fill this chair, but Cambridge took soundings. A letter was written, for instance, to Helen Gardner, recently appointed Reader in Renaissance Literature at Oxford, to ask whether she knew of anyone suitable for the post. She interpreted this letter as a darkly worded offer of the job to herself, and replied that, while being flattered by the enquiry, she thought that the obvious man for the job was Lewis. She communicated this information, not without some self-importance, to Tolkien. As a matter of fact she spoke of all academic appointments, in her own or other universities, as if they were in her gift, and 'I got Lewis the Cambridge chair' was one of her favourite songs. It was at least true that Helen Gardner, with all her distaste for Lewis as an individual, recognized his greatness and had a genuine respect for his written work. (Her characteristically dreary view remained unshakeable, though, that he would never have been suitable for an *Oxford* chair because he would not do any 'work', by which she meant supervising graduate students. In fact he did supervise some graduates, but lacked her voracious appetite for rewriting every thesis in sight.)

After all the due approaches had been made, Lewis accepted, with very mixed feelings, the chair at Magdalene College, Cambridge. It was a great honour, but the University was one that he only knew very slightly. Although he would keep on The Kilns and continue to reside there during the vacations and weekends, Oxford, as a university, would no longer be home. It was a big severance; a sort of exile. And though it would be an exaggeration to compare Lewis's

* It was not unique. Think of Rowse himself – certainly the most entertaining and eloquent historian of his age, and author of several histories – such as *The England of Elizabeth* – destined to become classics in the tradition of Gibbon and Macaulay, of history which is also literature. Rowse was never, in his half-century as a fellow of All Souls, once asked to lecture in the History Faculty, let alone offered promotion. Or think of Austin Farrer, described as the 'one true genius' of the Church of England in the twentieth century, author of incomparably the most interesting theological books ever to come out of the Oxford Theology Faculty, and passed over for professorial chairs over and over again.

promotion with the effective banishment from Oxford of Shelley and Newman (who in their different ways offended the prevailing orthodoxy of their times), it could be said that Lewis *was* exiled, in some sense, for his refusal to toe the line. It was not his failure to be a good graduate supervisor which cost him an Oxford chair, it was *Mere Christianity* and *The Screwtape Letters*: the fact that he wrote them, and the far more damaging fact that millions of people, as they do to this day, wanted to read them.

His inaugural lecture at Cambridge was arranged to take place on Monday, 29 November 1954, just before he finally relinquished his post at Oxford. It was indicative of the way that he was developing at this time that he chose to give the lecture not about Chaucer or Ariosto or Spenser, but about himself. His thesis was a sort of rambling elaboration of 'the old order changeth, yielding place to new'. He could not hope to rival other scholars, but he could place himself before the University of Cambridge as a dinosaur, as a specimen representing a vanished age, an obsolete set of beliefs, a wholly outmoded way of looking at the world. There was a strong element of irony in all this. But one of the things which makes Lewis such an interesting character is that – like some of the great Romantic poets – he was an object not just of fascination but also of mystery to himself. The 'dinosaur' he presented to his Cambridge audience was one of self-image. No one who knows anything of Lewis can suppose that it was an altogether false image. But nor was he altogether aware that, having painted the picture of the dinosaur, he had in some senses already done it to death. He was, at the age of fifty-six, in the process of turning into something very different. This was not a case of a poseur dropping one 'act' and wondering whether to try another. It was much more organic and natural than that. One hesitates to speak of a butterfly emerging from its chrysalis, for that would be to imply (falsely) that the former selves of Lewis were only preparations for the latter selves. But the emergence of other selves was something over which he had very little control, and which he watched with bewilderment and fascination.

The friends who organized a dinner of farewell from the Oxford English Faculty on 9 December 1954 had little or no conception of what had been going on inside Lewis. The dinner was held at Merton. F. P. Wilson came, and Nevill Coghill, J. R. R. and Christopher

Tolkien, Hugo Dyson and a number of others, including, as Warnie noted, 'an unfortunate young man with a face like a fish, who never, so far as I saw, made a remark all evening'.[16]

The young fish-face did not strike Warnie as interesting, but he provides us with an important clue about the way Lewis conducted his life. He was understandably shy on that occasion, because he had just been appointed Lewis's successor at Magdalen, and the thought of following in such footsteps was more than a little awe-inspiring. Many academics in Lewis's position would have made a great song and dance about finding a successor, suggested looking about a very wide field (the conceited implication being that they themselves were virtually irreplaceable) and generally wasted time. Lewis loathed time-wasting and lived his life on the 'Lord will provide' principle. The young man was very young indeed, but Lewis, who had taught him for three years, knew him to be very clever, and he was aware that Magdalen could travel further and fare worse in its search for a replacement. The young man also had the advantage – though he shared much of Lewis's wide-ranging fondness for reading of all kinds – of being quite unlike his master. Where one was red, the other was white; where one was loud, the other was quiet; where one was fat, the other was thin. Emrys Jones went on to be a much-loved English tutor at Magdalen, where he remained until his appointment to the Goldsmiths' Chair of English Literature some thirty or more years later.

'I would choose always to breakfast at exactly eight and be at my desk by nine, there to read or write till one. If a cup of good tea or coffee could be brought to me about eleven, so much the better,'[17] Lewis wrote in his autobiography. The passivity of this attitude was something he carried with him through life, and it explains both how he managed to achieve so much, to read and write so much, and at the same time why his outward surroundings, his household, family and friends, have struck so many people as bizarre. Most people, in the quest for colleagues or companions for life, imagine themselves to be making a great search. But in Lewis's case, why Paddy Moore? Because he just happened to be sharing Lewis's rooms at Keble for a few weeks in the summer of 1917. From the simple fact that Moore was there flowed all the subsequent events of Lewis's life until 1951. Why the 'unfortunate young man with a face like a fish' when there must have been a dozen men, at that date, whom most selection boards would have guessed to be more exciting? Because he was there. Now Lewis, in his new frame of mind, was reaching a point where it was extremely likely that he would think about getting married. It mattered extremely, in this case, who happened to be there. She was in the audience at Cambridge when he gave his inaugural lecture. Unbeknown to any of the Oxford friends who drank Jack's health at Merton at the beginning of December she was coming to spend Christmas at The Kilns, and this time she was bringing the boys.

SEVENTEEN

SMOKE ON THE MOUNTAIN
1954–1957

Joy had finally left the United States in April 1953, bringing with her the two boys Douglas and David, then aged eight and nine. By the autumn of 1953, Renée had made her divorce from her former husband final, and was ready to marry Bill Gresham. Very short of funds, and of friends, Joy put up at a hotel in Belsize Park (the Avoca House Hotel) under the impression that north-west London was a useful place for a 'writer' to be. She had made various unsuccessful efforts to get stories and poems published, but she had found a publisher in New York for her *Smoke on the Mountain: An Interpretation of the Ten Commandments*. This was published in the States in November 1954, with a dedication to C. S. Lewis. A few months later, Hodder & Stoughton published it in London, largely because it had a preface by Lewis praising it in the most extravagant terms. This should not be interpreted as having any special significance, incidentally, since when Lewis liked a book, particularly one written by a friend, he tended to lard on the praise, without realizing that this made people 'smell a rat'. His research pupil in Oxford, for example, Katherine Ing, wrote a very worthy little book on *The Elizabethan Lyric*. She eventually became a Fellow of St Hilda's; but she missed several jobs because the electors could not believe that she was as good as Lewis's references said she was. He praised her *Elizabethan Lyric* so fulsomely that the cynical dons assumed, since she was a beautiful young woman, that Lewis had a 'soft spot' for her. Nothing could have been further from the truth. It would be like arguing that he had a homosexual crush on Barfield, whose books, if you believed Lewis's accounts of them, would put Coleridge in the shade.

Relations with Joy, however, were deepening. She was quick to latch on to another of Lewis's characteristics, extreme generosity with money, and, having put the boys into an expensive preparatory school which she could not possibly afford, she accepted Lewis's offer to pay the fees. She was still based in London, moving out of the hotel into a nearby basement flat after only a few months. Lewis saw her on and off throughout the year, and even consented to entertain her parents, who came over in October 1954. 'Poor lamb,' Joy recorded, 'there were moments, as when my father lectured him on the blessings of Prohibition, when I saw his smile grow slightly fixed.' As for her mother Jen, decked out 'in a fancy black suit with rhinestone buttons, a pearl bracelet, a pearl choker, dingle-dangle pearl earrings, a pink lace blouse and a shocking pink hat . . . I'll let you imagine Jack's reaction for yourself,' Joy wrote.[1] This was of course meant to be gently mocking of her parents. But in fact Jack rather liked them. He who had reacted to the first sight of England at the age of nine with 'immediate hatred' was more than ready to befriend and adopt these jolly people, the Davidmans, who came as strangers.

Joy was a vivacious and physically attractive woman, then only thirty-nine years of age. On her visits to Oxford, there had been walks with Jack hand in hand which produced in her feelings of 'the most wonderful ecstasy'. In December 1953, she and the boys had spent four days of the Christmas holidays at The Kilns. 'It went swimmingly,' Lewis said, 'though it was very, very exhausting; the energy of the American small boy is astonishing.' For the children, it was a strange experience. Douglas, aged eight, felt that he was entering a world of magic. In the hall, he saw the large lumpish wardrobe which now stands in the Marion E. Wade collection at Wheaton College, Illinois. Was it . . . *the* wardrobe? 'It might be!' Lewis replied. It was years before Douglas dared open its door.[2] But if the wardrobe might be magic, the magician himself was a little bit of a let-down. 'Heroes are supposed to be dressed in a knight's armour,' he said, 'but this man looked so ordinary.'[3] It was to be some years before he saw that this was just the point. The ordinariness was not entirely accidental. 'I am tall, fat, bald, red-faced, double-chinned, black-haired and wear glasses for reading,' Lewis had written not long before to a class of fifth-graders in Rockville, Maryland. They had asked him for a description of himself. 'Best love to you all. When you say your prayers, sometimes ask God to bless me.'[4] It was a juvenile version of his Cambridge inaugural lecture.

'Look at me!' his childhood reflections, even those written before the death of his natural mother, appear to be saying. In the years immediately following his election at Cambridge, the self-disclosure in what he wrote became still more marked, and more relaxed; and at the same time he had found a woman with whom he felt able to be completely open about himself. We do not know whether, in his early years with Minto, he disclosed much of himself. Certainly when six years before her actual death she thought she was dying, she went to the kitchen in The Kilns, and shovelled all Jack's early letters to her into the stove. When he first knew her, even when he was going to visit her in the afternoons, he had written to her every day. There was a lot to destroy, and no doubt there was a lot which she did not wish Maureen or Warnie to read. Whatever there had been between herself and Jack, it was private. The openness which was a feature of his relationship with Joy perhaps excelled what he had had in the early days of Minto and had been missing for so long.[5]

So, naturally, these were the years of autobiography, the years when he took stock of himself, and genuinely began to wonder who and what he was.

Surprised by Joy was a book which he had been toying with for years. It began as a verse autobiography, like Wordsworth's *Prelude* or Betjeman's *Summoned by Bells*, only unlike them it was not in blank verse but in rhyming couplets. The passage about Kirkpatrick reads:

> Across my landscape like the dawn
> Some image of the sovranty of truth was drawn,
> And how to have believed an unproved thing by will
> Pollutes the mind's virginity; how reasons kill
> Beloved supposals: day makes lesser lights
> And mountain air is med'cinal. Oh, Attic nights
> And rigour of debate! Shrewd blows. Parry and thrust
> No quarter. And above us like the battle dust
> Fine particles of poets and philosophers
> Went flying in the midnight room. I had my spurs
> Of intellectual knighthood in that bannered field
> From Kirk's strong hand . . .

When he found himself rhyming 'spurs' with 'philosophers' it was probably as well to switch to prose. I have in the course of this book already commented in detail on many points in *Surprised by Joy*. Perhaps like most autobiographies, its evasions and omissions are as eloquent as anything which Lewis chose to put in: the dismissal of his love for Minto in a single phrase ('My earlier hostility to the emotions was very fully and variously avenged'), the preposterous assertion that 'my father's death . . . does not really come into the story I am telling,' the paradox that he represents his conversion to Christianity as a cerebral and intellectual affair, without recounting the famous conversation with Dyson and Tolkien during the midnight hours in Addison's Walk. About the Lewis who actually lived and moved and had his being, it tells us almost nothing – still less about the religious believer who emerges in his letters – say, those to Sister Penelope. It is really a glorious sort of comic novel. Although there is a strong element of malice in the comic portrait of his father, one could wish it twenty times longer, because it is surely born out of the sense that, insufferably annoying as he may have been in life, there was also something glorious about him. Lewis was able to love his father as a literary character in a way he could never love him as a man. The chapter called 'Release' is one of the funniest things written in English in the twentieth century.

But in a sense, even as he was writing it, and impishly choosing its title, which by then was charged for him with double meaning, Lewis was becoming aware that it is not so easy to tell the truth about ourselves. And it was out of this dilemma that his novel *Till We Have Faces* would grow.

Perhaps the autobiographical preoccupations were exacerbated by an increase in solitude, combined with the sense, dramatically presented in his inaugural lecture, that he was now, to so many people, a new face, a man they did not know, someone who needed explaining. Life at The Kilns continued. A new kitten called Guppy came to replace the one who had died at the end of the previous year. And Jill Freud gave the Lewises a Labrador bitch puppy whose charms excited all the dogs in the neighbourhood. 'One', Jack told her, 'gave a barking serenade at about 3 a.m. this morning. Another barked at me in our own drive. I am sick of (canine) love.' Warnie, who had Jack and the house to himself, was blossoming out as an author in his own right.

In 1953 he had published a really excellent book about life in France during the reign of Louis XIV called *The Splendid Century*. He was at work on another – *Sunset of the Splendid Century: The Life and Times of Louis Auguste de Bourbon, Duc de Maine, 1670–1736*. Well researched and pleasantly written, they were much more than a mere therapy to keep their author from alcoholic temptation. It is astonishing that the author of these books, who writes in such a way as to make the Versailles of Saint-Simon come completely alive, should never himself have visited Versailles – a mere seven or eight hours' journey from The Kilns. He always said that actually visiting the place about which he had so many pleasant daydreams would spoil it.

For much of the time, Warnie was left in 'solitary splendour'[6] while Jack went to Cambridge. In those days, there was a little cross-country train which made the journey possible. Jack was always civil if he met acquaintances on this train, but evidently a train, like a sitting room, was for him a place where a 'man is at his books', and the Professor did not wish to spend the journey in idle chatter.

Being a professor fulfilled, as Warnie said, 'the ideal we all have of less work and more pay ... Also he has a Fellowship at Magdalen*e* which he so much prefers to his old Magdalen Oxford that he now always calls the latter the Impenitent.'[7] 'Cambridge is fun,' Jack agreed, 'such a country town feeling.'[8]

It was in a spirit of fun that he approached Cambridge: grateful that they had wanted him, and pleased that he had arrived in a place of such beauty. 'It is not Cambridge, but *Oxford* which is the hardboiled materialistic scientific university. At Cambridge the majority of dons and undergraduates are Christians,'[9] Warnie wrote, evidently on his brother's say-so. If this was something of an exaggeration, it was nevertheless true that there were plenty of people who welcomed Lewis to Cambridge and who thoroughly enjoyed his lectures and companionship. One thinks not only of his colleagues at the Penitent Magdalene but also of such varied figures as Muriel Bradbrook, Graham Hough, and Joan Bennett in the English Faculty. There were others besides. He formed a very typical Lewisian friendship, shortly after his arrival, with a young research fellow of Girton and Newnham called Nan Dunbar, a clever, angular young Scotswoman who, even now, both in what she says and the way she says it, seems to have stepped straight out of the pages of the Waverley novels. She attended

Lewis's lectures and was arrested by something he said about the 'Silver' Latin poet Statius, whose 'moderately interesting but often rather turgid' epic *Thebais* tells the story of Seven against Thebes. In Dante's *Purgatorio*, Statius is counted as a sort of honorary or secret Christian, and Lewis claimed that the reason for this was that Statius 'seemed to give his female virgin characters an attitude to the sexual life which Dante would not easily have found in any other ancient text'.[10]

An inveterate letter-writer, and a bit of a flirt, Miss Dunbar wrote to the Professor to tell him that he was wrong. Maidens of the ancient world, claimed Miss Dunbar, were expected to behave themselves in the pre-Christian era just as much as in the Christian. One of Statius's maidens blushed because she had seen her betrothed in a dream. Was it an erotic dream? Or was it less that sex was wicked in itself than that it made the gods jealous? For eleven days, letters flew backwards and forwards between the colleges of Professor Lewis and Miss Dunbar. 'We know from Dante', Lewis said, 'that Statius got to heaven: if we ever get there we can ask him which he meant.' That was no comfort to Miss Dunbar. As she wittily parried, Lewis was bound to get to heaven before she did, and then he would have probably argued poor old Statius into agreeing with him by the time she arrived. Thirty years after the correspondence, she concludes, 'I have to admit that on the general point of Statius's then unusual attitude to sex, I now think that Lewis was right and I was wrong. He had read the whole of Statius – I still haven't and I doubt if I ever shall.'

At the end of term, they met at a dinner. 'Ah! Miss Dunbar! I'm glad to find you actually exist – I'd thought that perhaps you were only the personification of my conscience.' They had a merry evening, she quoting the (to him unknown) enjoyably bad Scottish poet William McGonagall, and he introducing her to his Ulster equivalent – the novelist Amanda McKittrick Ros. The next day she received a Latin poem which he had written about her through the post: 'Nan is more learned than all girls, more formidable than fierce Camilla, less able to control her tongue than Xanthippe. Bold, garrulous, obstinate, aggressive, grim, ferocious, companion of the sister Furies, daughter of Momus, mother of Zoilus, writing terrifying things, with a glance as sharp as watercress [this phrase is a quotation in Greek from

New Buildings, Magdalen College, Oxford

Charles Williams

J. R. R. Tolkien

Jack and Warnie Lewis
at Annagassan,
Ireland, 1949

more than a few moments. How could it when its whole effort was to achieve a contradiction?— to awake merely personal, selfish, prudential hopes and fears for things that can only be realised in proportion as the merely personal, selfish, and prudential have been (at least for the time being) sloughed off?

One thing that blunts grief in childhood is the mass of other miseries which surround it. I was taken into the bedroom where my Mother lay dead, to see the body. There was nothing that a grown-up would call disfigurement—except for that total disfigurement which is death itself. Sorrow was Sorrow was overwhelmed in terror; nor have I ever been able to this day to conceive how any corpse can be thought beautiful. The ugliest man alive is an angel of beauty (for me) compared with the liveliest of the dead. I have seen plenty of dead people since, and my impression has always been the same; namely, that a dead man re-veals man as an animal. That first view of death in my Mother's sick-room, that and all the horrible subsequent paraphernalia of coffin, flowers, hearse and black clothes, added richly to the furniture of my nightmares. The dreams about insects did not disappear, but the spectres multiplied.

The years spent in the new house before my Mother's illness had been very happy; they had also been very solitary since my brother was away for the greater part of the year. I loved solitude (ex-cept after dark). I once overheard my Father say of me to my grand-father "He is the most easily amused child I ever saw. give him pencil and paper and he'll be quiet for hours". And so I was, quiet at a little card-table in the corner of a room we called the "study" though in fact it was the room in which everyone usually sat. But I think I even preferred to be elsewhere. I had found out an attic for myself which I had, in a childish way, fitted up as a study of my own. Works of art, of my own composition, or cut from the highly-coloured Christmas numbers of magazines, were pinned on the walls. My pen and ink. pot and pad and paint-box were also there: for by now I could write as well as draw. Here my earliest stories were written and illustrated with enormous delight. They were an attempt to combine my two favourite literary pleasures—"dressed animals" and "knights in armour"; for Beatrix Potter's little books were now reaching me and Conan Doyle's Sir Nigel was appearing monthly in The Strand. As a natural result I wrote about medieval mice or rabbits who rode out in plate armour and killed, not giants but Cats. Already the mood of the systematiser was strong in me — the mood which made Trollope build up from novel to novel his

A manuscript leaf from *Surprised by Joy*

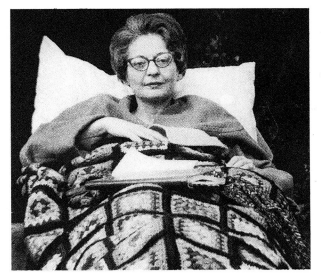

Joy Lewis in around 1957

C. S. Lewis

Aristophanes, the playwright on whom Miss Dunbar is an expert]' –
and then finally the punch-line from Catullus – 'A girl who does not
allow you to be careless'.

> Nan est doctior omnibus puellis
> Formidabilior fera Camilla,
> Xanthippa magis impotens loquelae,
> Audax, garrula, pertinax, proterva,
> Trux, torva. Eumenidem comes sororum,
> Momi filia Zoilique mater.
>
> Scribens horrida, kapsaua Blenouca
> Per quam non licet esse negligentes.[11]

History does not relate whether Mrs Gresham, like Statius's maiden,
blushed at her own dreams; but there could now be no doubt about
the identity of the beloved revealed in them. Her divorce had been
made final on 5 August 1954.[12] The following August, 1955, she and
the boys moved to Oxford – 10 Old High Street, Headington. It is
a dingy house, and the Greshams occupied the bottom half of it. For
ten years, Jack and Minto had traipsed about, living in various versions
of just such lodgings. Seeing Joy move in to 10 Old High Street must
have brought back to Jack memories of his past. It was he who had
found the place for them. It had considerably more room than the
flat in Belsize Park, and the rent was proportionally much higher, but,
as Joy's biographer tells us, 'this was no problem' because 'C. S. Lewis
... paid the rent.'[13]

By now Joy had confided in Bel Kaufman that she was 'deeply in
love with Jack'. Warnie saw that 'it was now obvious what was going
to happen.'[14] Jack, interestingly enough, did *not* see, or anyway not
fully. His autobiography shows his tremendous capacity (inherited,
though he could not see it, from his father) for thinking he saw human
situations extremely clearly, but actually getting them plumb wrong.
Just as, in the examples I have already quoted, he genuinely supposed
that the major relationships of his life, with his father and Minto, had
no bearing on his religious development, a similar myopia now took
possession of him in relation to Joy Gresham.

He was now paying for the education of Joy's children, and paying
her rent. Bill Gresham, the alcoholic who had been rough with the

children, and was now apparently incapable of paying cheques to his family on any regular basis, seemed like a repetition of the mythical Beast, alias Courtney Edward Moore. 'If Jacks were not an impetuous, kind-hearted creature who could be cajoled by any woman who has been through the mill,' Albert Lewis had written in 1919, 'I should not be so uneasy.'[15] It is even likely that in her abrasive line of talk, and the bold way in which she liked to argue with Jack, Joy reminded him of what had first attracted him to Mrs Moore. But he did not allow himself to see that the fates were preparing her as a Mrs Moore substitute.

Those of his friends who, at this juncture, were aware of Mrs Gresham's presence in Oxford still found her charm somewhat elusive. There was an occasion, for example, when George Sayer was lunching with Lewis in Oxford. Because Sayer had something to do in town that afternoon, he suggested that his wife Moira go to The Kilns and read a book until he called for her. They had often arranged things this way, just as Warnie and Jack were used to staying in Sayer's house in Malvern. Jack excused himself, saying that he wanted a nap, and left Mrs Sayer sitting in the library. During his absence, Mrs Gresham walked into the house, whistling loudly. When she saw Mrs Sayer, she asked abruptly, 'Who the hell are you and what the bloody hell are you doing in this house?' She was carrying a pile of Jack's laundry. Moira Sayer politely pointed out that she was a friend of Jack's and that she had, in fact, met Mrs Gresham once before.[16] 'Her mind was quick and muscular as a leopard,' Lewis wrote admiringly of his *inamorata*. 'It scented the first whiff of cant or slush, then sprang.'[17] Not everyone found this approach to conversation markedly con-genial.

Throughout the latter part of 1955 and the early months of 1956, Jack was revelling in her company. 'I soon learned not to talk rot to her unless I did it for the sheer pleasure of being exposed and laughed at.' Rousseau's taste, he had written in 1917, 'is altogether for suffering rather than inflicting: which I can feel too'.[18]

According to an oral memory of Joy's son Douglas, transcribed in the Marion E. Wade collection at Wheaton College, Illinois, the two of them were already lovers in 1955. Douglas on one occasion came into his mother's bedroom at 10 Old High Street and found it occupied by Jack and Joy in a compromising position. This memory, which transpired during a conversation between Douglas Gresham and Lyle W. Dorsett, is not repeated in either of the books which the two men have written about the Lewis marriage, and it is not clear whether the omission is because Gresham distrusts the memory (he was eight years old at the time) or because it was considered indelicate to imply that the union between Lewis and his future wife was consummated, as would appear to have been the case, before they were married.

Early in 1956, the British Home Office refused Mrs Gresham a permit to remain in England. There was only one way that she could quickly secure herself the right to stay, and that was by marrying a citizen of the United Kingdom. 'Jack assured me that Joy would continue to occupy her own house as "Mrs. Gresham",' wrote Warnie, 'and that the marriage was a pure formality designed to give Joy the right to go on living in England: and I saw the uselessness of disabusing him.'[19]

Useless it certainly would have been, but by now Lewis found himself in a position which not only was extraordinarily painful from an emotional point of view, but also struck at the very heart of his theological position. It was a genuine spiritual crisis.

What scandalized some of Lewis's Christian friends about his bluff eagerness to become an apologist for the faith in the late 1930s and early 1940s was their sense that he did not really understand enough about theology. On a much deeper and more personal level, as he had admitted to Sister Penelope when the bulk of his apologetic writings had been finished and published, he had not really believed in or understood the doctrine that God forgives human sin. Nearly all forms of religious belief except Orthodox Judaism and orthodox Christianity are in some measure dualistic: that is, they do not really believe that One God is responsible for everything in a cohesive, unified creation. The existence of pain and suffering – or, in many schemes of religious thought, the existence of matter itself – is explained by the existence of rival or lesser divinities who made the world of sin and change while, all unseen, the First Mover sits indifferently above. The doctrine, evolved by the Jews and developed most fully in Christianity, that God is One, *and* that He made and loved the world, is imaginatively extremely hard to hold on to. Lewis's imagination had a naturally dualistic tendency, which was why he was so brilliant at dreaming up letters from the Devil. And we see no clearer example of his dualism than in his thinking about marriage. 'My own view', he had said in his broadcast talk, 'is that the Church should frankly recognise that the majority of British people are not Christians and therefore cannot be expected to live Christian lives. There ought to be two distinct kinds of marriage: one governed by the Church with rules enforced by her on her own members. The distinction ought to be sharp, so that a man knows which couples are married in a Christian sense and which are not.'[20]

This is a wildly unhistorical, untheological and impractical sugges-tion. By what possible criterion could 'a man' – or, come to that, a woman – distinguish between such 'marriages'? For most of the history of the Church, marriages did not happen within the church building. They were civil contracts sealed at the church door. One thinks of the Wife of Bath with her 'housbondes at chirche doore I hadde five'. Even when marriage was raised to the dignity of a sacrament by the medieval western church (largely to make up the number of the sacraments to the magical seven), it was never suggested that the *church*, or the *priest*, made the marriage. The ministers of this particular 'sacrament' are the man and the woman who perform it; and in this sense any marriage, in Catholic teaching, is a marriage. A marriage between a pair of Hindus or a pair of modern secular agnostics is still, in orthodox Christian thinking, a marriage. By Lewis's argument, agnostic married couples who subsequently became Christians would presumably have to get 'remarried' in a church. This suggests a profound split in his thinking, not only about the relationship between flesh and spirit, but also about the relationship between Christianity and what he called the *Tao*. Tolkien, in a lengthy and excellently argued critique of Lewis's 'Christian Marriage' idea, goes to the heart of the matter when he pounces on Lewis's analogy 'I should be very angry if the Mahommedans tried to prevent the rest of us from drinking wine.' So, Lewis concludes by extension, Christians should not make it difficult for non-Christians to divorce. This is, as Tolkien says, 'a most stinking red herring':

No item of compulsory Christian morals is valid only for Christians ... Toleration of divorce – if a Christian does tolerate it – is toleration of a human abuse ... And wrong behaviour (if it is really wrong on universal principles) is progressive, always: it never stops at being 'not very good', 'second best' – it either reforms, or goes on to third-rate, bad, abominable.[21]

On the question of divorce, when he was considering it on a purely cerebral level, Lewis had failed to face up to the dilemma. Either Christ, in condemning it (as the Gospels say He did), was uttering a universal moral law, binding for everybody – in which case a Christian cannot believe in 'divorce for non-Christians' any more than he can believe in theft for non-Christians – or it is *not* a universal law that divorce is in all circumstances wrong. This is the view that, over the years, various Christian denominations have worked towards, including the Greek Orthodox and the Presbyterian Churches. They have extracted from the New Testament the texts which *do* allow for divorce in some circumstances, and in this sense they have come clean. The wholeness of their vision – like the wholeness and consistency of Tolkien's absolute no-divorce belief – is left intact.

Not so for Lewis, with his two-tier view of marriage. He, in any case, belonged to a church which, in spite of being famed for its wishy-washy Laodicean approach to the faith, has historically some of the strictest marriage laws of any denomination in Christendom. As I write these words in the late 1980s, things have loosened up. In the United States, there are even divorced and remarried bishops of the Anglican Church. In England, there are many priests in such a position, and divorced men and women remarry and approach the altar to receive the sacraments, even though the exact state of Anglican canon law about their status and the lawfulness of remarrying such persons in church remains, in some minds or some dioceses, somewhat hazy. In 1956, this was not the case. The most famous 'royal' story of the 1950s raised the question of whether Princess Margaret, the sister of Queen Elizabeth II, could marry the man she loved, Group Captain Townsend. He was divorced, and it was this alone that made her forsake him, 'mindful of the Church's teaching'.

Lewis must have discussed the matter with his friend Austin Farrer, whose views would, roughly speaking, have coincided with those of Tolkien. Farrer, in all his moral thinking, was purely 'tridentine' and would have no truck either with the idea of two-tier marriages or with the legality of Christian divorce. But both as a friend and as a priest, he crossed St Giles, the large avenue running north out of Oxford, from his flat in Trinity College to the register office which in those days nestled between the Quaker meeting house and the Army Recruitment Centre. It was St George's Day and Shakespeare's birthday. By what turned out to be a hideous prophetic instinct, the two friends Lewis asked to witness the ceremony were Farrer and his doctor, Havard.

Lewis was by now in a tremendous muddle. At some stage he had been to see Havard – and how typical this was of the man – to ask whether he would be well advised to undertake conjugal duties. After due examination and consideration, Havard decided that his patient, though at fifty-eight a little heavy and rather prone to high blood pressure, could risk the excitements of an erotic life if he took things gently. But with another part of himself, Lewis was reassuring Warnie that the marriage was simply a matter of convenience, to get Joy a permit to stay in England. 'There were never two people alive in the history of the world', Douglas Gresham has said about his mother and stepfather, 'more in love than Jack and Joy.'[22] What was Lewis to do? His belief in the status of these second-tier marriages by the State was now put to the test. Were he and Joy married in the eyes of God or were they not? If God had joined them together, then there was no reason why they should be put asunder, and his enquiries in Havard's consulting room could cease to be of purely academic concern. But there was a lingering doubt. Though he continued to see her every day, and though Joy confided in her brother that Jack was a wonderful lover, the fiction was maintained that she was Mrs Gresham, and he was merely an *ami de la maison* calling each afternoon or evening, and often not getting home until after eleven o'clock. Only a very few of his friends, like the Farrers, were even let into the secret that he *was* married; this reticence caused bewilderment and resentment among old friends like Tolkien and Dyson when – as inevitably happened – the news leaked out.

What on earth did Jack think he was playing at? His behaviour during that summer was exuberant and strange. 'The most precious gift that marriage gave me', he wrote when it was all over, 'was this constant impact of something very close and intimate yet all the time unmistakably other, resistant – in a word, real.' This sense of reality, which involved not only a sense of self-discovery, but also a readjustment of what he thought about God and hence about everything else, was something which had been developing through all the previous year, and is reflected in the novel he wrote now and dedicated to Joy: *Till We Have Faces*. With a large part of himself Lewis did not want things to go any further. For the first time in his life, he was enjoying a unique combination of pleasures. He was happy in his academic work, and enjoying the company of his colleagues. At home, all was peace. In September he had a very happy holiday on his own in Ireland. He told Greeves about Joy, and about the civil marriage, but more of what he said we cannot know. He did not take Joy's aches and pains, reported at intervals over the summer, any more seriously than he took his own. When the Useless Quack was consulted, he gave it as his opinion that she was suffering from fibrositis.

He went back to Cambridge at the beginning of October, ready for another happy round of lectures punctuated by long delicious days in his college rooms. No undergraduate here would knock at his door or read him an essay beginning 'Jonathan Swift was born . . .'. But on 19 October he received a telephone call to say that Joy's rheumatic pains had been investigated at the Wingfield Orthopaedic Hospital in Headington. The call was from Havard, whom he went to see as soon as he could get back to Oxford. Preliminary X-rays had revealed that Joy had broken her left thigh bone, and that she had a lump on her breast.

He went to see her. She was plucky, and good-humoured. Jokes were inevitably made about the Useless Quack; but there was a problem of much more practical concern. She had entered the hospital as Mrs Gresham, an American citizen. As Mrs C. S. Lewis, of course, she could have claimed free treatment on the National Health, but her true marital status was still a secret. Lewis was prepared to pay the bill – but that was not the point. What was now at issue was whether he was prepared to acknowledge as his wife the woman he loved and who might, for all they knew, be suffering from a mortal illness. They did not have to wait long. She was moved half a mile down the road to the Churchill Hospital, an unutterably bleak collection of Nissen huts and makeshift buildings put up at the end of the Second World War for Canadian servicemen, and used ever since as a cancer hospital for Oxford's residents. A biopsy revealed that her tumour was indeed malignant and her chances of survival were, as Warnie said, 'put at evens'. 'I have never loved her more than since she was struck down,' he added. 'Her pluck and her cheerfulness are beyond praise, and she talks of her disease and its fluctuations as if she were describing the experiences of a friend of hers.'[23]

On 14 November, Jack wrote to one of the many correspondents whom he had never met, 'I wish you would pray very hard for a lady called Joy Gresham and me . . . I am shortly to be both a bridegroom and a widower, for she has cancer. You need not mention this till the marriage (which will be at the hospital bedside if it occurs).'[24] This positively Wagnerian blend of love and death could not, however, be accomplished without Lewis's flying in the face of his own church.

He went to see Harry Carpenter, the Bishop of Oxford. (The front door was opened for him on this occasion by the bishop's son, a little boy called Humphrey who would one day write a book about him called *The Inklings*). Harry Carpenter, who was a fairly old-fashioned high churchman was quite as clear in his mind as Archbishop Fisher and Princess Margaret had been in theirs when faced with a parallel dilemma.

'Mindful of the Church's teachings', as they then stood, he said that there was no possibility of allowing Mrs Gresham, a divorced woman, to be given a church marriage. The fact that her bridegroom was a famous Christian apologist made the case all the more impossible, for the marriage would undoubtedly attract publicity, and if it should be known that it had received the bishop's sanction, he would have been flooded with requests by couples in similar positions, anxious to bend the rules to fit their own particular cases. Lewis left the bishop's house in a state of very great anger. Austin Farrer, as an obedient priest in Carpenter's diocese, could not oblige his friend by performing the ceremony. It was not a matter of charity; it was a matter of canon law. Such a marriage would simply be illegal. But Lewis was by now desperate that Joy should be able to come home – that is, to The Kilns – to die, and he wanted her to do so 'without scandal'. The irony is that if they had been Roman Catholics, it would almost certainly have been possible by Roman canon law for them to be united in the eyes of the Church. In his near-despair, he looked to the Church to fulfil a higher law, the law of love, and he felt that he was having the door slammed in his face.

Several months went by, and Joy's condition was visibly deteriorating. Since no help was at hand from any of his normal circle of friends, Lewis turned to an acquaintance of twenty years' standing called Peter Bide. Bide had come up to Oxford slightly late in his life to read English Literature just before the war, having started out as a chemist. He was not a pupil of Lewis's, and his tastes were very different, but he attended his lectures. He had, for example, tried to persuade Lewis to like the poetry of T. S. Eliot, but as Lewis had written:

> For twenty years I've stared my level best
> To see if evening – any evening – would suggest
> A patient etherized upon a table;
> In vain. I simply wasn't able.[25]

Subsequently Bide had become a Christian, got married, been ordained and discovered that he had a gift of healing. Lewis asked him to intercede for Joy, and to lay hands on her. He also put to Bide their dilemma about the illegality of a marriage service. 'Joy's first marriage [had been] to an already divorced man and therefore in the eyes of the church, no such marriage was possible,' Lewis forcefully argued. For the Church to deny their request for marriage was now 'to try to have your cake and eat it'. Father Bide agreed. 'Joy desperately wanted to solemnize her marriage before God and to claim the grace of the sacrament before she died,' he wrote afterwards: a statement which more than implies that Joy, since her register office marriage, had dutifully excommunicated herself. 'It did not seem to me in the circumstances possible to refuse her the outward and visible sign of grace which she so ardently desired and which might lead to a peaceful end to a fairly desperate situation.'[26]

On 21 March, the doctors pronounced the death sentence and said that Joy's condition was beyond hope of recovery. At 11 a.m., Warnie accompanied Jack to Joy's ward at the Churchill. There was only one other witness – the ward sister. Bide said mass and gave Holy Communion to those present. Warnie knew that 'to feel pity for anyone so magnificently brave as Joy is almost an insult,' but her eagerness for 'the pitiable consolation of dying under the same roof as Jack [was] heartrending.'[27] The two of them made their vows, 'as ye will answer at the dreadful day of judgement when the secrets of all hearts shall be disclosed'. They promised to keep themselves only unto themselves, in sickness and in health, so long as they both should live. In *The Times* the next day, Jack's oldest friends read with astonishment an announcement of which they had been given absolutely no warning: 'A marriage has taken place between Professor C. S. Lewis of Magdalene College, Cambridge, and Mrs. Joy Gresham, now a patient in the Churchill Hospital at Oxford. It is requested that no letters be sent.'

EIGHTEEN

MARRIAGE
1957–1959

Maureen Blake, Minto's daughter, did not read *The Times*, but she heard from Jack that his friend Mrs Gresham was ill in hospital. When she arrived at the Churchill, Maureen was told by the nurse that 'Mrs Lewis was very ill'. 'Mrs Lewis?' queried Maureen. 'Who is Mrs Lewis? There must be some mistake.'

She was shown into the ward to meet Joy. Jack was too distraught to apologize or explain why he had not bothered to tell Maureen of his plan to marry even though she was in some senses 'family'. After a sad, short encounter with Joy in the ward, Maureen returned to The Kilns with Jack, and asked what was happening to Joy's children. The answer appeared to be that no one knew what to do with the Gresham boys, so Maureen put the children in the back of her car and drove them to her own house in Malvern, where she and her husband both taught music. Douglas Gresham, the younger boy, was a sunny, cheerful child; David, the elder, was morose and profoundly disturbed. Maureen was not to know that David and Douglas had been on poor terms all their lives. David had reacted very vulnerably to the break-up of his parents' marriage, and profoundly resented his mother's decision to become a Christian and to emigrate; still more, to marry again. His disturbance was to take the form, a little later, of declaring himself to be a Jew (which ethnically was the case, though his parents had never practised the Jewish faith), refusing to eat with the family, and insisting on kosher food (not an easy requirement in Headington, but Lewis was eventually to find acceptable comestibles for David at Palm's Delicatessen in the Covered Market in Oxford).[1]

Maureen Blake herself had two children a little younger than the Greshams. The first sign of trouble was when she took them for a walk on Barnard's Green, Malvern, near where the Blakes lived, and

David began to bully her daughter, attacking her physically. During his entire stay with the Blakes, David was impossible; he either refused to take part in conversations and meals, or he entered upon them with rudeness and ferocity. His violence was never far beneath the surface. Some money disappeared, and Maureen had reason to believe that David had stolen it. At this point, she lost her temper and went up to see him in the bath, dragged him out of the tub and gave him a sound thrashing. After this, there was not much hope, as she had half-supposed there would be, of the boys' coming to live with her on any permanent or semi-permanent basis.

It was not possible, however, for the Blakes to ignore Lewis's marriage, since it affected their future most directly. Neither Leonard nor Maureen had any money; they were both poor teachers. Maureen's mother Minto had been a joint owner of The Kilns with Jack and Warnie. Minto's will and a gentlemen's agreement between the Blakes and the Lewises both recognized that when Jack and Warnie were dead, The Kilns should pass to the Blakes as their retirement home.

It was therefore a shock for Maureen, in one of her very first conversations with Joy once she was back at The Kilns, to be told, 'When I die, and Jack dies, this house will belong to the boys.'

Maureen faltered. 'I think not . . . You see, by the terms of my mother's will . . .'

'You evidently did not hear what I said,' said Joy very firmly. 'This house belongs to me and the boys.'

'I think if you asked Jack –' Maureen began.

'I've told Jack,' said Joy, looking at her shamefaced, silent husband.*

Joy had come home to die, and these questions of what would happen when she did so were of urgent practical importance. Who would look after the children? The obvious answer was their father. When Bill Gresham learnt how ill Joy was, he wrote to express his concern, adding: 'Naturally I shall want [Doug and Davy] to be with me in the event of your death.' The letter caused Joy great distress. Scenes of marital horror returned to haunt her – Bill drunk, Bill violent and terrifying the children. On 6 April 1957, Lewis wrote two letters to Gresham. The first read:

---

* In the event, the Blakes did retain Mrs Moore's share of the house, which was one of the reasons it was sold after Lewis's own death.

Joy is too ill to write and has asked me to answer yours of the 2nd. This is a ticklish job. If through clumsiness, in the effort to put things strongly, I sound like one who writes with animosity, believe me this is not so. I think there has never been any ill-feeling between you and me, and I very much hope there never will be.

Your letter reached Joy after a day of agony. The effect was devastating. She felt that the only earthly hope she now has has been taken away. You have tortured one who was already on the rack; heaped extra weights on one who is being pressed to death. There is nothing she dreads so much as the return of the boys to your charge. You perhaps do not understand that certain scenes (when you were not yourself) came early enough in their lives to make you a figure of terror to them. Their return to the U.S.A. when their education is finished is of course quite a different matter. Now, bitterly against their will, coming on top of the most appalling tragedy that can happen to childhood (I was put through it and I know) tearing them from all that has already become familiar and shattering all sense of security that remains to them, it would be disastrous. If you realise the cruelty of what you are proposing to do, I am sure you would not do it.

If you do not relent, I shall of course be obliged to place every legal obstacle in your way. Joy has, legally, a case. Her (documented) desire for naturalization (which there may still be time to carry out) and the boys' horror of going back, will be strong points. What is certain is that a good deal of your money and mine will go into the lawyers' hands. You have a chance to soothe, instead of aggravating, the miseries of a woman you once loved. You have a chance of recovering at some future date, instead of alienating forever, the love and respect of your children. For God's sake take it and yield to the deep wishes of everyone concerned except yourself.

You may suspect that the letter you will get from David was 'inspired' by Joy or me. In reality, it was expurgated, i.e. the letter he meant to send was much stronger and Joy made him tone it down. Douglas burst into tears on hearing your plans. I assure you that they have never heard a word against you from me. No *propaganda* at all has ever gone on.

Yours,

Jack[2]

It was an extraordinary letter to have composed, and reveals how deeply the knowledge of Joy's imminent death revived in Lewis all the traumas and horrors of August 1908, not least among them an irrational dread of his own father. The odd impertinence of the letter makes sense if we think that Lewis was subconsciously identifying Bill with the P'daytabird. The Gresham boys' dread of their father was *not* wholly irrational. As Lewis put it in the second letter that he wrote and posted that day:

> The boys remember you as a man who fired rifles through the ceilings to relieve his temper, broke up chairs, wept in public, and broke a bottle over Douglas's head. David knew, and resented the fact, that you were living with your present wife while still married to his mother. Children have indelible memories of such things and they are (like us adults) self-righteous.[3]

All this may very well have been the case, but the fact that the boys were crying in the week they heard their mother would soon be dead is hardly surprising. Had Bill Gresham's lawyer wished to contest the case, it could have been said that life with their first cousin once removed (Renée) and their own father (if alcoholic), in the land of their birth, offered a more stable continuity with the past than life with their stepfather, whom they had only known in school holidays for a little over a year, and his elderly brother (again alcoholic). But Lewis was not, strictly speaking, thinking. As he said in another context, 'it was a yell rather than a thought.'[4] The wildness of the suggestion that their own father should wait until they had grown up before being allowed access to his own sons revealed, as well as pain, a generous love. The last thing that many men in the circumstances would have been prepared to do was to take on responsibility for the future of the boys. In the event Bill Gresham agreed, as a result of receiving these letters, that he would not press for custody of Douglas and David. By the time they did in fact lose their mother, they were teenagers and the whole situation was different. (Bill did not then insist on their returning to the States with him.)

For, as the weeks went past in The Kilns, Joy mysteriously did not die. She was still incapable of walking in August 1957, when she was visited by her college friend Bel Kaufman, but she was radiant. Bel was pleasantly surprised by Lewis himself – 'so much handsomer than his photos!' – and she was very much struck by what Joy said concerning her love for her new husband – 'The movies and the poets are right: it does exist!' Lewis himself was to write something very similar in *The Four Loves*: 'Years ago when I wrote about medieval love poetry and described its strange half make-believe "religion of Love" I was blind enough to treat this as an almost purely literary phenomenon. I know better now.'[5]

The miraculous, the literally miraculous, appeared to be happening. Joy, very slowly, but quite discernibly, was getting better. The pain in her bones was vanishing. Bel Kaufman noted that Jack, too, had 'osteo-something, a degenerative disease – lack of calcium – back pains'.[6]

Both these testimonies from Joy's old friend from New York days are corroborated by confidences Lewis made to his old friend Nevill Coghill. In the happiness of his love for Joy, pathetically fragile as he knew her physical condition still to be, he was boy-like, exuberant. 'Do you know,' he said to Coghill and Peter Bayley as they were crossing a quadrangle at Merton, 'I am experiencing what I thought would never be mine. I never thought I would have in my sixties the happiness that passed me by in my twenties.'

At the same time, there was the eerie phenomenon of his apparently being allowed to bear Joy's suffering and pain. The doctrine of Substitution, that we can, in the most literal sense, opt to 'bear one another's burdens', had been an idea dear to the heart of Charles Williams. In 1949, over a drink in the Eagle and Child, J. R. R. Tolkien had told Warnie a remarkable story about his own dentist, Mr Pelger. A child was brought to him with an inflamed gum and a bad tooth. Pelger warned her that it would be necessary to cut away the diseased tissue and that this would be extremely painful. As he began to cut, Pelger felt a pang of such severity in his own jaw that he dropped his lancet and stomped up and down the surgery. 'When the agony had worn off a little, he returned to his patient sitting in the chair with a slash in her jaw – and asked her if she was in much pain. The child laughed and replied that she had felt nothing at all.'[7]

Lewis had a directly comparable experience with his wife. By September, she could move about in an invalid chair. By the end of 1957, she was walking with a stick, and by the time a year had elapsed from her hospital wedding day, when the doctors had pronounced her case hopeless, she was told that the cancer had been arrested. X-rays revealed that the cancerous spots in her bones had disappeared. Lewis, on the other hand, had developed osteoporosis, not a fatal bone disease, but one which brought with it excruciating pain. He had to wear a surgical belt and sleep on a board for four or five months of 1956. This he confided to Coghill, and to another Christian intimate, Sister Penelope. 'I am very crippled and had much pain all summer, but am in a good spell now,' he told the latter in November. 'I was losing calcium just about as fast as Joy was gaining it, a bargain (if it was one) for which I am very thankful.'

Once it became plain that Joy was not in danger of imminent death, Warnie's whole position at The Kilns became delicate. 'The gap between the Ancien Regime and the Restoration had lasted for less than four years,' wrote the French historian, referring to the gap between the death of Minto and Jack's marriage. 'There are times when I get tired of the role of "family man",' he admitted to a friend. 'Not that I don't get on well with my sister-in-law; it is her detestable spoilt brat of an elder boy who is the fly in the ointment. But the other one is a decent little kid, so I suppose I shouldn't grumble.'[8]

When the doctor's report confirmed that Joy's cancer had been arrested, Warnie announced his plans to leave Oxford and set up on his own in Ireland. 'But Jack and Joy would not hear of this,' and he was caught in the slightly awkward position of being the third party in a love-nest. Joy, as she frequently told Bill Gresham in her letters, set about helping her new brother-in-law not only with the index to his latest book, but also with his alcohol problem. 'She's the sort of woman who lives for others,' as Screwtape observed all those years ago; 'you can always tell the others by their hunted expression.'[9] Warnie gave in to several bouts of steady drinking at this period, and in Ireland he found a refuge which would take him in after each one – the Lourdes Hospital in Drogheda. The rest of his life (he died in 1973) was to be punctuated by his dependence on this routine. The marriage of his brother had not helped. He felt intensely alone. In March 1960, his diary was to record, 'Joy away fetching Douglas and J spent the evening with me in the study. With the exception of the 15 minute walk back from St. Mary's twice a month, this has been the only time I have spent with him since the end of March 1957 – just three years ago.'

Jack's other Oxford friends found the continual presence of Joy by his side irksome and baffling. When it was clear that she was going to recover, Jack conceived the naïve idea that he could re-establish the Inklings as a sort of salon around her. He entirely failed to see how this looked to them. Throughout the 1930s and 1940s, he had kept up the all-male Thursday evenings in a manner which was always convivial but frequently 'awkward' from a domestic point of view. He had expressed little or no interest in Tolkien's family life or troubles, and insisted that his friend should come out alone to the gatherings. Dyson, Havard and Colin Hardie had all been expected likewise to abandon their wives in order to be with Lewis. But now, when the ardour of their friendship had in any case cooled, they were expected to flock around to The Kilns and enjoy the company of Lewis's wife.

Even if this had been a prospect in itself inviting, Lewis could hardly have introduced the matter to his friends in a clumsier way. Tolkien, his closest friend from 1927 until about 1940, and still a figure of tremendous importance in Jack's life, had only learnt about his marriage when he read about it in *The Times*. And there were other friends with whom Lewis was 'funny' about his wife. The Freuds, for instance, found that for the duration of Lewis's marriage they were effectively dropped. When Jill Freud came to see Lewis in Oxford, he invited her not to The Kilns, but to Magdalen, where he still had lunching rights. He told her that he was married, and disclosed to her the strange phenomenon of his having taken on his wife's pain, but he did not suggest that Joy might be introduced either to Jill or to Clement Freud.[10]

Those like the old Inklings who were forced to meet Joy did not enjoy it, and pretty soon made excuses to avoid meeting her again. She had shown enormous fortitude and courage in her illness, but while this may have been a reason for her loved ones to love her more, and for those who read about her afterwards to admire her, it did not have the effect of making her an interesting companion. In spite of the gallant suggestions made by her biographer, and by Lewis himself, that Joy had 'wit', a 'sense of humour', a 'mind like a panther', etc., none of her recorded utterances exactly bears out these claims. Warnie's judgement was surely more accurate when he said 'she is well-read, but no high-brow'. In a way which now seems touching, but which was at the time, to his friends, embarrassing and annoying, Lewis was so in love with his wife that he could not quite see how she might appear to anyone else; and anyway, as his friends had discovered in the days of Minto, qualities in women which they found repugnant were precisely the ones which he found alluring. He had rebutted with humourless anger any suggestion that it was a 'cursed fate' which had given him to the Moore. In exactly the same way, and for very similar reasons, he loved Joy. He once praised her for her masculine virtues. 'She soon put a stop to that by asking how I'd like to be praised for my feminine ones. It was a good *riposte*, dear. Yet there was something of the Amazon, something of Penthesilea and Camilla. And you, as well as I, were glad that it should be there.'[11]

It was, in fact, an essential ingredient in what attracted Lewis to his wife in so profoundly erotic a manner. 'For those few years' they 'feasted on love; every mode of it – solemn and merry, romantic and realistic, sometimes as dramatic as a thunderstorm, sometimes as comfortable and unemphatic as putting on your soft slippers. No cranny of heart or body remained unsatisfied.'[12] In his typically self-revealing way he advanced a generalization in *The Four Loves* about what can only be specific to certain cases; and of what case, other than his own, could he have been aware? The sexual act, he wrote, 'can invite the man to an extreme, though short-lived masterfulness, to the dominance of a conqueror or a captor, and the woman to a correspondingly extreme abjection and surrender. Hence the roughness, the fierceness, of some erotic play; "the lover's pinch which hurts and is desired".'[13]

To someone as wrapped up in his beloved as Lewis was, friendship of the kind he had enjoyed with Tolkien or Williams became, for the time being, impossible. This is surely the reason why most men in the West today do not, in Lewis's sense of the word, have any friends at all. Like the great majority of married couples, Jack and Joy took to seeing 'friends' together – couples such as the Greens or the Farrers. No one for a moment would suggest that such foursomes do not constitute a convivial way of passing the time. Most married people, when they speak of their 'friends', mean precisely those with whom, as groups of four, six or eight, they pass their evenings or holidays. Lewis described the difference between such get-togethers and true friendship with his usual vigour when he said, 'an endless prattling "Jolly" replaces the intercourse of minds'.[14] He was writing, as so often, from experience.

On more than one occasion, when having a drink alone with Christopher Tolkien, Lewis would press the younger man for reasons why 'Tollers' had allowed their friendship to lapse. Lewis was hurt by it, but Christopher was too embarrassed to enter upon any explanation. Both the explanation and Lewis's pain were embarrassing.[15] Lewis, as he contemplated his old friendships and wrote their obituary in the chapter on 'Friendship' in *The Four Loves*, knew the reasons well enough, and in his cooler, more rational moments could spell them out with all his old merciless analytical power:

> Her presence has thus destroyed the very thing she was brought to share. She can never really enter the circle because the circle ceases to be itself when she enters it – as the horizon ceases to be the horizon when you get there. By learning to drink and smoke and tell risqué stories, she has not, for this purpose, drawn an inch nearer to the men than her grandmother . . . She may be quite as clever as the men whose evening she has spoiled, or cleverer. But she is not really interested in the same things.

This was profoundly true of Joy *vis-à-vis* Dyson, the Tolkiens and others. She knew nothing of medieval literature, was 'no highbrow', and in disputation seemed quite unable to distinguish between vigour and rudeness, strength of expression and obscenity or profanity. No wonder the Lewises were thrown back on 'an endless prattling "Jolly"'.

There was nevertheless not the smallest guarantee that when, as of old, Lewis was asked to conduct a speaking engagement, his wife would not come along too. An academic acquaintance of Lewis (female, agnostic) who was back in Oxford for a visit from another university went along, at about this period, to a very crowded meeting at which Lewis was billed to speak about Love and Faith-Healing. Though Lewis was the advertised speaker, his wife did most of the talking. 'It left me', wrote this witness, 'with a vague feeling of disgust and uncertainty which I can still recapture. "There's nowt so queer as folks."'[16]

Joy was also said to have helped Lewis with his book *Reflections on the Psalms*, notably the scrappiest of all his books. 'At one point,' he writes in his introduction, 'I had to explain how I differed on a certain matter both from Roman Catholics and from Fundamentalists: I hope I shall not for this forfeit the good will or prayers of either . . . But then I dare say I am a much more annoying person than I know. (Shall we, perhaps in Purgatory, see our own faces and hear our own voices as they really were?)' The acute self-awareness which these sentences display is remarkable, and they reflect a new tone of voice.

The Four Loves, which he wrote as the 1950s drew to a close, is rather different. It is not so much a treatise as a piece of oblique autobiography, as the extracts from it which I have already quoted show. It contains some good *Screwtape*-style comic caricatures. One remembers in particular the maddening figure of Mrs Fidget.

> She was always making things too; being in her own estimation (I'm no judge myself) an excellent amateur dressmaker and a great knitter. And of course, unless you were a heartless brute, you had to wear the things. (The Vicar tells me that, since her death, the contributions of that family alone to 'sales of work' outweigh all his other parishioners put together.) Mrs. Fidget, as she often said, would 'work her fingers to the bone' for her family. They couldn't stop her. Nor could they – being decent people – quite sit still and watch her do it. They had to help. Indeed, they were always having to help – the Vicar says Mrs. Fidget is now at rest. Let us hope she is. What's quite certain is that her family are . . .[17]

Many of the book's apophthegms are questionable – one thinks, for instance, of Lewis's rather limited understanding of homosexuality: 'All those hairy old toughs of centurions in Tacitus, clinging to one another and begging for last kisses when the Legion was broken up . . . all pansies? If you can believe that you can believe anything.' It is remarkable that Lewis could have written in such simple-minded terms, particularly when one bears in mind that at least two of his closest friends (Coghill and Greeves) were homosexuals. Can he really have supposed that homosexual feeling was limited to 'pansies', or that it would invariably be the less the hairier or tougher a man was? The notion is as ridiculous as his apparent belief that friendship between the sexes is all but impossible, and his implication that 'men's talk' and 'women's talk' are two quite separate and immiscible things. 'What were the women doing meanwhile? How should I know? I am a man and never spied on the mysteries of the Bona Dea.'[18] This last is a risible fantasy which has done Lewis much damage in many of his readers' eyes, written by a married man who had lived his entire grown-up life (with one short break) in the society of women and who numbered among the friends or acquaintances that he regularly saw or spoke to Dorothy Sayers, the poet Ruth Pitter, Rose Macaulay, the Anglo-Saxon scholar Dorothy Whitelock and Sister Penelope.

Interlaced with such strange ideas, there are sentences in *The Four Loves* of memorable wisdom and calm common sense. 'Say your prayers in the garden early, ignoring steadfastly the dew, the birds and the flowers, and you will come away overwhelmed by its freshness and joy; go there in order to be overwhelmed, and after a certain age, nine times out of ten nothing will happen to you ... Affection almost slinks or seeps through our lives. It lives with humble, un-dress, private things: soft slippers, old clothes, old jokes, the thump of a sleepy dog's tail on the kitchen floor, the sound of a sewing machine, a golliwog left on the lawn.' It is for paragraphs such as this that one remembers the book with gratitude. John Braine, the Yorkshire novelist and author of *Room at the Top*, used to keep *The Four Loves* by his bed in his later years. I suspect many people do. It stays in the mind, particularly for the times when, as in the final chapter on the love of God, Lewis writes with a new quietness, a new wistfulness.

If we cannot 'practise the presence of God', it is something to be able to practise the absence of God, to become increasingly aware of our unawareness till we feel like a man who should stand beside a great cataract and hear no noise, or like a man in a story who looks in a mirror and finds no face there, or a man in a dream who stretches out his hand to visible objects and gets no sensation of touch.[19]

This is a very different Lewis from the man who breezily wrapped up the whole mystery of the Incarnation by asking his wireless audiences to imagine how they would feel if they were reborn as slugs. He had already begun to glimpse both the incomprehensibility and the challenge of his faith. The Christian story is one of a mysterious love so strong that it led to self-abnegation on the part of the Godhead Himself; a story of one who was rich, for our sake becoming poor; a story of certainties and status abandoned, of sinlessness involved, totally, in the world of sin, to the point where it received the ultimate degradation and punishment for sin; of cosmic suffering; of darkness and abandonment by God; of Gethsemane and Golgotha. Lewis was to have the easy, theoretical – and almost frivolous, in the case of the slug parallel – certainties of his early days of faith tried to their limits.

From the end of 1957 until 1959, there was a period of happiness which in retrospect seemed as though it had only been sent to accentuate the times of torment which followed. As well as being so happy with Joy, Lewis was on top form in his academic work. Cambridge suited him in every way, and the lectures he gave there were superb. In 1960, he published one course of them under the title *Studies in Words*.

This is one of his most interesting books. It explores the history of certain English words – *Nature, Sad, Wit, Free, Sense*, and others – and reminds the modern reader how unsafe it is to take it for granted that he knows what these words 'mean' when they occur in an old book. 'Sad', for example, means 'full' in Old English; heavy, sated. It has gone through many semantic movements before acquiring its simple sense of 'melancholy'.

> From the very nature of metaphor, a word that means 'heavy' will be very likely to acquire the meaning 'grievous'. A word that means 'fed up' will be very likely to acquire the meaning 'displeased, ill-content'. A word which means 'grave' or even 'steady-going' will necessarily mean the opposite of 'light' or 'sportive'. Thus we find *sad* used to mean 'serious', i.e. not joking. 'Speak you this with a sad brow?' are you in earnest? (*Much Ado* I.i.183) And what is serious will always be thought gloomy by some, and gloom may by litotes be called seriousness.[20]

Lewis did not understand, or attempt to understand, linguistic philosophy, or what the followers of Wittgenstein were to think of as 'language games'. Nor was he a philologist. Tolkien once noted 'CSL's curious ability (remarkable in a great scholar with a wide range of languages) to misunderstand etymology'. But Lewis did indeed have a wide range; his examples in *Studies in Words* are chosen from all over the library and, as so often in his writings, he makes us long to read the books he quotes – *Beowulf* or Jane Austen, Gower, Malory, Dryden, Launcelot Andrewes or Dickens. There is, in all his paragraphs, the stimulating sense of a lively intelligence at work, prepared to look up from his books and talk in an intelligible way to anyone who will listen. And there is such common sense in what he writes, as when he dissents from the ingenuities and false readings of I. A. Richards or William Empson; above all from the idea that language is always to be mixed up with the thing it attempts to signify. 'Statements about crime are not criminal language; nor are statements about emotions necessarily emotional language . . . "It is not cancer after all", "The Germans have surrendered", "I love you" – may all be true statements about matter of fact. And of course it is the facts, not the language, that arouse the emotion.'

It is interesting that Lewis believed that the sentence 'I love you' was not necessarily emotional language. But by the time he was reading the proofs of *Studies in Words* for the Cambridge University Press, he was more interested in the sentence 'It is not cancer after all' . . .

NINETEEN

MEN MUST ENDURE
1959–1960

In January 1959, Lewis wrote in the *Atlantic Monthly*,

> I have stood by the bedside of a woman whose thigh-bone was
> eaten through with cancer and who had thriving colonies of the
> disease in many other bones as well. It took three people to move
> her in bed. The doctors predicted a few months of life: the nurses
> (who often know better) a few weeks. A good man laid his hands
> on her and prayed. A year later the patient was walking (uphill, too,
> through rough woodland) and the man who took the last X-ray
> photographs was saying 'These bones are as solid as rock'. It's
> miraculous.[1]

Lewis knew, intellectually, that all this was too good to be true; or,
at any rate, that there could be no good reason for it to be true. To
the question of why God might choose at certain moments to reverse the processes of nature he had devoted his mind in *The Problem
of Pain* and *Miracles*; and although he had established a good case for
arguing that – if you believe in the supernatural at all – it is irrational
to disbelieve in the mere possibility of miracles, the experience of
loving Joy had drawn him into the knowledge that where suffering
was concerned there were no answers. But his heart could not resist
the hope that a miracle had occurred, and he was 'riding high' to such
an extent that the next stage was bound to be all the more shattering.
So 'high' was he that he began to behave in a completely uncharacter-
istic way. For example, Roger and June Lancelyn Green, inveterate
travellers and lovers of the Mediterranean, persuaded the Lewises to
come with them the following spring on a 'Wings Tour' in Greece.
Lewis was by now sixty-one years old. He had never set foot in an

aeroplane and, apart from his time in the trenches, he had never been abroad. For most of his life, he would have regarded foreign travel as an unpardonable extravagance. Even the holidays he took in Ireland once a year were rigidly budgeted for and sometimes cancelled. He would also, one suspects, have shared Warnie's view that foreign travel 'spoiled' reading; and that if one had read Theocritus, Homer or Pindar it would actually spoil things to have one's vision of their Greece transformed by a Wings Tour Greece – the white concrete tavernas, the songs of Greek waiters, the fellow tourists, not to mention something he had always particularly detested, the heat. Yet here he was, signing up for a holiday with his wife like any other twentieth-century human being. What was happening to the 'dinosaur' who had so proudly laid out his credentials upon arrival in Cambridge?

It was in October 1959 that he accompanied Joy to the Churchill Hospital for her final cancer check-up. Having approached all previous check-ups with dread, they were not worried about this one. 'Her health seemed so complete.'[2]

But on this occasion the X-rays revealed that Joy had been enjoying a 'remission' and that her cancer was not cured at all. At first the doctors thought it possible that she would have 'a few years' life still' but, as Lewis knew, 'We are in retreat. The tide has turned.'[3]

Throughout the winter of 1959–60, Joy struggled bravely against her illness and the Lewises tried to keep life going as normally as they could. Jack went to and fro between Oxford and Cambridge, nearly always accompanied by her. The boys continued to go to school. David Gresham was now nearly sixteen; Douglas was fourteen.

By March 1960, it was very doubtful whether she would be well enough to travel to Greece on the planned holiday with the Greens; but, in spite of her doctors' warning not to go, what did Joy have to lose? 'I'd rather go out with a bang than a whimper,' she wrote to Bill Gresham, 'particularly on the steps of the Parthenon.'[4] So, although she recognized that 'I've got enough cancers now to form a Trades Union of the darned things,'[5] she and Jack set off in April on their Wings Tour for twelve days.

There could have been no more perfect travelling companions than the Greens. Roger knew Greece very well, and loved it. June, as well as being a passionate philhellene, is a person of a tremendous bubbly kindness and conversational vitality. She was not at all the insensitively breezy kind, but it was not possible, even in the Lewises' wretched condition, to be miserable in her company for long. They drank a lot, which helped to deaden the pain which Joy was evidently suffering, and they amused her, while she threw bread at waiters and swigged her ouzo, by making up harmless doggerel.[6] Jack was amazed by how much he liked it all. 'Joy performed prodigies, climbing to the top of the Acropolis and getting as far as the lion gate of Mycenae . . . She was absolutely enraptured by what she saw . . . Attica is hauntingly beautiful and Rhodes is an earthly paradise.' Three years later, Lewis remembered, 'Joy knew she was dying. I knew she was dying, and *she* knew I knew she was dying – but when we heard the shepherds playing their flutes in the hills it seemed to make no difference.'[7]

They returned home in 'a nunc dimittis frame of mind'. Joy was completely exhausted by the trip, and suffered several weeks of acute pain and frequent nausea. On 20 May she was taken into the Acland Nursing Home where she had her right breast removed. But still she fought for life; by the beginning of the next month, she was back at The Kilns. Warnie was pushing her about in a wheelchair. She even managed to buy him a dozen handkerchiefs for his sixty-fifth birthday on 16 June. She began to make arrangements for Bill Gresham's first visit to England, planned for August. But even in the midst of these preparations, she was once more stricken by appalling pain and taken into the Acland. David and Douglas were brought home from their boarding school for the death-bed scene. 'Finish me off quick,' she said to the doctor, 'I won't have another operation.'[8] Warnie decided that this was the last he would ever see of her. But he was wrong. 'Once again Joy has made fools of the doctors and nurses, having returned to us on Monday 27th June looking, and saying, that she feels better than she has done for a long time past.' With anxiety momentarily removed from his mind, Warnie settled down to read *Little Lord Fauntleroy*, with tremendous admiration for 'Mrs. Burnett's power of drawing a perfectly good child who is neither a prig nor a bore'.[9] On 3 July, Joy felt well enough to go over to a favourite hotel, Studley Priory, to have dinner with Jack and Warnie. The next day she had a pleasant drive with a friend in the Cotswolds. On 12 July Warnie made tea – his usual late-night ritual, took it in to Jack and Joy, and went off to bed. When he left them they sounded as though they were 'reading a play together'. Jack remembered 'how long, how tranquilly, how nourishingly we talked together that last night!'

In all her illness so far, she had never cried out. But at 6.15 a.m. Warnie was woken by the sound of Joy screaming. The doctor had come by about seven and administered dope; but she had been drugged so much in the previous months that although the painkillers brought some relief, they did not make her lose consciousness. Incredibly, there was a difficulty about finding her a hospital bed, and Jack had to spend the whole morning ringing round, eventually persuading Joy's surgeon, Till, to give her a private bed at the Radcliffe Infirmary. Jack sat with her throughout the afternoon and evening in the ward. She asked him to give her fur coat to Katharine Farrer, and expressed the wish to be cremated. Very near the end, he said to her, 'If you can – if it is allowed – come to me when I too am on my death bed.' 'Allowed!' she said. 'Heaven would have a job to hold me; and as for Hell, I'd break it into bits.'[10] Austin Farrer came in to hear her confession and see her out of the world. She asked him to take her funeral service. 'Don't get me a posh coffin,' she asked. 'Posh coffins are all rot.' Then she said to him, 'I am at peace with God.'

At about twenty to two that night, Warnie heard Jack returning to the house. 'What news?' he asked, coming out into the hall. 'She died about twenty minutes ago,' said Jack. They announced her death in the *Daily Telegraph*, the newspaper which Warnie habitually read, but neglected to put it in *The Times*. In consequence, even close friends like Roger and June Lancelyn Green were unaware that Joy had died. Jack was horrified by how few people attended her funeral, which took place on 18 July. Just two taxis carried the mourners the short distance from The Kilns to the Oxford Crematorium. Jack, Warnie and the boys went in the first. Mollie and Len Miller, the cleaning lady and handyman at The Kilns, followed in the second car with the nurse (Hibbie) and the Master of Magdalene, Cambridge. Quite by chance, the two cars met up with the hearse at the roundabout. It was a sunny, blustery day, with big white clouds. Only Katharine Farrer was present in the crematorium chapel as they trooped in behind the coffin. Austin Farrer read the Prayer Book service, his voice frequently and uncharacteristically choked with emotion. There was no music. Sun shone through the windows of the bleak little chapel as the coffin was withdrawn and curtains, pulled invisibly, hid it for ever.[11]

TWENTY

LAST YEARS
1960–1963

Lewis's natural reaction to any experience was to write it up, or down. As he had discovered, with a mixture of joyful shock and embarrassment ('What an ass I have been'), this often led to a curious effect of unreality, as in the case of his over-eager desire to defend religious positions which he had really only fallen in love with from the outside, before learning what it was like to *live* them. *A Grief Observed*, as he came to call the jottings which he made from almost the moment Joy died, has an almost novelistic quality from its brilliant first sentence – 'No one ever told me that grief felt so like fear.' But the fragmentary nature of the book, its lack of any cohesion, is a new development in Lewis. People speak of being shattered by bereavement. *A Grief Observed*, in its shooting stabs of pain, its yelps of despair, its tears, its emotional zig-zagging, bears testimony to just such a shattering. There can be no doubt that it was written from the heart. In its very scrappiness, it is far truer than the apparently cohesive *Surprised by Joy* of five years earlier.

He confronts, in the experience of grief, some of the most funda-mental questions a man can ever ask. He does so, not without flinching, for one of the endlessly appealing things about the book is its admission of fear, its willingness to lay hurt bare, but without fudging. In marriage he recognized that he had been 'forced out of [his] shell'. Was he now doomed to crawl back, or to be sucked back into it? One of the reasons for keeping the notebooks was to keep alive that newborn self that Joy had nursed into being, a tender and more vulnerable self. But how could he do so, without either indulging in morbid displays of emotion or making Joy into a sanctified figure which she was not? He recognized quite truthfully that she was 'rather a battle-axe'.[1] It had been more than he had ever dared to admit about Minto (or about his own mother?).

But the truth-telling was excruciatingly painful. The boys, as he realized, found him embarrassing. He saw in their faces the same feelings as he and Warnie had had about the P'daytabird in the weeks after his own mother died. He seemed, according to Douglas Gresham, 'incapable of understanding that if he kept on talking about my mother, I was going to burst into tears – what embarrassed me was that fear.'[2] Presumably one of the things which makes *A Grief Observed* such a consoling and helpful book to thousands of bereaved people is that Lewis knew by instinct what is now a commonplace of bereavement counselling, that grief must be expressed and lived through. His whole life had been warped by his failure to express grief for his mother. Ever since that disastrous day in August 1908, he had been buttoned up. Perhaps even the release caused by loving Joy was not enough to melt him; it was in losing her that the essential work of healing mysteriously began. He had to weep. Sometimes, if a person mentioned Joy in his presence, he would burst into uncontrollable tears.[3] Only once, even so, could he bring himself to comfort the boys physically. One day when Douglas was crying, Lewis came and hugged him and they stood there for some moments crying together. Thereafter they found it easier to talk to each other. Such a scene – Jack Lewis, in tears, holding in his arms a weeping adolescent boy – would have been quite unthinkable to those close friends with whom, over thirty or forty years, he had not been able to share even the simplest intimacies.

Such a tremendous emotional shake-up was bound to have an enormous effect on his relationship with God. In *Surprised by Joy*, he had been so terrified of anyone placing a Freudian interpretation on the fact that his ability to believe in God only came upon him with the death of his father that he had deliberately played down his father's part in the story, making the P'daytabird into a purely comic character and reducing his important last illness to a single short paragraph. Now, beaten down into a position of absolute honesty, he faced a much more terrible thought than the facile idea that God was really a projection of his father. What, instead, if the reactions of irritation and disgust which he had foisted on the unfortunate Albert Lewis were really emotions more properly reserved for his Heavenly Father?

Total unbelief flickered across his consciousness – 'Go to Him when your need is desperate, when all other help is vain, and what do you find? A door slammed in your face and a sound of bolting and double bolting on the inside. After that, silence.'⁴ But his imagination could not absorb the idea of no-God. Instead, with Promethean courage, he faced a more dreadful alternative. 'Fate (or whatever it is) delights to produce a great capacity and then frustrate it. Beethoven went deaf. By our standards a mean joke; the monkey trick of a spiteful imbecile.'⁵ If God is all-powerful, and if he made the world in which we suffer, what other alternative can there be? In his Beethoven example, the crucial phrase is *by our standards*. It reflects the sort of attitude which produced Thomas Hardy's magnificently haunting poem, 'God's Education'. But Hardy, like most of those in modern literature who have railed against Providence, did not really believe in God. Lewis did, which is what makes his cries of anguish against 'the Cosmic Sadist' so much more devastating. Outside the Psalms and the Book of Job, there is not a book quite like *A Grief Observed*, a book by a man who still believes in God but cannot find evidence for His goodness. Like the Psalmist, and like Job, Lewis lets himself be tossed about from mood to mood. He moves on from the Cosmic Sadist idea. He realizes that if his faith has been knocked to pieces like a house of cards, then no such hypothesis is necessary.

From this point of blackness, he moves on again. Some days, he feels that the grief is lightening and he fears its going; he is tempted morbidly to hug it. Sometimes he thinks life is getting back to normal and he is suddenly hit by the full force of his grief all over again. Gradually, however, he starts to feel that the whole process has been so painful because it has involved the smashing of all his illusions; that religion, if true, must be the ultimate truth, and therefore something which could never be contained in the pat phrases and slick analogies of his earlier self.

My idea of God is not a divine idea. It has to be shattered time after time. He shatters it Himself. He is the great iconoclast. Could we not say that this shattering is one of the marks of His presence? . . . All reality is iconoclastic. The earthly beloved, even in this life, incessantly triumphs over your mere idea of her. And you want her to; you want her with all her resistances, all her faults, all her unexpectedness. That is, in her foursquare and independent reality. And this, not any image or memory, is what we are to love still, after she is dead.

This understanding makes him realize how little either of Joy, or of the dead, or of God, he has hitherto understood.

Can a mortal ask questions which God finds unanswerable? Quite easily, I should think. All nonsense questions are unanswerable. How many hours are there in a mile? Is yellow square or round? Probably half the questions we ask – half our great theological and metaphysical problems – are like that.

No, it was not Wittgenstein who wrote that. It was C. S. Lewis. His confrontation, his war, with the Unknown God produced writings which were far more searching, far more intelligent, far more deeply religious, than any of those papers which he read aloud to amused undergraduate audiences or to wireless listeners during the Second World War. This was the real thing.

Having finished his essay, Lewis sent it to his agents, Curtis Brown, who submitted it anonymously to Faber & Faber. The author of the typescript was N. W. Clark. T. S. Eliot, Managing Director of Faber & Faber, found the short typescript distasteful enough to be worth a second reading. No one can read the book without being haunted by it. Like everything Lewis ever published, it is supremely readable, and the experiences it describes are of such pain and such universality that one cannot fail to turn the pages. But the reader's report was unfavourable. Several people were consulted and no one seemed sure that N. W. Clark, whoever he was, should be allowed to burden the world with his unhappiness. It so happened that T. S. Eliot then asked Charles Monteith, a younger director of the firm and a Fellow of All Souls, to read the typescript and give his opinion. Monteith, who had not only been a pupil of Lewis's, but was also a fellow Ulsterman, instantly recognized the handwritten corrections which appeared at several points in the typescript. Once he had done so, everything else fell into place. He knew that Lewis had lately lost his wife, and also that he published poems in *Punch* under the pseudonymous initials N.W. for Nat Whilk (Old English for 'I know not who'). He told Eliot of his discovery and the decision was made to publish.[6]

Strangely enough the book did not do very well. Faber & Faber sent it to Donald Coggan, the Archbishop of York, for his comments, preserving the author's anonymity. Coggan was forthright in condemning what he thought of as its mawkish and unmanly tone. Trevor Huddleston, the campaigner for black rights in South Africa and later Archbishop of Mauritius, however, remarked, 'I began to read it at once and quite literally could not put it down ... I believe that it would be of the greatest help to many people in bereavement, not least because it refuses to compromise or to sentimentalise over the issue of death, yet it remains a profoundly religious and theological document.'[7] Huddleston's words were to be proved true, but not at once. Faber & Faber did not sell more than twelve or thirteen hundred copies until, after Lewis's death, Owen Barfield as the literary executor of the estate authorized them to publish it under Lewis's name. Then it became an instant bestseller and has continued to sell very well ever since. For the burning truths it contains, as well as for the thousands of people it has 'helped', one could almost say that (in the unlikely event of all Lewis's works save one being destroyed and wiped from the face of the earth) one would choose *A Grief Observed* above all his other books.

There is a certain irony in the fact that it was published by Eliot. The two men had never felt drawn to each other. From an early stage Lewis had made rather a 'thing' of being unable to see merit in Eliot's poetry, and their disagreement about Milton could not have been more absolute. In other ways, it could be said that there were areas of similarity in these two men temperamentally so very different. Both came to England as strangers; both found their way by a circuitous spiritual path to lives patterned by the restraints of the Anglican confessional and the consolations of the Anglican altar. Both were men with two women in their lives, separated by a long gap of pious, not particularly happy celibacy; both had found soul mates in their second marriages to much younger women.

Charles Williams had made an attempt long since to bring the two men together, at the Mitre Hotel in Oxford in 1945. It had been a somewhat frosty occasion, with Eliot remarking, 'Mr Lewis, you are a much older man than you appear in photographs,' before going on to pay him a back-handed compliment – 'I consider your *Preface to "Paradise Lost"* your best book.' Read Eliot's essays on Milton, and think about it.

In the late 1950s, after Lewis wrote his book on the Psalms, he was invited to sit on a church committee advising about the revision of the Psalter. Lewis hosted this committee on a number of occasions at Magdalene, Cambridge, and he and Eliot dined together sometimes with their wives. Both liturgically conservative, they would have been unlikely to have derived much pleasure from the knowledge of how radical liturgical change in their church was destined to be.

Their differences could be demonstrated by comparing Eliot's extremely judgemental and 'authoritative' literary criticism with Lewis's totally different approach. As he crept back to life again after the experience of bereavement, Lewis found himself contemplating the 'subject' and the Faculty of English to which he was returning. *An Experiment in Criticism* may seem to some readers (and in particular to those who have never had anything to do with the study of English in universities) to be an exercise in stating the obvious. It has to be understood as a document of its time before its merits, which are abundant, begin to emerge. Lewis went to Cambridge at a time when 'evaluative' criticism was at its height in the English school. For adherents of this approach to the subject, 'reading English' meant being encouraged as a young person of twenty or twenty-one to decide whether Chaucer, Milton or Dickens were 'any good'. Lewis had moved away from a university where boring undergraduates wrote essays beginning 'Swift was born . . .' He had entered a university where anything so prosaic as a *fact* would have marred the moral attitudinizing of those who looked to I. A. Richards and F. R. Leavis as to the leaders of some new way of study. In this atmosphere, whole categories of book, and the works of authors hitherto considered great (like Dickens or Milton), were dismissed as valueless. This was particularly true in the case of Dr Leavis, who had some of the fanaticism of a Savonarola or a Robespierre. Lewis tactfully and cunningly does not mention Leavis by name but there can be no doubt who is meant when he describes the new Vigilant critics:

We have learned from the political sphere that committees of public-safety, witch-hunters, Ku Klux Klans, Orangemen,

Macarthyites *et hoc genus omne* can become dangers as great as those they were formed to combat. The use of the guillotine becomes an addiction. Thus under Vigilant criticism a new head falls nearly every month. The list of approved authors grows absurdly small. No one is safe.[8]

What had begun as an apparently sensible desire to distinguish between 'good' and 'bad' literature had ended with a vast Index of proscribed books, including the names of all but a tiny handful of writers approved by Dr Leavis – D. H. Lawrence, T. S. Eliot, Joseph Conrad, and two or three more. Strange to say, far from repelling the young, this ungenerous approach to a vast literary tradition stretching back a thousand years attracted zealous adherents. Lewis had left the university which supported King Charles I in the Civil War and gone to the University of Oliver Cromwell. 'The Literary Puritans', Lewis realized,

are too serious as men to be seriously receptive as readers. I have listened to an undergraduate's paper on Jane Austen from which, if I had not read them, I should never have discovered that there was the least hint of comedy in her novels. After a lecture of my own I have been accompanied from Mill Lane to Magdalene by a young man protesting with real anguish and horror against my wounding, my vulgar, my irreverent suggestion that *The Miller's Tale* was written to make people laugh ... We are breeding up a race of young people who are as solemn as the brutes ('smiles from reason flow'); as solemn as a nineteen year old Scottish son of the manse at an English sherry party who takes all the compliments for declarations and all the banter for insult.[9]

It was in this atmosphere that Lewis was writing, and the *Experiment* was not to replace one sort of literary evaluation with another but to abandon evaluative literary criticism altogether.

Can I honestly and strictly speaking, say with any confidence that my appreciation of any scene, chapter, stanza or line has been improved by my reading of Aristotle, Dryden, Johnson, Lessing, Coleridge, Arnold himself (as a practising critic), Pater or Bradley?

I am not sure that I can ... It is always better to read Chaucer again than to read a new criticism of him.[10]

This seems like common sense today, but in the Cambridge of 1960 it was explosive stuff. Lewis proposed that instead of dividing books and authors into 'good' and 'bad' on the say-so of critics, we should judge literature by the way we read it. The duty of reading, as well as its pleasure, was, he believed, in submission to what the author actually intended. 'We seek an enlargement of our being. We want to be more than ourselves.' Books which compel us to re-read them frequently, to be attentive to their exact wording and style, books which *cannot* be read as non-literary people read trash, will always emerge and remain as the great books. The advantage of Lewis's approach is that it need not give way either to snobbery (pretending we like books which happen to be fashionable) or to inverted snobbery (in the way that Lewis's temptation was to see more merit in Captain Marryat than in T. S. Eliot). It does not really matter what *judgement* we pass on a book. What matters is not what we do to the book but what the book does to us. The *Experiment* ends with one of the finest paragraphs in the whole Lewis *œuvre*:

> Literary experience heals the wound, without undermining the privilege, of individuality. There are mass emotions which heal the wound; but they destroy the privilege. In them our separate selves are pooled and we sink back into sub-individuality. But in reading great literature I become a thousand men and yet remain myself. Like a night sky in the Greek poem, I see with a myriad eyes, but it is still I who see. Here, as in worship, in love, in moral action, and in knowing, I transcend myself; and am never more myself than when I do.[11]

When it appeared posthumously, J. R. R. Tolkien was repelled by *Letters to Malcolm*, finding in it precisely the attitude which Lewis professed to find distasteful in his grandparents – 'Cosily at ease in Zion'. Among a lot of criticisms which seem wide of the mark, Tolkien managed to score some very palpable hits, most notably when he said that the *Letters* were not 'about prayer' but 'about Lewis praying'. In the same way it could be said that *An Experiment in Criticism* is not about literature but about *Lewis Reading*, and *A Grief Observed* is candidly, though anonymously, what its title says it is. Doubtless if *Letters to Malcolm* were being offered to us as a manual of prayer, a substitute for St François de Sales or William Law, Tolkien's objection would be only proper. But a taste for Lewis is, in large part, a taste for reading about him. Though it was denied him to become a great poet, he shares with 'the last Romantics' a vivid awareness of his own consciousness, a sense that the chief end of writing is to communicate sensation and experience. A high proportion of Lewis's *œuvre* when properly considered can be found to be of the same kind as Wordsworth's *Prelude*, a book which was always very dear to him. What the Catholic Tolkien found distasteful – in particular the inference drawn from *Malcolm* that an 'unqualified' Protestant layman might take upon himself a teaching office in a matter so delicate as how we should pray – was precisely what Lewis would have felt justified his position as a writer. He disclaimed the role of *directeur*, which was why he framed his book in the form of fictitious letters to the invented figure of Malcolm, who has apparently (his letters are not attempted) been hitting back, Barfield-style, at the chinks in Lewis's armour. At the same time, he was not frightened of soliloquy, either as a literary mode or as a means of discovering or conveying religious truth, as he made plain by quoting one of his own poems, pretending that the identity of the author was unknown to him:

> They tell me, Lord, that when I seem
>   To be in speech with you,
> Since but one voice is heard, it's all a dream,
>   One talker aping two.
>
> Sometimes it is, yet not as they
>   Conceive it. Rather, I
> Seek in myself the things I hoped to say,
>   But lo! my wells are dry.
>
> Then, seeing me empty, you forsake
>   The listener's role and through
> My dumb lips breathe and into utterance wake
>   The thoughts I never knew.

> And thus you neither need reply
>   Nor can; thus, while we seem
> Two talkers, thou art one forever, and I
>   No dreamer, but thy dream.

'*Dream*', adds Lewis the critic, 'makes it too like Pantheism and was perhaps dragged in for the rhyme. But is he not right in thinking that prayer in its most perfect state is a soliloquy? If the Holy Spirit speaks in the man, then in prayer God speaks to God. But the human petitioner does not therefore become a "dream".'

Maybe not a dream. But there remains a sense in which all Romantic writers (Romantic in the sense of post-Wordsworthians who make themselves and their own sensations the subject of their work) are difficult to pin down. There are those who, discerning that Lewis, like Yeats, worked by assuming a number of masks, have come to the conclusion that there was something bogus about him; that either in his literary attitudes, or his bluff conservatism, or his religious faith, he was 'putting it on'. This misjudgement of Lewis surely stems from a mistaken view of how anything comes to be written, or possibly even perceived. Just as, all those years ago, Tolkien and Dyson drew Lewis into Christianity by making him see that it was truth told by means of story, so he himself as a writer is so constantly accessible and interesting because he is unashamed of the story-telling element in all literary modes. It is not a *lie* to recognize that literature itself is unnatural. So, having tried to write a straight book on prayer and found in the early 1950s that he had to abandon it, in *Malcolm* he found the perfect mode. It was almost certainly suggested by reading Rose Macaulay's 'real' *Letters to a Friend*, a correspondence with her former confessor and largely taken up with spiritual matters. But the fact that the mode is only a mode does not mean that the content of *Malcolm* is bogus, any more than the semi-fictionalized pattern of *A Grief Observed* should make us suppose that he did not really go through the experience of bereavement.

A failure to understand the kind of writer Lewis was – a Romantic egoist in the tradition of Wordsworth and Yeats – has led to two of the grosser extremes among those expressing views about him since his death. (And similar extremes are noticeable among those who love or loathe Wordsworth and Yeats.) On the one hand there are those who would dismiss all three writers as mere poseurs, shallow men pretending to be deep, mortals putting on immortal masks. This view must be false – in Lewis's case – because every single piece of biographical evidence which exists supports the opposite point of view. In love, in friendship and above all in religion there can be no doubt of his passionate sincerity.

On the other hand there are those readers who are so uplifted by the sublimity of Lewis at his best as a writer that they assume that he was himself a sublime being, devoid of blemishes. Readers of this kind either ignore Lewis's faults altogether, and attribute any mention of them to some ulterior motive (possibly anti-religious) on behalf of the speaker, or – oddest of all to neutral observers who perhaps haven't read much Lewis or made up their minds about him – they acknowledge the faults but wish to make them into virtues. We suddenly find ourselves in an uncongenial world where a bullying, hectoring technique in public debate is held up as a courageous defence of the faith, or spells of club-room misogyny are taken as evidence of holy celibacy.

All this seems a pity because it dehumanizes a man who was not posing when he described his wife and himself as 'a sinful woman married to a sinful man; two of God's patients, not yet cured'.[12] If we ignore the kind of man Lewis was, in our anxiety to dismiss him as a fraud or canonize him as a plaster saint, we miss the unmistakable and remarkable evidence of something like sanctification which occurred in him towards the end of his days. The suffering which smashed him up and made him so vulnerable did not destroy his faith. Nor did it destroy the kind of man he was. He went on being a red-faced Ulsterman, he continued to smoke and drink heavily, his aesthetic tastes remained much the same – that is to say broad. He never did see the point in Arthur Greeves's fondness for Proust; but nor could you ever classify Lewis as a man who 'only liked' fantasy, or epic poems, or E. Nesbit, much as he liked all three. A fortnight before his death, he was reading *Les Liaisons Dangereuses* and writing to a colleague at Magdalene, Cambridge – 'Wow what a book! Come to lunch on Friday (fish) and tell me about it.'[13]

This colleague, Richard William Ladborough, went to lunch 'and of course it was Jack who told *me* about it; and not the other way round ... I somehow felt it was the last time we should meet, and when he escorted me, with his usual courtesy, to the door, I think he felt so too. Never was a man better prepared.' One might take this as a commonplace, but it is not. Like many (most?) religious people, Lewis was profoundly afraid of death. His dread of it, when in the midst of life, had been almost pathological and obsessive. Physical extinction was a perpetual nightmare to him and, whatever his theological convictions and hopes, he was unable, before his wife's death, to reconcile himself to the transition which death must inevitably entail.

Towards the end, this changed. It was not that he developed a death wish: his hold on life was as vigorous as ever. But he became altogether more accepting of the cards that were being dealt to him. The last years at Cambridge were happy ones. His last year of all was dogged by humiliating illnesses which he took in a remarkably passive frame of mind. Since 1961, he had been troubled with an enlarged prostate gland, and from spring 1962 he was forced to wear a catheter.

In spite of the fact that Havard had diagnosed Joy's cancer as a touch of fibrositis, Lewis was still loyally employing the services of the Useless Quack when he was in Oxford. The catheter fitted by Havard was an almost Heath Robinson contraption, with a small tap at the end of Lewis's penis to enable him to release the contents of his bladder as the need arose. He sometimes forgot, and there was more than one occasion, such as at a sherry party at Cambridge, when the thing burst and he wet his trousers, displaying no more than a jocular embarrassment at the incident.

The Useless Quack's attentions to his urinary problems brought more problems of their own, and by the early summer of 1962 Lewis was in very acute pain. His doctor in Cambridge was a young general practitioner called Tony Haines, who was astonished when he examined Lewis by the extent to which his case had been neglected. He had assumed that so famous and distinguished a professor would have been given the best possible medical attention; it was the sort of assumption young men make. Here, suspended from Lewis's person, were pieces of tubing held on by rubber bands, an old wooden peg, a bit of cork. It was all filthy and stinking and, far worse, it was poisoning his system. It was killing him. He was put on to a low-protein diet, which he loathed; for his own eating tastes had come to resemble exactly those of his father, and he did not consider that he had eaten a 'proper' meal unless it included slices of meat off the joint. The Haineses had him to dinner in Cambridge and gave him a pizza. Pamela Haines, the doctor's wife, and herself a writer, was so nervous that she burnt the pizza, so they did not have much to eat that evening.[14] But neither Haines nor the other doctors could do much to help their patient, being afraid that the prostate operation which he so desperately needed would damage his weak heart. The heart trouble sometimes left him 'gasping like a new-caught fish which no one has the kindness to knock on the head'.[15]

In the same year J. R. R. Tolkien's publishers wrote to Lewis asking him if he would be prepared to write a 'puff' for *The Adventures of Tom Bombadil*, a book of verse. It is indicative of how far the estrangement had gone that Lewis did not know Tolkien's Oxford address; he wrote to Merton College and marked the envelope 'Please forward'.

Dear Tollers,

Breckman has sent me a copy of The A. of T.B. and I have explained to him why I think the 'word' from me which he asked for wd. probably do the book no good and might do it harm. The public – little dreaming how much you dislike my work, bless you! – regard us as a sort of firm and wd. only laugh at what wd. seem to them mutual back-scratching.

Lewis went on to praise the poems and suggest one emendation in the voice of 'Bentley', one of the fictitious editors of *The Lay of Leithien*, whom he had invented as far back as 1937. It was an allusion to the time when his friendship with Tolkien was perhaps the most important ingredient in both their lives. He concluded the letter, 'I wish we cd. ever meet.'[16]

Prompted by this letter and at last yielding to his son's persuasions, Tolkien agreed to meet Lewis. He and Christopher presented themselves at The Kilns some time later, deep in the winter of 1962–3. It was an awkward meeting, like an encounter between estranged members of a family. Neither Tolkien nor Lewis had much to say to one another. The icy winter weather as the two Tolkiens made their way back through the gloomy housing estates which now pressed in on The Kilns seemed to match the great chill which had descended on a once-warm friendship.[17]

Lewis was unwell for most of the winter, but with the coming of spring hope revived, and he and Douglas Gresham planned a trip to Ireland to see Arthur Greeves. ('I can manage stairs now provided I take them in bottom gear.')[18] But it was not to be. On 15 June 1963, Lewis had a heart attack and was taken into the Acland Nursing Home.

Warnie was away in Ireland at the time, and when the seriousness of Jack's condition became clear to him, he could not face it. For some weeks, no one was able to trace him, and by the time he turned up at the Lourdes Hospital in Drogheda, it was obvious how he had been spending his time. Jack, meanwhile, was losing his hold on life. He became unconscious. A curate from a church near the Acland came and administered extreme unction (the anointing of the sick with oil) and, as quite often happens when this sacrament is administered, the patient recovered. Lewis sat up in bed and asked for tea, the beverage which he had consumed in enormous quantities over the years and which presumably accounted in part for the ruinous state of his bladder. But although he was awake, he was not 'himself'. Dressed in a sports coat and pyjama trousers, he began to give instructions to his nurses that he must be taken to the Bodleian Library. He also dictated some letters which, while being perfectly coherent, had no basis in fact. When he recovered, he remarked that his last real dread – that of madness – had been removed from him; having been mad, he saw that there was nothing to fear. The generalization was typical of his way of arguing; the identification of this post-comatose period of confusion with all the other horrors the mind is capable of suffering – schizophrenia, claustrophobia, simple depression – shows that in this way he was still the same. But in other ways he was different. To Sister Penelope, he wrote, 'Ought one to honour Lazarus rather than Stephen as the protomartyr? To be brought back and have all one's dying to do again was rather hard. When you die, and if "prison visiting" is allowed, come down and look me up in Purgatory. It *is* all rather fun – solemn fun – isn't it?'[19]

The Farrers were on hand, but they could not undertake the work of looking after Lewis in his decrepitude. He now needed a night nurse and a day nurse; and the flood of correspondence still continued. He needed Warnie, but Warnie 'doesn't even write and is, I suppose, drinking himself to death'. Lewis had never been so alone in his life. He felt compelled, when sanity had been restored to him, to write to

Magdalene resigning his fellowship. Oxford – as always in the Long Vacations – was deserted. No friends seemed to be there for him. As so often in life, he conducted himself on the 'ram caught in a thicket' principle.

A young American from the University of Kentucky called Walter Hooper had recently arrived in Oxford to attend a summer school and for the purpose of getting to know Lewis. He had visited The Kilns, and Lewis had taken him out to pubs to meet his friends on several occasions. Since Hooper wished to write some sort of dissertation on Lewis, and regarded him as 'the Master', what more suitable figure could Lewis find to help him through the summer? He impulsively asked Hooper to come and work at The Kilns as his secretary, and a Scotsman called Alec Ross was hired as the night nurse. Thus passed the month of August and some of September. Then Hooper went back to the United States, intending to return as Lewis's full-time secretary after Christmas.

The consequence of Lewis's Lazarus-like 'reprieve' was that he was able to spend the last months of his life, as he had spent so many years before, in the company of Warnie. Jack had reached the point of despairing, and was writing to Greeves in tones of great desolation – 'But oh Arthur, never to see you again!' – when the prodigal returned. Warnie was like a dog who had just eaten the Sunday roast off the dinner table. But he need not have worried. There were no recriminations. For two quietly happy months, the brothers lived together as they had always dreamed of doing. Warnie coped with the letters. Jack sat and read. In a strange sort of way, as he remarked to one correspondent, there was something positively comforting about being out of things, and no longer obliged to keep up with the latest developments in scholarship; 'I have re-read the Iliad instead.' Though infinitely enfeebled, he was being given two months of Bookham days, with vast leisure in which to read and no responsibility for domestic chores. Only they were Bookham days with a difference, for they had none of the loneliness which characterized Lewis's time with Kirkpatrick. The Little End Room had been re-established after all. He and Warnie were together. Not that everything which Warnie read to him could give pleasure. That terrible habit of reading the newspapers brought some severe shocks. On 16 November 1963 Jack wrote to a lady in Darien, Connecticut:

My brother tells me gloomily that it is an absolute certainty that we shall have a Labour Government within a few months, with all the regimentation, austerity and meddling which they so enjoy. Perhaps it will not be so bad this time for Sir Stafford Cripps, the late nursery governess of England, is dead. But if they get in with a big majority, it will take ten years to break it down – which means that both of us have in all probability seen our last Conservative government.[20]

Warnie's newspaper did not err, but Jack was to be spared what he so much dreaded; spared, too, the resurrection of the troubles in his native Ulster. For a week or more, he remained at The Kilns, propped up in the very room where Joy had spent so many heroic hours of suffering. Paxford, repeatedly singing 'Abide with Me' *sotto voce*, did some cooking. It was all excellent; houses have memories and atmospheres. As he sat there with a book on his lap, Lewis could not fail to remember the scenes of a past existence: Paxford egging Minto on to buy the dud wireless set; Minto, still in the days of her vigour, feeding the fowls, exercising the dogs, amusing the evacuee children; shy, kind June Flewett coming up behind him in the study and kissing him on the back of his head; or much earlier, in the late 1920s, Bruce MacFarlane and another Fellow of Magdalen calling at the house unannounced. Lewis had hovered, and not gone to the door. Maureen had answered it. He had watched the Fellows walk away, clearly astonished to discover that Jack the archetypal bachelor was sharing his house with two women. Whatever the real secret was, they never penetrated it. Nobody would ever quite know, truly know, what he had shared with Minto in those early days. The poor P'daytabird certainly knew nothing of it. Sometimes, in the glass, Jack saw his father's face staring back at him, and all that world came back – of hot days in Strandtown, when their heavily tweeded father led the two boys indoors for steaming roast meat. 'Well, boys, this is grand.'

Friday, 22 November was a day to be graven in the history of the Western world, since it was the day that John F. Kennedy drove to Dallas and met his assassin. Shortly after six, Warnie looked in on his brother and met a cheerful 'I'm all right'. Breakfast was as usual, after which he managed to get dressed and answer four letters. He had difficulty, however, in keeping awake, and when Warnie found him slumped asleep in his chair after lunch he advised him to get into bed. At four, Warnie brought him tea and found him very drowsy, and very thick in his speech. He was 'calm and cheerful'. One and a half hours later, Warnie heard a crash and ran into the room. Jack was lying at the foot of the bed, unconscious. He was still breathing, but some three or four minutes later he ceased to do so.

TWENTY-ONE

FURTHER UP
AND FURTHER IN

Since Lewis died on the very day that John F. Kennedy was assassin-ated (it was also, as it happened, the day that Aldous Huxley died in California), his death was noted by the newspapers, but did not attract as much notice as it would have done on a less eventful day. Since he himself despised 'news', this would not much have troubled him.

Warnie was in any case anxious that the funeral should be private, and he gave instructions to Father Head, the vicar of the parish church, that there should be no prior notice of when the obsequies were to take place. Word got round among a small handful of friends, who assembled at the Headington Quarry church to bury Lewis on 26 November 1963, a Tuesday. Head had previously celebrated a requiem mass, and J. R. R. Tolkien, who attended the funeral with his son Christopher, had arranged for a Roman Catholic mass to be said at the church of St Aloysius. Others present included Lewis's old pupil and future biographer George Sayer, his stepson Douglas Gresham, Maureen and Leonard Blake, and Fred Paxford the gar-dener. Everyone waited for Warnie to appear, but he did not come. One can safely say that, since the catastrophe of 1908 when he lost his mother, Warnie had suffered no more devastating loss. He is not the only person who has been unable to face the funeral of someone truly dear to him. Queen Victoria was unable to bring herself to attend the funeral of Prince Albert; Samuel Johnson missed the funeral of his wife. Warnie spent 26 November lying in bed drinking whisky.

Lewis was buried in the churchyard, and when Warnie chose the gravestone, he had carved on it the words from *King Lear* which had been on the calendar of Flora Lewis's bedroom on the day she died: *Men must endure their going hence.* Warnie was not equipped to endure Jack's departure, but he was doomed to live for another miserable nine and a half years without him. He would let The Kilns and move out to live with Len and Mollie Miller, who had been the servants there in latter years. Sometimes he would move back again to The Kilns or take to his travels, inconsolable without Jack. Sometimes the Sayers in Malvern would have him to stay. Jill and Clement (Clé) Freud let him spend his holidays at their house in Walberswick, on the Suffolk coast. Clement Freud, he noted in 1968, 'now wears a beard and moustache, looks astonishingly like Edward VII's photos in early life. It's not only the hairiness which produces the resemblance, but the rather prominent dull heavily lidded eyes. Not that Clé is dull, far from it . . .'

In some moods he wished to sell The Kilns, not necessarily the easiest thing to do, since it had fallen into a poor state; there was fungus growing on the walls of the bathroom even before Jack died. Warnie and Maureen Blake, who owned the place jointly, seemed to be unable to agree on the details of the sale, and Warnie confided angrily to his journal that 'time was when Maureen would have stood a good chance of being burnt as a witch'. His irascibility, always a marked feature of his character, was poured into the pages of his diary, and no one escaped except his beloved Jack. He remembered furiously 'the winter when Joy and her brats burnt the whole of our winter coal ration while we were in Ireland'.

These cries of hurt sprang largely from the intolerable feeling that he wanted to be with Jack, and the knowledge that this was impossible. There were very long spells when Warnie was sober, and if he felt the need for a truly heroic 'bender', he tried to arrange for it to happen in Ireland. When the worst of it was over, he found a welcome with the nuns of Our Lady of Lourdes.

Warnie's natural instinct as a historian had been to keep records and compile documents. From early days in the Little End Room, he had been doing so, and his life's work when he came out of the Army had been to put together the monumental *Lewis Papers*. It was natural that he should have taken a great interest in the preservation of his brother's archives, and in making some kind of permanent literary memorial to him, and he began to prepare an edition of Jack's letters. This was published in 1966.

Warnie, however, was not the only scholar to take an interest in Jack's letters, manuscripts and literary remains. There was, for example, Walter Hooper, the young man from Kentucky who had come to Oxford in 1963. Hooper is one of nature's devotees, and he had hero-worshipped C. S. Lewis for many years. He had an ambition to write the life of Lewis, and to undertake a study of his works, possibly as a B.Litt. or D.Phil. student in the English Faculty at Oxford. The evidence suggests that Lewis had been flattered and pleased by Hooper's attentions, while at the same time wondering, particularly after he had allowed Hooper to stay at The Kilns, what he had let himself in for. He had written to his friend Roger Lancelyn Green only a few weeks after Hooper's arrival to spell out the embarrassing fact that although Green had been designated, by Lewis himself, to write a biography of him when he was dead, Hooper was engaged on the same quest, and there might be some clash of interests unless they were to collaborate. This they eventually did.

With C. S. Lewis dead, Hooper's plans to become closer-acquainted with his hero were shattered, but he reappeared in Oxford in 1964 and befriended Warnie. In his introduction to *They Stand Together* (Lewis's letters to Arthur Greeves), Hooper tells us, 'Warnie welcomed me as though I were already as much his friend as I had been Jack's and it soon became clear that it had been given to me to care for Warren Lewis.' This arrangement certainly had its advantages for Warnie, since Hooper is a kind man who was prepared to offer him companionship in his alcoholic phases, when other friends fought shy of him. When even the nuns of Drogheda found Warnie's visits too disruptive, Hooper wrote,

This threw us on the only resource that Oxford offered, the Warneford Hospital which is a mental institution but which affords treatment to alcoholics when there is nowhere else for them to go. Warnie resisted this as long as he could, with unfortunate results for both of us. His 'resistance' meant that he would sit in his study chair for as long as a fortnight without getting up, eating nothing, and drinking as much as six bottles of whisky a day. As he could not distinguish night from day I had to be constantly on call, and as a result I passed more than a year without a single night of unbroken sleep. Not even then could I bear him any ill will.[1]

Alas, this spirit of Christian charity was not always reciprocated. Warnie profoundly resented his spells of incarceration in the Warneford Hospital, and in his darker moods, he suspected Hooper of mixed motives. His diaries express fear that Hooper was taking too much control of the C. S. Lewis literary estate, and even on occasion express the surely unreasonable dread that Hooper was actually appropriating manuscripts behind his back. A drama not dissimilar to that of Henry James's *The Aspern Papers* was being enacted, with Hooper cast, in Warnie's mind, in the role of 'the publishing scoundrel'.

There is no evidence that Hooper has ever sought to make financial gain from his association with Lewis, and his work for the C. S. Lewis estate during the last quarter-century has been tireless. Nevertheless, Warnie felt strong misgivings that Owen Barfield, who had no inclination for the work himself but who was Lewis's literary executor, should have entrusted Hooper with the task of presiding over the estate and of publishing, as he has done in a regular stream, many of the fragmentary works of C. S. Lewis which have appeared since his death and which have perhaps done little to enhance his reputation. Hooper is not the villain that some have imagined, though it could be said that in his unwavering devotion to Lewis's memory, love has occasionally blossomed into fantasy. As one who has lived and breathed C. S. Lewis for most of his adult life, even changing his handwriting so that it now resembles that of the Master, it is understandable that he should have come to believe that he was much closer to Lewis than was in life the case. By the time Lewis's posthumous volume of essays, *God in the Dock*, edited by Hooper, appeared in 1970, for example, the American publishers' blurb was describing Hooper as 'a long-time friend and for some years personal secretary of C. S. Lewis'. In 1975, Hooper was able to share with a New York audience his memories of what had passed between himself and Lewis when they attended church together 'one Easter', a curious slip of the tongue when it is remembered that in the days of his flesh Lewis only knew Hooper in the high summer of 1963, some months after Easter had passed.

For Warnie, the development of the C. S. Lewis industry, presided over by Hooper, simply became a bore. 'CSL's home,' he grumbled to his diary, 'complete with the great man's brother, is now a show piece for any American who happens to visit Oxford . . . And what is the worst of it is that this situation is going to continue for the rest of my life . . . I suppose that on my death-bed – or at any rate on the day before – I shall have some verbose American standing over me and lecturing on some little observed significance of J's work. Oh, damn, damn, DAMN!'

Hooper exhausted him with his quest for C. S. Lewis memorabilia, and with his assumption that Warnie would be available for the troop of American pilgrims who now wished to beat a path to 'the great man's brother'. He complained to his diary of Hooper's 'gadfly adhesiveness'. 'A ferret could take Walter's correspondence course with advantage.' Walter 'should have been either a detective or better still a journalist'. He 'has the hide of a hippopotamus or rather I'm afraid he's quite indifferent as to whether I like having American vagrants thrust on me or not.'

One of the Americans who came to see Warnie was Clyde S. Kilby of Wheaton College, Illinois. He had been a penfriend of C. S. Lewis's and took a particular interest in the Inklings. At the Wheaton library he was building up a collection of manuscripts and memorabilia relating to this circle, and in the summer of 1966, when he was over to see J. R. R. Tolkien for discussions about *The Silmarillion*, he came out to Headington to visit Warnie. 'I took to him,' Warnie wrote, 'tho' he is a teetotaller and a non-smoker, being a Baptist to whom both these things are forbidden. He is one of that nice type of American about whom there is a faint suggestion of childishness, something of the dog which with wagging tail appeals to you to like him.'

From this point onwards, though it did not become immediately clear, a rivalry grew up between Clyde S. Kilby and Walter Hooper. Warnie tacitly expressed which side he was on by leaving his own diaries and papers to Wheaton College in his will. He eventually died on 9 April 1973.

The disputes between scholars and the guardians of C. S. Lewis's memory are unedifying, but they reflect something much more than a learned debate or a purely mercenary desire to lay hands on valuable manuscripts. Indeed, despite the claims of cynics, there would appear to have been very little element of avarice in these wrangles. What was emerging was a profound divergence of imaginative views of rival mythologies. Those who have been witnesses to the spectacle have been able to observe in microcosm something which is perhaps symptomatic of the religious temperament as a whole, the need to erect images and to worship them. The Marion E. Wade Center at Wheaton College keeps alive the image of an evangelical Lewis, simple in his devotion to 'mere Christianity', and theologically preoccupied almost to the exclusion of all other interests. It is not a wholly false picture; Lewis himself had a hand in building up this persona both in his published religious writings and in his letters to those thousands who wrote to him for clarification in their own religious search. In the reverent atmosphere of the Center, seated at the very table which once stood in Lewis's college rooms, the visitor shares a place with innocent-looking college kids in white socks, blue jeans and sneakers, turning the pages of the Narnia books. Meanwhile the Curator of the Center, Lyle Dorsett, brings out transcripts of conversations which he has been able to have with survivors from the Inklings and their friends. He has cast his net wide. Turning away from the Pauline Baynes illustrations of Narnia, the bright maps and the sweet fauns and beavers, one reads of a conversation with an old gentleman called Major Henry, a vague connection of Mrs Moore's who used to drive Jack and Warnie about on their Irish holidays. Henry remembers, 'Well, when they were in the car Jack didn't talk as if he was particularly . . . as if he was very keen on Christianity. He just was ordinary.' There follows an account of what happened when they got to the hotel, and of Warnie's behaviour in the dining-room. 'He never really passed out properly except when we were staying – when we were going to remain on at a hotel. And on one occasion he passed out at the dinner table. And I got up and went over to the head waiter and asked him to take my friend to his room. And he and another waiter did so.'

There is something verging on the farcical about reading such sad stuff in such a setting, where the figures revered seem so much at variance with the evidence contained in the sanctum. It produces the same feeling of shock that one derives from attending Walter Hooper's meetings of the C. S. Lewis Society in Oxford, where a High Church, celibate C. S. Lewis is reverenced.

Evidence is only of peripheral interest when the idolatrous imagination gets to work. If you want to believe in a High Church, celibate Lewis, there were enough periods of his life when he was 'High Church' *and* celibate for it to be a plausible belief. The fact that he had two liaisons with married women need not really disturb the potency of the image. Similarly, one can sit in the Marion E. Wade Center believing that Lewis gave his life to support all that the firmly non-smoking and teetotal Wheaton College stands for, and one's faith need not be diminished by reading stories of drunken evenings in Ireland and old gentlemen being carried out of the dining-room by the head waiter. As another of the authors in the Wheaton pantheon once observed, 'Human kind cannot bear very much reality.'

Where spiritual truths are in question, what in any case constitutes reality? The matter is notoriously difficult to decide, as the whole history of metaphysics, from Plato to Wittgenstein, would attest. Since there is nothing in the universe to suggest that 'rational' explanations of life explain anything, the sceptic or mocker finds as much to disconcert him in the cult of C. S. Lewis as does the troubled believer. The ultimate idolatry would appear to be the eight-foot-high stained-glass window of C. S. Lewis in St Luke's Episcopal Church, Monrovia, California. Does this not constitute a visible embodiment of what C. S. Lewis's devotees have been doing to him ever since his death, transforming him into a sinless image? The answer is more complex than the question implies. Many perfectly sane religious believers have received insight and help from Lewis's writings, and it seems a natural progression from here to commemorate him in a window. If the child's definition of a saint is true (based on the belief that saints were people invariably depicted in windows), then C. S. Lewis could well have been a saint: 'a man through whom the Light shines'. If people have found it so, it is so.

Moreover, there have been those points where simple devotion to Lewis has passed over into paranormal experience. The most striking of these are the apparitions of C. S. Lewis which were vouchsafed to the biblical scholar and translator J. B. Phillips. In his book *Ring of Truth*, Phillips tells the following anecdote to substantiate his belief in the authenticity of the Gospel accounts of Christ's resurrection:

Many of us who believe in what is known as the Communion of the Saints must have experienced the sense of nearness, at some time, of those we love after they have died. This has happened to me several times. But the late C. S. Lewis, whom I did not know very well and had only seen in the flesh once but with whom I had corresponded a fair amount, gave me an unusual experience. A few days after his death, while I was watching television, he appeared sitting in a chair within a few feet of me, and spoke a few words which were particularly relevant to difficult circumstances through which I was passing. He was ruddier in complexion than ever, grinning all over his face and positively glowing with health. The interesting thing to me was that I had not been thinking about him at all. And I was neither alarmed nor surprised. He was just there. A week later, when I was in bed reading before going to sleep, he appeared again, even more rosily radiant than before and repeated to me the same message, which was very important to me at the time . . .

It would be churlish to point out that in a subsequent volume of autobiography Canon Phillips explained to his readers the nature of these 'difficult circumstances' through which he was passing: depressions and nervous breakdowns so severe as to constitute periodic bouts of lunacy; churlish because irrelevant. However we explain the experience, it was an experience. Phillips, an intelligent and truthful man, believed that he had seen Lewis in some sense of the word risen from the dead. He makes a very direct comparison in his book between the apparition of Lewis in 1963 with the Resurrection narratives in the Gospels.

While some might choose to conduct the metaphysical debate on the plane of intellectual enquiry, others might choose to recall Lewis's momentous conversation with Hugo Dyson and J. R. R. Tolkien on that September night in 1931, when Tolkien pointed out to his friend that the human race receives truth through the medium of myth. C. S. Lewis has become a mythological figure, and it has therefore seemed legitimate to some to retell his story without too much regard for empirical evidence, just as poets have told and retold the tales of Greek or Norse mythology.

A good example of this was the brilliant television play *Shadowlands* by Bill Nicholson, subsequently written up by Brian Sibley as a book, which tells the story of C. S. Lewis's marriage to Joy Davidman. Lewis is played by Joss Ackland and Joy by Claire Bloom. In the play, her sons are still little boys at the time of her death; little boys of the same age that Jack and Warnie had been when they lost their own mother, even though David and Douglas Gresham were actually in their late teens. Lewis's circle of friends are reduced to a single generic Inklings type, a man called Christopher who is a piece of fiction; so is the college chaplain called Harry, whose name was perhaps suggested by that of Harry Carpenter, the Bishop of Oxford who forbade Lewis a Christian marriage ceremony to Joy. Claire Bloom, graceful, beautiful and poised, is recognizable as Joy in her doughty courage and in her power to make Jack love her, but she lacks any of the 'real' Joy's abrasiveness. There is nothing in the film which could explain why Lewis's friends disliked Joy – and indeed this fact forms no part of the story. After her death, the script heightens those passages in *A Grief Observed* which make it seem that Lewis lost his religious faith, though he recovers it in time to enjoy rambles with his young stepson Douglas Gresham. The book based on the screen-play contains eight pages of illustrations whose captions make only passing reference to the fact that these are photographs of actors. Thus a photograph of Claire Bloom is captioned 'Joy Davidman first corresponded with C. S. Lewis whose books greatly influenced her'. A picture of Claire Bloom, David Waller and Joss Ackland walking in the gardens of Magdalen College is captioned 'Joy, Warnie and Jack in the botanical gardens with Magdalen College in the rear'.

Not only was the play extremely moving as drama. The fascinating thing about it was how vividly it conveyed some sort of reality about Lewis, not only to those who did not know him, but also to some of those who did. Douglas Gresham has told me how authentic it all felt, in spite of the fact that so many of the details were 'untrue'. A pupil of Lewis's has told me that although Joss Ackland looked nothing like Lewis, sounded nothing like Lewis, and was unable to convey Lewis's cheeriness, there was an uncanny sense for him, while watching, that this *was* Lewis, that somehow the actor had, by means of untruth, conveyed the truth. It reminded me of how a medieval stained-glass window or tapestry can depict a biblical scene entirely within its own contemporary terms of reference – Mary and Joseph in fourteenth-century court costume, and views of a Burgundian town outside the window where the Angel of the Annunciation is appearing – without losing the essence of the story: indeed, perhaps coming closer to it than would a photograph of a Middle Eastern young woman engaged in domestic chores.

Shadowlands was more than a good play; it was an important landmark in the story of C. S. Lewis and his cult. Thereafter, Lewis was free to outsoar the shadow of our night, and such questions as what was and was not the case 'in real life' became less important than what made the most imaginative impact. C. S. Lewis societies, C. S. Lewis journals, C. S. Lewis institutes proliferate on both sides of the Atlantic. His books continue to sell in ever-increasing quantities, with devoted readers all over the Christian world. If professional theologians and Christian liberals do not find Lewis to their taste, they are heavily outnumbered by those who find him in various ways helpful. Thus while Dr Robert Runcie, the Archbishop of Canterbury, is reported to have said that he 'couldn't stand C. S. Lewis', it is not surprising that *Mere Christianity* should have found an appreciative reader in the more conservative-minded Pope John Paul II. Lewis's Ulster nurse, who told him to take his feet out of muddy puddles and not to get dirty with 'wee popes', might not have liked this development, and with the residual part of himself that reacted against Roman Catholicism, Lewis himself would have found it uncomfortable that he had been taken up by the Sovereign Pontiff in Rome.

A Polish lady informed Walter Hooper that 'Uncle' (as Polish students call the Pope) 'was always talking about Lewis when he was Archbishop of Krakow'. When the chance of a papal audience came Hooper's way, he was therefore delighted. It took place on 14 November 1984 in the Paul VI Hall in the Vatican: a public audience and not, as Hooper might have hoped, a private interview. When the Pope appeared the audience applauded 'with such fervour that my hands were sore for the rest of the day', Hooper wrote. As he studied the figure of John Paul II coming down among the crowds, Hooper was aware that there was something familiar about him, but he could not at first tell what it was. Then he knew. '"This is Aslan," I thought, "this really is Aslan."'

Hooper informed the Pope, 'Lewis was very much like you. I feel that I am talking with him now.' He presented the Holy Father with various books, including *Mere Christianity* and *The Screwtape Letters*, illustrated by Papas. The Pope laughed at the illustrations, and Hooper asked him whether he read Lewis in Polish or in English, 'but I don't think he understood the question'. They spoke together for about ten minutes.

'Do you miss your friend Lewis?' the Pope asked.

Hooper replied, 'Holy Father, I was sure nothing very special would ever happen to me after C. S. Lewis died. It did not seem right to feel sorry for myself because the best man I knew died a long time ago. Still my mind kept saying that was *all*. From now on, it's just remembering. I know that you realize that you are the last person in the world I would flatter, and this I feel ought to be said. I did not see it until I met you but it is clear to me this moment that the special gift which I received from God in knowing Lewis continues to be given to me through the years. All my years of editing Lewis's writings have been a pleasure which has blossomed fully in meeting you. It is now full grown. Meeting you is the culmination of one, single, happy reality.'

The Pope replied, 'Our [sic – or did he really say, "Ah"?] Wal-ter Hoo-per – you are doing very good WORK!' He then moved on to speak to a nun on Hooper's left. Shortly after doing so, he reached out and touched Hooper, who sank to his knees and kissed the papal ring. It would appear that at this moment a Charles Williams-style miracle of substitution took place and that Hooper was given to suffer the Pope's pain, both for the moment when he had been shot and, in more general terms, the pain he suffered in carrying 'the care of all the churches'. Some years after this, Walter Hooper became a Roman Catholic.

Like the story of Narnia itself, the story of C. S. Lewis would appear to be one 'which goes on for ever: in which every chapter is better than the one before'. We do not approach him, as we would approach other writers, only through his books, but also through the intense experiences of his followers and devotees, who have found in his pages something much more potent than purely literary interest or delight. Those who knew Lewis in the days of his flesh might suppose that he would chiefly be remembered as a vigorously intelli-gent university teacher and critic who also wrote some children's stories. For others, it might be of interest to trace the story of how the inconsolable child from the Little End Room became the life-companion of Mrs Moore, the husband of Joy Gresham and the creator of Narnia. But the pious atmosphere of Wheaton College,

Illinois, or the mystic experiences of Walter Hooper in the presence of Pope John Paul II, offers the biographer a very different approach:

> You are not here to verify,
> Instruct yourself, or inform curiosity
> Or carry report. You are here to kneel
> Where prayer has been valid.[2]

Sources

C. S. Lewis tended to throw away the manuscripts of his books once they had been published. Most surviving Lewis manuscripts, however, both of his literary productions and of his letters, are preserved in the Bodleian Library at Oxford, where it is also possible to read photocopies or microfiches of Lewis holdings from other libraries. I am very grateful to the staff of the Bodleian for all the help which they have given me, and in particular to Dennis Porter and Judith Priestman from the Department of Western Manuscripts who guided me through the material. The papers and letters belonging to the late Major Warren Lewis ('Warnie') were bequeathed to the Marion E. Wade Center at Wheaton College, Illinois. These include the monumental family history compiled by Major Lewis in eleven volumes and entitled the *Lewis Papers*; many of C. S. Lewis's letters, including the very important correspondence with Arthur Greeves, and the letters C. S. Lewis wrote to his brother; and Major Lewis's Diary, some of which has been published as *Brothers and Friends* (see Bibliography), and the rest of which I have been able to read at Wheaton. I am indebted to the Curator of the Marion E. Wade Center, Lyle W. Dorsett, for his graciousness at the time of my visit, and for the help of his staff in showing me their collection of Lewis memorabilia, as well as for the opportunity to read the transcripts of interviews between Lyle W. Dorsett and some of those who knew C. S. Lewis.

I wrote this book at the suggestion of Sarah Baird-Smith, at that time an editor at Collins, and of Walter Hooper, the literary adviser to the C. S. Lewis estate. I am very grateful to them both for the trust which this invitation implied, and for the help which they have both given me. Elizabeth Stevens, at Curtis Brown Ltd, Lewis's literary agents, has also been kind and helpful.

I am greatly indebted to all those who, over the years, have shared their memories of C. S. Lewis with me, either as a friend, a teacher, or a figure on the horizon. In particular, I should thank Lady Dunbar of Hempriggs (née Maureen Moore) and her husband Leonard Blake for their generous hospitality and the ready way in which they shared their memories with me; likewise Douglas Gresham. Others whose conversation was of particular help or interest include John Bayley, John Blackwell, Jean Bromley, John Buxton, the late Lord David Cecil, Nan Dunbar, the late Hugo Dyson, Clement Freud and Jill Freud, the late Helen Gardner, Pamela Haines and Tony Haines, Canon Head, Peter Henderson, John Jones, John Lucas, Charles Monteith, Claude Rawson, A. L. Rowse, Margaret Sayer, George Sayer, Christopher Tolkien and Rachel Trickett. Among those who did not 'see Lewis plain' but who know his work well, Humphrey Carpenter and Katherine Duncan-Jones have helped me enormously over the years with their reflections upon this in some ways puzzling subject. Pam Hewitt typed the manuscript, Starling Lawrence, Carol O'Brien and Amanda McCardie gave invaluable editorial advice, and Bill Lyons drove me to Little Lea, whose owner was kind enough to open the front door and show me the Little End Room.

Acknowledgements

The author and publishers gratefully acknowledge permission to reproduce extracts from copyright material in this book. All works listed are by C. S. Lewis unless otherwise indicated, and are copyright © C. S. Lewis Pte Ltd. (W) denotes that world permission has been obtained from the source given.

In the United Kingdom:

The Bodley Head: *Perelandra*, *That Hideous Strength* (both W)

Cambridge University Press: *The Discarded Image*, *An Experiment in Criticism*, *Studies in Words* (all W)

William Collins, Sons & Co. Ltd: *The Abolition of Man* (W), *Beyond Personality* (W), *Christian Behaviour* (W), *Fern-Seed and Elephants*, *The Four Loves*, *The Great Divorce* (W), *The Last Battle* (W), *Letters*, *Letters to Malcolm*, *The Magician's Nephew* (W), *Narrative Poems*, *The Pilgrim's Regress*, *Poems*, *The Problem of Pain* (W), *The Screwtape Letters* (W), *The Silver Chair* (W), *Surprised by Joy*, *They Stand Together*

Curtis Brown, London: *Lewis Papers*, *The Personal Heresy*, *Essays Presented to Charles Williams*, letters by C. S. Lewis and Joy Davidman Lewis, Walter Hooper's article in the *G. K. Chesterton Review* (all W)

Faber & Faber Ltd: *A Grief Observed*, 'Little Gidding' from *Four Quartets* by T. S. Eliot

John Murray Ltd: *Summoned by Bells*, 'Original Sin on the Sussex Coast' from *Collected Poems*, both by John Betjeman (W)

Oxford University Press: *The Allegory of Love*, *English Literature in the Sixteenth Century Excluding Drama*, *A Preface to 'Paradise Lost'* (all W)

Unwin Hyman Ltd: *The Letters of J. R. R. Tolkien* (edited by Humphrey Carpenter)

Lady Dunbar of Hempriggs: the letters of Mrs Moore (W)

Christopher Tolkien and the Tolkien Estate: the unpublished papers of J. R. R. Tolkien (W)

In the United States:

Harcourt Brace Jovanovich Inc.: *The Four Loves, Letters, Letters to Malcolm, Narrative Poems, Poems, Reflections on the Psalms, Surprised by Joy, The World's Last Night and other Essays*, 'Little Gidding' from *Four Quartets* by T. S. Eliot

Harper & Row, Publishers: *Brothers and Friends: The Diaries of Major Warren Hamilton Lewis* (W), *A Grief Observed*

Houghton Mifflin Company: *The Letters of J. R. R. Tolkien* (edited by Humphrey Carpenter)

Macmillan Publishing Company: *They Stand Together*

Marion E. Wade Center, Wheaton College, Illinois: the unpublished diaries of W. H. Lewis (W)

Sheed & Ward: *The Pilgrim's Regress*

Every effort has been made to contact the copyright owners of material quoted in this book. If in any instance this has not proved possible, we offer our apologies to those concerned.

Notes

Where they are not self-explanatory, references are to the bibliography which follows. For example, 'Dorsett 70' indicates that the source is page 70 of Lyle W. Dorsett's book *And God Came In*. If more than one book by an author is listed in the bibliography, the reference is amplified by the date of publication. Thus 'Tolkien (1981)' refers to the *Letters of J. R. R. Tolkien*. Where a cited book does not appear in the bibliography the author, title and date of publication are given. Titles by C. S. Lewis are referred to by name only; full details appear in the bibliography.

The following short titles are used in the notes:
LP: The *Lewis Papers* (followed by volume and page numbers)
SJ: *Surprised by Joy: The Shape of My Early Life*
BF: *Brothers and Friends: The Diaries of Major Warren Hamilton Lewis*
TST: *They Stand Together: The Letters of C. S. Lewis to Arthur Greeves 1914–1963*
OHEL: *English Literature in the Sixteenth Century Excluding Drama*
Letters: The *Letters of C. S. Lewis* (1966)

CHAPTER ONE: ANTECEDENTS
1 SJ 9

CHAPTER TWO: EARLY DAYS
1 SJ 11
2 Christopher Tolkien to author
3 LP 2.17
4 *The Pilgrim's Regress* 1.30
5 SJ 13
6 LP 10.192
7 SJ 12

8 SJ 12
9 LP 2.310
10 LP 3.25
11 LP 3.54

CHAPTER THREE: LITTLE LEA
1 LP 3.11
2 SJ 14
3 LP 3.34
4 *Decline and Fall* 17
5 SJ 18

6 Bodley MS. facs. d.265 f.4
7 LP 3.79
8 LP 3.58
9 LP 3.109–10
10 LP 3.120

CHAPTER FOUR: SCHOOLS
1 SJ 25
2 LP 3.140
3 LP 3.36
4 LP 3.147
5 SJ 33
6 LP 3.170
7 SJ 48
8 SJ 52
9 LP 3.235
10 LP 3.225
11 SJ 100
12 LP 3.325
13 LP 3.301
14 SJ 103
15 LP 3.193
16 SJ 87
17 Bodley MS. facs. d.265 f.139
18 LP 4.193
19 SJ 91
20 LP 4.174

CHAPTER FIVE: THE GREAT KNOCK
1 SJ 106
2 *Ibid.*
3 LP 4.184
4 LP 4.223
5 LP 4.58
6 SJ 110
7 *Ibid.*
8 LP 4.279
9 LP 4.135
10 SJ 131
11 LP
12 TST 135
13 TST 137
14 LP 4.224
15 LP 4.234

16 LP 4.239
17 LP 4.236
18 TST 82
19 TST 424
20 *Ibid.*
21 *Ibid.*
22 Hugo Dyson
23 TST 92
24 SJ 146
25 Holbrook xii
26 SJ 145
27 LP 4.250
28 LP 4.256
29 *Letters* 32
30 TST 159
31 TST 171
32 TST 180
33 TST 179
34 TST 189

CHAPTER SIX: THE ANGEL OF PAIN
1 LP 5.229
2 LP 5.260
3 SJ 151
4 LP 5.260
5 LP 5.282
6 SJ 153
7 *Ibid.* 154
8 *Ibid.* 159
9 Lady Dunbar to author
10 LP 5.42
11 LP 6.134
12 TST 217
13 SJ 160
14 *The Problem of Pain* 31
15 LP 6.38
16 TST 230
17 LP 6.66
18 LP 6.75

CHAPTER SEVEN:
UNDERGRADUATE
1 TST 242
2 TST 249

316

3 TST 242
4 TST 253
5 SJ 161
6 TST 241
7 Carpenter 11
8 Quennell 140
9 Lady Dunbar to author
10 LP 6.123
11 LP 6.129
12 TST 256
13 LP 6.145
14 LP 6.170
15 LP 6.184
16 Bodley MS. facs. d.264 f.140
17 LP 6.187
18 LP 6.193
19 LP 6.208
20 LP 8.117
21 TST 286
22 TST 287
23 LP 6.262
24 *The Great Divorce* 98–9
25 LP 6.318

CHAPTER EIGHT: HEAVY LEWIS
1 LP 8.148
2 LP 8.165
3 LP 8.127
4 C. S. Lewis related both these
  pieces of Oxford lore to
  Helen Gardner
5 SJ 171
6 LP 8.122
7 *Ibid.*
8 LP 8.53
9 *Ibid.*
10 *Ibid.*
11 LP 8.80
12 LP 8.75
13 LP 8.90
14 SJ 163
15 *The Allegory of Love* 7
16 LP 8.126
17 LP 8.163

18 LP 8.172
19 LP 8.89
20 LP 8.160
21 Green and Hooper 76
22 LP 8.290

CHAPTER NINE: REDEMPTION BY
PARRICIDE
1 LP 8.315
2 BF 237
3 LP 9.312–3
4 LP 9.29
5 LP 9.72
6 CSL to Charles Monteith (oral
  tradition)
7 John Betjeman to David Cecil
  (oral tradition)
8 Green and Hooper 91
9 MS in Bodleian dated 3 Feb.
  1926
10 MS in Bodleian dated 19 March
  1926
11 SJ 126
12 Humphrey Carpenter: *J. R. R.
  Tolkien* (1977) 64
13 SJ 173
14 J. H. Newman: *Apologia Pro
  Vita Sua* (1966) 164
15 Gibb 10
16 SJ 174
17 *Ibid.* 180
18 *Ibid.* 174
19 *Ibid.* 182
20 TST 147
21 *Letters* 137

CHAPTER TEN: MYTHOPOEIA
1 Letter to Miss Bodle. MS in
  Bodleian: 25 March 1954,
  f. 234
2 LP 10.192
3 LP 10.203
4 LP 10.207
5 *Ibid.*

6   LP 10.230
7   J. R. R. Tolkien: *The Lays of
    Belenand* (1985) 150
8   *Ibid.* 151
9   TST 379
10 *Ibid.* 341
11 Carpenter 32
12 BF 38
13 *Ibid.* 40
14 LP 10.231
15 *Letters* 12
16 BF 58
17 *Ibid.* 86
18 TST 331
19 *Ibid.* 328
20 *Ibid.* 395
21 *Ibid.* 399
22 *Mere Christianity* 158
23 J. R. R. Tolkien: *The
    Silmarillion* (1977) 41
24 TST 427
25 BF 88
26 SJ 189
27 TST 425
28 Green and Hooper 197
29 *Mere Christianity* 86
30 *Ibid.* 90
31 TST 332
32 Bodleian MS facs d.263
33 Gibb 72
34 Como 43
35 *Ibid.* 212
36 Letter to W. H. Lewis
    (Wheaton College)

CHAPTER ELEVEN: REGRESS
1   J. R. R. Tolkien: *The
    Silmarillion* (1977) 265
2   *The Pilgrim's Regress* 47
3   *Ibid.* 184
4   *Ibid.* 216
5   *Ibid.* 130
6   TS in the possession of
    Christopher Tolkien

7   Letter to W. H. Lewis, 22 Nov
    1931 (Wheaton College)
8   BF 141
9   *Ibid.* 145
10 Oral testimony of Canon
    Head
11 LP 1.1
12 BF 67
13 *The Allegory of Love* 348
14 *Ibid.* 319
15 Gibb 9

CHAPTER TWELVE: THE INKLINGS
1   Humphrey Carpenter: *W. H.
    Auden* (1981) 224
2   Carpenter 97
3   TST 471
4   *The Discarded Image* 98–9
5   TST 479
6   Tolkien (1987) 7
7   Tolkien (1981) 29
8   Como 94
9   Tolkien (1981) 36
10 Carpenter 67
11 BF 174
12 TST 482
13 *Letters* 161
14 *The Problem of Pain* 62
15 *The Discarded Image* 8

CHAPTER THIRTEEN: SCREWTAPE
1   Tolkien (1981) 48
2   Oral testimony
3   *A Preface to 'Paradise Lost'* 5
4   *Ibid.* 98
5   *Ibid.* 4
6   *Ibid.* 79
7   *Ibid.* 63
8   *Ibid.* 60
9   BF 171
10 Oral testimony of Charles
    Monteith
11 *The Screwtape Letters* 135
12 *Ibid.* 87

13 *Ibid.* 22
14 *Ibid.* 46
15 *Ibid.* 112
16 Green and Hooper 199
17 TS in the possession of Christopher Tolkien
18 Green and Hooper 202
19 *Mere Christianity* 83
20 *Ibid.* 33
21 *Ibid.* 41
22 *Ibid.* 44
23 *Ibid.* 152
24 Kathleen E. Burne (ed.): *The Life and Letters of Father Andrew SDC* (1948) 126
25 Hooper and Green 214
26 *Letters* 195
27 *Perelandra* 161–2
28 TST 427
29 *Letters* 232

CHAPTER FOURTEEN: SEPARATIONS
1 MS letter in the possession of Lady Freud
2 *Ibid.*
3 TST 495
4 *Ibid.* 499
5 Green and Hooper 174
6 *That Hideous Strength* 249
7 *Ibid.* 173
8 *Ibid.* 188
9 *Ibid.* 226
10 *The Four Loves* 74
11 Tolkien (1981) 64
12 Carpenter 120
13 TST 501
14 Tolkien (1981) 82
15 *Ibid.* 110
16 *Ibid.* 81
17 BF 179
18 *The Abolition of Man* 22
19 *Ibid.* 39
20 MS in the possession of Lady Freud

21 MS in the possession of Lady Freud
22 TST 507
23 Carpenter 204
24 *Letters* 206
25 BF 185

CHAPTER FIFTEEN: NARNIA
1 Peter Henderson to author
2 Kathleen Tynan: *Kenneth Tynan* (1987) 54
3 *Ibid.* 404
4 Oral testimony
5 Tolkien (1981) 108
6 Oral testimony of Helen Gardner
7 Sayer 172
8 BF 217
9 Letter to Mrs Frank Jones, 16 Nov. 1963
10 Letter to June Flewett (Lady Freud), 1946
11 Letter to June Flewett (Lady Freud), 1946
12 BF 232
13 Carpenter 226
14 J. R. R. Tolkien: 'The Ulsterior Motive'. MS in the possession of Christopher Tolkien
15 Tolkien (1981) 128
16 BF 238
17 Bodleian MS Eng. Lett. c.220/2
18 Green and Hooper 236–56
19 OHEL 380
20 *Ibid.* 393
21 BF 226
22 *Ibid.* 232
23 *The Magician's Nephew* 1
24 *The Silver Chair* 103
25 *The Last Battle* 176
26 *Ibid.* 201

CHAPTER SIXTEEN: THE SILVER
CHAIR
1 BF 238
2 SJ 179
3 *Letters* 232
4 Schofield 76
5 Dorsett 70
6 *Ibid.* 87
7 *Ibid.* 20
8 *Ibid.* 18
9 *Ibid.* 59
10 *Ibid.* 74
11 Griffin 331
12 BF 276
13 OHEL 221
14 SJ 93
15 A. L. Rowse to author
16 BF 243
17 SJ 93

CHAPTER SEVENTEEN: SMOKE ON
THE MOUNTAIN
1 Dorsett 75
2 Sibley 109
3 Dorsett 112
4 Griffin 353
5 Schofield 58
6 W. H. Lewis letter to Jill
Freud
7 W. H. Lewis letter to Jill Freud,
30 Dec. 1956
8 Letter to Jill Freud, 5 April
1955
9 BF 244
10 Nan Dunbar (unpublished
paper)
11 *Ibid.*
12 Dorsett 196
13 *Ibid.* 112
14 BF 245
15 LP 6.129
16 Sayer 186
17 *A Grief Observed* 6
18 TST 170

19 BF 245
20 *Mere Christianity* 91
21 Tolkien (1981) 60–1
22 Gresham 127
23 BF 245
24 MS Bodleian Library: Eng.
Lett. c. 220/2
25 *Poems* 1
26 Dorsett 126
27 BF 246

CHAPTER EIGHTEEN: MARRIAGE
1 Lady Dunbar to author
2 Dorsett 135
3 *Ibid.*
4 *A Grief Observed* 27
5 *The Four Loves* 102
6 Dorsett 128
7 BF 232
8 Letter to Jill Freud, 12 Dec
1957
9 *The Screwtape Letters* 135
10 Letter to Jill Freud, 30 Dec
1956
11 *A Grief Observed* 42
12 *Ibid.* 9
13 *The Four Loves* 95
14 *Ibid.* 71
15 Christopher Tolkien to author
16 Jean Bromley to author
17 *The Four Loves* 49
18 *Ibid.* 61
19 *Ibid.* 128
20 *Studies in Words* 33

CHAPTER NINETEEN: MEN MUST
ENDURE
1 Sibley 132
2 *A Grief Observed* 39
3 Sibley 133
4 Dorsett 136
5 BF 249
6 June Lancelyn Green to
author

7   Dorsett 140
8   BF 248
9   *Ibid.* 249
10 *A Grief Observed* 63
11 BF 251

CHAPTER TWENTY: LAST YEARS
1   *A Grief Observed* 44
2   Sibley 148
3   *Ibid.* 147
4   *A Grief Observed* 7
5   *Ibid.* 16
6   Charles Monteith to author
7   Letter in the files of Faber &
    Faber
8   *An Experiment in Criticism* 127
9   *Ibid.* 12
10 *Ibid.* 122
11 *Ibid.* 141

12 *A Grief Observed* 37
13 Quoted in Griffin 306
14 Tony and Pamela Haines to
    author
15 TST 562
16 MS letter in the possession of
    Christopher Tolkien
17 Christopher Tolkien to author
18 TST 564
19 *Letters* 307
20 MS in Bodleian, dated 16 Nov.
    1963

CHAPTER TWENTY-ONE: FURTHER
UP AND FURTHER IN
1   Walter Hooper: Preface to
    TST 34
2   T. S. Eliot: 'Little Gidding',
    Four Quartets

Select Bibliography

Unless otherwise stated, the place of publication is London.

I BOOKS BY C. S. LEWIS

Spirits in Bondage: A Cycle of Lyrics (under the pseudonym Clive Hamilton). 1919

Dymer (under the pseudonym Clive Hamilton). 1926

The Pilgrim's Regress: An Allegorical Apology for Christianity, Reason and Romanticism. 1933

The Allegory of Love: A Study in Medieval Tradition. 1936

Out of the Silent Planet. 1938

Rehabilitations and Other Essays. 1939

The Personal Heresy: A Controversy (with E. M. W. Tillyard). 1939

The Problem of Pain. 1940

The Screwtape Letters. 1942

A Preface to 'Paradise Lost'. 1942

Broadcast Talks. 1942

Christian Behaviour: A Further Series of Broadcast Talks. 1943

Perelandra (reprinted as a Pan paperback in 1953 as *The Voyage to Venus*). 1943

The Abolition of Man: Reflections on Education with Special Reference to the Teaching of English in the Upper Forms of Schools. 1943

Beyond Personality: The Christian Idea of God. 1944

That Hideous Strength: A Modern Fairy-Tale for Grown-Ups. 1945

The Great Divorce: A Dream. 1945

Miracles: A Preliminary Study. 1947

Arthurian Torso: Containing the Posthumous Fragment of the Figure of Arthur by Charles Williams and A Commentary on the Arthurian Poems of Charles Williams by C. S. Lewis. 1948

Transposition and Other Addresses. 1949

The Lion, the Witch and the Wardrobe. 1950

Prince Caspian: The Return to Narnia. 1951

Mere Christianity. 1952

The Voyage of the Dawn Treader. 1952
The Silver Chair. 1953
The Horse and His Boy. 1954
English Literature in the Sixteenth Century Excluding Drama. Oxford, 1954
The Magician's Nephew. 1955
Surprised by Joy: The Shape of My Early Life. 1955
The Last Battle. 1956
Till We Have Faces: A Myth Retold. 1956
Reflections on the Psalms. 1958
The Four Loves. 1960
Studies in Words. Cambridge, 1960
The World's Last Night and Other Essays. New York, 1960
A Grief Observed (under the pseudonym N. W. Clark). 1961
An Experiment in Criticism. Cambridge, 1961
They Asked for a Paper: Papers and Addresses. 1962
Letters to Malcolm: Chiefly on Prayer. 1964
The Discarded Image: An Introduction to Medieval and Renaissance Literature.
   1964
Poems (ed. Walter Hooper). 1964
Screwtape Proposes a Toast and Other Pieces. 1965
Studies in Medieval and Renaissance Literature (ed. Walter Hooper).
   Cambridge, 1966
Of Other Worlds: Essays and Stories (ed. Walter Hooper). 1966
Christian Reflections (ed. Walter Hooper). 1967
A Mind Awake: An Anthology of C. S. Lewis (ed. Clyde S. Kilby). 1968
Narrative Poems (ed. Walter Hooper). 1969
Selected Literary Essays (ed. Walter Hooper). Cambridge, 1969
God in the Dock: Essays on Theology and Ethics (ed. Walter Hooper). 1970
Fern-Seed and Elephants and Other Essays on Christianity (ed. Walter
   Hooper). 1975
The Dark Tower and Other Stories (ed. Walter Hooper). 1975
The Joyful Christian: Readings from C. S. Lewis. New York, 1977
On Stories, and Other Essays in Literature (ed. Walter Hooper). 1982
First and Second Things (ed. Walter Hooper). 1984
The Business of Heaven (ed. Walter Hooper). 1985
Boxen: The Imaginary World of the Young C. S. Lewis (ed. Walter Hooper).
   1985
Present Concerns (ed. Walter Hooper). 1986

2 LETTERS AND DIARIES

Letters of C. S. Lewis (edited and with a memoir by W. H. Lewis). 1966
   (revised by Walter Hooper). 1988
Letters to an American Lady (ed. Clyde S. Kilby). 1969

They Stand Together: The Letters of C. S. Lewis to Arthur Greeves 1914–1963 (ed. Walter Hooper). 1979

Letters to Children (ed. Lyle W. Dorsett and Marjorie Lamp Mead). New York, 1985

Brothers and Friends: The Diaries of Major Warren Hamilton Lewis (ed. Clyde S. Kilby and Marjorie Lamp Mead). San Francisco, Calif., 1982

3 A SELECTION OF BOOKS RELATING TO C. S. LEWIS

Carpenter, Humphrey *The Inklings: C. S. Lewis, J. R. R. Tolkien, Charles Williams and Their Friends.* 1979

Christensen, Michael T. *C. S. Lewis on Scripture: His Thoughts on the Nature of Biblical Inspiration, the Role of Revelation, and the Question of Inerrancy.* Waco, Texas, 1979

Christopher, Joe R. *C. S. Lewis.* Boston, Mass., 1987

Como, James T. (ed.) *C. S. Lewis at the Breakfast Table and Other Reminiscences.* New York, 1979

Cunningham, Richard B. *C. S. Lewis: Defender of the Faith.* Philadelphia, Pa., 1967

Dorsett, Lyle W. *And God Came In: The Extraordinary Story of Joy Davidman, Her Life and Marriage to C. S. Lewis.* New York, 1983

Ford, Paul F. *Companion to Narnia.* San Francisco, Calif., 1980

Gibb, Jocelyn (ed.) *Light on C. S. Lewis.* 1965

Gibson, Evan K. *C. S. Lewis, Spinner of Tales.* Washington, DC, 1980

Gilbert, Douglas and Clyde S. Kilby *C. S. Lewis: Images of His World.* Grand Rapids, Michigan, 1973

Green, Roger Lancelyn, and Walter Hooper *C. S. Lewis: A Biography.* 1974

Gresham, Douglas H. *Lenten Lands: My Childhood with Joy Davidman and C. S. Lewis.* New York, 1988

Griffin, William *Clive Staples Lewis: A Dramatic Life.* San Francisco, Calif., 1986

Hannay, Margaret Patterson *C. S. Lewis.* New York, 1981

Holmer, Paul L. *C. S. Lewis: The Shape of His Faith and Thought.* San Francisco, Calif., 1976

Hooper, Walter *Through Joy and Beyond: A Pictorial Biography of C. S. Lewis.* New York, 1982

Howard, Thomas *The Achievement of C. S. Lewis: A Reading of His Fiction.* Wheaton, Illinois, 1980

Karkainen, Paul A. *Narnia Explored.* Old Tappan, New Jersey, 1979

Kilby, Clyde S. *The Christian World of C. S. Lewis.* Grand Rapids, Michigan, 1964

—, *Images of Salvation in the Fiction of C. S. Lewis.* Wheaton, Illinois, 1978

Kreeft, Peter *C. S. Lewis: A Critical Essay.* Grand Rapids, Michigan, 1979

Lindskoog, Kathryn Ann *C. S. Lewis: Mere Christian*. Glendale, Calif., 1973

—, *The Lion of Judah in Never-Never Land: The Theology of C. S. Lewis Expressed in His Fantasies for Children*. Grand Rapids, Michigan, 1973

—, *The C. S. Lewis Hoax*. Portland, Oregon, 1988

Meilander, Gilbert *The Taste for the Other: The Social and Ethical Thought of C. S. Lewis*. Grand Rapids, Michigan, 1978

Payne, Leanne *Real Presence: The Holy Spirit in the Works of C. S. Lewis*. Westchester, Illinois, 1979

Purtill, Richard *Lord of the Elves and Eldils: Fantasy and Philosophy in C. S. Lewis and J. R. R. Tolkien*. Grand Rapids, Michigan, 1974

—, *C. S. Lewis's Case for the Christian Faith*. 1981

Schakel, Peter J. (ed.) *The Longing for a Form: Essays in the Fiction of C. S. Lewis*. Kent, Ohio, 1977

—, *Reading with the Heart: The Way into Narnia*. Grand Rapids, Michigan, 1979

—, *Reason and Imagination in C. S. Lewis: A Study of Till We Have Faces*. Grand Rapids, Michigan, 1979

Schofield, Stephen (ed.) *In Search of C. S. Lewis*. South Plainfield, New Jersey, 1984

Sibley, Brian *Shadowlands: The Story of C. S. Lewis and Joy Davidman*. 1985

Tolkien, J. R. R. (ed. Humphrey Carpenter and Christopher Tolkien) *The Letters of J. R. R. Tolkien*. 1981

—, (ed. Christopher Tolkien) *The Lost Road and Other Writings*. 1987

Vanauken, Sheldon *A Severe Mercy*. New York, 1977

Walsh, Chad *C. S. Lewis: Apostle to the Sceptics*. New York, 1949

—, *The Literary Legacy of C. S. Lewis*. New York, 1979

White, William Luther *The Image of Man in C. S. Lewis*. New York, 1969

4 C. S. LEWIS PERIODICALS

CSL: The Bulletin of the New York C. S. Lewis Society. 1969–

The Chronicle of the Portland C. S. Lewis Society. 1972–

The Lamp-Post of the Southern California C. S. Lewis Society. 1974–

The Canadian C. S. Lewis Journal (Godalming, Surrey). 1979–

Seven: An Anglo-American Literary Review. 1980–

Inklings-Jahrbuch für Literatur und Asthetic (Ludenscheid, W. Germany). 1984–

Index

NOTE: Works by C. S. Lewis appear directly under title; works by others under the name of the author